A Basic Introduction to
Biblical Hebrew

A Basic Introduction to
Biblical Hebrew

with CD

Jo Ann Hackett

HENDRICKSON PUBLISHERS

A Basic Introduction to Biblical Hebrew

© 2010 by Hendrickson Publishers Marketing, LLC
P. O. Box 3473
Peabody, Massachusetts 01961-3473
www.hendrickson.com

ISBN 978-1-59856-028-2

Printed in the United States of America

Fourth Printing—September 2017

Library of Congress Cataloging-in-Publication Data

Hackett, Jo Ann.
A basic introduction to Biblical Hebrew, with cd / Jo Ann Hackett.
      p. cm.
    Text in English and Hebrew (Masoretic text).
    Includes bibliographical references and index.
    ISBN 978-1-59856-028-2 (paper binding : alk. paper)
    1. Hebrew language—Grammar. 2. Hebrew language—Grammar—Problems, exercises, etc. 3. Bible O.T.—Language, style. I. Title.
    PJ4567.3.H33 2010
    492.4'82421—dc22   2010001283

◀ CONTENTS ▶

◄ ACKNOWLEDGMENTS ►

Several years of my beginning Biblical Hebrew classes at Harvard and the University of Texas have been the guinea pigs for this book, and their reactions, corrections, and good humor have made it a much better work, for which I thank them tremendously. Many individuals have also been instrumental in helping me through the process of turning out a finished product. A number have been using the book in its photocopied form and have often added their own and their classes' comments (and, as always, corrections): Mark Arnold, Walter Aufrecht, Joel Baden, Cory Crawford, Robert Daum, Peggy Day, Carrie Duncan, John Ellison, Eve Feinstein, Karen Grumberg, Martien Halvorson-Taylor, Ted Hiebert, Vivian Johnson, Jonathan Kaplan, Na'ama Pat-El, Greg Schmidt-Goering, Jennifer Singletary, Jeffrey Stackert, Keith Stone, Christine Thomas (and my sincere apologies to anyone I may have missed). Catherine Beckerleg is responsible for much of the final proofreading. I know how good her Hebrew is and was delighted that her trained eye was combing through the galleys. Both Josef Tropper and Carol Norman read earlier versions and encouraged me with their positive feedback to get the book finished. Two readers deserve special mention: Jonathan Kline and Ben Thomas both went through the book with a fine-toothed comb; no matter how much I worked on the final version, the two of them found more errors. They were both amazingly attuned to the fine points (pun intended) of Biblical Hebrew.

Michael Heidenreich, at the College of Liberal Arts Instructional Technology Services at the University of Texas in Austin, recorded John Huehnergard and me reading from the book's lessons for the CD included with this book. He worked with us at very short notice, making us feel perfectly comfortable in what is, for us, an alien environment, even providing candy to keep our growling stomachs from ruining the readings—all the while calmly and professionally producing the recordings that made it possible for us to stay on a very tight schedule. Without him, we would have been lost.

I am particularly grateful and indebted to Bob Buller, who pulled off the daunting task of typesetting the book. He not only dealt with details like standardizing my idiosyncratic font use but also enhanced the usefulness and look of each page.

What a treat to have a typesetter with his knowledge of Hebrew! And as the schedule for finishing the book stretched on far beyond our original projections, he kept his sense of humor with each change of the hundreds we asked him to make. I can't imagine anyone doing a better job.

Allan Emery at Hendrickson Publishers was the editor for this book. I have known Allan well for more years than either of us will admit to. It was his encouragement that got me to put on paper finally the ideas I had had for years about a one-semester, basic grammar of Biblical Hebrew. He stuck with the project through many years of my procrastination, my sickness, and my change of venue. He has been splendid. He has kept track of thousands of details that made my head spin, and he always approaches his work with a kindness and professionalism that made me want to do him proud.

As with everything scholarly I've ever written, John Huehnergard has read every word of this book, and read them again, and yet again. John is a brilliant scholar and knows Biblical Hebrew inside and out, and so my work through the years has benefited enormously from his comments, but he also has a fine eye for the way a book should look. He has been involved in virtually every aspect of this project and has actually seemed to enjoy it. The number of errors he has caught and the number of illogical explanations he has pointed out are far too many to remember, let alone mention, and he has steadfastly encouraged me through the above-mentioned procrastination, sickness, and change of venue, and so much more. It is to him, with love, that this book is dedicated.

◄ HOW TO USE THIS BOOK ►

This textbook is meant as a one-semester or one-term introduction to the basics of Biblical Hebrew. It is divided into 30 lessons in order to fit into 15-week semesters and 10-week terms. Any instructor will find, however, that the last 6 lessons are more challenging than the first 24, so the ideal division into two or three lessons per week will probably never be followed. In the following paragraphs, I explain some of my thinking behind various aspects of this grammar, in the hope that it will make that thinking transparent, to use a timely term.

The boxes and paradigms in this textbook present words from right-to-left, or top-to-bottom and right-to-left, in the hope that using the Hebrew order will help to familiarize students with that aspect of the writing system. In general, anything in boxes with single lines around them is information that is interesting for the student to know but not necessary for learning the language. Information in boxes with double lines around them, however, is something that is essential to the language.

As noted in the book, I have presented verbs in the vocabularies according to the 3ms suffix conjugation, even before the suffix conjugation is introduced. Since this is the way most verbs in Biblical Hebrew are "named" ('to guard' is שָׁמַר), I have continued that tradition. The exception is the middle-weak verbs, which are usually "named" according to their infinitives construct ('to arise' is קוּם). More controversial is that I have listed the verbal paradigms in the order first-person, second-person, then third-person, unlike the traditional Biblical Hebrew textbook order, which begins with the third-person, since that is in the suffix conjugation the simplest form of the verb. Most of us have learned the verbal paradigms in the traditional way, but I have found that listing pronominal suffixes from first-person to third-person (בִּי, בְּךָ, and so on), while listing verbal forms from third-person to first-person, is confusing to many students. This is especially so as modern languages, including English, present the verbs in the order first-person, second-person, third-person, and that is the order students are used to when they first approach Biblical Hebrew.

I deliberately introduced the strong verb first, through all its stems and forms, and only at the end do I bring in the weak verbs. The other common way to introduce Biblical Hebrew is to introduce the *qal* completely, strong and weak verbs alike, and then to move on to the other stems. I have always found that I learn languages more easily when they are presented in the former order, so I have followed it here.

I have also deliberately not used the rubrics "perfect," "imperfect," or "converted," because they carry with them either complete misinformation ("converted") or old-fashioned methods of dealing with the Biblical Hebrew verbal system ("perfect" and "imperfect"). Luckily, the merely descriptive terms "prefix conjugation" and "suffix conjugation" are available (and were in fact the terms we used in the first Hebrew classes I took as a student). I have also been happy to see the term *və-qatal* applied to the form that is וֹ plus suffix conjugation (often called "converted perfect"), and I have used it here. Several years ago, John Huehnergard and I together came up with the term "consecutive preterite" for the verb form that is usually called the "converted imperfect." I hesitated to use a new name in this beginning textbook for such a common form, but our rubric fits so perfectly that I decided to introduce it here. It is the only time I have used a term that is otherwise not a part of the scholarly literature. We have since been made aware that a few other scholars had previously proposed the same terminology.

I have presented the verbs in an order that is unusual: first the prefix conjugation, then the volitives, then the consecutive preterite. I was first given the idea to begin the Biblical Hebrew verbs with the prefix conjugation by George Landes in an offhand conversation many years ago, and I have thought it a good idea ever since. It is a logical progression to begin with the prefix conjugation and lead up to the consecutive preterite. The consecutive preterite is the form beginning students must know thoroughly in order to read most biblical prose, and in order to lead them to that form, I needed to introduce the jussive, and in order to introduce the jussive, I first needed to present the prefix conjugation. So the order of lessons 12–15 was determined by my desire to get to the consecutive preterite as quickly as possible, plus the seed planted long ago by George Landes. The suffix conjugation and *və-qatal* forms follow in the next lessons, along with the infinitives and participles.

Using the accent marks of the biblical text, the טְעָמִים, can be a great help to students attempting to discover the syntax of a given passage; I have introduced the most common ones in this book and have used them in the sentences in the exercises. I did this knowing that I was often not using the accents in the appropriate way, according to the biblical rules, but I wanted to present both disjunctive and conjunctive accents to the students, and at this early time in their Biblical Hebrew study, the impossibility of some of my combinations will not affect their learning the usefulness of the system as a whole. Those who know biblical accentuation well will cringe, but the students will know what to do with the most common accent marks when they approach the biblical text.

This leads me to explain another decision: most of the exercises are artificial; they are not generally biblical passages. As my professor Thomas Lambdin once said (and here I am supplying my own examples), if the biblical text has a sentence such as "He struck the cat" and we know the word for "dog," it does not matter that "He struck the dog" is nowhere in the biblical text. We still know how it would have been said/written. On the other hand, in making up examples of biblical prose, I have risked introducing Hebrew phrases and syntax that never, in fact, existed. I can only say that I hope I have avoided that pitfall.

Thus, not every form for a given "model" verb in a paradigm will be found in Biblical Hebrew. If, however, that form that is not found in the "model" verb is found in another verb, it will usually be provided in the paradigm as part of the "model" verb (with exceptions such as חָוָה in the *hishtaphel*). A blank space in a paradigm indicates that the form is not found in *any* verb of the type that the paradigm represents.

I have always found it useful for students to memorize a few paradigms because their forms are used again and again. The endings of the paradigm of the preposition בְּ plus pronominal suffixes are almost exactly the same as those of singular nouns with possessive pronominal suffixes, but the בְּ paradigm is much easier to remember. Likewise, אֶל plus pronominal suffixes prepares one for the plural nouns and their possessive pronominal suffixes. Furthermore, learning the entire paradigm of the *qal* strong verb makes recognizing the same forms in other stems, and even in the weak verbs, a much easier task.

This textbook includes a CD with a great deal of pronunciation supplied for the beginning student: of some necessary but unfamiliar English words (for lesson 1); of many of the paradigms; and of all of the vocabulary words. It also includes pronunciation of all the Hebrew-to-English exercises in lessons 1–15 and of the first two exercises in lessons 16–30. Assuming the computer has speakers, the vocabulary words can be heard by passing one's cursor over the word in the vocabulary list. The phrases and sentences of the exercises can be heard by passing one's cursor over those phrases and sentences. At first, the reading seems painfully slow—painful for the instructor, but probably not for the student. Gradually the speed of reading is increased. Moreover, many Biblical Hebrew instructors use Genesis 22:1–19 as a sample text to help students learn to read more quickly and correctly, and I have included it on the CD as well. It is a well-known text for most students, and it has the helpful feature that the consecutive preterite of most of the common Biblical Hebrew verbs are part of the passage. On this textbook's CD, John Huehnergard and I are the readers, except for the recording of Gen 22:1–19 made by Prof. David Levenson of Florida State University. Both Prof. Huehnergard and Prof. Levenson have kindly given me permission to use their voices for this textbook.

Like all language textbook authors, I considered not including answers for the exercises, because too many students simply use the answers given to them without struggling with the exercises first, and then, of course, they are in trouble when they take exams. On the other hand, anyone attempting to use the book outside an organized class will definitely need an answer key. Hendrickson suggested a compromise: the answers to the exercises are included in this package, but they are on the CD rather than in the textbook itself. This at least forces people to go to some trouble to find the answers, and I hope it will promote working on the exercises in the book without access to the answers, then checking the work with the answers on the CD, if one wants to.

It was Allan Emery's idea to number each lesson in Arabic numerals augmented on the left and right with the same numbers in the Hebrew system, which uses Hebrew consonants to represent numbers: *aleph* is "1," *bet* is "2," and so on. This system adds to the distinctive appearance of the beginning of each lesson and painlessly teaches students the look of the Hebrew numbers 1–30. The student will notice that in the traditional Hebrew numbering system "15" is written טו rather than יה, because the latter looks too much like the Tetragrammaton, the name of Israel's god, יהוה. "16" is טז rather than יו for the same reason.

Finally, a second book is in the works that will depend on this basic textbook. It will consist of graded readings of biblical passages, with glosses where necessary, additional vocabulary, and references to this book when something basic might need to be reviewed. I hope instructors and students alike will appreciate the approach and the contents of this basic introduction.

Jo Ann Hackett
Austin, Texas
January 2010

◄ ABBREVIATIONS ►

1cp	first person common plural (in paradigms)
1cs	first person common singular (in paradigms)
2fp	second person feminine plural (in paradigms)
2fs	second person feminine singular (in paradigms)
2mp	second person masculine plural (in paradigms)
2ms	second person masculine singular (in paradigms)
3cp	third person common plural (in paradigms)
3fp	third person feminine plural (in paradigms)
3fs	third person feminine singular (in paradigms)
3mp	third person masculine plural (in paradigms)
3ms	third person masculine singular (in paradigms)
adj.	adjective
B.C.E.	Before the Common Era
BH	Biblical Hebrew
BHS	*Biblia Hebraica Stuttgartensia*
ca.	*circa*, about
C.E.	Common Era
cf.	*confer*, compare
cohort.	cohortative
cons. pret.	consecutive preterite
cs.	construct
def. art.	definite article
dir.	direct
dir. obj.	direct object
du.	dual
e.g.	*exempli gratia*, for example
esp.	especially
f	feminine (in paradigms)
fem.	feminine
fp	feminine plural (in paradigms)

fs	feminine singular (in paradigms)
I-א	Hebrew letter *aleph* for first consonant (in a verbal root)
I-G	Hebrew guttural letter for first consonant (in a verbal root)
I-נ	Hebrew letter *nun* for first consonant (in a verbal root)
I-weak	Hebrew "weak" letter for first consonant (in a verbal root)
II-ו	Hebrew letter *vav* for the second consonant (in a verbal root)
II-G	Hebrew guttural letter for second consonant (in a verbal root)
II-י	Hebrew letter *yod* for second consonant (in a verbal root)
II-weak	Hebrew "weak" letter for second consonant (in a verbal root)
III- א	Hebrew letter *aleph* for third consonant (in a verbal root)
III-G	Hebrew guttural letter for third consonant (in a verbal root)
III-ה	Hebrew letter *he* for the third consonant (in a verbal root)
III-weak	Hebrew "weak" letter for third consonant (in a verbal root)
III-ת	Hebrew letter *tav* for the third consonant (in a verbal root)
impv.	imperative
inf. abs.	infinitive absolute
inf. cs.	infinitive construct
juss.	jussive
LBH	Late Biblical Hebrew
LXX	Septuagint
m	masculine (in paradigms)
masc.	masculine
mp	masculine plural (in paradigms)
ms	masculine singular (in paradigms)
MH	Mishnaic Hebrew
MT	Masoretic Text
obj.	object
pref. conj.	prefix conjugation
pl.	plural
ptcp.	participle
SBH	Standard Biblical Hebrew
suff. conj.	suffix conjugation
sf.	suffix
sg.	singular

Biblical references

Gen	Genesis
Exod	Exodus

Lev	Leviticus
Num	Numbers
Deut	Deuteronomy
Josh	Joshua
Judg	Judges
1, 2 Sam	1, 2 Samuel
1, 2 Kgs	1, 2 Kings
Ps(s)	Psalm(s)
Isa	Isaiah
Jer	Jeremiah
Hab	Habakkuk
Zeph	Zephaniah

ℵ ◄ **1** ► ℵ

INTRODUCTORY MATTERS

1.1. OVERVIEW

In this lesson we will place Biblical Hebrew, which is the focus of this grammar, in summary fashion within its linguistic, historical, and written (scribal) settings. Much has been written on each of these subjects, for which see the suggestions for further reading.

1.2. LINGUISTIC SETTING

Biblical Hebrew (BH) is a member of the Canaanite branch of the Semitic language family, along with Phoenician, Moabite, Ammonite, and Edomite. It is also closely related to Aramaic, Ugaritic, and even Arabic. The literature of the Hebrew Bible extends from ca. 1100 B.C.E. to ca. 150 B.C.E.

In the Bible itself, the word 'Hebrew' is not used by Israelites or Judahites to describe their own language. Instead, we have 'the language of Canaan' (Isa 19:18) and 'Judahite' (e.g., 2 Kgs 18:26 = Isa 36:11). The prologue to the Wisdom of Ben Sira (written in Greek) contains our first extant attestation of 'Hebrew' being used of the language: Ben Sira's grandson claims to have translated his grandfather's words from the original Hebrew.

> B.C.E. and C.E. stand for "Before the Common Era" and "Common Era." B.C.E. and C.E. are modern scholarly conventions for B.C. and A.D., respectively, an attempt to represent time in something other than a purely Christian way.

1.3. HISTORICAL DEVELOPMENT

Biblical Hebrew is usually divided into three large chronological periods: early poetry, Standard Biblical Hebrew (SBH), and Late Biblical Hebrew (LBH). Not all scholars agree on what should be included in the "early poetry," but many would accept that the poems in Exod 15 and Judg 5 are earlier than the tenth century B.C.E., because linguistic and stylistic features in those poems can be compared to those of the thirteenth-century Ugaritic epics from Ras Shamra and to the Canaanite language known from the fourteenth-century Amarna letters found in Egypt. Other passages that are often considered tenth century or earlier are Deut 33 and Gen 49, and some would add one or more of the following: parts of the oracles of Balaam in Num 23 and 24; and the poems in Deut 32; 1 Sam 2; 2 Sam 22 = Ps 18; Pss 29; 68; 72; 78; 2 Sam 1; 23; and Hab 3.

SBH is generally used to refer to the narrative prose of the Deuteronomistic History and of the Pentateuch. LBH includes grammar and vocabulary that is different from SBH and can be found, in part or completely, in Chronicles (those portions that are not parallel to material elsewhere in the Bible); Ezra; Nehemiah; Esther; Ecclesiastes; Daniel; and Ben Sira. The Hebrew of the Dead Sea Scrolls (DSS) is the latest LBH. The Hebrew of the rabbinic writings (the Mishnah and the Talmuds), called Mishnaic Hebrew (MH), is a different dialect of Hebrew from any BH. MH was still spoken in the second century C.E., but after the failure of the Bar Kokhba revolt, Hebrew became a literary language and *lingua franca* for Jews all over the world, until its revival in modern times.

1.4. WRITTEN (SCRIBAL) DEVELOPMENT

The earliest Hebrew script was an offshoot of the Phoenician script, as was Aramaic, and the Phoenician script was itself a continuation of an earlier Old Canaanite tradition that goes as far back as the eighteenth century B.C.E. The earliest Hebrew inscriptions copied the Phoenician custom of writing only the consonants. In ninth-century Aramaic inscriptions, we begin to see the use of *matres lectionis* ("mothers of reading"; pronounced máh-tres lek-tee-óh-nis), that is, consonants used to indicate a (long) vowel sound. This Aramaic innovation seems to have influenced Hebrew writing so that Hebrew inscriptions have final *matres lectionis* beginning in the eighth century and regularly use internal *matres lectionis* by the end of the seventh. The earliest Hebrew system of final matres lectionis used *w* (Hebrew ו) to mark a final long *u*, *y* (Hebrew י) for final long *i*, and *h* (Hebrew ה) for all other final long vowels. The earliest Hebrew system of internal *matres lectionis* copied the system of final *matres lectionis* and used *w* to mark long *u* and *y* to mark long *i*. Eventually, the system was expanded so that both final and internal *w* could represent long *o* as well as long *u*, and final and internal *y* could mark long *e* as well as long *i*. An *h* was used for all other final long vowels and was never used as an internal *mater lectionis* (máh-ter lek-tee-óh-nis), often referred to as simply a *mater*.

The received text of the Hebrew Bible is called the Masoretic Text (MT) because medieval scholars known as Masoretes added vocalization and accentuation to the consonantal text. (They were called Masoretes because they handed down the tradition, the Masorah, of their pronunciation of the Hebrew text.) It is possible to narrow the dates for the addition of vowel signs and accents to ca. 600–750 C.E., on the basis of citations in external sources.

The history of the Hebrew Bible that we use today is even more complicated. The Masoretic tradition most commonly available today is the Tiberian Masoretic tradition, but it is only one of three (or more) used in antiquity: Tiberian, Babylonian, and Palestinian. The Tiberian system was passed down by at least two schools, named after the family names of their most famous adherents: the Ben Asher school and the Ben Naphtali school. *BHS* is based on the Leningrad Codex, a manuscript from ca. 1000 C.E., which is a Ben Asher Tiberian Masoretic text, as is the Aleppo Codex, an even earlier (tenth century) but incomplete manuscript, which is the basis for the Hebrew University Bible. So the "Biblical Hebrew" we will learn in this book is actually the vocalized Hebrew of the MT of the Ben Asher Tiberian tradition, as represented by the Leningrad Codex.

As we have seen, there is a span of almost one thousand years of literature included in the Hebrew Bible, and over that long time period, the Hebrew language must have changed considerably. The Masoretic tradition, however, used the same vocalization system for the entire text, leveling any differences in pronunciation or accentuation or even possibly grammar that might have existed at an earlier time. (Note the Shibboleth story in Judg 12, which turns on precisely the existence of dialectal differences in pronunciation.) Furthermore, the Masoretic tradition of the biblical text was not the only ancient Hebrew biblical tradition. The Hebrew text from which the earliest Greek translation was made (called the Septuagint and abbreviated LXX) was not identical to the MT, nor are many of the Dead Sea Scrolls found at Qumran. The differences are mostly small but sometimes significant. So the Masoretes not only added a system of vowel and accent signs but also preserved a tradition of the consonants themselves that was

Because the Masoretes were concerned that the biblical text be copied and transmitted correctly from one copyist to the next, they wrote thousands of marginal notes (also called Masorah), pointing out when a word or combination of words only occurs once in the Bible or only two or three times, for instance. A selection of the Masorah to the MT is included in many modern Bibles, and the *Biblia Hebraica Stuttgartensia* (*BHS*) includes notes in the margins (the Masorah parva [Mp]) and in an apparatus at the bottom of each page (pointing to discussions in the Masorah magna [Mm], available in several collections).

only one among several extant around the turn of the eras.

The Tiberian Masoretic vowel system is usually interpreted according to Joseph Qimkhi's (twelfth century C.E.) system of corresponding short and long vowels. Because by their time the consonantal text was considered sacred, the Masoretes had to insert vowel marks without changing the line of the consonantal text; consequently, vowels in BH are small lines and combinations of dots inserted above, below, and within the consonantal text.

Unlike the Qimkhi system, the Masoretic vocalization (or vowel "pointing") itself suggests seven basic vowels, differentiated by vowel quality ([a] versus [o], for instance) rather than quantity (long or short), and medieval grammarians corroborate this interpretation of the system. Despite these problems, most modern students and scholars of Hebrew still use the Qimkhi short and long vowel pronunciation system, so that is the system we will learn in this grammar.

When we speak of "the Hebrew alphabet," we mean only the twenty-two consonantal letters. That is, reciting the alphabet is simply reciting the consonants.

Be sure to read and refer back to the section "How to Use This Book," beginning on page xix, for information on decisions about various features of the book, such as the ordering of paradigms.

1.5. EXERCISE FOR LESSON 1

In lesson 2 we will begin to learn how to recognize, draw, and pronounce the consonants and vowels of BH. It is important to learn the alphabet in its proper order, of course, in order to use a dictionary, so we will also memorize and recite the alphabet. At the end of each of the first four lessons, we will memorize the names of the letters of the alphabet that are to be taken up in the following lesson. These names are not written out here in any transliteration system, but rather, they are written in a fashion that will make them easily pronounceable by English speakers. We will learn their proper transliterated spellings as we learn to draw them. So, before going on to lesson 2, memorize the following set of "words":

áhlef, bait, gímmel, dóllet, hay. (The *g* in gímmel is a hard *g* as in "get.")

Repeat this list until you can say it when called upon.

ב ◄ **2** ► ב

Consonants א through ה
and the Short Vowels

2.1. Scope of the lesson

We will now begin learning to recognize, draw, and pronounce the BH alphabet. You have already memorized the names of the first five letters; you can turn to the Consonants Chart in appendix A and see their names written out in a scholarly transliteration. In this textbook, however, we will use neither the phonetic spelling you will memorize at the end of each of the first four lessons nor the scholarly transliterations. Rather, we will use more generally recognized spellings of consonants, vowels, and grammatical terms, with indications of correct accentuation: *aleph* (spelled "áhlef" at the end of the last lesson; note the accent on the first syllable), *bet* ("bait"), *gimel* ("gímmel"; note the accent on the first syllable), *dalet* ("dóllet"; note the accent on the first syllable), and *he* ("hay").

2.2. Two systems for pronunciation

There are at least two popular pronunciation systems for BH: one based on the pronunciation of Modern Israeli Hebrew; and one that was invented in the nineteenth century and was meant to be scientific, that is, to approximate as closely as possible the pronunciation of Hebrew in biblical times. Today, virtually all academic and religious venues use the Modern Israeli pronunciation system, and that is the system we will learn in this book. For reference, the scientific pronunciation of a given consonant or vowel will be noted, where it differs from the Modern Israeli.

2.3 THE *ALEPH*

We will begin with *aleph* (א). English speakers actually pronounce *aleph*s all the time, but we don't mark it in our alphabet. When you say "Ouch!" you have made an *aleph* at the beginning of the word. In fact, it is very difficult for English speakers to begin a sentence with a vowel without pronouncing an *aleph* before the vowel. The *aleph* is the catch in the throat that you can feel if you put your hand to your throat and say "Ouch!" again. Most of the time, *aleph* is pronounced as a glottal stop. When English speakers see *aleph* plus a vowel in a BH syllable, if they simply pronounce the vowel they will automatically be pronouncing the *aleph* as well.

Occasionally we find that an *aleph* in a word has "quiesced," that is, it is written but not pronounced at all. We will take up these examples as we come to them.

2.4. THE *BET*

The letter *bet* (ב) has two pronunciations in BH. When the letter is written with a dot in the middle (בּ), called a *dagesh*, it is pronounced like the *b* in "bat." When it is written without the *dagesh* (ב), it is pronounced like the *v* in "vat." (The pronunciation of *dagesh* is obvious from its spelling, although many people pronounce it as though the accent falls on the first syllable: *dágesh*.)

The *Beged-Kephet* Consonants

Bet is the first of six letters that in ancient times were pronounced differently depending on whether the *dagesh* was written. These are called *béged-képhet* letters, an acronym for the sounds of the six letters. (The accent marks on *béged-képhet* are provided so that each word is pronounced on the first syllable. They will be left off the words from now on.) We will discuss the *beged-kephet* letters in more detail below; for the moment, you should simply learn the pronunciations of the letters both with and without the *dagesh*. When writing the letter in isolation (for instance, when writing out the alphabet), always use the form without the *dagesh*. (The pronunciation without the *dagesh* is referred to as "spirantized" or "soft." The pronunciation of the letter *with* the *dagesh* is referred to as the "hard" pronunciation.)

2.5. THE *GIMEL*

The letter *gimel* (ג) is also a *beged-kephet* letter, but in the Modern Israeli pronunciation system, no distinction is made between *gimel* with a *dagesh* (גּ) and *gimel* without a *dagesh* (ג). Both are pronounced like the *g* in "get." (In the scientific pronunciation system, *gimel* without a *dagesh* is pronounced like the guttural French *r*.)

2.6. SHORT VOWELS

BH has four vowel "lengths": short, long, irreducibly long, and reduced. In this lesson, we will take up the short vowels, using ב as a dummy consonant: *pátakh* בַּ (pronounced like the *a* in "father"; the accent mark is added here so that the word will be pronounced with the accent on the first syllable); *híreq* בִּ (pronounced like the *i* in "bit"; again, the accent mark here is to ensure the first syllable is accented); *seghol* בֶּ (pronounced like the *e* in "bet" and written with a ה *mater* when it is the last sound in a word; the vowel name is pronounced se-gól, with a long *o*-sound); and *qibbuts* בֻּ (pronounced like the *oo* in "book"). For the moment, we will postpone the discussion of *o* as a short vowel. (For discussion of the vowel *qamets*, see 3.5 and 11.8.) For a summary of how BH vowels are transliterated, see appendix B.

Mini-exercise: Pronounce the following meaningless "words": גֶּג, אֶג, בַּב, גֶּב, אִג, בֶּג, אַב.

> Note that Hebrew is written from right to left, so that בַּג is pronounced "bag" and גַּב is pronounced "gav."

2.7. THE *DALET*

The letter *dalet* (ד) is the third *beged-kephet* letter we've encountered (hence the first half of *beged-kephet*—b-g-d connected by *e*-vowels). In the Modern Israeli pronunciation system, *dalet* is pronounced like the *d* in "dog," both with and without the *dagesh*. (In the scientific system, spirantized *dalet* is pronounced like the *th* in "the" or "this.")

Mini-exercise: Pronounce the following: אֶד, דָּג, בִּד, אֶד, בֶּד, דַּב.

2.8. THE *HE*

The fifth letter of the Hebrew alphabet, *he* (ה), is pronounced like the *h* in "hat," but *he* can also be a final *mater lectionis* for a final vowel sound (see 1.4 above), in which case it is not pronounced at all. (Rarely, a final *he* is not a *mater lectionis* but is in fact to be pronounced *h* [a simple release of breath, or "aspiration"]; in this case, a dot is put in the middle of the letter [ה]. This dot is not referred to as a *dagesh* but rather as a *mappiq*.) Note that the left-hand vertical does not touch the top horizontal.

Mini-exercise: Pronounce the following: הַב, בֶּה, הָד, הָג, דֶּה, הָד.

2.9. EXERCISES FOR LESSON 2

A. Practice writing *aleph* through *he* according to the instructions on the Consonants Chart (appendix A).

B. Memorize these informal names of the next five letters of the alphabet:

vahv, záyin, khet, tet, yod (with a long *o* as in "code")

3

$\gimel$ ◀ ▶ $\gimel$

Consonants ו through י
and the Long Vowels

3.1. Scope of the lesson

You have now learned to pronounce the names of the first ten letters of the Hebrew alphabet. We will move on to learning the drawing and pronunciation of the second five letters. The scholarly transliterations of their names are given on the Consonants Chart (appendix A): *vav* (spelled "vahv" at the end of the last lesson), *zayin* ("záyin"; note the accent on the first syllable), *khet* ("khet"), *tet* ("tet"), and *yod* ("yod" with long *o*).

3.2. The *vav*

The sixth letter of the Hebrew alphabet is *vav* (the same *v* pronunciation as ב without *dagesh*). In the Modern Israeli pronunciation system, it is pronounced like the *v* in "vat." (In the scientific system, it is pronounced like the *w* in "water.") *Vav* can also be a *mater lectionis*, either in the middle of a word or at its end, and in that case, it is not pronounced as a consonant at all.

Mini-exercise: Pronounce the following: וַד‎, גַו‎, וּב‎.

3.3. The *zayin*

The next letter is *zayin* (ז), pronounced like the *z* in "zebra."

Mini-exercise: Pronounce the following: זַג‎, וַו‎, דֵד‎, זַד‎, הֵז‎, זַג‎, בֵּז‎, אַג‎.

3.4. The *khet*

The next letter is *khet* (ח), which has no equivalent in the English consonant system, but the *ch* in German "Bach" or Scottish "loch" is the right sound. The sound is a kind of throat-clearing along with a release of breath that is difficult for English speakers but can be made with practice. Note that the left-hand vertical must be written so as to touch the top horizontal stroke; otherwise, *khet* is easily confused with *he*.

3.5. Long vowels

In this lesson, we will learn the long vowels in BH: *qámets* בָ (in the system we are using, pronounced exactly like *patakh*, i.e., like the *a* in "father"; usually written with a ה *mater* when it is the last sound in a word; note the accent on the first syllable); *tsére* בֵ (pronounced like the *e* in "they" and written with a ה *mater* when it is the last sound in a word. Note the accent on the first syllable; the vowel's name is pronounced tséh-reh); and *hólem* בֹ (pronounced like the *o* in "pose"; note the accent on the first syllable).

Mini-exercise: Pronounce the following: אָד, בְּג, חֶה, הָח, וְח, חֹב, זֶג, חֶב, חֶד, אַח.

3.6. The *tet*

The ninth letter in the Hebrew alphabet is *tet* (ט), and it is pronounced like the *t* in "top." *Tet* is the first "emphatic" consonant we have come to: in antiquity it was probably pronounced with an extra glottal stop (the א-sound) along with the *t*-sound, but in modern pronunciation systems it is simply pronounced *t*.

Mini-exercise: Pronounce the following: דְּב, טֹט, וְד, הָט, אָט, בְּט, טֶח, טַג.

3.7. The *yod*

The tenth letter of the alphabet is *yod* (י). It is the smallest letter, and it hangs from the top line. *Yod* is pronounced like the *y* in "yet," but it can also be a *mater lectionis*, both in the middle of and at the end of words, in which case it is not pronounced.

Mini-exercise: Pronounce the following: יֶה, בֹּז, גֶג, יַז, זֵי, בְּט, וְד, חָט, אֶב, יְט, יָד.

3.8. VOCABULARY FOR LESSON 3

Memorize the following vocabulary words, from Hebrew to English and from English to Hebrew:

אָב   'father, kinsman'

אָח   'brother, kinsman, cousin'

יָד   'hand'

3.9. EXERCISES FOR LESSON 3

A. Practice writing *vav* through *yod* according to the instructions on the Consonants Chart (appendix A).

B. Practice writing the vocabulary words above.

C. Memorize these informal names of the next seven letters of the alphabet:

koff, lómmed, maim, noon, sáhmekh, áyin, pay

4

Consonants כ through פ and Irreducibly Long Vowels

4.1. Scope of the lesson

In this lesson we will learn how to draw and pronounce letters 11–17 of the Hebrew alphabet, the names of which you have already memorized. The scholarly transliterations of their names are given in the Consonants Chart (appendix A): *kaph* (spelled "koff" at the end of the last lesson), *lamed* ("lómmed"; note the accent on the first syllable), *mem* ("maim"), *nun* ("noon"), *samekh* ("sáhmekh"; note the accent on the first syllable), *ayin* ("áyin"; note the accent on the first syllable), and *pe* ("pay").

4.2. The *KAPH*

The eleventh letter of the alphabet, *kaph* (כ), is another *beged-kephet* letter, and it is also the first of five letters that are written differently when they occur at the end of a word. *Kaph* with a *dagesh* (כּ) is pronounced like the *k* in "kid." In Western systems, the spirantized pronunciation (without the *dagesh*: כ) is pronounced exactly like ח, that is, like the *ch* in "Bach" or "loch." Final *kaph* is usually written with two dots arranged like a colon, nestled into its space: ךְ. These two dots are called *shwa* in Hebrew, a vowel to be taken up in lesson 6.

The *Sophit* Forms

Five letters in BH have "final" forms; that is, when they occur at the end of a word, they are written differently from their usual forms. Such a form is called *sophit* in Hebrew, pronounced "sofeet." So final *kaph* is also called *kaph sophit*. Final forms are easily identifiable, and in four of the five cases the final forms extend well below the line.

Mini-exercise: Pronounce the following: טָה, יֶךְ, כָּח, וֵד, כֹּז, הָךְ, דֶּךְ, אָט, כֵּג, בַּה.

4.3. THE *LAMED*

The next letter is *lamed* (ל), pronounced like the *l* in "lid."

Mini-exercise: Pronounce the following: אֶט, חַד, וֵל, בָּג, לֹז, יֵט, אֵב, לֵךְ, דִּל.

4.4. THE *MEM*

The thirteenth letter of the alphabet is *mem* (מ), and it is the second letter we have come to that has a final form (ם). *Mem* is pronounced like the *m* in "map."

4.5. IRREDUCIBLY LONG VOWELS

The vowels we will learn in this lesson are "irreducibly" long. We will see that there are rules in BH that cause some long vowels to "reduce" to much shorter vowels. (These "reduced" vowels will be taken up in lesson 6.)

There is a category of long vowels, however, that are not reduced by these rules; hence they are called "irreducibly" long vowels. These are *hireq gadol* ("big *hireq*") בִּי, which is pronounced like the *i* in "machine" and is written as a *hireq* followed by a י-*mater*; *tsere-yod* בֵּי, pronounced the same as *tsere* and written as a *tsere* followed by a י-*mater*; *shúreq* בוּ, pronounced like the *oo* in "mood" and written between consonants as a dot nestled into a ו-*mater* (note the accent on the first syllable); *holem-vav* בוֹ, which is simply *holem* written on top of a ו-*mater* placed between consonants. *Holem* is pronounced the same way with or without the *mater*. When *holem* is the last sound in a word, it is always written with a *mater*, almost always with a ו-*mater*, but on rare occasions with a ה-*mater*. (Occasionally, simple *holem*, one of the long vowels we learned in lesson 3, is also irreducible.)

Rarely, the irreducibly long vowels *hireq* (*gadol*) and *shureq* are written "defectively," that is, without a *mater*. In such cases, the irreducibly long *i*-vowel is written as a simple *hireq*, and the irreducibly long *u*-vowel is written as a *qibbuts*. For examples of this phenomenon, see 28.11 note 14, 29.8 note 9, and 30.13 note 38 for the missing *vav mater*, and 30.13 note 44 for the missing *yod mater*. (See also appendix B.)

Mini-exercise: Pronounce the following: כֵּט, לִי, חֶז, דֹּו, זוּ, גֵּל, הֵי, אֵיךְ, לֵב, אוּג, מִיב.

The *Vav* as Vowel or Consonant

Some confusion may arise at this point about how to know when *vav* is a consonant and when it is part of a vowel. BH syllable structure is the key. Words in BH almost always follow the same pattern: consonant + vowel (+ consonant). So, if *vav* is being used as a consonant, it should have its own vowel. If it follows another consonant immediately, it is part of a vowel.

4.6. THE *NUN*

The next letter in the alphabet is *nun* (נ), and, like *kaph* and *mem*, it has a different form when it is the last letter in a word (ן). *Nun* is pronounced like the *n* in "nap."

Mini-exercise: Pronounce the following: נָל, בֵּין, כֹּל, יֵדְ, חִיט, מָה, דּוֹב, אֵם, גֵג, מוּן.

4.7. THE *SAMEKH*

The fifteenth letter of the alphabet is *samekh* (ס), which is pronounced like the *s* in "sit."

Mini-exercise: Pronounce the following: וֵד, מְז, כַּס, חוֹל, נוּב, אֹס, בּוֹ, סֵים, יֵן, הַג, סוֹ, טֵז.

4.8. THE *AYIN*

The next letter of the alphabet is *ayin* (ע). In biblical times, *ayin* was pronounced in the back of the throat in a way that is difficult for most English speakers; consequently, *ayin* is simply pronounced like *aleph*, that is, as a glottal stop.

Mini-exercise: Pronounce the following: עֹס, טֵע, יֵיג, חַז, הֵן, סָה, עוּ, בָּה, אוֹדְ, עוּל.

The "Gutturals"

א, ה, ח, and ע are referred to rather loosely as "guttural" consonants. The gutturals in BH share certain features, to be taken up in future lessons, so this short list should be memorized.

4.9. THE *PE*

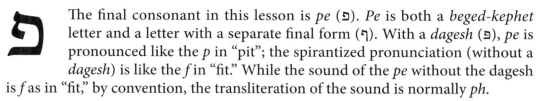 The final consonant in this lesson is *pe* (פ). *Pe* is both a *beged-kephet* letter and a letter with a separate final form (ף). With a *dagesh* (פ), *pe* is pronounced like the *p* in "pit"; the spirantized pronunciation (without a *dagesh*) is like the *f* in "fit." While the sound of the *pe* without the dagesh is *f* as in "fit," by convention, the transliteration of the sound is normally *ph*.

Mini-exercise: Pronounce the following: פֵּי, עֵיג, כּוּז, בֹּל, פֵּד, גוֹ, הִיא, טַס, עֵף, פּוֹף.

4.10. VOCABULARY FOR LESSON 4

Memorize the following vocabulary words, from Hebrew to English and from English to Hebrew:

בֵּן	'son'
הוּא	'he, it'
הִיא	'she, it'
יוֹם	'day'

4.11. EXERCISES FOR LESSON 4

A. Practice writing *kaph* through *pe* according to the instructions on the Consonants Chart (appendix A).

B. Practice writing the vocabulary words you have learned so far.

C. Memorize these informal names of the last five letters of the alphabet:

tsáh-day, kof (with a long *o* as in "vote"), **raysh, sheen, tahv**

ה ◄ 5 ► ה

CONSONANTS צ THROUGH ת
AND DIPHTHONGS

5.1. SCOPE OF THE LESSON

You have now memorized, in order, the pronunciation of the names of all the letters of the alphabet. In this lesson we will learn the drawing and pronunciation of the remaining letters of the alphabet. The scholarly transliterations of their names are given in the Consonants Chart (appendix A): *tsade* (spelled "tsáh-day" at the end of the last lesson; note the accent on the first syllable), *qoph* ("kof" with long *o*), *resh* ("raysh"), *shin* ("sheen"; with similar *sin*, "seen"), and *tav* ("tahv").

5.2. THE *TSADE*

Tsade is the first consonant to be taken up in this lesson. It is pronounced like the *ts* in "hits." *Tsade* (צ) is the fifth and last letter in the alphabet with a final form (ץ). It is also the second "emphatic" consonant we have learned (ט was the first), probably pronounced in biblical times with an extra א-sound (*ts* plus a glottal stop) but pronounced simply *ts* in modern times.

Mini-exercise: Pronounce the following: יוֹז, צֶף, אֵץ, דָּג, צִי, נֵט, וֹב, לָס, צִים, חֵץ.

5.3. THE *QOPH*

The next letter of the alphabet is *qoph* (ק), our third and last emphatic consonant. *Qoph* today is pronounced like the *k* in "kid," although in biblical times it was probably pronounced with an extra א-sound (i.e., *k* plus a glottal stop).

-16-

Mini-exercise: Pronounce the following: בַּן, אֹז, מֶג, וְק, חָה, בִּיט, קוּ נֶד, קוּל צֶק, קֵב, יוֹק.

5.4. THE *RESH*

The next letter in the alphabet is *resh* (ר). English speakers generally pronounce *resh* like the *r* in "red," but those who have learned to make a guttural *r*, like the pronunciation of *r* in French, often use that pronunciation instead.

5.5. DIPHTHONGS

The next group of vowels we will take up are called diphthongs. A diphthong is a pair of vowel sounds that follow each other immediately, with no consonant in between. In BH, the diphthongs are combinations of vowels followed by the sound of *w* or *y*. In the scientific pronunciation, and in biblical times, all combinations of vowels followed by *vav* or *yod* really were pronounced as diphthongs. The term "diphthong" is not really appropriate, however, for the modern Israeli pronunciation of many of these vowels, since in that system *vav* is pronounced *v* rather than *w* or *u*. Because the term is still appropriate in the scientific pronunciation system and makes sense in the biblical system, we will continue to use it here, with the caveat that for most speakers today half of these examples are not truly diphthongs.

The diphthongs, with a dummy ב, are: *îv* בִּיו, pronounced "eve"; *êv* בֵּיו and *ēv* בֵּו, both pronounced "ave" as in "save"; *āv* בָּו, *âv* בָּיו, and *av* בַּו, all pronounced like the "av" in "bravo"; *ay* בַּי and *āy* בָּי, both pronounced like the "y" in "sky"; *ôy* בּוֹי and *ōy* בֹּי, both pronounced like the "oy" in "boy"; and finally *ûy* בּוּי and *uy* בֻּי, both pronounced like the "uey" in "gluey."

Mini-exercise: Pronounce the following: רֵל, נֹוִי, זָיו, הֹז, מֵיל, רֹוִי, אֵי, וִיר, רִיו, קָר.

5.6. THE *SHIN/SIN*

When reciting the alphabet, we always move from *resh* to *shin*, but in fact the basic part of the letter *shin* can indicate either *shin* (שׁ), pronounced like the *sh* in "ship," or *sin* (שׂ), pronounced the same as *samekh*, like the *s* in "sip." When the dot is over the right arm, the letter is *shin*; when the dot is over the left arm, the letter is *sin*. Although we skip *sin* when reciting the alphabet, it is a separate letter in Biblical Hebrew dictionaries: *sin* appears just before *shin*, as in the Consonants Chart (appendix A).

Sometimes, though not always, a *shin* (שׁ) preceded by a *holem* will have only one dot, which functions as *both* the *holem and* the dot over the right-hand arm of the שׁ. So מש is pronounced *mōsh*. This same double-duty dot can function as both the *holem* and the dot over the left-hand arm of *sin* (שׂ): שׂם is pronounced *sōm*.

Mini-exercise: Pronounce the following: שׁוּם, שִׁיל ,נֵשׁ ,שׂוִֹי ,אוֹר ,שֵׂי ,יָט ,חָשׁ ,עֹשׂ ,הֵז ,שַׁי.

5.7. THE *TAV*

ת The final letter of the alphabet, *tav* (ת), is a *beged-kephet* letter. In the Modern Israeli system, *tav* is always pronounced like the *t* in "top," both with and without a *dagesh*. (In the scientific system, *tav* without the *dagesh* is pronounced like the *th* in "think.")

> The Hebrews borrowed their alphabet from the Phoenicians, and Phoenician had by that time lost the *sin* sound: it had fallen together with the *shin* sound. Consequently, the Phoenicians only needed one letter for what was earlier two sounds. The Hebrews, however, still kept the distinction between the two sounds, so they had to adapt the Phoenician alphabet to work for the consonants they were pronouncing in their own language. They took the basic form of the letter from the Phoenicians but added a dot to it—on the right for *shin* and on the left for *sin*.

Mini-exercise: Pronounce the following: תֶּק, הֹת, כַּשׁ, אוֹת ,מוּי ,תּוֹי ,רֶט ,רִית, תָּג.

5.8. THE *BEGED-KEPHET* CONSONANTS

בֶּגֶד כֶּפֶת is a mnemonic for the six letters in Biblical Hebrew whose pronunciation was dependent on the presence or absence of a *dagesh*, the so-called *dagesh lene*. This *dagesh* is not the doubling *dagesh* (*dagesh forte*, which will be explained in the next lesson), but simply determined pronunciation based on the sounds around the consonant in question. (The *beged-kephet dagesh* is pronounced léh-nay; *forte* is pronounced fór-tay.)

In the modern Israeli pronunciation of Biblical Hebrew, these pronunciation distinctions have been kept with only three of the original six consonants: ב, כ, and פ. This means that there is no difference in pronunciation between ג and גּ (both [g] as in "get"), or between ד and דּ (both [d] as in "dog"), or between ת and תּ (both [t] as in "top"). The *beged kephet dagesh* is still an essential part of the spelling of a word, however, for *all six* בֶּגֶד כֶּפֶת consonants.

When a בֶּגֶד כֶּפֶת consonant is preceded immediately by a vowel *sound*, it is written *without* a *dagesh* (see below for exceptions). When the בֶּגֶד כֶּפֶת consonant is not preceded immediately by a vowel *sound*, it is written *with* a *dagesh*.

For the three consonants where the *dagesh lene* makes a difference in pronunciation, we refer to the pronunciation without a *dagesh* as "spirantized." בּ is [b], but ב, the spirantized pronunciation, is [v]. כּ is [k], but כ, the spirantized pronunciation, is [kh] as in German "*auch.*" פּ is [p], but פ, the spirantized pronunciation, is [f].

There are, however, exceptions to the above rules. (1) There are several "doubling" rules in Biblical Hebrew, such as the shape of the definite article: הַ plus doubling of the next consonant (with the doubling *dagesh, dagesh forte*). You put the *dagesh forte* into even בֶּגֶד כֶּפֶת consonants when you prefix the definite article's הַ to a noun, so in this case you have a בֶּגֶד כֶּפֶת consonant, preceded immediately by the vowel *patakh*, but the consonant has a *dagesh*, because the definite article rule "trumps" the בֶּגֶד כֶּפֶת rule. There are other doubling rules we will encounter in this course, and they, too, will "trump" the בֶּגֶד כֶּפֶת rules.

(2) When a word begins with a בֶּגֶד כֶּפֶת consonant, that consonant should receive a *beged-kephet dagesh*, because it would seem that by definition the first letter in a word "is not preceded immediately by a vowel sound." In practice, however, it is sometimes the case that a vowel sound at the *very end* of the previous word can affect the בֶּגֶד כֶּפֶת consonant, producing the form without *dagesh*. When this happens depends on the syntax of the sentence in the Bible and should not concern you in this class. Do not, however, be surprised when you see a בֶּגֶד כֶּפֶת consonant at the beginning of a word *without* the *dagesh*, if that *word* is preceded immediately by a vowel *sound*.

5.9. Vocabulary for lesson 5

Memorize the following vocabulary words, from Hebrew to English and from English to Hebrew:

הַר	'mountain'		רַע	'bad'
טוֹב	'good'		שֵׁם	'name'
סוּס	'horse'			

5.10. Exercises for lesson 5

A. Practice writing *tsade* through *tav* according to the instructions on the Consonants Chart (appendix A).

B. Practice reciting the 22-letter Hebrew alphabet, in its proper order.

C. Practice writing the vocabulary words you have learned.

ן ◄ **6** ► ן

THE HEBREW SYLLABLE
AND REDUCED VOWELS

6.1. THE SCOPE OF THE LESSON AND A CAVEAT

This lesson discusses the syllables found in Hebrew, the reduced vowels, and the triconsonantal root structure of Semitic languages in general. Bear in mind the following caveat. There are a great many details included in this lesson, and it is probable that they will not all be understood thoroughly at this point. Much of the information will come in handy in future lessons, however, so it is presented here with the understanding that it will only truly be digested when it is applied in the upcoming lessons.

6.2. THE TWO HEBREW SYLLABLES

BH has two kinds of syllables: open, which consists of a consonant + a vowel (Cv), and closed, which consists of a consonant + a vowel + a consonant (CvC) or consonant + diphthong.

> All syllables in BH begin with a consonant.[1]

6.3. THE ACCENT

Most words in Hebrew are accented on the final syllable. In this book, words with the accent on the last syllable will not be marked for accent at all; words with the accent on any other syllable will have that syllable marked with an accent mark: ˋ . For instance, סוּסִים 'horses' is accented on the final syllable and is therefore unmarked for accent; מֶלֶךְ 'king' is accented on the next-to-last syllable (the pen-

---

1. There is actually one minor exception to this rule, some forms of the word for 'and', which we will take up in a future lesson.

-20-

ultimate syllable or penult), and so there is an accent mark ˋ over the accented syllable. We will learn the common biblical accent marks in future lessons.

6.4. THE *DAGESH*

The next-to-last column in the Consonants Chart (appendix A) shows how most letters look when used with a *dagesh*. We have already seen that *beged-kephet* letters appear both with and without a *dagesh* (*dagesh lene*) and that there is also a "doubling" *dagesh* (*dagesh forte*). The doubling *dagesh* is used whenever a letter needs to be doubled in BH. Unlike English spelling, BH never indicates a doubled letter by writing that letter

> BH words cannot begin with a doubled consonant, and with rare exceptions, they do not end in a doubled consonant. A doubled consonant will almost always be in the middle of a word.

twice; instead, the letter is written only once, but with a doubling *dagesh* inside the letter. In English, we rarely actually pronounce the doubling of consonants, but there are exceptions, like the word "meanness," for instance. In BH, however, the doubling is an important part of any word in which it occurs. The word for 'cubit' in BH was pronounced with a doubled *m* sound: *ʾahm-mah*. It is written אַמָּה, with the doubled *m*-sound represented by *mem* with a *dagesh*: מּ.

6.5. COMPENSATORY LENGTHENING

When a rule of the language dictates that one of the gutturals or ר be doubled, the vowel preceding that consonant will sometimes be affected. Sometimes the vowel will be lengthened from a short vowel to a long vowel, called "compensatory lengthening" (i.e., a lengthening of the vowel to "compensate" for the undoubled consonant), but sometimes nothing at all will happen to the pre-

> The gutturals (א, ה, ח, and ע) plus ר cannot be doubled in BH. (There are actually rare exceptions to this in the Bible, but they need not worry us here.)

ceding vowel, in which case we speak of "virtual doubling" (i.e., the word looks exactly as it would if the consonant in question actually were doubled). When a rule of the language dictates that a *beged-kephet* letter be doubled, it is always the hard pronunciation that is doubled (i.e., the pronunciation with the *dagesh*). We will never see a doubled spirantized פ, for instance, with a doubled *f* pronunciation. It will always be a doubled hard פּ, with a doubled *p* pronunciation.

6.6. THE REDUCED VOWELS AND *SHWA*

The final set of vowels we must take up are the reduced vowels: *shwa* and the *hateph*-vowels. (*Hateph* is sometimes pronounced rather sloppily háh-tef and sometimes more correctly khah-táyf.) These are very short vowels, shorter even than BH "short" vowels. (Note that the reduced vowels are transliterated with a brève sign, ˘ , indicating that they are the shortest vowels in BH.) The *hateph*-vowels are simple: they are a combination of a short vowel plus *shwa* and are pronounced as an even shorter version of the short vowel.

Shwa itself is more difficult, because it has two uses in the BH system of pronunciation we are using: *shwa* can be either "vocal," that is, pronounced, or "silent," not pronounced at all. When it is vocal, it is pronounced like the *e* in "petition"—the shortest possible distance between two consonants.

Silent *shwa* has a very specific use. The last consonant in a BH word need not have a vowel sign after it, but every other consonant is always followed by a vowel sign.[2] For open syllables (Cv) this is no problem. For closed syllables (CvC), however, a vowel sign is not really necessary after the second consonant; there is no vowel *sound* there, simply a closed syllable ending in a *consonant* sound. All the same, the Masoretes inserted a vowel sign even there, and the sign they inserted was *shwa*. This is the "silent" *shwa*; it is not pronounced. This means that a closed (CvC) syllable that is not at the end of a word is actually written C + v + C + silent *shwa*. (Silent *shwa* is not ordinarily written at the end of a word; the most common exception is the silent *shwa* that is nestled into the final *kaph* ךְ, as in מֶלֶךְ 'king'.) The two *shwa*s, vocal and silent, look exactly alike, so the decision to pronounce or not pronounce the *shwa* must take into account other features of the word in which it occurs.

6.7. FIVE GUIDELINES FOR THE USE OF *SHWA*

The following guidelines hold true in the vast majority of cases; there are some *accented* syllables, however, such as in the word תִּשְׁמֹרְנָה 'you/they will keep' (fem. pl.), that ignore these guidelines. You will simply learn these very few exceptions as they arise.

Guideline 1

Shwa is always vocal when it is the first vowel in a word or when it is preceded immediately in the word by a long vowel.

---

2. An exception is the "quiescent *aleph*" discussed in lesson 2 and first noted in the word for "head" in lesson 8.

Mini-exercise: Pronounce the following: דְּבָרִים 'words'; שֹׁמְרִים 'watchers'.

Guideline 2

When two *shwa*s occur together in the middle of a word, the first is always silent, and the second is always vocal.

Mini-exercise: Pronounce the following: יִכְתְּבוּ 'they will write'; מִזְבְּחוֹת 'altars'.

Guideline 3

When *shwa* occurs under a doubled consonant it is always vocal.

Mini-exercise: Pronounce the following: יִרְצְחוּ 'they will murder'; לַזְּקֵנִים 'for the elders'.

Guideline 4

Vocal *shwa* can only occur in open syllables.

Guideline 5

Shwa is silent when it is preceded in the word by a short vowel. (But see rule 3 for an exception. Rule 3 "trumps" rule 5; that is, when *shwa* occurs under a doubled consonant, it is vocal even if it is preceded in the word by a short vowel.)

Mini-exercise: Pronounce the following: מִדְבָּר 'wilderness'; מַלְכָּה 'queen'; שֻׁלְחָן 'table'.

6.8. THE *HATEPH*-VOWELS

The *hateph*-vowels are most often used to substitute for *shwa* in situations where *shwa* is impossible.

The guttural consonants (א, ה, ח, and ע) are never followed by a vocal *shwa*.

We saw above that there are words in BH that have a consonant plus vocal *shwa* as part of their pattern. דְּבָרִים 'words', for example, begins with a consonant plus *shwa*, and that *shwa* is vocal because it is the first vowel in the word (see above, 6.7). When we have words that follow the same pattern as דְּבָרִים but begin with a guttural consonant, a *hateph*-vowel substitutes for the vocal *shwa*. For instance, חֲדָשִׁים 'new things' has exactly the same pattern as דְּבָרִים, except that the vocal *shwa*

> *Hateph*-vowels can occur only in open syllables.

in דְּבָרִים has been replaced in חֲדָשִׁים by a *hateph-patakh*. *Hateph-patakh* is by far the most common *hateph*-vowel, but all three can be used in this way. As another example, אֱדוֹם 'Edom' has the exact same pattern as בְּכוֹר 'firstborn', except that the vocal *shwa* in בְּכוֹר has been replaced in אֱדוֹם by a *hateph-seghol*.

6.9. Unaccented syllables and the vowels they may contain

While *accented* syllables in BH can contain any kind of vowel except the reduced vowels, in some *unaccented* syllables, the kind of syllable (open or closed) and the quantity of the vowel (long or short) are interconnected. For instance,

> an unaccented closed syllable in BH will almost always contain a short vowel (*patakh, hireq, seghol, qibbuts,* or *qamets* as short *o*).[3]

Less predictably,

> an unaccented open syllable in BH will usually contain a long vowel (*qamets, tsere, holem, holem-vav, shureq, hireq gadol,* or *tsere-yod*) or a reduced vowel (*shwa* or one of the *hateph*-vowels).

Taking together what we know about syllables and *shwa*, we can see that an unaccented *closed* syllable in BH will (with two exceptions) consist of consonant + *short* vowel + consonant + silent *shwa*. (Remember, however, that the silent *shwa* is not generally used at the end of a word.) See the first syllable of מִדְבָּר and of שֻׁלְחָן above.

We can also see that most unaccented *open* syllables consist of consonant + *long* vowel or of consonant + *reduced* vowel. See the first two syllables of דְּבָרִים and of שֹׁמְרִים above.

---

3. In the entire language there are only two words that are exceptions to this rule: the plural of בַּיִת 'house' is בָּתִּים 'houses', with the mark to the left of the *qamets* (called a *metheg*, to be discussed in a later lesson) indicating that the unaccented *qamets* is to be pronounced long *a*, even with the accent on the final syllable; and the rare interjection of entreaty אָנָּה, with the *metheg* indicating the same thing.

6.10. THE FURTIVE *PATAKH*

There is one vowel we have not yet dealt with, and that is what is known as a "furtive *patakh*." When a word ends in certain long vowels plus one of the gutturals ח, ע, or הּ (i.e., ה with *mappiq*, a true *h* sound), there is a very short *a*-sound that is pronounced between the long vowel and the guttural. This is the furtive *patakh*. Unlike a regular *patakh*, a furtive *patakh* is not written directly under a consonant but rather slightly to the right of the position of a normal *patakh*: לוּחַ 'tablet', pronounced *loo{}^{a}kh* (only one syllable), where the superscript *a* represents a very short *a*-sound. The furtive *patakh* does not add a syllable to the structure of the word, although the Anglicized pronunciation of some words treats the syllable as if it were two: the final *a* in the name Joshua, for instance, is actually a furtive *patakh*, יְהוֹשׁוּעַ, so that in Hebrew the name is pronounced "yə-ho-shoo{}^{a}."

6.11. THE TRICONSONANTAL ROOT IN SEMITIC LANGUAGES

All Semitic languages operate with a triconsonantal system; that is, there are three-consonant roots that carry a general meaning, which is made specific by the patterns of vowels, prefixes, suffixes, and doubling of consonants that occur within a given word. For example, in Hebrew, the root מ-ל-ך has something to do with 'ruling':

מֶלֶךְ means 'king'

מָלַכְתִּי means 'I ruled'

תִּמְלֹךְ means 'she will rule'

הִמְלַכְתִּי means 'I caused (someone else) to rule'

מְלוּכָה means 'kingship'

Much of learning BH, then, is a matter of figuring out the root of a given word and deciding whether the pattern of the word is one that is already familiar. A word from an unfamiliar root and/or pattern must be looked up in a dictionary, and the most popular English-language scholarly dictionary, Brown-Driver-Briggs, arranges all its words alphabetically according to the perceived root of the word, so learning to identify roots is a very important step in any Hebrew study.

6.12. EXERCISES FOR LESSON 6

A. Divide the Hebrew words used in this lesson (listed below) into syllables, and indicate the length of each vowel and whether each syllable is open or closed and whether it is accented or unaccented. For instance, דְּבָרִים can be divided and analyzed in the following way:

third (and last) syllable	second syllable	first syllable
רִים	בְ	דְּ
accented closed syllable, irreducibly long vowel	unaccented open syllable, long vowel	unaccented open syllable, reduced vowel

Do the same thing for the following words; for this exercise, none of the *dagesh*es in *beged-kephet* letters is a doubling *dagesh*; they are all simply *beged-kephet dagesh*es:

מֶלֶךְ (remember that at the end of a word, silent *shwa* is usually not written, but in a word that ends in *kaph*, it is nestled into the ךְ)

אַמָּה (note that the doubled *mem* includes one *mem* that closes the first syllable and a second *mem* that begins the second syllable)

סוּסִים	שֻׁלְחָן	יְהוֹשׁוּעַ[4]
שֹׁמְרִים	חֲדָשִׁים	מָלַכְתִּי
יִכְתְּבוּ	אֱדוֹם	תִּמְלֹךְ
מִזְבְּחוֹת	בְּכוֹר	הִמְלַכְתִּי
יְבַשְּׁלוּ	מִדְבָּר	מְלוּכָה
לִזְקֵנִים	מַלְכָּה	

B. We saw above that מָלַכְתִּי comes from the root מלך and means 'I ruled'. Given the root שמר 'to observe, guard, watch', how would you write and pronounce 'I observed'? We also saw above that תִּמְלֹךְ means 'she will rule'. How would you write and pronounce 'she will observe'?[4]

C. Practice reading the first line of Gen 22:1 (appendix C).

---

4. The name Joshua is spelled this way only twice in the Bible, normally being spelled with a *qibbuts*, יְהוֹשֻׁעַ. Because of the two instances where it is written with a *shureq*, we know there is a long vowel before the *ayin*, so in all the other instances the *qibbuts* represents a long vowel even though it is written without the *vav mater*.

7

INDEPENDENT PERSONAL
PRONOUNS AND ADJECTIVES

7.1. THE INDEPENDENT PERSONAL PRONOUNS

In the box below are the BH independent personal pronouns, with singular and plural number distinguished in all three persons, and masculine and feminine gender distinguished in second and third persons.

INDEPENDENT PERSONAL PRONOUNS

we	אֲנַחְנוּ	אָנֹכִי, אֲנִי	I
you (mp)	אַתֶּם	אַתָּ(ה)	you (ms)
you (fp)	אַתֵּנָה	אַתְּ	you (fs)
they (m)	הֵם	הוּא	he, it
they (f)	הֵנָּה	הִיא	she, it

Note that 'I' has two forms, with the shorter form more common. 'You' (ms) is written with or without the ה-*mater*. The doubled ת (ת + ּ) at the end of אַתְּ is there for historical reasons, even though it breaks the rule about doubled consonants at the end of words. There are, further, less common alternate plural forms such as אַתֵּן ('you' fp) and הֵמָּה ('they' mp). Independent personal pronouns are generally used as the subject of a sentence.

> The Feminine Plural in Biblical Hebrew
>
> The feminine plural is used in BH only when the entire group in question is feminine in gender. The masculine plural is used for groups of items that are all masculine in gender *and* for groups that are mixed in gender.

7.2. ADJECTIVES

Adjectives in BH are either masculine or feminine, singular or plural. Using the adjective טוֹב 'good', the chart below demonstrates the forms for both genders and both numbers (the chart reads from right to left).

ONE-SYLLABLE ADJECTIVES

mp	טוֹבִים	טוֹב	ms
fp	טוֹבוֹת	טוֹבָה	fs

In two-syllable adjectives with *qamets* in the first syllable, the *qamets* often reduces to *shwa* when gender and number endings are added, as in גָּדוֹל 'big, large, great' below. This reduction of the vowel will be noted in the vocabularies, when appropriate.

TWO-SYLLABLE ADJECTIVES WITH *QAMETS*

mp	גְּדוֹלִים	גָּדוֹל	ms
fp	גְּדוֹלוֹת	גְּדוֹלָה	fs

7.3. ATTRIBUTIVE ADJECTIVES

BH has both attributive adjectives and predicate adjectives. Attributive adjectives are part of a noun-adjective phrase, like 'the good woman'. 'Good' in that phrase is an attributive adjective. A predicate adjective comes after the verb 'to be', either expressed or unexpressed. In the sentence 'The man is good', 'good' is a predicate adjective.

> Note that BH does not use a form of the verb 'to be' unless it is important that tense be indicated (see lesson 8 for more on this issue).

We will use the nouns 'horse', 'mare', 'horses', and 'mares' to demonstrate the use of attributive adjectives in Hebrew. An attributive adjective follows the noun it modifies and agrees with it in gender, number, and definiteness (to be discussed later).

ATTRIBUTIVE ADJECTIVES

a good mare	סוּסָה טוֹבָה	a good horse	סוּס טוֹב
good mares	סוּסוֹת טוֹבוֹת	good horses	סוּסִים טוֹבִים

7.4. PREDICATE ADJECTIVES

Predicate adjectives are used with a subject to form a sentence. In the sentence 'He is good' טוֹב הוּא, 'good' טוֹב is a predicate adjective.[1] A predicate adjective agrees with the noun it modifies in number and gender but not definiteness; it is always indefinite, as in טוֹבוֹת הֵנָּה 'They are good', where 'they' stands for a group of females or a group of items that are all feminine in gender.

7.5. THE ADVERB מְאֹד

The adverb מְאֹד 'very' modifies adjectives and follows them in a phrase or sentence. It does not change with gender or number. For instance, טוֹב מְאֹד 'very good'; סוּסוֹת גְּדוֹלוֹת מְאֹד 'very large mares'.

7.6. VOCABULARY FOR LESSON 7

noun

    סוּסָה   'mare' (fem. of סוּס 'horse')

pronouns

    אֲנִי   'I'

    אָנֹכִי   'I'

    אֲנַחְנוּ   'we'

    אַתָּה   'you' (ms); sometimes written אַתְּ

    אַתְּ   'you' (fs)

---

1. The word order used in טוֹב הוּא, i.e., predicate adjective first, then pronoun subject, is the normal order. The opposite order, pronoun subject first, then predicate adjective (i.e., הוּא טוֹב) does occur, but much less frequently.

אַתֶּם   'you' (mp)

אַתֵּנָה   'you' (fp)

הוּא   'he, it'

הִיא   'she, it'

הֵם   'they' (mp)

הֵנָּה   'they' (fp)

adjectives

גָּדוֹל   'big, large, great' (the *qamets* reduces to *shwa*)

זָקֵן   'old' (the *qamets* reduces to *shwa*)

טוֹב   'good'

קָטֹן ,קָטָן   'small, little' (irregular: קְטַנָּה ,קְטַנִּים ,קְטַנּוֹת)

adverb

מְאֹד   'very'

7.7. EXERCISES FOR LESSON 7

A. Translate from Hebrew to English:

1. Phrases

1. סוּסָה טוֹבָה

2. סוּס טוֹב

3. סוּס גָּדוֹל

4. סוּסָה גְּדוֹלָה מְאֹד

5. סוּסָה זְקֵנָה

6. סוּסוֹת טוֹבוֹת

7. סוּסִים קְטַנִּים מְאֹד

2. Sentences

1. טוֹב מְאֹד הוּא

2. קָטֹן הוּא

3. זְקֵנָה הִיא

4. גְּדוֹלִים מְאֹד אֲנַ֫חְנוּ

5. טוֹבוֹת הֵ֫נָּה

6. זְקֵנִים הֵם

B. Translate from English to Hebrew:

1. I am good. (spoken by a woman)

2. I am good. (spoken by a man)

3. She is great.

4. He is old.

5. They (masc.) are very good.

C. Practice reading the second line of Gen 22:1.

ח ◄ **8** ► ח

NOUNS, THE DEFINITE ARTICLE,
AND THE CONJUNCTION ‍ו

8.1. NOUNS GENERALLY

Nouns in BH, like adjectives, have gender and number: masculine or feminine, singular or plural. A few nouns, especially paired body parts like hands or eyes, also occur in the dual (to be discussed separately in lesson 11.5). We will use the BH noun סוּס 'horse' as a convenient paradigm noun.

NOUNS BY NUMBER AND GENDER

mp	סוּסִים	horses	horse	סוּס	ms
fp	סוּסוֹת	mares	mare	סוּסָה	fs

As is obvious from the paradigm above, the feminine singular, masculine plural, and feminine plural endings for nouns can be, and usually are, the same as the endings on adjectives.

There are two other feminine endings that are somewhat common: ת ֵ-, as in בַּת 'daughter', and ת ֶ-, for example, on feminine participles such as שֹׁמֶרֶת 'watcher', to be discussed below, in lesson 18.

8.2. TWO-SYLLABLE NOUNS WITH *QAMETS* IN THE FIRST SYLLABLE

In two-syllable nouns with *qamets* in the first syllable, the *qamets* often reduces to *shwa* when gender and number endings are added, for instance, דָּבָר 'word, thing, matter, affair', plural דְּבָרִים.

8.3. SEGHOLATE NOUNS

Two-syllable nouns with the accent on the first syllable, commonly known as "segholates," have a set pattern for the plural: *shwa* or *hateph*-vowel in the first syllable, *qamets* in the second syllable, and the plural ending.

מֶלֶךְ	king	pl.	מְלָכִים
עֶבֶד	slave, servant	pl.	עֲבָדִים[1]

8.4 . GENDER OF NOUNS

Unlike adjectives, however, the gender of a noun is not always obvious from the endings or lack of ending. Some feminine nouns have no feminine ending in the singular, yet the gender is still feminine (as can be deduced from the feminine adjectives that modify the noun). Names of countries and towns tend to be feminine in gender, for example, as do paired body parts. The most common of these endingless feminine nouns are:

אֵם	mother		אֹזֶן	ear
אֶרֶץ	earth, land		עַיִן	eye; spring, source
עִיר	city, town		יָד	hand; side

So, 'a good land' is אֶרֶץ טוֹבָה; 'an old mother' is אֵם זְקֵנָה; and so on.

There are also nouns with ות- plurals that are actually masculine in gender. The most common are:

אָב	father	pl.	אָבוֹת
מָקוֹם	place	pl.	מְקוֹמוֹת
קוֹל	voice, sound	pl.	קֹלוֹת

Likewise, some feminine words with the feminine ending ה ָ- in the singular have plurals in ים ִ-. The most common of these is the irregular plural of אִשָּׁה:

אִשָּׁה	woman	pl.	נָשִׁים

---

1. Note that the *hateph-patakh* in עֲבָדִים substitutes for the vocal *shwa* found in מְלָכִים.

It is important to note that these words *do not change gender* from singular to plural. 'A good woman' is אִשָּׁה טוֹבָה, and 'good women' is נָשִׁים טוֹבוֹת. 'A good father' is אָב טוֹב, and 'good fathers' is אָבוֹת טוֹבִים.

8.5. THE DEFINITE ARTICLE

There are several ways that a noun in BH can be *definite*. First, all proper nouns are considered definite. Second, a noun can be defined by the addition of a definite article, "the" in English.[2]

In BH, the definite article for most nouns is הַ on the beginning of the word, plus doubling of the first letter of the noun itself. So:

מֶלֶךְ	king, a king	הַמֶּלֶךְ	the king
סוּס	horse, a horse	הַסּוּס	the horse

8.6. THE DEFINITE ARTICLE WITH INITIAL GUTTURALS AND *RESH*

Because the definite article is הַ plus *doubling*, it is a problem that א, ה, ח, ע, and ר cannot be doubled. We learned in lesson 6.5 that the two responses to this problem are compensatory lengthening of the preceding vowel and virtual doubling of the consonant. The definite article on words beginning with א, ע, and ר is almost always הָ, with *patakh* lengthening to *qamets* before the א, ע, or ר. For instance:

אִשָּׁה	woman, a woman	הָאִשָּׁה	the woman
רֹאשׁ	head, a head	הָרֹאשׁ	the head
עִיר	city, a city	הָעִיר	the city

For words beginning with ה or ח, the definite article is almost always הַ without doubling of the next letter; hence the ה or ח is "virtually" doubled. For instance:

הֵיכָל	palace, temple	הַהֵיכָל	the palace, temple
חֶרֶב	sword	הַחֶרֶב	the sword

There are a few situations where the definite article is הֶ. These will be pointed out as we come to them.

---

2. There is no indefinite article in BH, so מֶלֶךְ is both 'king' and 'a king'.

8.7. THE DEFINITE ARTICLE WITH CERTAIN WORDS

Finally, there are a few nouns in BH that have slightly different vowel patterns when the definite article is added. These words must simply be learned as part of BH vocabulary. The most common such words are identified in the box below.

אֶרֶץ	earth, land	הָאָרֶץ	the earth, the land
עַם	people, nation	הָעָם	the people, the nation
הַר	mountain	הָהָר	the mountain

The Definite Article: Nine Words to Remember

Memorizing a list made up of the following nine words will help you to remember the rules for the definite article in almost every instance:

הָאָרֶץ	הַהֵיכָל	הָאִשָּׁה	הַמֶּלֶךְ
הָעָם	הַחֶרֶב	הָרֹאשׁ	
הָהָר		הָעִיר	

8.8. AGREEMENT BETWEEN DEFINITE NOUNS AND ADJECTIVES

The definiteness of a noun has an effect on the way adjectives are used in BH. An *attributive* adjective agrees with the noun it modifies in gender and number, and also in *definiteness*. So:

מֶלֶךְ טוֹב	a good king	הַמֶּלֶךְ הַטּוֹב	the good king
אֲנָשִׁים טוֹבִים	good men	הָאֲנָשִׁים הַטּוֹבִים	the good men
אִשָּׁה טוֹבָה	a good woman	הָאִשָּׁה הַטּוֹבָה	the good woman

A *predicate* adjective also agrees with the noun it modifies in gender and number, but it is always indefinite. In fact, when a definite noun is paired with an *indefinite* predicate adjective of the same number and gender as the noun, the result is actually a sentence:

טוֹב הַמֶּלֶךְ	'The king is good.'[3]
טוֹבִים הָאֲנָשִׁים	'The men are good.'
טוֹבָה הָאִשָּׁה	'The woman is good.'

> Remember: the word 'to be' need not be used in BH, unless it is important to determine tense in a clause. The combination of a definite noun and an indefinite adjective *assumes* the verb 'to be'.

8.9. THE WORD 'AND'

The word for 'and' in BH is simply וְ, which is written at the beginning of the word that follows 'and'. For instance, 'the man and the woman' is הָאִישׁ וְהָאִשָּׁה.

While the ordinary form of the conjunction is וְ, its form can change for phonological reasons.

> *Vav* Rule 1
>
> Before ב, מ, or פ, וְ becomes וּ. This is the "BuMP" rule: before a *b*-sound, an *m*-sound, or a *p/f*-sound (the B, M, and P of BuMP), וְ becomes וּ (the u of BuMP). For example, 'a queen and a king' is מַלְכָּה וּמֶלֶךְ.

> *Vav* Rule 2
>
> At the beginning of most words whose first vowel is *shwa*, וְ becomes וּ. For example, 'voices and words' is קֹלוֹת וּדְבָרִים.

> *Vav* Rule 3
>
> At the beginning of a word, וְיְ becomes וִי. For example, 'Judah' is יְהוּדָה, and 'the city and Judah' is הָעִיר וִיהוּדָה.

---

3. As with the phrase טוֹב הוּא 'He is good', explained in 7.4 above, the more common word order for a sentence like 'The king is good' is predicate adjective first and defined noun second. The opposite order does occur, but less frequently.

> *Vav* Rule 4
>
> Finally, at the beginning of a word whose first vowel is a *hateph*-vowel, the vowel of 'and' will "mirror" the *hateph*-vowel. For example, 'kings and slaves' is מְלָכִים וַעֲבָדִים.

> Summary: 'and' is usually וְ, but in some phonological environments it can change to וּ or ו plus a "mirroring" *hateph*-vowel; finally, at the beginning of a word, וְיִ becomes וִי.

8.10. VOCABULARY FOR LESSON 8

nouns

אִישׁ	'man, a male human being'
אֲנָשִׁים	'men'; irregular pl. of אִישׁ
אֵם	'mother' (fem.); pl. אִמּוֹת
אֶרֶץ	'earth, land, country' (fem.); with def. art. הָאָרֶץ; pl. אֲרָצוֹת
אִשָּׁה	'woman' (fem.)
נָשִׁים	'women' (fem.); irregular pl. of אִשָּׁה
דָּבָר	'word, thing, matter, affair'
הֵיכָל	'temple, palace'; pl. הֵיכָלוֹת (masc., like the sg.)
הַר	'mountain, mountain range'; with def. art. הָהָר; pl. הָרִים; with def. art. הֶהָרִים (note the *seghol* of the def. art.)
חֶרֶב	'sword' (fem.); pl. חֲרָבוֹת
מֶלֶךְ	'king'; pl. מְלָכִים
מַלְכָּה	'queen' (fem.); pl. מְלָכוֹת [4]
מָקוֹם	'place'; pl. מְקוֹמוֹת (masc., like the sg.)
עֶבֶד	'slave, servant'; pl. עֲבָדִים
עִיר	'city, town' (fem.)
עָרִים	'cities' (fem.); irregular pl. of עִיר; with def. art. הֶעָרִים (note the *seghol* of the def. art.)

---

4. מַלְכָּה is, in fact, the feminine counterpart of the segholate מֶלֶךְ. Note the similarity between this plural and the plural of מֶלֶךְ, immediately above.

עַם   'people, nation' (collective); with def. art. הָעָם; pl. עַמִּים; both singular and plural adjectives (and verbs) are used with this noun, with no difference in meaning

קוֹל   'voice, sound'; pl.: we would expect קוֹלוֹת, but in fact it is never written in the extant text with both *vav*s. We find instead קֹלוֹת, קוֹלֹת, or even קֹלֹת (masc., like the sg.).

רֹאשׁ   'head'; pl. irregular רָאשִׁים (Note the quiescent א in both the singular and plural; see above, 2.3.)

adjectives

יָפֶה   'beautiful, handsome'; fem. sg. יָפָה, masc. pl. יָפִים, fem. pl. יָפוֹת. There are many adjectives and nouns that end in ה ָ - (the ה is a *mater lectionis*). Note that in the feminine and plural forms, the ה ָ - simply drops away before the endings are added.

רַע   'evil, bad, troublesome'; fem. sg. רָעָה, masc. pl. רָעִים, fem. pl. רָעוֹת. Note that the *patakh* becomes *qamets* in the feminine and plural forms.

definite article

הַ   + doubling of the next letter

conjunction

וְ   'and'; can also mean 'but' and 'or' when the sense calls for it

8.11. EXERCISES FOR LESSON 8

A. Translate the following into English:

   1. Phrases

1. אֶרֶץ טוֹבָה

2. הָאָרֶץ הַטּוֹבָה

3. דְּבַר רַע

4. הַדָּבָר הָרַע

5. הַסּוּסוֹת הַיָּפוֹת

6. רֹאשׁ גָּדוֹל

7. הֶהָרִים וְהֶעָרִים

8. דְּבָרִים וְקוֹלֹת

9. אֲנָשִׁים וְנָשִׁים

10. הָאֵם הַטּוֹבָה

2. Sentences

1. גְּדוֹלוֹת הֶעָרִים

2. קְטַנָּה הַחֶרֶב

3. יָפֶה הַהֵיכָל

4. רַע הַמֶּלֶךְ

5. רָעִים הֵם

6. גָּדוֹל הָעָם

7. זָקֵן הָעֶבֶד

8. גְּדוֹלָה הָאָרֶץ

9. יָפִים הֶעָרִים וְהֶהָרִים

10. זְקֵנָה הִיא

B. Translate the following into Hebrew:

   1. the big city and the beautiful land

   2. the handsome king and the beautiful queen

   3. good places

   4. He is a small horse.

   5. You are a good queen.

C. Practice reading the third line of Gen 22:1.

ט ◄ **9** ► ט

PREPOSITIONS, THE RELATIVE PRONOUN, AND THE "RULE OF *SHWA*"

9.1. THREE KINDS OF PREPOSITIONS

Prepositions in BH occur in three forms.

1. Some prepositions are separate words that come directly before their objects. For instance, אֵצֶל is 'near, next to', and 'near the city' is אֵצֶל הָעִיר.

2. Some prepositions are connected to their noun objects by a sort of above-the-line hyphen called a *maqqeph* ("mah-káyf"). For instance, עַל is 'on, above, on top of', and עַל־הַסּוּס is 'on the horse'; אֶל is 'to', and 'to the city' is אֶל־הָעִיר.[1]

3. The most common prepositions, however, are the three *inseparable* prepositions. That is, they are connected directly to their (usually) noun objects and go together with them to form a single word (as ו 'and' does).

ב is 'in, on, at; with [instrumental], by means of': 'in a palace' is בְּהֵיכָל; 'with [instrumental] a loud voice' is בְּקוֹל גָּדוֹל.

ל is 'to, for' (not used, however, for traveling 'to' a place; that is אֶל, above). 'To a king' (as in someone gave something *to* a king) is לְמֶלֶךְ; 'for a man' (as in someone did something *for* a man) is לְאִישׁ.

כ is 'like', and 'like a queen' is כְּמַלְכָּה.

---

1. When words are tied together in this way, there is only one accent for the entire combination, and that is the accent on the final word. Remember, the Masoretes were simply indicating what they were saying and hearing; the use of a *maqqeph* between two (or more) words indicates that they were pronouncing the first word(s) without any accent.

9.2. INSEPARABLE PREPOSITIONS AND THE DEFINITE ARTICLE

When the object of one of these inseparable prepositions has the definite article, there is a loss of the ה of the definite article, and the preposition takes the vowel of the definite article.

'for a king' is לְמֶלֶךְ

'for *the* king' is not לְהַמֶּלֶךְ, as you might expect, but rather לַמֶּלֶךְ

'for a woman' is לְאִשָּׁה

'for the woman' is לָאִשָּׁה

'in the palace' is בַּהֵיכָל

'like the men' is כָּאֲנָשִׁים

9.3. PREPOSITIONS WITH PRONOUNS (THE PARADIGM בְּ)

When prepositions take pronouns as their objects, the pronouns are not written as separate words but rather occur as pronominal suffixes, on the end of the preposition. For instance, 'in it' (masc.) is בּוֹ; 'to me' is אֵלַי. It will be very useful to memorize two different paradigms of preposition + suffixes: once they are memorized, it will be easy for you to recognize the forms of the several similar paradigms given below. The first paradigm to be memorized is from בְּ 'in'.[2]

THE PREPOSITION בְּ

in us	בָּנוּ	בִּי	in me
in you (mp)	בָּכֶם	בְּךָ	in you (ms)
in you (fp)	בָּכֶן	בָּךְ	in you (fs)
in them (m)	בָּם	בּוֹ	in him/it
in them (f)	בָּן	בָּהּ	in her/it

'In them' can also be written בָּהֶם and בָּהֶן, even בָּהֵמָּה and בָּהֵנָּה, but the shorter forms should be memorized. לְ follows the same pattern as בְּ, except we usually get לָהֶם and לָהֶן (rarely לָהֵמָּה and לָהֵנָּה), never לָם or לָן.

---

2. When used in a paradigm, the number in parentheses after each form is the person (1st, 2nd, or 3rd); the m or f is masculine or feminine gender; the s or p is singular or plural.

עִם 'with' and אֶת/אֵת 'with' (used interchangeably) have similar patterns but are not exactly the same. In these two paradigms, the second consonant is doubled; otherwise, once the בְּ paradigm is memorized, the forms of עִם and אֵת are easily recognized. Be sure to note the unexpected but common form עִמָּדִי.

with us	אִתָּנוּ		אִתִּי	with me
with you (mp)	אִתְּכֶם		אִתְּךָ	with you (ms)
with you (fp)	אִתְּכֶן		אִתָּךְ	with you (fs)
with them (m)	אִתָּם		אִתּוֹ	with him/it
with them (f)	אִתָּן		אִתָּהּ	with her/it

with us	עִמָּנוּ		עִמִּי or עִמָּדִי	with me
with you (mp)	עִמָּכֶם		עִמְּךָ	with you (ms)
with you (fp)	עִמָּכֶן		עִמָּךְ	with you (fs)
with them (m)	עִמָּם		עִמּוֹ	with him/it
with them (f)	עִמָּן		עִמָּהּ	with her/it

The preposition כְּ 'like' has a similar paradigm, but with more variation. Note especially the addition of the accented syllable מוֹ in most forms; the endings for 'me', 'him', and 'her' are somewhat different from those in the בְּ paradigm.

like us	כָּמֹונוּ		כָּמֹונִי	like me
like you (mp)	כָּכֶם		כָּמֹוךָ	like you (ms)
like you (fp)	כָּכֶן		כָּמֹוךְ	like you (fs)
like them (m)	כָּהֶם		כָּמֹוהוּ	like him/it
like them (f)	כָּהֵנָּה		כָּמֹוהָ	like her/it

9.4. PREPOSITIONS WITH PRONOUNS (THE PARADIGM אֶל־)

The second paradigm to be memorized is from אֶל־ 'to'. Note that אֵלָיו, אֵלֶיךָ, and אֵלֶיהָ are pronounced as if the י were not there.

THE PREPOSITION אֶל־

to us	אֵלֵ֫ינוּ	אֵלַי	to me
to you (mp)	אֲלֵיכֶם	אֵלֶ֫יךָ	to you (ms)
to you (fp)	אֲלֵיכֶן	אֵלַ֫יִךְ	to you (fs)
to them (m)	אֲלֵיהֶם	אֵלָיו	to him/it
to them (f)	אֲלֵיהֶן	אֵלֶ֫יהָ	to her/it

עַל־ 'on, above, over' has the same paradigm, including the *hateph-patakh* under the ע in the second and third persons plural, but *qamets* under ע everywhere else: עָלַי and עֲלֵיהֶם. (Without a suffix, עַל־ is usually, but not always, written with a *maqqeph*.)

תַּ֫חַת 'under; in the place of' and אַחַר/אַחֲרֵי 'after' also follow this same paradigm. They begin

תַּחְתַּי	אַחֲרַי
תַּחְתֶּ֫יךָ	אַחֲרֶ֫יךָ

and the remainder of these paradigms can be figured out from there.

9.5. THE PREPOSITION מִן

One very common preposition, which we have yet to take up, is מִן 'from'. מִן is usually written directly on the front of its object. It behaves slightly differently, however, from other inseparable prepositions, because, as we will see again and again, when נ comes immediately before another consonant, it tends to "assimilate" to that consonant; that is, the נ disappears, and the next consonant is doubled. 'From a king' is, theoretically, מִנְמֶ֫לֶךְ, but since the *shwa* under the נ is silent, the נ would be pronounced immediately before the מ in מֶ֫לֶךְ; so the נ assimilates, and the form we actually get is מִמֶּ֫לֶךְ. 'From a horse' is מִסּוּס; 'from a voice' is מִקּוֹל; and so on.

> Note: *nun* regularly assimilates to the following consonant if no vowel sound intervenes.

Because there is doubling involved in adding the word מִן to its object, problems will inevitably occur when the noun object begins with one of the gutturals or ר. In those cases, because the first letter of the noun object cannot be doubled, we get compensatory lengthening instead, and the *hireq* lengthens to *tsere*. 'From a woman' is מֵאִשָּׁה; 'from a sword' is מֵחֶרֶב. Occasionally we find "virtual doubling" (see 6.5), as in מֵחוּץ.

The definite article, since it begins with the guttural consonant ה, is an obvious subset of this doubling problem. Besides the usual solution, that is, 'from the horse' מֵהַסּוּס, we also find the entire word מִן hung from the front of its noun object with a *maqqeph*. So 'from the horse' can also be written מִן־הַסּוּס.

When the object of מִן is a pronoun, the pronominal suffixes are very similar to those of the בְּ paradigm.

from us	מִמֶּנּוּ	מִמֶּנִּי	from me
from you (mp)	מִכֶּם	מִמְּךָ	from you (ms)
from you (fp)	מִכֶּן	מִמֵּךְ	from you (fs)
from them (m)	מֵהֶם	מִמֶּנּוּ	from him/it
from them (f)	מֵהֵנָּה	מִמֶּנָּה	from her/it

Note that 'from him' and 'from us' are both מִמֶּנּוּ; the difference must be discovered from context. 'From you' (fs) has a *tsere* מִמֵּךְ instead of the *qamets* we have come to expect. Note, finally, the compensatory lengthening that occurs when the pronominal suffix begins with the guttural ה.

9.6. ANOTHER MEANING OF מִן

Besides its meaning 'from', מִן is also used to express comparison in BH: 'more/better than' or 'too (much) for' (the difference to be decided from context). 'The slave is better *than* the king' in BH is actually 'good is the slave *from* the king', טוֹב הָעֶבֶד מֵהַמֶּלֶךְ; 'the man is *too* old *for* the woman' = 'old is the man *from* the woman', זָקֵן הָאִישׁ מִן־הָאִשָּׁה.

9.7. THE RELATIVE PRONOUN אֲשֶׁר

In BH, the relative pronoun ('which', 'who') is אֲשֶׁר. אֲשֶׁר does not change with the gender, number, or definiteness of its antecedent; it is always אֲשֶׁר. We will take up the use of אֲשֶׁר in verbal sentences in a later lesson, but at this point it is important to know that a noun that is modified by a prepositional phrase in BH is ordinarily separated from that prepositional phrase by אֲשֶׁר. The word for 'house' is בַּיִת, so 'the woman in the house' would be written הָאִשָּׁה אֲשֶׁר בַּבַּיִת. 'The tree (עֵץ) near the river (נָהָר)' is הָעֵץ אֲשֶׁר אֵצֶל הַנָּהָר.

Note that although it is perfectly grammatical in English usage to leave out the relative pronoun in phrases like the ones above—'the woman in the house', 'the tree near the river'—in BH the relative pronoun אֲשֶׁר must be used between the noun and the prepositional phrase that modifies it.

9.8. ANOTHER WAY TO CONSTRUCT A SENTENCE

We saw above in lesson 8.8 that it is possible to make a sentence in BH by juxtaposing a definite noun and an indefinite predicate adjective: טוֹב הָאִישׁ 'The man is good'. It is also possible to make a sentence by juxtaposing a noun and a prepositional phrase (although here the prepositional phrase follows the noun): הָאִשָּׁה בַּבַּיִת 'The woman is in the house'. As before, the verb 'to be' is usually not expressed.

We can combine the sentences in 9.7 and 9.8 to make sentences like the following: 'The woman in the house is good' טוֹבָה הָאִשָּׁה אֲשֶׁר בַּבַּיִת; 'the tree near the river is large' גָּדוֹל הָעֵץ אֲשֶׁר אֵצֶל הַנָּהָר.

9.9. THE RULE OF *SHWA* FOR INSEPARABLE PREPOSITIONS

Because the prepositions בְּ, לְ, and כְּ come at the beginning of a word, the *shwa*-vowels of the prepositions will always be vocal. If, however, the noun object to which they are attached also has a *shwa* as its first vowel, the result would be two vocal *shwa*s at the beginning of a word, and that is something the language will not allow. Instead, what is called the "rule of *shwa*" takes over: whenever a word would begin with two vocal *shwa*s, the first one becomes *hireq* instead. Therefore, 'in places' is not בְּמְקוֹמוֹת but בִּמְקוֹמוֹת (with a now *silent shwa* under the first מ); 'like kings' is כִּמְלָכִים (with a silent *shwa* under the first מ); and so on.[3]

It is equally impossible in BH to have as the first two vowels of a word a vocal *shwa* followed by a *hateph*-vowel. In such cases, as we learned with the forms of וְ 'and', the vocal *shwa* "mirrors" the *hateph*-vowel. 'For slaves' is not לְעֲבָדִים but rather לַעֲבָדִים.

9.10. VOCABULARY FOR LESSON 9

nouns

בַּיִת	'house'
בָּתִּים[4]	'houses'; irregular pl. of בַּיִת

---

3. Remember that we learned in lesson 8 that forms of the וְ 'and' are an exception to this rule. Instead of becoming וְ in these circumstances, it ordinarily becomes וּ. (When וְ becomes וִי, however, it is because of the rule of *shwa*.)

4. The small vertical line to the left of the *qamets* is called a *metheg* (pronounced méh-teg and, less correctly but quite commonly, méh-theg). In this textbook, when used next to a *qamets*, a

דֶּרֶךְ   'road, way; journey; way of life'

נָהָר   'river'; pl. נְהָרוֹת (masc., like the sg.)

עֵץ   'tree'

שָׂדֶה   'field'; pl. שָׂדוֹת (masc., like the sg.)

proper nouns

דָּוִד   'David' (also written דָּוִיד in mostly later texts; we will use דָּוִד)

יְהוּדָה   'Judah'

מֹשֶׁה   'Moses'

pronoun/conjunction

אַחַר   'after'

אֲשֶׁר   relative pronoun/conjunction: 'who, which'

adverb

שָׁם   'there; in that place'

prepositions

אַחַר/אַחֲרֵי   'after, behind; to the west of'

אֶל־   'to'; regularly with verbs of motion (*not* with indirect object; see לְ below)

אֵצֶל   'near, next to' (follows pattern of בְּ with pronoun sf., e.g., אֶצְלִי)

אֶת־/אֵת   'with, along with'

בְּ   'in, on, at; with' (i.e., instrumental 'with' = 'by means of')

כְּ   'like'

לְ   'to, for, as' (as 'to', used with indirect object; used with infinitive of verbs; not ordinarily used with verbs of motion)

מִן   'from'; used to express the comparative

עַל־   'on; above; on top of; beside; against'

עִם   'with; along with'

תַּחַת   'under; in the place of, instead of'

---

metheg indicates that the *qamets* is to be pronounced long *a*. This will be discussed in more detail in a later lesson. Remember that בָּתִּים is one of two words in the language that contain a long vowel in a closed, unaccented syllable.

9.11. EXERCISES FOR LESSON 9

A. Complete the paradigms for תַּחַת and אַחֲרֵי that were started in section 9.4.

B. Translate from Hebrew to English:

1. Phrases

1. אֶל־הַבָּתִּים

2. אֶל־הָהָר

3. הָאִישׁ אֲשֶׁר בַּבַּיִת

4. הָאִשָּׁה אֲשֶׁר שָׁם

5. הָאִישׁ אֲשֶׁר אֶת־מֹשֶׁה

6. הָאִישׁ אֲשֶׁר עִם־הַמֶּלֶךְ הַגָּדוֹל

7. הָעֶבֶד אֲשֶׁר עַל־הַדֶּרֶךְ

8. הַבַּיִת אֲשֶׁר אֵצֶל הַנָּהָר הַיָּפֶה

9. הַנָּשִׁים אֲשֶׁר בָּעִיר הָרָעָה

10. הַסּוּסִים אֲשֶׁר מֵהַשָּׂדֶה הַקָּטֹן

2. Sentences

1. גָּדוֹל הַבַּיִת מֵהַהֵיכָל

2. אֶרֶץ טוֹבָה מְאֹד יְהוּדָה

3. הָאִשָּׁה עַל־הַסּוּס הַזָּקֵן

4. זָקֵן הָאִישׁ אֲשֶׁר בַּשָּׂדֶה

5. דָּוִד בַּהֵיכָל

6. מַלְכָּה טוֹבָה הִיא

7. אֲנָשִׁים רָעִים הֵם

8. הַחֶ֫רֶב לְמֹשֶׁה

9. הָאִשָּׁה כְּמַלְכָּה

10. יָפָה הַסּוּסָה אֲשֶׁר תַּ֫חַת הָעֵץ

C. Translate the following into Hebrew:

1. a good king

2. the good king

3. The king is good.

4. The good king is on the horse.

5. The mares in the field are very small.

D. Practice reading all of Gen 22:1.

10

THE CONSTRUCT CHAIN AND DEMONSTRATIVE ADJECTIVES AND PRONOUNS

10.1. THE CONSTRUCT CHAIN IN GENERAL

In BH, a phrase like 'the king of the land' would be written without a word for 'of'. Instead of using 'of', BH expresses this relationship between nouns by juxtaposing the nouns: מֶלֶךְ הָאָרֶץ. The first noun in such a chain is said to be "in construct with" the second, and the chain itself is called a "construct chain." A construct chain may include any number of nouns, but there are seldom more than three.

10.2. THE DEFINITENESS OR INDEFINITENESS OF A CONSTRUCT CHAIN

The entire chain will be either definite or indefinite. The definiteness of a construct chain is determined by the definiteness of the last member of the chain, and as it happens, construct chains in BH are nearly always definite. All members of a definite construct chain *except* the final one, however, are considered definite by the mere fact of their being "in construct" with the next noun in the chain, so the nonfinal members of a construct chain are *never* written with the definite article. Note the example above: we translate '*the* king of *the* land' in English, but the word מֶלֶךְ in מֶלֶךְ הָאָרֶץ is not written with a definite article; only the final word is. In a three-member construct chain, such as 'the horse of the king of the land', as before, only the final word is definite: סוּס מֶלֶךְ הָאָרֶץ. Since proper nouns are always definite, we can also write a definite construct chain with a proper noun at the

> The entire construct chain is either definite or indefinite. The definiteness of the chain is determined by the definiteness of the final member of the chain. Only the final member of a definite construct chain will be marked as definite.

end. יִשְׂרָאֵל is 'Israel', and the phrase סוּס מֶלֶךְ יִשְׂרָאֵל is 'the horse of the king of Israel'.

10.3. THE REGULAR FORMS OF A NOUN IN THE CONSTRUCT STATE

We recognize the chain as expressing the 'of' relationship simply because there is nothing else that those three nouns in a row could mean. Many nouns, however, have special "construct" forms when they are the nonfinal members of a construct chain. These forms must be recognized as readily as the regular forms of the nouns are. The regular form is said to be in the "absolute" state and to be the "absolute" form of the noun, while the special form for use in construct chains is said to be in the "construct" state and to be the "construct" form of the noun. (The "absolute" forms are the dictionary forms of the nouns.) When a noun has an unpredictable construct form, that will be pointed out in the vocabulary list.

For instance, the construct form of דָּבָר is דְּבַר, and 'the word of the king' is דְּבַר הַמֶּלֶךְ. This is more recognizable as a construct chain: not only is it two juxtaposed nouns, only the second of which is formally defined; we can also recognize דְּבַר as a construct form.

10.3.1. Like the feminine singular, masculine plural, and feminine plural forms of words like גָּדוֹל or the plural of דָּבָר, the construct form of a word with a *qamets* in an unaccented open syllable substitutes vocal *shwa* (or a *hateph*-vowel) for the *qamets*; hence the first syllable of דְּבַר (tsere in an unaccented open syllable reduces to *shwa* also).[1]

10.3.2. The second syllable shows us that a *qamets* in a closed final syllable will reduce to *patakh* in the construct form.

10.3.3. Feminine singular nouns that end in הָ- in the absolute state end in ת-ַ in the construct state: absolute מַלְכָּה; construct מַלְכַּת.

10.3.4. Masculine plurals, or more correctly, all plural nouns that end in ים-ִ, end in ֵי- in the construct: absolute עַמִּים; construct עַמֵּי. We refer to this form as the masculine plural construct, even though, as we have seen, not all ים-ִ plurals are masculine in gender.

10.3.5. Feminine plural nouns, or rather, plural nouns that end in וֹת-, retain the וֹת- ending in the construct but undergo the changes discussed above concerning *qamets* in an open syllable (as do feminine singular and masculine plural nouns): עֵצָה 'advice, counsel', plural עֵצוֹת; construct plural עֲצוֹת. We refer to this

---

1. In some circumstances, a *qamets* or a *tsere* will not reduce. These construct forms will be noted in the vocabulary lists.

form as the feminine plural construct, even though, as we have seen, not all וֹת- plurals are feminine in gender.

Sometimes a construct form is not easy to figure out. The plural of דָּבָר is דְּבָרִים. The ending changes to ־ֵי, and the *qamets* reduces to (vocal) *shwa*, which would give us דְּבְרֵי. We learned in lesson 9 that two vocal *shwa*s in a row at the beginning of a word brings the rule of *shwa* into play, so the plural construct form here will be דִּבְרֵי (the first *shwa* becomes *hireq* by rule of *shwa*).

אֲנָשִׁים is similar, but with the complication that there is a *hateph*-vowel under the א. אֲנָשִׁים substitutes the construct ending ־ֵי, yielding אֲנָשֵׁי, then reduces the *qamets* to give us אֲנְשֵׁי. But just as we do not get two vocal *shwa*s together at the beginning of a word, we also never get a vocal *shwa* and a *hateph*-vowel together at the beginning of a word. This combination is resolved by the rule of *shwa* for gutturals: if the *hateph*-vowel is first, it becomes a full vowel, and the vocal *shwa* becomes silent. So, אֲנְשֵׁי becomes אַנְשֵׁי.[2]

10.4. THE FORMS OF CERTAIN NOUNS IN THE CONSTRUCT STATE

Some nouns have construct forms that follow patterns that cannot be deduced by the rules above, but words of the same form are consistent with each other, all the same:

The construct of בַּיִת is בֵּית (all similarly formed words have similar construct forms).

The construct of מָוֶת 'death' is מוֹת (likewise all similarly formed words).

The construct of שָׂדֶה is שְׂדֵה (ה ֶ- singulars have ה ֵ- construct forms)

Masculine singular segholates are unchanged in the construct (as are endingless feminine singular segholates, e.g., אֶרֶץ).

Some construct forms are not predictable:

The construct forms of אָב 'father' and אָח 'brother' are אֲבִי and אֲחִי.

The plural construct forms of masculine and endingless feminine segholates do not follow the expected rules, and their forms will be noted in the vocabulary lists.

Other, less common construct forms will be noted in the vocabulary lists.

---

2. The other possibility, with the *hateph*-vowel second, has nothing to do with construct forms, but we have seen it before, at 9.10. For instance, we would expect that 'for slaves' would be לְעֲבָדִים. In this situation, however, rule of *shwa* for gutturals says that the first vowel "mirrors" the *hateph*-vowel, so that what we actually get is לַעֲבָדִים.

10.5. POSITION OF ADJECTIVES MODIFYING MEMBERS OF A CONSTRUCT CHAIN

An adjective that modifies one member of a construct chain must go at the end of the entire chain. (In fact, it is very rare that *anything* interrupts the flow of a construct chain.) 'The house of the good woman' is בֵּית הָאִשָּׁה הַטּוֹבָה, and 'the good house of the woman' (= 'the woman's good house') is בֵּית הָאִשָּׁה הַטּוֹב. (Remember, all members of the chain are considered definite if the final member is definite.)

The example above pairs a feminine and a masculine noun, so it is clear which word the adjective modifies. This will not always be the case, and some cases will be ambiguous. What does הַטּוֹב modify in the following phrase: בֵּית הָאִישׁ הַטּוֹב? There is no way to know.[3]

10.6. THE DEMONSTRATIVE ADJECTIVES AND PRONOUNS

A distinct set of adjectives that must be learned are the demonstrative adjectives/ pronouns: 'this', 'that', 'these', 'those'. זֶה is 'this' masculine singular; זֹאת is 'this' feminine singular; and אֵלֶּה is 'these' for both genders. 'That' and 'those' are simply the third-person independent pronouns, plus the definite article, used as attributive adjectives: הַהוּא, הַהִיא, הָהֵם, הָהֵנָּה.[4]

Demonstrative adjectives are the last adjectives in a noun-adjective phrase and agree with the nouns they modify in gender, number, and definiteness, like all attributive adjectives.[5] 'This good man' is הָאִישׁ הַטּוֹב הַזֶּה. Like all adjectives, indefinite demonstratives paired with definite nouns produce a sentence: 'This is the good man' is זֶה הָאִישׁ הַטּוֹב.[6]

In a construct chain, the demonstrative goes at the end of the chain and after any other adjectives that modify a member of the chain. 'The house of that good woman' is בֵּית הָאִשָּׁה הַטּוֹבָה הַהִיא.

---

3. It is also possible to get around this problem by a circumlocution using the preposition לְ in the sense 'belonging to': הַבַּיִת הַטּוֹב אֲשֶׁר לָאִישׁ 'the good house that belongs to the man' = 'the man's good house'.

4. Note that when הֵם and הֵנָּה are used as attributive adjectives, the definite article that appears on them is הָ instead of the expected הַ.

5. With the exception of nouns with pronominal suffixes: זֶה and זֹאת are generally not definite when they modify a noun with a pronominal suffix, which, as we will learn in the next lesson, is also considered definite in BH.

6. In this example, the demonstrative is more properly a pronoun.

10.7. VOCABULARY FOR LESSON 10

Here are the attested construct forms of vocabulary words we have learned in lessons 7–9:

אֲנָשִׁים; construct: אַנְשֵׁי   מַלְכוֹת; construct: מַלְכוֹת

אֲרָצוֹת; construct: אַרְצוֹת   מְלָכִים; construct: מַלְכֵי

אִשָּׁה; construct: אֵשֶׁת   מָקוֹם; construct: מְקוֹם

בַּיִת; construct: בֵּית   נָהָר; construct: נְהַר

דָּבָר; construct: דְּבַר   נָשִׁים; construct: נְשֵׁי

דְּבָרִים; construct: דִּבְרֵי   עֲבָדִים; construct: עַבְדֵי

הֵיכָל; construct: הֵיכַל   עָרִים; irregular construct: עָרֵי

הָרִים; irregular construct: הָרֵי   רָאשִׁים; irregular construct: רָאשֵׁי

חֳרָבוֹת; construct: חָרְבוֹת   שָׂדֶה; construct: שְׂדֵה

מַלְכָּה; construct: מַלְכַּת

Note: 'woman of' can = 'wife of'; 'women of' can = 'wives of'.

---

nouns

אָב   'father, kinsman'; cs. אֲבִי; pl. אָבוֹת (masc., like the sg.); cs. pl. אֲבוֹת

אוֹר   'light' (pl. אוֹרִים only occurs once)

אָח   'brother, kinsman, cousin'; cs. אֲחִי; irregular pl. אַחִים; cs. pl. אֲחֵי

בֵּן   'son'; cs. usually בֶּן־; pl. בָּנִים; cs. pl. בְּנֵי

בַּת   'daughter' (fem.); with sf. בִּתִּי; pl. בָּנוֹת; cs. pl. בְּנוֹת

חֹשֶׁךְ   'darkness'

יוֹם   'day'; irregular pl. יָמִים; cs. pl. יְמֵי

יַיִן   'wine'; cs. יֵין

מָוֶת   'death'; cs. מוֹת

פָּנִים   'face' (always pl.); cs. פְּנֵי

שֵׁם   'name'; cs. usually שֶׁם; pl. שֵׁמוֹת (masc., like the sg.); cs. pl. שְׁמוֹת

proper nouns

יִשְׂרָאֵל   'Israel'

pronouns

The demonstrative adjectives are also used as pronouns but will be listed under adjectives in this list.

adjectives

זֶה	'this' (ms)	הוּא	'that' (ms)
זֹאת	'this' (fs)	הִיא	'that' (fs)
אֵלֶּה	'these'	הֵם	'those' (mp)
		הֵנָּה	'those' (fp)

prepositions:

לִפְנֵי   'in front of, in the presence of, in the sight of'; 'before' (in both space and time)

10.8. EXERCISES FOR LESSON 10

A. Translate from Hebrew to English:

1. Phrases

1.   שֵׁם הַמֶּלֶךְ

2.   בֶּן־הַמַּלְכָּה

3.   פְּנֵי בַת הָאִשָּׁה

4.   אַחֲרֵי מוֹת מֹשֶׁה

5.   אֲחִי הָאִשָּׁה הַזָּקֵן

6.   אוֹר וְחֹשֶׁךְ

7.   מֶלֶךְ הָעִיר הַגְּדוֹלָה הַזֹּאת

8.   עָרֵי הָאָרֶץ הַקְּטַנָּה הַהִיא

9.   דְּבַר הָעֲבָדִים הָאֵלֶּה

10.   נְהַר יִשְׂרָאֵל

2. Sentences

1.   טוֹב יֵין הַמֶּלֶךְ

2.   רָעָה אֵשֶׁת הָעִיר הַהִיא

3.   יָפָה בַּת דָּוִד

4.   יָפֶה מְאֹד אוֹר הַיּוֹם

5.   אֵלֶּה דִּבְרֵי הַמֶּלֶךְ הַטּוֹבִים

6.   לִפְנֵי הַמֶּלֶךְ הָרַע הַזֶּה אֲנַחְנוּ

7.   יָפֶה סוּס הַמַּלְכָּה

8.   תַּחַת הָעֵץ הַגָּדוֹל אֲשֶׁר אֵצֶל הַנָּהָר אָנֹכִי

9.   אִם הָעֶבֶד הַטּוֹב הַזֶּה הִיא

10. גְּדוֹלוֹת נְשֵׁי הָאָרֶץ הַקְּטַנָּה הַהִיא

B. Translate the following into Hebrew:

1. the house of David

2. the words of the women

3. the darkness of the beautiful city

4. He is the king of Israel.

5. They are the kings of the lands.

C. Practice reading the first line of Gen 22:2.

יא ◄ **11** ► יא

NOUNS WITH PRONOMINAL SUFFIXES

11.1. POSSESSIVE PRONOUNS GENERALLY

In BH, possessive pronouns ('my', 'his', 'your', etc.) are not written as separate words but are expressed as suffixes on the noun being possessed.

There are two sets of these suffixes: one set is used on singular nouns, whether masculine or feminine; another set is used on plural nouns (masculine or feminine). The suffixes used on singular nouns are almost exactly the same as the suffixes that you have memorized with the preposition בְּ.

We will use the word סוּס as the masculine singular (or endless feminine singular) paradigm noun; the possessive suffixes are as follows:

NOUNS WITH PRONOMINAL SUFFIXES

our horse	סוּסֵֽנוּ	סוּסִי	my horse
your (mp) horse	סוּסְכֶם	סוּסְךָ	your (ms) horse
your (fp) horse	סוּסְכֶן	סוּסֵךְ	your (fs) horse
their (m) horse	סוּסָם	סוּסוֹ	his horse
their (f) horse	סוּסָן	סוּסָה	her horse

Note that סוּסֵךְ and סוּסֵֽנוּ differ from the בְּ paradigm: *tsere* has replaced *qamets*. Also, remember that the masculine plural is used both for groups of objects or people that are all masculine in gender and for groups of objects or people that are mixed in gender, with one or more feminine objects or people and at least one masculine object or person.

11.2. POSSESSIVE PRONOUNS ON THE FEMININE SINGULAR NOUN

With a feminine singular noun, the suffixes are the same, but the הָ- ending changes to תָ- or תְ- before the suffixes. As our paradigm word, we will use the word תּוֹרָה, 'instruction, teaching, law'. תּוֹרָה is often used to refer to the entirety of the first five books of the Bible. It is also used to refer to the bodies of law that are present in those books. The word is developed, however, from a root that means 'to teach', so we will translate it 'teaching' here or sometimes simply leave it untranslated and transliterated into Latin characters: Torah.

> The ת plus *a*-vowel is a more original form of the fs noun. By the time of BH, however, the *t*-sound has dropped off at the end of a such a word, and we are left with the *a*-vowel plus ה-mater. The original form remains when it is "guarded" by a suffix of some kind.

FEMININE SINGULAR NOUNS WITH PRONOMINAL SUFFIXES

our teaching	תּוֹרָתֵנוּ	תּוֹרָתִי	my teaching
your (mp) teaching	תּוֹרַתְכֶם	תּוֹרָתְךָ	your (ms) teaching
your (fp) teaching	תּוֹרַתְכֶן	תּוֹרָתֵךְ	your (fs) teaching
their (m) teaching	תּוֹרָתָם	תּוֹרָתוֹ	his teaching
their (f) teaching	תּוֹרָתָן	תּוֹרָתָהּ	her teaching

11.3. POSSESSIVE PRONOUNS AND VOWEL REDUCTION ON TWO-SYLLABLE WORDS

Two-syllable words with an open first syllable, and *qamets* or *tsere* as the vowel of that syllable, have the usual vowel reductions (see above, lesson 8.2), which make the paradigm a bit different:

TWO-SYLLABLE WORDS WITH AN OPEN FIRST SYLLABLE

our word	דְּבָרֵנוּ	דְּבָרִי	my word
your (mp) word	דְּבַרְכֶם	דְּבָרְךָ[1]	your (ms) word
your (fp) word	דְּבַרְכֶן	דְּבָרֵךְ	your (fs) word
their (m) word	דְּבָרָם	דְּבָרוֹ	his word
their (f) word	דְּבָרָן	דְּבָרָהּ	her word

11.4. POSSESSIVE PRONOUNS ON PLURAL NOUNS

The pronominal possessive suffixes that are used on *plural* nouns are exactly the same as those already memorized with the preposition אֶל־. We will use סוּסִים as the paradigm word. First, the ים- ending is removed, and then the endings from the אֶל־ paradigm are substituted.

PLURAL NOUNS WITH PRONOMINAL SUFFIXES 1

our horses	סוּסֵינוּ	סוּסַי	my horses
your (mp) horses	סוּסֵיכֶם	סוּסֶיךָ	your (ms) horses
your (fp) horses	סוּסֵיכֶן	סוּסַיִךְ	your (fs) horses
their (m) horses	סוּסֵיהֶם	סוּסָיו	his horses
their (f) horses	סוּסֵיהֶן	סוּסֶיהָ	her horses

Note that the י in these pronominal suffixes on plural nouns (here and in the two paradigms just below) is not pronounced in most forms, except סוּסַי, where it is part of a diphthong, and סוּסַיִךְ, where it is a proper consonant. In all the other forms, the words should be pronounced as if the י were not there. In these words, the י is probably simply an unpronounced marker of the plural nature of the noun, and it distinguishes between 'our word' דְּבָרֵנוּ and 'our words' דְּבָרֵינוּ, for instance. The *seghol-yod* in סוּסֶיךָ is pronounced exactly the same as a simple *seghol* (su-séh-kha), and the *qamets-yod* in סוּסָיו is pronounced as simple *qamets*, with no י sound whatsoever (su-sahv).

---

1. Note that דְּבָרְךָ has a *metheg* next to the *qamets* under the ב, which indicates that the *qamets* is pronounced as a long *a*-vowel.

The suffixes כֶם-, כֶן-, הֶם-, and הֶן - are known as "heavy suffixes." The basic stem before the heavy suffixes is the construct form of the word in question (except for feminine plurals; see below). דְּבַרְכֶם, above, is דְּבַר (construct form of דָּבָר) plus כֶם; and סוּסֵיהֶן is סוּסֵי (construct form of סוּסִים) plus הֶן. Next we will take up the word דְּבָרִים plus suffixes, and we will see that the stem before the heavy suffixes is דִּבְרֵי, the construct form of דְּבָרִים.

PLURAL NOUNS WITH PRONOMINAL SUFFIXES 2

our words	דְּבָרֵינוּ	דְּבָרַי	my words
your (mp) words	דִּבְרֵיכֶם	דְּבָרֶיךָ	your (ms) words
your (fp) words	דִּבְרֵיכֶן	דְּבָרַיִךְ	your (fs) words
their (m) words	דִּבְרֵיהֶם	דְּבָרָיו	his words
their (f) words	דִּבְרֵיהֶן	דְּבָרֶיהָ	her words

Finally, we will see the pronominal suffixes on a feminine plural noun (or rather, a noun with an וֹת- plural) such as תּוֹרוֹת. Feminine plural nouns retain the וֹת- ending and *also* add the pronominal suffixes for plural nouns.

FEMININE PLURAL NOUNS WITH PRONOMINAL SUFFIXES

our teachings	תּוֹרוֹתֵינוּ	תּוֹרוֹתַי	my teachings
your (mp) teachings	תּוֹרוֹתֵיכֶם	תּוֹרוֹתֶיךָ	your (ms) teachings
your (fp) teachings	תּוֹרוֹתֵיכֶן	תּוֹרוֹתַיִךְ	your (fs) teachings
their (m) teachings	תּוֹרוֹתֵיהֶם	תּוֹרוֹתָיו	his teachings
their (f) teachings	תּוֹרוֹתֵיהֶן	תּוֹרוֹתֶיהָ	her teachings

11.5. NOUNS WITH DUAL NUMBER

In a few circumstances, BH uses a dual ending on a noun rather than a plural ending. The most common situation that calls for a dual is the case of naturally occurring pairs. When we say something like "David's hands are large," we are really saying that his *two* hands are large, and BH incorporates this fact into its grammar. There are also a few other words (mostly denoting time periods) that have a normal plural but are expressed in the dual when exactly *two* units are being discussed. יֹם - is the dual ending for masculine nouns, and תַ֫יִם- for feminine nouns. There are no dual adjectives or verbs in BH; duals take plural adjectives and plural verbs. The construct dual endings are the same as the construct plural endings (they will be noted in the vocabulary lists). The most common of the BH duals are presented below.

יָד	hand	יָדַ֫יִם	(two) hands	שָׁנָה	year	שְׁנָתַ֫יִם	two years
אֹ֫זֶן	ear	²אָזְנַ֫יִם	(two) ears	יוֹם	day	יוֹמַ֫יִם	two days
עַ֫יִן	eye	עֵינַ֫יִם	(two) eyes	פַּ֫עַם	once	פַּעֲמַ֫יִם	twice
רֶ֫גֶל	foot	רַגְלַ֫יִם	(two) feet	[no sg.]		²צָהֳרַ֫יִם	noon
[no sg.]		²מָתְנַ֫יִם	loins				

The possessive suffixes used with these duals are the אֵלִי set, just as with plural nouns: 'my (two) hands' is יָדַי. Two words often thought to be duals, because they have dual forms, are in fact simply plurals: מַ֫יִם 'water'; and שָׁמַ֫יִם 'sky, heaven'.

11.6. POSSESSIVE PRONOUNS ON SEGHOLATE NOUNS

Segholate nouns (two-syllable nouns with the accent on the first syllable) have special forms both in the construct plural and in the singular with pronominal suffixes. Each segholate noun has a "characteristic vowel" (either *patakh, hireq,* or *qamets* as short *o*) that shows up in these two places. Consequently, segholate nouns should be learned along with their characteristic vowels.

For the construct plural or the singular with pronominal suffixes, the base word collapses into one syllable, with the characteristic vowel as the vowel of that syllable; then the appropriate endings are added. The characteristic vowel of מֶ֫לֶךְ is *patakh*, which means that 'my king', 'his king', and 'their (m) king', for example, are מַלְכִּי, מַלְכּוֹ, and מַלְכָּם; the construct plural 'kings of' is מַלְכֵי. It is useful to memorize a word like מֶ֫לֶךְ along with its 'my' form of the singular: מֶ֫לֶךְ, מַלְכִּי.[3] The characteristic vowels of the segholates we have already learned follow:

אֶ֫רֶץ   with first-person suffix: אַרְצִי; construct plural: אֲרָצוֹת

---

2. אָזְנַ֫יִם, מָתְנַ֫יִם, and צָהֳרַ֫יִם are the first three words we have encountered with *qamets* used for a short *o*-sound (short in BH, that is; still pronounced like the *o* in pose). They are pronounced oz-ná-yim; mot-ná-yim; and tso-hŏ-rá-yim. See below for discussion.

3. The characteristic vowel is actually the original vowel of the word; the "segholate" form of the word is a later development. When it is "guarded" by the pronominal suffix or the construct ending, the original form remains. Also, the reason for the *beged-kephet dagesh* in the *kaph* in some forms but not in others is historical, but a discussion of the reason would not benefit us at this point.

דֶּרֶךְ	דַּרְכִּי; דַּרְכֵי	
חֶרֶב	חַרְבִּי; חַרְבוֹת	
חֹשֶׁךְ	חָשְׁכִּי (short *o*); no plural	
עֶבֶד	עַבְדִּי; עֲבָדַי	

11.7. POSSESSIVE PRONOUNS ON IRREGULAR NOUNS

The pronominal suffixes on the singular of words like בַּיִת and מָוֶת occur with the construct singular as the base: 'my house' בֵּיתִי; 'my death' מוֹתִי.

The words אָב and אָח have irregular forms with suffixes, both with the singular nouns and with the plural nouns.

our father	אָבִינוּ	אָבִי	my father
your (mp) father	אֲבִיכֶם	אָבִיךָ	your (ms) father
etc.		אָבִיךְ	your (fs) father
		אָבִיהוּ or אָבִיו	his father
		אָבִיהָ	her father

The suffixes on the singular אָח 'brother' follow the same pattern.

The suffixes on the plural אָבוֹת 'fathers' are like the suffixes on any וֹת- plural. The plural אַחִים 'brothers' with suffixes, however, is sometimes irregular.

our brothers	אַחֵינוּ	אַחַי	my brothers
your (mp) brothers	אֲחֵיכֶם	אַחֶיךָ	your (ms) brothers
etc.		אַחַיִךְ	your (fs) brothers
		אֶחָיו	his brothers
		אַחֶיהָ	her brothers

(Note the *seghol* in the 3ms suffixed form: אֶחָיו "his brothers.")

Four Ways a Noun Can Be Definite

A noun with a pronominal suffix is considered definite in BH. We have now learned the four ways in BH that a noun can be definite: (1) it can have the definite article; (2) it can be a proper noun; (3) it can be in construct with a definite noun; (4) it can have a pronominal suffix.

11.8. THE TWO PRONUNCIATIONS OF THE VOWEL *QAMETS*

It is time to discuss the two pronunciations of *qamets* in BH, according to the Qimkhi system of pronunciation, which we are using (see above, lesson 1). We know that an unaccented, closed syllable must contain a short vowel (with only two exceptions) but that an unaccented *open* syllable will *usually* contain a long vowel. We also know that *shwa* is silent when preceded by a short vowel but vocal when preceded by an unaccented long vowel. Knowing these rules of thumb, how do we analyze a word like חָכְמָה 'wisdom'? There is no problem with the מָה syllable; it is open with a long vowel (*qamets* as long *a*). The beginning of the word, however, poses a problem. If the first *qamets* is long *a*, then the *shwa* is vocal and we have two syllables: חָ plus כְ. If, however, the *qamets* represents short *o*, then the *shwa* is silent and we have only one syllable: חָכְ, pronounced "khokh." Looked at another way, if the *shwa* is vocal, then the *qamets* must be a long *a*, but if the *shwa* is silent, then the *qamets* is a short *o*. The problem, in other words, is how to pronounce the two vowels when *qamets* is followed by *shwa*. The two ways just given of figuring the pronunciation of the *qamets* and *shwa* are interdependent; there is no firm ground to begin from.

Qamets Followed by *Shwa*

A rule of thumb is that in a noun, *qamets* followed by *shwa* is almost always pronounced short *o* plus silent *shwa* (see חָכְמָה above, pronounced khokh-ma). The same combination in verbs is not as predictable but is *usually* pronounced long *a* plus vocal *shwa*. (We will take this up again when we have learned some verbs.)

The only common exception to the noun part of this rule of thumb is some singular nouns with the second-person masculine singular (2ms) suffix, such as דְּבָרְךָ. Note the *metheg* beside the *qamets* under the ב. We learned in lesson 9, in the footnote discussing the word for 'houses' בָּתִּים, that a *metheg* is used (inconsistently in the Hebrew Bible but consistently in this textbook) whenever there is some question about the pronunciation of *qamets*. The *metheg* indicates a long *a* pronunciation. So דְּבָרְךָ is actually four syllables: דְּ plus בָ (long *a*) plus רְ (vocal *shwa*) plus ךָ. If it had been written without the *metheg*, it would have been pronounced as three syllables: דְּ plus בָרְ (short *o* and silent *shwa*) plus ךָ. בָּתִּים contains a *metheg* because the word is pronounced as two closed syllables, בָּ plus תִּים, and we would ordinarily expect the unaccented, closed syllable בָּת to have a short-*o* vowel. The *metheg* tells us that, against all expectations, the *qamets* here is pronounced as long *a*.

> ### Qamets Followed by Hateph-Qamets
>
> Another rule of thumb: the combination *qamets* followed by *hateph-qamets* is almost always pronounced o + ŏ. See צָהֳרַיִם 'noon' above, in section 5.

11.9. VOCABULARY FOR LESSON 11

nouns

From this point on, the nouns in the vocabulary lists will be assumed to be feminine if they have the ה ָ - ending and masculine if they have no ending, unless otherwise noted.

אֹזֶן 'ear' (fem.); with sf. אָזְנִי; du. אָזְנַיִם; cs. du. אָזְנֵי

חָכְמָה 'wisdom'; cs. חָכְמַת

יָד 'hand' (fem.); cs. יַד; du. יָדַיִם; cs. du. יְדֵי

לַיְלָה [4] 'night' (masc.); cs. לֵיל; pl. לֵילוֹת (masc., like the sg.)

מַיִם 'water(s)' (always pl.); cs. מֵי

מָתְנַיִם 'loins; waist'; middle part of the body (always du.); cs. מָתְנֵי; du. with sf. מָתְנַי

עַיִן 'eye' (fem.); cs. עֵין; with sf. עֵינִי; du. עֵינַיִם; cs. du. עֵינֵי; du. with sf. עֵינַי; also means 'spring, water source'; cs. עֵין; pl. עֲיָנוֹת; cs. pl. עֵינוֹת

עֵצָה 'advice, counsel'; cs. עֲצַת; pl. עֵצוֹת

פַּעַם 'time' (= occurrence, as in 'one time', 'two times' = 'once', 'twice'); 'pace, footstep' (fem.); du. פַּעֲמַיִם 'twice, two times'; pl. פְּעָמִים; cs. du./pl. פַּעֲמֵי

צָהֳרַיִם 'noon' (always du.)

רֶגֶל 'foot' (fem.); with sf. רַגְלִי; du. רַגְלַיִם; cs. du. רַגְלֵי; du. with sf. רַגְלַי

שָׁמַיִם 'sky, heaven(s)' (always pl.); cs. שְׁמֵי; with sf. שָׁמַי

שָׁנָה 'year'; cs. שְׁנַת; du. שְׁנָתַיִם; pl. שָׁנִים; cs. pl. שְׁנֵי (less common, שָׁנוֹת); pl. with sf. שָׁנַי or שְׁנוֹתַי

תּוֹרָה 'instruction, teaching; law; Torah' (the first five books of the Bible); cs. תּוֹרַת; pl. and cs. pl. תּוֹרוֹת

---

4. Note that the accent is on the first syllable. This is a masculine noun, *not* a feminine noun; the feminine ה ָ - ending is accented.

proper nouns

    אַבְרָהָם   'Abraham'

    אַבְרָם   'Abram' (Abraham's name before it was changed)

    יְרוּשָׁלַם⁵   'Jerusalem'

    שְׁלֹמֹה   'Solomon'

adjective

    רָשָׁע   'wicked; criminal'; often inter-
        changeable with רַע

preposition

    בְּעֵינֵי   'in the eyes of, in the opinion
        of'

> Any adjective in BH can be "substan-tivized," that is, used as a noun. So, טוב is both "good" (masc.) and "a good person/thing" (masc.); טוֹבָה is both "good" (fem.) and "a good person/thing" (fem.); רָשָׁע is "wicked" (masc.) or "a wicked person/thing" (masc.); and רְשָׁעָה is both "wicked" (fem.) and "a wicked person/thing" (fem.).

11.10. EXERCISES FOR LESSON 11

A. Translate from Hebrew to English:

  1. Phrases

1. יְדֵי הַמַּלְכָּה

2. רַגְלֵי הַנָּשִׁים

3. עֶבֶד אָבִיו

4. אֵשֶׁת דָּוִד

5. בְּעֵינֵי הָרָשָׁע

6. לִפְנֵי עֵינֵי בִתּוֹ⁶

7. חָכְמַת הַשָּׁמַיִם

---

5. Note the *hireq* that is not quite centered under the מ. The Masoretes were pronouncing the name of the city יְרוּשָׁלַיִם, but the people who wrote the consonants centuries before were pronouncing it יְרוּשָׁלֵם. So the Masoretes were faced with indicating their own pronunciation in a word that was lacking the י that was essential to them. They could not add a י to the sacred consonantal text, so they indicated their pronunciation by inserting a *hireq* after the ל syllable, but to the right of the normal place where a vowel would be under the מ (much like a furtive *patakh*). Thus, the word is to be pronounced יְרוּשָׁלַיִם, even though we will only rarely see the second y in the biblical text.

6. It is often the case that *beged-kephet* consonants lose their *dageshes*, even at the beginning of a word, if the word immediately before them ends in a vowel sound and the two words are pronounced quickly together.

8. ‏דִּבְרֵי הַיּוֹם הָרַע הַהוּא‎

9. ‏מֵי הַנָּהָר הַקָּטֹן‎

10. ‏אַחֲרֵי חֹשֶׁךְ הַלַּיְלָה הַטּוֹב הַזֶּה‎

2. Sentences

1. ‏זְקֵנָה אֵם הָעֶבֶד‎

2. ‏טוֹבָה חָכְמָה מִיַּיִן‎

3. ‏רְשָׁעִים הַבָּנִים אֲשֶׁר מִמָּתְנָיו‎

4. ‏אֲחֵי אַבְרָהָם הֵם‎

5. ‏זֹאת מַלְכַּת יְרוּשָׁלַם‎

6. ‏אֵלֶּה יְדֵי אֲבִי מֹשֶׁה הַיָּפוֹת‎

7. ‏זֹאת עֲצַת הָאִשָּׁה הַטּוֹבָה‎

8. ‏אֵשֶׁת אַבְרָם הִיא‎

9. ‏גָּדוֹל אֲבִי שְׁלֹמֹה‎

10. ‏זֹאת שְׁנַת עַמִּי‎

B. Translate from English to Hebrew:

1. my father's wife

2. his horses' ears

3. your (masc. sg.) Torahs

4. Our brother is small.

5. Your (fem. pl.) word is great.

C. Practice reading the second line of Gen 22:2.

12

יב ◄   ► יב

THE *QAL* PREFIX CONJUGATION, THE IMPERATIVE, AND THE DIRECT OBJECT MARKER

12.1. THE QAL PREFIX CONJUGATION'S USE

We will begin our study of verbs with the *qal* (קַל) or "simple" stem. The prefix conjugation (pref. conj.; often referred to as the imperfect) is used in BH to express:

1. simple future   he will write

2. ongoing action *in any tense*   he was writing; he is writing

3. habitual action *in any tense*   he writes (for a living, all the time); he used to write

4. modal uses   he would write, should write

12.2. THE FORM OF THE QAL PREFIX CONJUGATION

The paradigm for the prefix conjugation should be memorized using the root שׁמר [1] 'to keep, observe (e.g., the commandments); guard, watch'.

---

1. Remember or reread the discussion of triconsonantal roots in lesson 6.11.

QAL PREFIX CONJUGATION

1cp	we will keep	נִשְׁמֹר	אֶשְׁמֹר	I will keep	1cs[2]
2mp	you (mp) will keep	תִּשְׁמְרוּ	תִּשְׁמֹר	you (ms) will keep	2ms
2fp	you (fp) will keep [3]	תִּשְׁמֹרְנָה	תִּשְׁמְרִי	you (fs) will keep	2fs
3mp	they (m) will keep	יִשְׁמְרוּ	יִשְׁמֹר	he will keep	3ms
3fp	they (f) will keep [3]	תִּשְׁמֹרְנָה	תִּשְׁמֹר	she will keep	3fs

Note that in the second and third persons, verbs in BH mark number and gender. In the first person, only number is expressed; as with the pronouns, the gender of the first-person verb is "common," that is, the same for masculine and feminine.

12.3. THE SUBJECT IN THE FORM OF THE *QAL* PREFIX CONJUGATION

In most cases, the pronominal subject is not written with the prefix conjugation: the form אֶשְׁמֹר includes the pronoun "I" within it. In fact, writing the pronoun in addition to the verb implies emphasis; that is, אֲנִי אֶשְׁמֹר is '*I* will keep' or 'It is *I* who will keep'. In BH, 'I will keep' without special emphasis is simply אֶשְׁמֹר, a fact that may cause difficulty for many English speakers and students who know modern Hebrew, but leaving out the separate pronoun is the usual custom for BH.

When the subject of the prefix conjugation verb is a noun rather than a pronoun, it will almost always *follow* the verb. 'The king will watch' is יִשְׁמֹר הַמֶּלֶךְ. Switching the word order so that the subject comes first implies emphasis on the subject: הַמֶּלֶךְ יִשְׁמֹר is '*The king* will watch' or 'It is *the king* who will watch'.

12.4. FURTHER REMARKS ON THE FORM OF THE *QAL* PREFIX CONJUGATION

The prefix conjugation is so called because each item in the paradigm begins with a prefix, called a "preformative" letter: א for 1cs; נ for 1cp; י for 3ms and 3mp; ת for everything else (all second-person forms and all feminine forms). The vowel of the preformative is *hireq*, except for 1cs אֶשְׁמֹר, when it is *seghol*. Finally, note that the 2fp and 3fp are identical: תִּשְׁמֹרְנָה (sometimes written תִּשְׁמֹרְן, without the ה *mater*).

---

2. The number after each form is the person (first, second, or third); the c, m, or f is common, masculine, or feminine gender; the s or p is singular or plural.

3. Note that this word violates one of the *shwa* rules you learned above in lesson 6.7: the *shwa* after the long vowel is silent; the word is pronounced tish-mór-nah.

Although the conjugation is named after its prefixes, half the forms also have suffixes. 2fp and 3fp תִּשְׁמֹרְנָה have unaccented נָה-; 2fs תִּשְׁמְרִי has an accented יִ- suffix; 2mp תִּשְׁמְרוּ and 3mp יִשְׁמְרוּ have accented וּ- suffixes. The accented suffixes have the effect of both adding a syllable to the end of the word and creating open syllables right before the (new) stressed syllable. That is, we start with יִשְׁמֹר (two closed syllables) in the 3ms and add the plural suffix to it, to end up with (or so we would expect) יִשְׁמֹרוּ (one closed and two open syllables) in the 3mp. But that is not exactly the form we get. Note:

> In prefix conjugation verbs, if there is an open syllable right before the accented syllable and that syllable has a vowel that can be reduced, that vowel will be reduced (to *shwa* or a *hateph*-vowel).

So the 3mp form that we actually get is יִשְׁמְרוּ, still consisting of one closed and two open syllables, but the *holem* in the middle syllable has reduced to *shwa*. The first *shwa* (under שׁ) is silent, and the second (under מ) is vocal, according to the second rule we learned in lesson 6.7.

The paradigm above for the prefix conjugation should be memorized.

12.5. THE IMPERATIVE FORM

Direct commands in BH are expressed by the imperative form. The imperative (impv.) proper in BH[4] is always second person and is formed by removing the preformative from the second-person prefix conjugation forms. Thus:

pref. conj.	תִּשְׁמֹר	'you (ms) will watch, keep'
impv.	שְׁמֹר[5]	'Watch! Keep!' (spoken to a male)
pref. conj.	תִּשְׁמֹרְנָה	'you (fp) will watch'
impv.	שְׁמֹרְנָה	'Watch!' (spoken to a group of women)

With the 2fs and 2mp forms, once we remove the preformative, we are left with impossible forms, and the rule of *shwa* takes over:

---

4. As opposed to other forms that express a wish, such as "Let's go!"; these forms that will be discussed in a future lesson.

5. The *shwa* has become vocal because it is now the first vowel in the word.

| pref. conj. | תִּשְׁמְרִי | 'you (fs) will watch' (without the preformative this would be שְׁמְרִי, an impossible form because it begins with two *shwas*; rule of *shwa* gives us a *hireq* instead) |
| impv. | שִׁמְרִי | 'Watch!' (spoken to one woman) |

| pref. conj. | תִּשְׁמְרוּ | 'you (mp) will watch' |
| impv. | שִׁמְרוּ | 'Watch!' (spoken to a group of men or to a mixed group) |

12.6. A BRIEF NOTE ON THE NEGATIVE IMPERATIVE FORM

We will discuss the negative imperative in a later lesson. For now, note that the negative of the imperative is never simply a negative word plus the imperative. It is a bit more complicated than that.

12.7. THE VERBAL SENTENCE IN BIBLICAL HEBREW

A verbal sentence in BH is one that includes a "finite" verb, that is, a verb that can be conjugated for person, gender, and number, like the prefix conjugation. In BH, verbal sentences almost always begin with the verb, which is followed by the subject (if it is something other than the pronoun included in the verb), then any direct or indirect objects (commonly referred to as V-S-O sentences).

כתב means 'to write', and the word for 'book' is סֵפֶר. Thus, 'He will write a book' is יִכְתֹּב סֵפֶר. 'The king will write a book' is יִכְתֹּב הַמֶּלֶךְ סֵפֶר. Again, this word order is difficult for English speakers and those who have studied modern Hebrew, but it must be observed.

Adverbial phrases, especially those concerned with time, will generally precede the verb, even in a verbal sentence. 'On that day the king will write a book' would usually be בַּיּוֹם הַהוּא יִכְתֹּב הַמֶּלֶךְ סֵפֶר.

12.8. THE DEFINITE DIRECT OBJECT MARKER

When the direct object of a verb in BH is definite, the word אֵת comes directly before the direct object. It is called a direct object marker.[6] 'The king will write the book' is יִכְתֹּב הַמֶּלֶךְ אֶת הַסֵּפֶר. אֵת is most commonly written, not as a separate word, but connected with *maqqeph* to the definite direct object that follows it.

---

6. There are, admittedly, instances in the Hebrew Bible where we would expect אֶת but it does not appear. This lack of אֶת is, in fact, common when the direct object is a part of the body.

Since this connection takes the stress off of אֵת, the long vowel *tsere* of אֵת reduces to *seghol*, and the form we get is יִכְתֹּב הַמֶּלֶךְ אֶת־הַסֵּפֶר.

This אֵת is not originally the same word as the *preposition* אֵת 'with', which we learned in lesson 9, although they look the same in BH. This direct object marker אֵת can also take pronominal suffixes, however, and that paradigm is not the same as the paradigm for the preposition אֵת plus pronominal suffixes. The direct object marker plus suffixes follows the בִּי paradigm, but the *tsere* or *seghol* changes to *holem* in most forms:

THE DIRECT OBJECT MARKER WITH PERSONAL PRONOUN

'us' as direct object	אֹתָנוּ	אֹתִי	'me' as direct object
'you' (mp) as direct object	אֶתְכֶם	אֹתְךָ	'you' (ms) as direct object
'you' (fp) as direct object	אֶתְכֶן	אֹתָךְ	'you' (fs) as direct object
'them' (m) as direct object	אֹתָם	אֹתוֹ	'him, it' as direct object
'them' (f) as direct object	אֹתָן	אֹתָה	'her, it' as direct object

For instance, the expression 'He will watch me' is יִשְׁמֹר אֹתִי.

12.9. THE NEGATION OF THE PREFIX CONJUGATION

The prefix conjugation is negated by the word לֹא, which goes immediately before the verb. 'The king will not write the book' is לֹא יִכְתֹּב הַמֶּלֶךְ אֶת־הַסֵּפֶר.

12.10. VOCABULARY FOR LESSON 12

The Lexical Form of the Verb in Biblical Hebrew

By convention, verbs in BH are referred to, not by their infinitive forms, as in English ('to go', 'to work', and so on), but rather by the 3ms suffix conjugation form of the verb. This is the simplest form of any verb. (Sometimes a slightly different form is used as the "name" of the verb, but the 3ms suffix conjugation form is the norm.) Even though we have not yet learned the suffix conjugation, the verbs in our vocabulary lists will be written out in this form for ease of reference. Thus, the first vocabulary word, זָכַר, *means* 'he remembered', but in a vocabulary list or when referring to the root in the abstract, we will render the word 'to remember'.

---

verbs

זָכַר   'to remember'; pref. conj. יִזְכֹּר

כָּרַת   'to cut; cut off (from a community)'; used idiomatically with בְּרִית to mean 'to make (a covenant)'; pref. conj. יִכְרֹת

כָּתַב   'to write'; pref. conj. יִכְתֹּב

מָלַךְ   'to rule, reign; be a monarch'; עַל־ 'over'; בְּ 'in; over'; pref. conj. יִמְלֹךְ

קָטַל   'to kill'; pref. conj. יִקְטֹל

שָׁמַר   'to watch, guard; keep, observe'; pref. conj. יִשְׁמֹר

שָׁפַט   'to judge'; pref. conj. יִשְׁפֹּט

nouns

בָּקָר   'cattle' (collective noun for bovines); pl. rare

בְּרִית   'covenant, treaty' (fem.); no pl.

כֹּהֵן   'priest'; pl. כֹּהֲנִים

מִצְוָה   'commandment'; cs. מִצְוַת; pl. מִצְוֺת

מִשְׁפָּט   'judgment, justice, ordinance; custom'; cs. מִשְׁפַּט; pl. מִשְׁפָּטִים; cs. pl. מִשְׁפְּטֵי

נַעַר   '(unmarried) young man; boy; servant'; with sf. נַעֲרִי

סֵפֶר   'book, document, scroll'; with sf. סִפְרִי

צֹאן   'sheep, goats, sheep and goats' (fem.) (collective noun for bovines); no pl. (Note the quiescent א.)

proper nouns

אֱלֹהִים   'God; gods': a pl. form that can indeed mean 'gods', it is more commonly used as a way of addressing the God of the Bible and is then treated as a singular noun; the reason for the pl. form is debated. Construct אֱלֹהֵי can also mean either 'gods of' or 'God of' (Israel, for instance). When אֱלֹהִים is preceded by one of the inseparable prepositions, the א quiesces, and the vowel under the preposition is *tsere*. 'To God' is לֵאלֹהִים (only three syllables). Observant Jews will often pronounce the word as if it were אֱלֹקִים (see immediately below).

יְהֹוָה   the personal name of the God of Israel, "the Tetragrammaton," "Yahweh" in modern scholarly writing; this word is usually vocalized by the Masoretes so that the reader will read Adonay 'my lord' (אֲדֹנָי), because pronouncing the personal name of God was taboo, at least by the Hellenistic period. Observant Jews today will pronounce Adonay or Hashem, 'the name', rather than Yahweh. The name is often represented in English Bibles as "the LORD." In this textbook, we will vocalize the Tetragrammaton in the way usually done in the Hebrew Bible, and the student can decide how to pronounce and translate it. As with אֱלֹהִים above, the א of אֲדֹנָי quiesces when an inseparable preposition comes before it; 'for Yahweh' is written לַיהוָה, with *patakh*, and it is to be pronounced לַאדֹנָי (only three syllables).

However יְהוָה is pronounced and translated, the two words יְהוָה and אֱלֹהִים must be kept separate, each with its own translation. יְהוָה is not 'God', and אֱלֹהִים is not 'the LORD'.

adverb

לֹא   'not'; negates the prefix conjugation

particle

אֶת־/אֵת   marker for definite direct objects

12.11. EXERCISES FOR LESSON 12

A. Completing the paradigm

Write out the complete paradigm for the prefix conjugation of מלך.

B. Translating Hebrew to English sentences

1. יִזְכֹּר אָבִי אֶת־דְּבָרַי

2. יִשְׁמֹר הַנַּעַר אֶת־הַבָּקָר וְאֶת־הַצֹּאן

3. יִשְׁמְרוּ הַכֹּהֲנִים אֵת מִצְוֹת יְהוָה

4. יִכְרֹת אֱלֹהִים בְּרִית עִם עַם יִשְׂרָאֵל

5. כְּתֹב אֶת־סִפְרְךָ

6. שִׁמְרִי אֶת־מִשְׁפְּטֵי יְהוָה הַטּוֹבִים

7. תִּמְלֹךְ הַמַּלְכָּה בִּירוּשָׁלַ͏ִם

8. לֹא יִכְתֹּב לִי הָעֶבֶד הַזָּקֵן אֶת־סִפְרוֹ

9. יִכְתְּבוּ אֶחָיו בְּסִפְרֵיהֶם יוֹם וְלַיְלָה

10. יִזְכְּרוּ בְּנֵי יִשְׂרָאֵל אֶת־אֱלֹהֵיהֶם

> In sentence 8, the word order (with לִי immediately after the verb, and even preceding the subject) is correct for the situation in which the indirect object ('me') is a pronoun and the direct object is a noun (סִפְרוֹ). In fact, when בְּ, לְ, אֶת־, or אֶל־, עַל־ plus pronominal suffix is part of a verb phrase, it is likely that the בִּי, אֹתוֹ, עָלֶיךָ, and so on, will come immediately after the verb.

11. לֹא יִשְׁפְּטוּ אֹתָנוּ בְּחָכְמָה

12. תִּשְׁפֹּטְנָה נְשֵׁי יְהוּדָה אֶת־דְּבָרֶיךָ

C. Translating English to Hebrew

   1. I will remember his words.

   2. You (masc. sg.) used to observe the commandments.

   3. We will not make a covenant.

D. Practice reading the third line of Gen 22:2.

13

יג ◄ **13** ► יג

THE PREFIX CONJUGATION OF VERBS WITH VARIANT PATTERNS; RESUMPTIVE PRONOUNS

13.1 SECOND- AND THIRD-GUTTURAL VERBS

In this lesson we will learn to *recognize* several forms of the prefix conjugation that differ in small ways from תִּשְׁמֹר, אֶשְׁמֹר, and so on. There are several categories of verb that have *patakh* as the last vowel instead of *holem*. The first such category comprises most verbs (with a few exceptions) in which the second of the three root consonants of the verbal root is a guttural (א, ה, ח, ע), like בָּחַר 'to choose', or in which the third root consonant is one of the gutturals ה, ח, or ע, like שָׁמַע 'to hear' (called "second-guttural" and "third-guttural" verbs, or "II-G" and "III-G" respectively):

THIRD-GUTTURAL VERB		SECOND-GUTTURAL VERB	
נִשְׁמַע	אֶשְׁמַע	נִבְחַר	אֶבְחַר
תִּשְׁמְעוּ	תִּשְׁמַע	תִּבְחֲרוּ	תִּבְחַר
תִּשְׁמַּעְנָה	תִּשְׁמְעִי	תִּבְחַׁרְנָה	תִּבְחֲרִי
יִשְׁמְעוּ	יִשְׁמַע	יִבְחֲרוּ	יִבְחַר
תִּשְׁמַּעְנָה	תִּשְׁמַע	תִּבְחַׁרְנָה	תִּבְחַר

Note the *hateph-patakh* in the בָּחַר paradigm: 2fs, 2mp, and 3mp.

13.2. STATIVE VERBS

The second such category is "stative verbs." Stative verbs are verbs that describe a state rather than an action. The translation value of these verbs is usually 'to be' plus an adjective: כָּבֵד, for instance, means 'to be heavy, weighty; important, honored'. The prefix conjugation of "stative" verbs usually has *patakh* rather than *holem*.

THE STATIVE VERB

נִכְבַּד	אֶכְבַּד
תִּכְבְּדוּ	תִּכְבַּד
תִּכְבַּ֫דְנָה	תִּכְבְּדִי
יִכְבְּדוּ	יִכְבַּד
תִּכְבַּ֫דְנָה	תִּכְבַּד

13.3. OTHER VERBS WITH *PATAKH*

The third such category is a small set of verbs that have *patakh* in the prefix conjugation for no obvious reason, for instance, שָׁכַב 'to lie down'; לָמַד 'to learn'; and רָכַב 'to ride'.

VERBS WITH *PATAKH*

נִשְׁכַּב	אֶשְׁכַּב
תִּשְׁכְּבוּ	תִּשְׁכַּב
תִּשְׁכַּ֫בְנָה	תִּשְׁכְּבִי
יִשְׁכְּבוּ	יִשְׁכַּב
תִּשְׁכַּ֫בְנָה	תִּשְׁכַּב

13.4. THIRD-*ALEPH* VERBS

Verbs with א as the third root consonant (third-א verbs) are a subset of the first group above. When א comes at the end of a word (or even a syllable), it quiesces, and the vowel before it tends to lengthen. See, for instance, the following paradigm for קָרָא 'to cry, call, summon':

THE THIRD-*ALEPH* VERB

נִקְרָא	אֶקְרָא
תִּקְרְאוּ	תִּקְרָא
תִּקְרֶ֫אנָה	תִּקְרְאִי
יִקְרְאוּ	יִקְרָא
תִּקְרֶ֫אנָה	תִּקְרָא

Note the anomalous *seghol* in the 2fp and 3fp.

13.5. FIRST-GUTTURAL VERBS

First-guttural verbs (other than I-א, see below) have two basic forms in the prefix conjugation: as before, those with *holem* as the last vowel; and those with *patakh* as the last vowel. The first-guttural (I-G) prefix conjugations with *holem* as the last vowel usually have *patakh* under the preformative, plus *hateph-patakh* (sometimes referred to as an "echo vowel") rather than the expected *shwa* under the guttural, as with עָמַד 'to stand' (note the usual *seghol* in the 1cs).[1]

THE FIRST-GUTTURAL VERB

נַעֲמֹד	אֶעֱמֹד
תַּעַמְדוּ	תַּעֲמֹד
תַּעֲמֹ֫דְנָה	תַּעַמְדִי[2]
יַעַמְדוּ	יַעֲמֹד
תַּעֲמֹ֫דְנָה	תַּעֲמֹד

---

1. Note that I-G verbs do not always have an echo vowel, e.g., יֶהְדַּר, יַחְשֹׁב.
2. The 2fs, 2mp, and 3mp get their forms from the rule of *shwa* for gutturals: יַעֲמְדוּ is an impossible form, with a *hateph*-vowel and a vocal *shwa* together in the middle of the word. The resolution for such patterns is to lose the *hateph*-vowel and substitute the corresponding full vowel.

13.6. First-Guttural Verbs with *Patakh*

First-guttural (I-G) verbs with *patakh* as the last vowel are generally stative verbs; their preformative vowel is *seghol*, with *hateph-seghol* under the first root consonant. For example, חָזַק 'to be strong':

THE FIRST-GUTTURAL VERB WITH *PATAKH*

נֶחֱזַק	אֶחֱזַק
תֶּחֱזְקוּ	תֶּחֱזַק
תֶּחֱזַֿקְנָה	תֶּחֱזְקִי[3]
יֶחֱזְקוּ	יֶחֱזַק
תֶּחֱזַֿקְנָה	תֶּחֱזַק

13.7. First-*Aleph* Verbs

Verbs that have א as the first root consonant (first-א verbs) occur in several forms in the prefix conjugation. Most are just like other I-G verbs, with the minor variation that those with *holem* in the last syllable have *seghol* plus *hateph-seghol* instead of *patakh* plus *hateph-patakh*.[4] We will use אָסַף 'to gather' as our model verb:

THE FIRST-*ALEPH* VERB

נֶאֱסֹף	אֶאֱסֹף
תַּאַסְפוּ	תֶּאֱסֹף
	תַּאַסְפִי
יַאַסְפוּ	יֶאֱסֹף
	תֶּאֱסֹף

The most interesting and most common I-א verbs, however, are five verbs that have the now-familiar *patakh* as the last vowel but *holem* as the first; also, the root

---

3. Again, note the 2fs, 2mp, and 3mp forms, with two *seghol*s as a result of rule of *shwa*.

4. This is a peculiarity of words with א followed by an *o*-vowel, which we will see frequently.

letter א quiesces in every form. Three of these five verbs are אָמַר 'to say', אָכַל 'to eat', and אָבַד 'to die'. (The other two are אָבָה 'to be willing' and אָפָה 'to bake'.)

THE FIRST-*ALEPH* VERB אמר

נֹאמַר	אֹמַר
תֹּאמְרוּ	תֹּאמַר
תֹּאמַ֫רְנָה	תֹּאמְרִי
יֹאמְרוּ	יֹאמַר
תֹּאמַ֫רְנָה	תֹּאמַר

Note that the 1cs form has only one א, whereas we would expect two: one to represent the 1cs and one to be the first root letter. Instead, the second א disappears, and we are left with only one.

To summarize, in this lesson we have seen:

(1) several types of prefix conjugation verbs with *patakh* in the last syllable—stative verbs (including I-G); II-G; III-G; a small group with no obvious reason for the *patakh*;
(2) III-א verbs with *qamets* in the last syllable;
(3) I-G verbs that begin with either *patakh* plus *hateph-patakh* or *seghol* plus *hateph-seghol*;
(4) five I-א verbs with *holem* in the first syllable.

13.8. RESUMPTIVE PRONOUNS

We learned in lesson 9 that אֲשֶׁר is the relative pronoun in BH. Besides the uses we have already seen, אֲשֶׁר is used to introduce entire clauses. 'This is the man who will rule over Israel' is זֶה הָאִישׁ אֲשֶׁר יִמְלֹךְ עַל־יִשְׂרָאֵל.

In most of BH, there is no word-for-word equivalent to English 'in which', 'to which', 'for which', and so on. Instead, BH uses אֲשֶׁר plus a preposition with a "resumptive pronoun." Thus, 'this is the city in which I will write the book' is written זֹאת הָעִיר אֲשֶׁר אֶכְתֹּב אֶת־הַסֵּפֶר בָּהּ (literally, 'This is the city which I will write the book in it'—bad English, but perfectly normal Hebrew).

13.9. VOCABULARLY FOR LESSON 13

verbs

אָכַל   'to eat'; pref. conj. יֹאכַל

אָמַר   'to say' ('to' someone, with לְ or אֶל־); pref. conj. יֹאמַר

בָּחַר   'to choose'; pref. conj. יִבְחַר (dir. obj. with בְּ: 'he will choose me' (יִבְחַר בִּי)

חָזַק   'to be strong'; pref. conj. יֶחֱזַק

עָמַד   'to stand'; pref. conj. יַעֲמֹד

קָרָא   'to call'; 'to summon' (with לְ); 'to name' (with לְ or אֶת; with or without the noun שֵׁם in the phrase); pref. conj. יִקְרָא

שָׁמַע   'to hear; to listen to' (with אֶל־ or לְ); 'to obey' (with בְּקוֹל or לְקוֹל); pref. conj. יִשְׁמַע

nouns

גִּבּוֹר   'strong or mighty man; warrior; soldier'

לֶחֶם   'bread; food'; with sf. לַחְמִי

מִדְבָּר   'wilderness'; cs. מִדְבַּר

מַחֲנֶה   'camp'; cs. מַחֲנֵה

מַלְאָךְ   'messenger; angel'; cs. מַלְאַךְ; with sf. מַלְאָכִי; pl. מַלְאָכִים; cs. pl. מַלְאֲכֵי

פֶּה   'mouth'; 'edge' (of a sword, for instance); cs. פִּי; with sf. פִּי, פִּיךָ, and so on, on the pattern of אָב and אָח; pl. very rare

צָבָא   'army'; cs. צְבָא; pl. צְבָאוֹת; cs. pl. צִבְאוֹת; used especially in the phrase יְהוָה צְבָאוֹת 'the LORD of hosts' (masc., like the sg.)

proper nouns

שָׂרָה   personal name, 'Sarah'

שָׂרַי   personal name, 'Sarai' (the spelling of Sarah's name before it was changed in Gen 17)

pronoun

מִי   'who?'; usually comes at the beginning of the sentence

adjective

צַדִּיק   'righteous'

preposition

עַד   'up to, as far as; until'

conjunction

כִּי   'because'; sometimes 'when'; after a negative, 'but rather'

particle

לֵאמֹר   literally 'to say', this word can be used to mark the onset of direct speech; often translated 'saying' but better left untranslated and represented by quotation marks.

13.10. Exercises for lesson 13

A. Translate from Hebrew to English:

1. יֹאכְלוּ גִבּוֹרִים אֶת־לֶחֶם הַמִּדְבָּר

2. נֹאמַר אֶל־מַלְאַךְ יְהוָה לֵאמֹר יִבְחַר הָעָם⁵ בְּדָוִד לְמֶלֶךְ⁶

3. וַיֹּאמֶר⁷ אֱלֹהִים אֶל־אַבְרָהָם
   לֹא תִקְרָא אֶת־שְׁמָהּ שָׂרַי כִּי שָׂרָה שְׁמָהּ (Gen 17:15)

4. נִזְכֹּר אֶת מֵי יְרוּשָׁלַם

5. יִקְרָא יְהוָה לְמֹשֶׁה לֵאמֹר בַּצָּהֳרַיִם יַעֲמֹד צְבָא יִשְׂרָאֵל לִפְנֵי הַמַּחֲנֶה

6. תִּכְתֹּב אֶת־הַסֵּפֶר אֲשֶׁר מִשְׁפַּט יְהוָה בּוֹ

7. יִשְׁפְּטוּ הַכֹּהֲנִים אֶת־הַצַּדִּיקָה אֲשֶׁר יִבְחַר בָּהּ יְהוָה⁸

8. תִּשְׁמַע הָאִשָּׁה לַעֲצָתֵךְ הָרָעָה

9. אֵלֶּה הַמִּצְוֹת אֲשֶׁר יִשְׁמֹר אַבְרָהָם

10. יִכְרֹת אֲבִי אַבְרָם בְּרִית עִם עַם אֲשֶׁר יֶחֱזַק מִמֶּנּוּ

11. מִי יַעֲמֹד לִפְנֵי מֶלֶךְ הַשָּׁמַיִם

12. יֹאמַר הַנַּעַר לְמֹשֶׁה לֵאמֹר אֶשְׁמַע אֶת פִּי יְהוָה עַד־מוֹתִי

---

5. עַם is used as both a singular and a plural. Sometimes in the same sentence, עַם will be used with a singular adjective and a plural verb.

6. לְ can be translated 'as' here.

7. 'And [God] said,'

8. See the explanatory box that goes along with sentence 8 in lesson 12.

B. Translate the following into Hebrew:

    1. He will say these words.

    2. I will name him David.

    3. We will listen to the king's wife.

C. Practice reading all of Gen 22:1–2.

INDIRECT IMPERATIVES, THE PRONOMINAL SUFFIXES ON VERBS, AND THE PARTICLES -נָא AND -הַ

14.1. THE INDIRECT IMPERATIVE OR VOLITIVE FORMS GENERALLY

Besides the direct imperative, BH uses indirect imperatives to express a wish, in all three persons. Taken together, the imperative and the indirect imperatives are called "volitive" forms—verb forms that express a wish. In English, the first-person plural indirect imperative is best illustrated by the contraction "Let's." "Let's go to the beach" does not ask for someone to *allow* us to go the beach; rather, it expresses a wish: I want for us to go to the beach. The first-person singular indirect imperative is uncommon in English, but the bumper sticker "Let me be the person my dog thinks I am" is one example. Again, the dog owner is not using "let" to ask for permission but rather is expressing a wish or hope.

In the second and third persons in English, the indirect imperative is most easily thought of as a toast at a celebration. "May you live long and prosper!" is a second-person example, and it works for singular and plural. "May she have many happy years in her new home!" is a third-person singular example; "May they be happy together!" is a third-person plural example.

In BH, the prefix conjugation can always have the indirect imperative meaning, if the context allows or demands it. נִכְתֹּב סֵפֶר can be both 'We will write a book' and 'Let's write a book!' תִּכְתֹּב אֶת־הַסֵּפֶר can mean both 'She will write the book' and 'May she (finally) write the book!'

14.2. THE COHORTATIVE FORM

Although the prefix conjugation can always have the meaning of the indirect imperative in BH, there are also special forms of the verb in each person that make it clear that the indirect imperative is being expressed. In the verbs we have learned thus far,[1] only the first person exhibits such a form: an accented הָ - is added at the end of the verb. This form is known as the cohortative.

THE COHORTATIVE

נִשְׁמֹר	We will guard/Let's guard.	נִשְׁמְרָה	Let's guard.
אֶכְתֹּב	I will write/Let me write.	אֶכְתְּבָה	Let me write.

> The cohortative is a special form of the first-person prefix conjugation that expresses a wish.

14.3. THE JUSSIVE FORM

In the *qal* "weak" verbs (see the note below), however, there is sometimes a special form of the prefix conjugation to express the indirect imperative, not only for the first person (the cohortative), but for the second and third persons as well. These special forms for the second and third persons are referred to as jussives. In the *qal* "strong" verbs, the jussive looks exactly the same as the prefix conjugation, in both second and third persons.

Weak verbs will be taken up in later lessons, but for the purpose of illustration, we will use a few as examples here. We will look at only the most common types.

'He will arise' is יָקוּם, and 'May he arise' (third-person singular jussive) is יָקֹם, from the root קום.

'You (ms) will build' is תִּבְנֶה, and 'May you build' (second-person singular jussive) is תֶּבֶן, from the root בנה.

'It (masc.) will be' is יִהְיֶה, and 'Let it be/Let there be' is יְהִי, as in 'Let there be light' (Gen 1:3): יְהִי אוֹר, from the root היה.

> In this textbook, the word *jussive* is used to indicate a special form of the second- and third-person prefix conjugation that expresses a wish.

---

1. Referred to as the *qal* "strong" verbs. We will learn the "weak" verbs later in the semester.

14.4. THE NEGATIVE IMPERATIVE FORMS

The negative imperative is the negative word אַל‑ plus the jussive.[2] 'Don't watch!' (said to a man) is אַל‑תִּשְׁמֹר. In BH, the imperative *form* is *never* negated.

There is also a negative imperative that uses the negative word לֹא plus the prefix conjugation. When this form is used, the command is meant to be especially strong or forceful, even a universal prohibition; this is the form used in many of the Ten Commandments. For instance, 'Don't close that window!' would be אַל‑ plus the jussive; 'Don't *ever* close that window!' would be לֹא plus the prefix conjugation.[3]

> אַל‑ "not": used with the jussive to negate the imperative; in general, used to negate forms that express a wish (volitive forms)
>
> לֹא "not": negates the prefix conjugation, as we saw above; also serves as an emphatic negative imperative when used with the second-person prefix conjugation

14.5. THE PARTICLE ‑נָא

The particle ‑נָא/נָא can be added after any of the volitive verb forms. It is often translated 'please', but its meaning is debated. It is useful, however, in distinguishing between the simple future and volitive meanings of those verbs that look alike in the prefix conjugation and jussive. יִכְתֹּב סֵפֶר is 'He will write a book' or 'May he write a book'. יִכְתֹּב נָא סֵפֶר is definitely 'May he write a book' (with *maqqeph*, written יִכְתָּב‑נָא סֵפֶר). When the negative אַל is used, נָא is added directly to the negative: אַל‑נָא.

14.6. OBJECT SUFFIXES ON PREFIX CONJUGATION AND IMPERATIVE FORMS

We learned pronominal suffixes on nouns in lesson 11. Very similar suffixes occur when the direct object of the verb is a pronoun. (We have learned אֹתִי, etc. for these situations, but the object suffixes are actually more common.) The following

---

2. As noted above, in the *qal* strong verb, the jussive and the prefix conjugation look exactly alike; consequently, the negative imperative is often referred to in textbooks as אַל‑ plus the prefix conjugation (or plus the "imperfect"). This formulation does, in fact, work for many kinds of verbs, but in reality only those for which the jussive and the prefix conjugation look exactly alike. The more correct formulation is as above, אַל‑ plus jussive.

3. There is the possibility for ambiguity from the point of view of English speakers: Is the sentence 'Don't ever close that window!' or 'You will not close that window'? They look exactly the same. This very point, however, shows us that the ancient Hebrews did not see a distinction between those two possibilities. To say 'You will not close that window' is the same as saying 'Don't ever close that window!'

suffixes occur on prefix conjugation or imperative verbs. They must be recognized but need not be memorized; nor is it necessary to memorize the changes that occur on the verbs themselves when suffixes are added. Recognition and understanding are the goals.

There are two paradigms, neither complete: one that usually has an accented *tsere* plus pronominal suffixes; and one with an accented *seghol* plus a doubled consonant. In fact, with very few exceptions, a *tsere* or *seghol* before a verbal objective suffix tells you that the verb itself is a prefix-conjugation verb or an imperative. That is, you can use the suffix to help you identify the verb. So:

THE OBJECT SUFFIXES ON THE PREFIX CONJUGATION AND IMPERATIVES

נִי- or נִֽי-	'me' as direct object (as in יִשְׁמְרֵ֫נִי 'he will observe *me*')
ךָ- or ךָֽ-	'you' (ms) as direct object
ךְ-	'you' (fs) as direct object
הוּ-, הֽוּ-, or נּוּ-	'him' as direct object
הָ- or נָּֽה-	'her' as direct object
נוּ-	'us' as direct object
ם-	'them' (m or mixed) as direct object
ן-	'them' (f) as direct object

When these suffixes are added to a verb that ends in a vowel, the *tsere* or *seghol* will disappear. There are only rarely examples of second-person plural suffixes.

14.7. THE PARTICLE -הֲ

The particle הֲ, when added directly to the first word in a clause, turns the clause into a question:

יִשְׁמֹר אֶת־הַצֹּאן	He will watch the sheep/goats.
הֲיִשְׁמֹר אֶת־הַצֹּאן	Will he watch the sheep/goats?

Before words that begin with gutturals or with *shwa*, the interrogative particle is usually הַ. (This particle can only rarely be confused with the definite article.) A negative question begins with הֲלֹא.

14.8. Vocabulary for Lesson 14

verbs

עָבַד 'to serve; work' (cf. ‎עֲבֹדָה below); pref. conj. ‎יַעֲבֹד

שָׁלַח 'to send' (something, someone); 'to reach out, extend' (e.g., a hand); pref. conj. ‎יִשְׁלַח

יִבֶן 'let him build' (from the root ‎בנה)

יְהִי 'let it be, let there be' (from the root ‎היה)

יָקֻם 'let him arise, stand up' (from the root ‎קום)

> ‎יָקֻם, ‎יְהִי, ‎יִבֶן, and are jussive forms that you should simply memorize as they are. They will be useful for the discussion of the verbal system in general, even though we have not studied them in depth yet.

nouns

מִלְחָמָה 'battle, war'; cs. ‎מִלְחֶמֶת; with sf. ‎מִלְחַמְתִּי; pl. ‎מִלְחָמוֹת; cs. pl. ‎מִלְחֲמוֹת

עֲבֹדָה 'work; service; labor' (cf. ‎עָבַד above); cs. ‎עֲבֹדַת; no pl.

עוֹלָם 'eternity', either future or antiquity; ‎עַד־עוֹלָם or ‎לְעוֹלָם 'forever'; with a negative, 'never'

proper noun

פַּרְעֹה 'Pharaoh'

adverbs

אַל־ forms the negative imperative: negates the jussive

הַיּוֹם 'today'; less commonly ‎כַּיּוֹם with the same meaning

לֹא with the pref. conj., either negates the pref. conj. (see lesson 12) or forms the universal negative imperative ('thou shalt not's')

עוֹד 'again; still'; after a negative, 'no longer'

particles

הַ interrogative particle

כָּל־/כֹּל 'all; each; every' (for instance, ‎כָּל־הָעָם 'all the people'; ‎כָּל־אִשָּׁה 'each woman, every woman'; with pronominal suffixes, ‎כֻּלּוֹ or ‎כֻּלָּה 'all of it', ‎כֻּלָּם 'all of them'. Whether written with *holem* as a separate word or, more commonly, attached to the next word with a *maqqeph*, the vowel is an *o*-vowel. The word is always pronounced like English "coal." (For a different set of two forms with the same sort of variation, see 12.8.) When ‎כֹּל is part of the direct object, it sometimes takes ‎אֶת in front of it; that is to say, כֹּל is sometimes considered definite, even without a definite article, although that use is not predictable.

נָא/־נָא   volitive particle, no clear translation

14.9. EXERCISES FOR LESSON 14

A. Translate from Hebrew to English:

1. הֲזֶה הַשָּׂדֶה אֲשֶׁר סוּסִי בּוֹ

2. אַל־תִּזְכְּרוּהוּ הַיּוֹם כִּי אִישׁ רַע הוּא

3. וַיֹּאמֶר[4] יְהוָה לֵאמֹר יְהִי אוֹר בַּשָּׁמָיִם

4. לֹא־אֶשְׁלַח יָדִי[5] אֶל־בֶּן־הַמֶּלֶךְ כִּי בְאָזְנֵינוּ צִוָּה[7] הַמֶּלֶךְ אֹתְךָ ... לֵאמֹר שִׁמְרוּ אֶת־הַנָּעַר (adapted from 2 Sam 18:12)

5. אַל־תִּבֶן[8] אֶת־הַבַּיִת הַהוּא

6. יֶחְזְקוּ גִבּוֹרֵינוּ לְעוֹלָם כִּי אֱלֹהִים עִמָּנוּ

7. אַל־יָקָם פַּרְעֹה עוֹד בַּהֵיכָל אֲשֶׁר בָּעִיר הַגְּדוֹלָה

8. תַּעֲמֹדְנָה כָּל־נְשֵׁי יְרוּשָׁלַם בְּבֵית הַכֹּהֵן וְלֹא תִשְׁמַעְנָה אֶת־דְּבָרָיו

9. תִּקְרְאוּ בְּשֵׁם[9] אֱלֹהֵיכֶם וַאֲנִי אֶקְרָא בְּשֵׁם־יְהוָה (taken from 1 Kgs 18:24)[9]

10. טוֹבִים כָּל־יְמֵי אַבְרָהָם עַל־הָאָרֶץ הַזֹּאת

11. אֶשְׁלְחָה־נָּא אֶת־מַלְאָכִי אֶל־הַמִּלְחָמָה הַהִיא

12. הִתְעַבְּדוּ אֶת עֲבֹדַת הַהֵיכָל לִפְנֵי יְהוָה אֱלֹהֵינוּ

---

4. 'And he said,'

5. Note that when the definite direct object is a part of the body, the direct object marker אֵת is often not used. (See footnote 6 of lesson 12.)

6. This is one of those situations mentioned above when the *beged-kephet* letter is pronounced without the *dagesh* even though it is at the beginning of a word, because the preceding word ends in a vowel, and the two words are pronounced closely together.

7. 'commanded'

8. This is the same verb as יִבֶן, which is 3ms, but in this case it is the *jussive* of the *second*-person masculine singular or of the third-person *feminine* singular.

9. בְּשֵׁם + קרא = "to call on the name of."

B. Translate from English to Hebrew:

   1. Will the man rule over us?

   2. The man will rule over us.

   3. The man will not rule over us.

   4. May the man not rule over us!

C. Practice reading the first three lines of Gen 22:3.

THE CONSECUTIVE PRETERITE VERBAL FORM

15.1. THE CONSECUTIVE PRETERITE GENERALLY

The most common narrative past-tense form in BH we will call the consecutive preterite (cons. pret.) in this book.[1] It is based on the jussive *form* but has nothing to do with the *meaning* of the jussive. It is made by attaching the word וַ 'and' (which in these verbs usually has the vowel *patakh*) to the front of the jussive plus, usually, doubling the preformative letter of the jussive. For instance, we learned in the last lesson that יִּבֶן means 'let him build'; now we will learn that וַיִּבֶן means 'and he built'. יִשְׁמֹר means both 'he will watch' (pref. conj. meaning) and 'may he watch' (jussive meaning); 'and he watched' is וַיִּשְׁמֹר.

> Remember: in the *qal* strong verb, the prefix conjugation form and the jussive form look exactly alike, so it is not obvious in the *qal* strong consecutive preterite that we are starting with the jussive form. It is only obvious when we begin with weak verb jussives like יִּבֶן. Still, it is correct to say in general that the consecutive preterite is built off the jussive form, not the prefix conjugation form.

We learned in the last lesson that יְהִי is 'let there be'; now we can see that 'and there was' is וַיְהִי:[2] יְהִי אוֹר וַיְהִי אוֹר 'Let there be light! And there was light' (Gen 1:3).

---

1. Preterite = past tense. The form is called "consecutive" because it begins with וַ 'and', implying that it follows another verb. It usually does, but it will be noted that the form has become so common that it can stand at the beginning of a sentence.

2. In theory, the י preformative should be doubled and so would contain a doubling *dagesh*, but in fact, when doubled *yod* (י) appears with *shwa* as its vowel, it tends to lose the doubling. This is true of several letters in BH: ס/שׂ, ק, נ, מ, ל, ו, and י. The mnemonic for remembering which letters lose the doubling when they appear with *shwa* is Skin 'em Levi or Skin 'em alive, which uses the sounds of all the consonants involved.

15.2. THE RETRACTION OF ACCENT IN THE CONSECUTIVE PRETERITE FORM

Sometimes a word's accent moves back toward the beginning of the word when the וֹ is added. (We will refer to this וֹ as the "*vav* consecutive.") We also learned in the last lesson that יָקֹם is 'may he arise'; after adding the *vav* consecutive to make 'and he arose', we get וַיָּקֹם. But this verb is one in which the accent moves in the consecutive preterite form, so we would have וַיָּקֹם. But notice that the retraction of the accent has left us with a final syllable that is unaccented and closed. It really should not have a long vowel, and in fact the form we get in BH does not. We get instead *qamets* with the value short-*o*, and the actual form for 'and he arose' is וַיָּקָם. (Remember: the first *qamets* is the usual long *a*-vowel, but the second is an *o*-sound: vay-yá-qom.)

Another verb that retracts the accent in the consecutive preterite form is the very common וַיֹּאמֶר 'and he said' that we have already seen in a few sentences in the exercises. We also get the expected וַיֹּאמַר, which is often, but not always, the form that is used when a quotation begins with the very next word.

15.3. OTHER NAMES FOR THE CONSECUTIVE PRETERITE

The form we are calling the consecutive preterite is usually called the "converted imperfect," as if the addition of the וֹ somehow "converted" a future-tense verb into a past-tense verb. It is also called the "imperfect with *vav* consecutive," a better choice, but also misleading, since the basic verb is not the "imperfect" (our prefix conjugation) but rather the jussive.

15.4. AN ASIDE: THE HISTORY OF THE CONSECUTIVE PRETERITE FORM

The reason the consecutive preterite looks the way it does is a historical one. Students need not know the following explanation, but they might find it helpful, so it is included here.

The consecutive preterite is a past-tense verb based on the jussive form, because in an earlier form of Hebrew the jussive and the past tense were the same form. That is, יִבֶן would have meant both 'may he build' and 'he built'.[3] By the time we get to the form of Hebrew used in the Bible, this old past-tense meaning is preserved in

---

3. We come to this conclusion from reading the fourteenth-century Ugaritic texts, which operate under this same system, but even more important is the evidence from the fourteenth-century B.C.E. Akkadian texts found at el-Amarna in Egypt, because many of them were written in an Akkadian that exhibits features of the underlying language of the Canaanite scribes, especially in the verbal system. (See also the beginning of lesson 1.)

prose[4] only after the word 'and' (also written in its earlier form וַ rather than וְ).[5] This is what is known as a "frozen form": it is as if the וַ "protects" the form from being updated, even though the rest of the language has left this old past tense behind.

> We are using the name "consecutive preterite" in this book to express the idea that this form has *always* been a past-tense form in Hebrew (hence "preterite"), and it is preserved in BH narrative prose with the word "and" at the beginning (hence "consecutive"). Students should be aware, however, that this is idiosyncratic terminology: "the converted Imperfect" or "the Imperfect with *vav* consecutive" is the norm.

15.5. WHERE THE CONSECUTIVE PRETERITE MAY BE FOUND AND WHERE IT WILL NOT BE FOUND

The consecutive preterite is ordinarily only used in positions where the word 'and' is *not inappropriate*; for instance, it would not come *between* subject and object: הַמֶּלֶךְ וַיִּכְתֹּב סֵפֶר 'the king and he wrote a book' would be wrong. Also, it would not come immediately after another conjunction: כִּי וַיִּכְתֹּב הַמֶּלֶךְ סֵפֶר 'because and the king wrote a book' is also wrong. There is no place in such a sentence for the 'and' in English or in Hebrew.

On the other hand, because the consecutive preterite is a frozen form, it comes all together, as a package. It has become, by the time of BH, simply a past-tense verb, with the sense of the 'and' at the beginning acknowledged only when it is useful. So the sentence וַיִּכְתֹּב הַמֶּלֶךְ סֵפֶר 'And the king wrote a book' could come at the very beginning of a document, where the tie between that sentence and whatever is perceived to have come before it (represented by the 'and') is very loose. In fact, even entire books of the Bible begin with consecutive preterites, such as וַיִּקְרָא '(and) he called' (Yahweh to Moses; the book is Leviticus, called וַיִּקְרָא in Jewish tradition). The 'and' in this case, while it can be thought of as connecting Leviticus to Exodus, is really extraneous in translation. Although 'and' is ordinarily not *inappropriate*, as was explained above, it is not necessarily to be *translated* in every case. It is left to the discretion of the translator whether to translate a particular consecutive preterite form with 'and', to use some other conjunction such as 'then', or not to translate the וַ at all.

---

4. Examples of this early past-tense/jussive form without 'and' do occur in the Hebrew Bible, in early poetry.

5. The origin of the doubling of the preformative that follows this וַ is debated.

15.6. The lengthening of *patakh* to *qamets* before the 1cs form

Because א cannot be doubled, the וַ plus doubling of the consecutive preterite becomes וָ in the 1cs form. אֶשְׁמֹר means 'I will guard' or 'may I guard'; '(and) I guarded' is וָאֶשְׁמֹר.

15.7. Vocabulary for lesson 15

verbs

מָצָא	'to find'; pref. conj. יִמְצָא
עָבַר	'to cross (over), travel through, traverse; to transgress' (a commandment); pref. conj. יַעֲבֹר
עָזַב	'to abandon, leave'; pref. conj. יַעֲזֹב
קָבַר	'to bury' (see קֶבֶר below); pref. conj. יִקְבֹּר
שָׁכַב	'to lie down'; pref. conj. יִשְׁכַּב

nouns

בֹּקֶר	'morning'; pl. very rare
לֵב	'heart; mind' (the seat of knowledge); with sf. לִבִּי; pl. לִבּוֹת (masc., like the sg.)
לֵבָב	'heart; mind'; cs. לְבַב; with sf. לְבָבִי; pl. לְבָבוֹת (masc., like the sg.)
עֶרֶב	'evening'; no pl. attested, but a dual is: עַרְבַּיִם
קֶבֶר	'grave' (see קָבַר above); with sf. קִבְרִי

proper nouns

יַרְדֵּן	'Jordan River'
שָׁאוּל	personal name, 'Saul'

adjectives (numbers)

אֶחָד	'one, first' (masc.); cs. אַחַד; pl. אֲחָדִים 'several'
אַחַת	'one, first' (fem.); can also be written אֶחָת (called a "pausal" form; such forms will be taken up in lesson 23)

15.8. EXERCISES FOR LESSON 15

A. Translate from Hebrew to English:

1. וַיִּקְרָא אֱלֹהִים לָאוֹר יוֹם וְלַחֹשֶׁךְ קָרָא⁶ לָיְלָה וַיְהִי־עֶרֶב וַיְהִי־בֹקֶר יוֹם אֶחָד
(Gen 1:5)

2. וַיִּמְצָאָהּ מַלְאַךְ יְהוָה עַל־עֵין הַמַּיִם בַּמִּדְבָּר (from Gen 16:7)

3. וַיָּקָם⁷ דָּוִד וְכָל־הָעָם אֲשֶׁר אִתּוֹ⁸ וַיַּעַבְרוּ אֶת־הַיַּרְדֵּן עַד־אוֹר הַבֹּקֶר
(from 2 Sam 17:22)

4. וַיַּעַזְבוּ אֶת־יְהוָה וַיַּעַבְדוּ לַבַּעַל⁹ וְלָעַשְׁתָּרוֹת ¹⁰ (Judg 2:13)

5. וַיִּשְׁכַּב אֲבִיָּם¹¹ עִם־אֲבֹתָיו וַיִּקְבְּרוּ אֹתוֹ בְּעִיר דָּוִד וַיִּמְלֹךְ אָסָא¹² בְּנוֹ תַּחְתָּיו
(1 Kgs 15:8)

6. וַיֹּאמֶר יְהוָה אֶל־מֹשֶׁה עֲבֹר לִפְנֵי הָעָם (from Exod 17:5)

7. וַתִּכְתֹּב הָאִשָּׁה אֶת־הַסֵּפֶר עַל־לִבָּהּ

B. Translate Hebrew short sentences with consecutive preterite:

1. וַיִּזְכֹּר אֶת־יְהוָה

2. וַנִּכְרֹת בְּרִית עִמָּהֶם¹³

3. וָאֶשְׁמֹר אֹתָהּ בִּלְבָבִי

---

6. The accent on this word is unusual and is here for the sake of authenticity. Often in the Hebrew Bible, having two accents directly next to each other is avoided, so קָרָא here is accented on the first syllable because its regular accent, on the final syllable, would come immediately before the accent on the next word, לָיְלָה. If the verse is being memorized, the accentuation should be remembered correctly, but otherwise, such intricate matters of accentuation will not be a part of this textbook.

7. See above, 15.2.

8. When a compound subject follows the verb, it is possible in BH for the verb to agree with only part of the compound subject—the part that is immediately after the verb (here: David). That is, וַיָּקָם can be understood to go with the entire compound subject.

9. הַבַּעַל is the usual spelling of the divine name Baal.

10. This is the plural of the divine name Ashtóret = Astarte. The plural usage is generally taken to mean various manifestations of the deity at different locations.

11. A personal name.

12. A personal name.

13. An alternate form of עִמָּם.

4. וַיִּשְׁמֹר אֶת־הַצֹּאן

5. וַיִּקְבֹּר אֹתוֹ בְּקֶבֶר אָבִיו

6. וָאֹכַל אֶת־לַחְמִי

7. וַתִּבְחַרְנָה בַּנַּעַר

8. וַתִּשְׁפֹּט אֶת־הָעָם

9. וַתֶּחֱזַק יָדִי

10. וַיַּעֲמֹד לִפְנֵי הַהֵיכָל

11. וַיִּבֶן בַּיִת בִּירוּשָׁלַם

12. וַתִּשְׁמְעוּ אֶת־דְּבָרָיו

C. Translating English to Hebrew:

1. (And) the old man wrote the book.

2. (And) I remembered the name of Yahweh.

3. (And) we made a covenant with the king of the great land.

D. Practice reading all of Gen 22:3.

THE *QAL* SUFFIX CONJUGATION, THE *Və-QATAL* FORM, AND ITS OBJECT SUFFIXES

16.1. THE SUFFIX CONJUGATION GENERALLY

In lesson 15 we learned that the consecutive preterite is the most common past-tense verb form in BH narrative prose. We also learned that the consecutive preterite is used in positions where the word 'and' is not inappropriate, for instance, at the beginning of a clause. That leaves a number of situations unaccounted for, however, including: past-tense clauses that begin with כִּי (we do not get 'because and he wrote'); past-tense clauses that, for one reason or another, begin with the subject (we do not get 'the king and he wrote'); past-tense clauses that begin with other conjunctions, such as אֲשֶׁר (we do not get 'the man who and he wrote the book'); past-tense clauses that begin with לֹא.

16.2. THE MEANINGS OF THE SUFFIX CONJUGATION

In these situations, BH uses the suffix conjugation (suff. conj.), which is actually the simplest form of the verb and, therefore, the form we have been using to identify verbs in the vocabulary lists. The meaning of the suffix conjugation is: (1) a past tense in most forms, as in 'I wrote', including what is called in English the present perfect 'I have written' and the pluperfect 'I had written'; and (2) present tense in stative verbs and verbs of perception, for instance, 'I know' as well as 'I knew' (verbal root ידע).

16.3. THE FORM OF THE SUFFIX CONJUGATION

The paradigm of the suffix conjugation is as follows and should be memorized (using the verbal root שׁמר):

THE SUFFIX CONJUGATION

we kept	שָׁמַרְנוּ	שָׁמַרְתִּי	I kept
you (mp) kept	שְׁמַרְתֶּם[1]	שָׁמַרְתָּ	you (ms) kept
you (fp) kept	שְׁמַרְתֶּן	שָׁמַרְתְּ[2]	you (fs) kept
they (m and f) kept	שָׁמְרוּ[4]	שָׁמַר[3]	he kept
		שָׁמְרָה[5]	she kept

The suffix conjugation has no preformatives but instead has distinctive endings, most of which are unaccented; they should be noted, as they will occur in every stem. The 1cs (תִּי-), 2ms (תָּ-), and 2fs (תְּ-) all have ת as part of their ending. The 3ms is the simple form, without a special ending; remember that it is this form that identifies most verbs in Biblical Hebrew. The 3fs ends in ָה -, a familiar feminine ending from nouns and adjectives. The 1cp ends in נוּ-, and the third-person plural ending וּ- does not distinguish between masculine and feminine. Finally, the second-person plural endings are accented תֶּם- and תֶּן-, masculine and feminine, respectively.[6]

16.4. THE NEGATION OF THE SUFFIX CONJUGATION

Like the prefix conjugation, the suffix conjugation is negated with לֹא, placed directly before the verb.

---

1. Note the *shwa* under the שׁ in the second-person plural forms.

2. Both *shwa*s at the end of the word are silent. The word is pronounced sha-mart. This is one of the very rare occurrences of a final consonant cluster in BH, that is, two consonants pronounced together at the end of a word without a vowel in between.

3. Note that this is the 3ms suffix conjugation form of the verb that we are using as the verb's "name."

4. There is only one form in the third-person plural suffix conjugation. It works for both genders. Note the *metheg* with the *qamets*, to indicate that this *qamets* plus *shwa* combination is pronounced as long *a* and vocal *shwa*: sha-mə-ru, where ə = vocal *shwa*.

5. Note the *metheg* with the first *qamets*, used to indicate that this *qamets* plus *shwa* combination is pronounced as long *a* and vocal *shwa*: sha-mə-ra, where ə = vocal *shwa*.

6. There is also a stative paradigm in the suffix conjugation, which usually differs from the non-stative paradigm only in the 3ms form, which has *tsere* rather than *patakh*, e.g., כָּבֵד.

16.5. EXAMPLES OF TRANSLATIONS OF THE SUFFIX CONJUGATION

We will look at a few examples:

He did not observe Yahweh's commandment.	לֹא שָׁמַר אֶת־מִצְוֺת יְהוָה
This is the man who served Yahweh.	זֶה הָאִישׁ אֲשֶׁר עָבַד אֶת־יְהוָה
He will not rule over us because he has not kept Yahweh's commandment.	לֹא יִמְלֹךְ עָלֵינוּ כִּי לֹא שָׁמַר אֶת־מִצְוֺת יְהוָה

16.6. FIRST, SECOND, AND THIRD GUTTURALS IN THE SUFFIX CONJUGATION

When one of the verb's root consonants is a guttural, predictable changes occur. In the four paradigms below, note 7 explains the quiescence of א throughout most of the paradigm; the other unusual forms are contained in boxes and explained in notes 8, 9, and 10:

THE SUFFIX CONJUGATION WITH GUTTURALS

1cs	קָרָ֫אתִי[7]	שָׁמַ֫עְתִּי	בָּחַ֫רְתִּי	עָמַ֫דְתִּי
2ms	קָרָ֫אתָ	שָׁמַ֫עְתָּ	בָּחַ֫רְתָּ	עָמַ֫דְתָּ
2fs	קָרָאת[9]	שָׁמַ֫עַתְּ[8]	בָּחַרְתְּ	עָמַדְתְּ
3ms	קָרָא	שָׁמַע	בָּחַר	עָמַד
3fs	קָרְאָה	שָׁמְעָה	בָּחֲרָה[10]	עָמְדָה
1cp	קָרָ֫אנוּ	שָׁמַ֫עְנוּ	בָּחַ֫רְנוּ	עָמַ֫דְנוּ
2mp	קְרָאתֶם	שְׁמַעְתֶּם	בְּחַרְתֶּם	עֲמַדְתֶּם
2fp	קְרָאתֶן	שְׁמַעְתֶּן	בְּחַרְתֶּן	עֲמַדְתֶּן
3cp	קָרְאוּ	שָׁמְעוּ	בָּחֲרוּ	עָמְדוּ

---

7. The א quiesces throughout this paradigm, except for 3fs and 3cp.

8. This is an irregular form.

9. No *shwa* is needed under this ת. The usual תְּ at this point in the paradigm comes after another consonant with *shwa* and indicates a consonant cluster at the end of the word. But here, with the א quiescent, there is no consonant cluster, just a simple ת sound after a vowel.

10. The *hateph-patakh* substitutes for vocal *shwa* under the guttural, here and in בָּחֲרוּ, עֲמַדְתֶּם, and עֲמַדְתֶּן.

16.7. ADDITIONAL MEANING OF THE WORD כִּי

The familiar word כִּי 'because, since' has another common use in BH. It is used to mean 'that' after certain verbs, notably verbs of perception and אָמַר, in phrases such as the following: 'I said that he was there' אָמַ֫רְתִּי כִּי שָׁם הוּא; 'I know that you are there' יָדַ֫עְתִּי כִּי שָׁם אַתָּה; 'I heard that she was there' שָׁמַ֫עְתִּי כִּי שָׁם הִיא.

16.8. THE *Və-QATAL* ("CONVERTED PERFECT") FORM

Corresponding to the consecutive preterite, there is a form of the suffix conjugation with a prefixed *vav*, the *və-qatal* (וְקָטַל)[11] form, which, instead of meaning 'and' plus past tense, as would be logical, has the same meaning as the simple prefix conjugation. That is, וְאָמַר is to be translated 'and he will say'. ('And he said', remember, is וַיֹּ֫אמֶר, the consecutive preterite.) For instance, 'He will remember my name, and he will write it in his book' is יִזְכֹּר אֶת־שְׁמִי וְכָתַב אֹתוֹ בְּסִפְרוֹ. Note that וְכָתַב is translated as future.

In this textbook we will refer to this form simply as the *və-qatal* (pronounced *və-qatál*) form. It is usually called the "converted perfect" or the "consecutive perfect" or the "perfect with *vav* consecutive." Unlike the history of the consecutive preterite, outlined in lesson 15, the history of the וְקָטַל form is not clear. It probably arose either as an imitation of the consecutive preterite (that is, if *vav* + prefix conjugation = past tense, then *vav* + suffix conjugation = future tense) or as a generalization of some specific use of וְקָטַל as future. (We will see such a use in conditional clauses, to be taken up at the very end of this book.) Whatever the reason, it is important to remember that throughout most of the Hebrew Bible וְקָטַל is to be translated with all the possible meanings of the prefix conjugation: future; ongoing or habitual action in any tense.

16.9. PRONOMINAL SUFFIXES ON THE SUFFIX CONJUGATION

In lesson 14 we learned the pronminal object suffixes on most prefix conjugation verbs. There is a set of suffixes for suffix conjugation verbs as well. The verb שָׁמַר will be used to provide some simple examples.

---

11. So called because the root קטל to 'kill' is one of the roots that grammarians have used over the centuries (in the 3ms form) to describe generic verbs. So the prefix conjugation might be referred to as יִקְטֹל, and the consecutive preterite would be וַיִּקְטֹל, and so on. וְקָטַל, then, is simply a way of saying "any suffix conjugation verb, with וְ at the beginning."

THE PRONOMINAL SUFFIXES FOR THE SUFFIX CONJUGATION

me	-נִי / -ַנִי [12]	שְׁמָרַנִי	he observed *me*
		שְׁמַרְתַּנִי	you (ms) observed *me*
you ms	-ָ֫ךְ / -ְךָ	שְׁמָרְךָ	he observed *you* (ms)
		שְׁמַרְתִּיךָ	I observed *you* (ms)
you fs	-ֵךְ	שְׁמָרֵךְ	he observed *you* (fs)
him	-וֹ / -ֹו / -ֵ֫הוּ / הוּ- [13]	שְׁמָרוֹ and שְׁמָרָהוּ	he observed *him* [14]
		שְׁמַרְתִּיו and שְׁמַרְתִּ֫יהוּ	I observed him
her	-ָהּ / -ֶ֫הָ [15]	שְׁמָרָהּ	he observed *her*
		שְׁמַרְתִּ֫יהָ	I observed *her*
us	-נוּ(ֵ)	שְׁמָרָ֫נוּ	he observed *us*
		שְׁמַרְתָּ֫נוּ	you (ms) observed *us*
them m	-ָם / -ֶם / ם-	שְׁמָרָם	he observed *them* (m or mixed)
		שְׁמַרְתָּם	you (ms) observed *them*
them f	-ָן / -ֶן / ן-	שְׁמָרָן	he observed *them* (fp)
		שְׁמַרְתָּן	you (ms) observed *them*

Note that the vowels of the base verb change slightly when these suffixes are added, but the verb is still identifiable. Second-person plural suffixes on verbs occur only rarely.

16.10. VOCABULARY FOR LESSON 16

verbs (the pref. conj. of these verbs will be learned later)

הָלַךְ 'to go, walk'

יָדַע 'to know'

---

12. Cf. the indep. pronoun אֲנִי.
13. הוּ- and הֵ֫הוּ- should look familiar (cf. the independent pronoun הוּא); also וֹ- (cf. סוּסוֹ).
14. There are other possibilities, much less common. We will note these when they arise.
15. הָ- should look familiar (cf. סוּסָהּ). הֶ- should look familiar (cf. סוּסֶ֫יהָ).

יָרַד   'to go down, descend'

יָשַׁב   'to sit; dwell; live in; inhabit'

נָפַל   'to fall'

noun

יָם   'sea'; cs. יַם; pl. יַמִּים (note the difference between this word and 'days' יָמִים); cs. pl. יַמֵּי (again, note the difference between this word and 'days of' יְמֵי)

proper nouns

מִצְרַיִם   'Egypt'

שְׁמוּאֵל   'Samuel'

adjective

רַב   'much; many'; fs. רַבָּה; mp. רַבִּים; fp. רַבּוֹת (note the doubled ב in every form except the ms)

adverbs

גַּם־/גַּם   'also'; when used more than once, can mean 'both … and'

עַתָּה   'now'

prepositions

בֵּין   'between'; generally used twice in a prepositional phrase, 'between the king and the queen' בֵּין הַמֶּלֶךְ וּבֵין הַמַּלְכָּה; sometimes paired with ל: בֵּין הַמֶּלֶךְ לַמַּלְכָּה

בְּתוֹךְ   'in the middle of, midst of'

16.11. EXERCISES FOR LESSON 16

A. Translate from Hebrew to English:

1. זֶה הָאִישׁ אֲשֶׁר הָלַךְ אֶל־הַשָּׂדֶה אֲשֶׁר בֵּין הַנָּהָר וּבֵין הָהָר

2. יִזְכֹּר אֶת־אָבִי וְיָשַׁב עִם־אֵשֶׁת אָבִי בְּתוֹךְ מִדְבַּר יְהוּדָה יָמִים רַבִּים

3. וַיַּעַבְרוּ מֹשֶׁה וְהָעָם אֶת־יַם סוּף[16] כִּי לֹא יָרַד פַּרְעֹה אֶל־דֶּרֶךְ הַיָּם

4. אֶכְרֹת בְּרִית עִמְּךָ וְגַם עִם־אָחִיךָ כִּי יָדַעְתִּי כִּי שָׁמַעְתָּ לְקוֹלִי

5. יִקְבְּרוּ אֶת־אֵם שְׁמוּאֵל בְּקֶבֶר אֲבוֹתֶיהָ וְלֹא יַעַזְבוּהָ עַד־עוֹלָם

---

16. 'Reed'; the entire phrase is generally translated 'Sea of Reeds'.

6. לֹא שָׁלַח הַכֹּהֵן אֶת־מַלְאָכָיו אֶל־מִצְרַיִם כִּי נָפְלוּ בְּתוֹךְ הַמִּלְחָמָה

7. יַעֲמֹד אַבְרָהָם תַּחַת הָעֵץ אֲשֶׁר בְּתוֹךְ שְׂדֵה הַהֵיכָל

8. וַיֹּאמֶר הַמֶּלֶךְ הֲיַד יוֹאָב[17] אִתָּךְ בְּכָל־זֹאת (from 2 Sam 14:19)

9. אֵלֶּה בְנֵי יִשְׂרָאֵל אֲשֶׁר יִמְלְכוּ עַל־הַמָּקוֹם הַזֶּה

10. לֹא מְצָאתֶם אֶת נַעַר הַגִּבּוֹר בַּשָּׁנָה הַהִיא

11. לֹא תִמְלֹךְ עָלֵינוּ דָוִד[18] כִּי לֹא תִשְׁפֹּט בְּחָכְמָה

12. וַיֹּאמֶר דָוִד אֶל־אַבְנֵר[19] הֲלֹא אִישׁ אַתָּה וּמִי[20] כָמוֹךָ בְּיִשְׂרָאֵל

(from 1 Sam 26:15)

B. Translate from English to Hebrew:

1. The king wrote the book.

2. And the king wrote the book.

3. And the king will write the book.

C. Practice reading Gen 22:1–3.

---

17. A personal name, Joab.

18. There is rarely any indication of the vocative in BH, so a noun or name that seems to stand alone, with no syntactic connection to what is around it, is often to be translated 'O…'; here translate '(O) David,'.

19. A personal name, Abner.

20. ו is often to be translated as something other than simple 'and'. For instance, sometimes it is logical to translate 'but', and sometimes the ו is to be ignored altogether. Here the ו seems simply to tie the two questions together.

17

יז ◄ ► יז

THE QAL INFINITIVE CONSTRUCT
AND THE INFINITIVE ABSOLUTE

17.1. THE USES OF THE INFINITIVE CONSTRUCT

Two verb forms in BH are called "infinitives": the infinitive construct and the infinitive absolute. Only the infinitive construct, however, acts like an English infinitive, and we will take that form up first. The infinitive construct in BH has several uses: (1) It is used like an English infinitive. In the sentence "I like to write," "write" is an infinitive. (2) It is used like an English gerund, the –ing form that is a noun. In the sentence "Writing is my favorite activity," "writing" is a gerund. (3) A very common use of the infinitive construct is as part of a temporal ("when ... then") sentence, in which the infinitive is used with the prepositions בְּ and כְּ.

17.2. THE FORM OF THE INFINITIVE CONSTRUCT

The form of the *qal* infinitive construct is שְׁמֹר. The preposition לְ 'to', 'in order to' is often used with the infinitive construct, so that 'to keep' is לִשְׁמֹר, with *hireq* under the לְ because of the rule of *shwa*. (The pattern for the infinitive construct in I-G verbs is לַעֲמֹד; in I-א verbs, it is לֶאֱכֹל.)

'I sent him to watch the sheep/goats' is וָאֶשְׁלָחֵהוּ לִשְׁמֹר אֶת־הַצֹּאן.

'I sent him to write the book' is וָאֶשְׁלָחֵהוּ לִכְתֹּב אֶת־הַסֵּפֶר.

'I will remember the writing of the book' is אֶזְכֹּר אֶת־כְּתֹב הַסֵּפֶר.

17.3. THE AMBIGUITY OF THE INFINITIVE CONSTRUCT

Infinitives are often somewhat ambiguous. A common illustration of this ambiguity is the phrase "the love of God." When we use that phrase, are we talking about our love for God or God's love for us? (In the former case, God would be called the infinitive's object, and in the latter God is the infinitive's subject.) Such cases are rare in BH and must be decided by context.

17.4. THE INFINITIVE CONSTRUCT WITH PRONOMINAL SUFFIXES

When the subject or object of an infinitive construct is a pronoun, the form of the infinitive changes with the addition of pronominal suffixes:

THE INFINITIVE CONSTRUCT WITH PRONOMINAL SUFFIX

our guarding	שָׁמְרֵנוּ	שָׁמְרִי	my guarding
your (mp) guarding	שָׁמְרְכֶם	שָׁמְרְךָ	your (ms) guarding
your (fp) guarding	שָׁמְרְכֶן	שָׁמְרֵךְ	your (fs) guarding
their (m) guarding	שָׁמְרָם	שָׁמְרוֹ	his guarding
their (f) guarding	שָׁמְרָן	שָׁמְרָהּ	her guarding

In these forms, the *qamets* under the root consonant (שׁ here) is pronounced as short *o*: 'my guarding' is shom-reé.

17.5. THE NEGATION OF THE INFINITIVE CONSTRUCT

The infinitive construct is negated with לְבִלְתִּי/בִּלְתִּי. 'Not to remember' is לְבִלְתִּי זְכֹר.

17.6. THE INFINITIVE CONSTRUCT IN TEMPORAL SENTENCES

We said above that the infinitive construct with the prepositions בְּ and כְּ is often used in temporal sentences. Consider the following examples:

בְּמָלְכִי עַל־יִשְׂרָאֵל	When I ruled/will rule over Israel…
בִּמְלֹךְ הַמֶּלֶךְ עַל־יִשְׂרָאֵל[1]	When the king ruled over Israel…
כְּשָׁמְעִי אֶת־דְּבָרָיו	When I heard/will hear his words…

---

1. In this case, the infinitive מְלֹךְ really is " in construct with" the noun הַמֶּלֶךְ. It is this usage that gives the infinitive construct its name.

כְּשְׁמֹעַ² הָאִשָּׁה אֶת־דְּבָרָיו   When the woman heard/will hear his words…

The four phrases read literally: 'In my ruling over Israel'; 'In the king's ruling over Israel'; 'As (of) my hearing his words'; 'As (of) the woman's hearing his words'. This type of phrase, however, is simply one of the normal ways of beginning a "when… then" sentence in BH, so they should be translated idiomatically, as they are above.

17.7. THE INFINITIVE CONSTRUCT IN CONJUNCTION WITH OTHER TEMPORAL VERBS

The phrases in 17.6 are ambiguous as to tense, because infinitives do not have tense, person, gender, or number (hence the "infinity" or unboundedness of the form). They take their tense from the context in which they are used. The tense context is often provided by the use of וַיְהִי or וְהָיָה at the beginning of the phrase, to indicate past tense and future tense, respectively.

וַיְהִי בְמָלְכִי עַל־יִשְׂרָאֵל   When I ruled over Israel…

וְהָיָה בִמְלֹךְ הַמֶּלֶךְ עַל־יִשְׂרָאֵל   When the king will rule over Israel…

or, more colloquially in English, 'When the king rules over Israel…', which is common English usage for future temporal sentences, for example, "When the king rules over Israel, he will rule in God's name." The meaning is future tense throughout.

וַיְהִי כְּשָׁמְעִי אֶת־דְּבָרָיו   When I heard his words…

וְהָיָה כְּשְׁמֹעַ הָאִשָּׁה אֶת־דְּבָרָיו   When the woman hears his words…

Although וַיְהִי and וְהָיָה literally mean 'and it was' and 'and it will be', respectively, it is best in this context to leave them untranslated and let them serve simply as tense markers in the temporal sentence.

17.8. THE "WHEN" CLAUSE OF A REGULAR TEMPORAL SENTENCE
When the "when" clause of a temporal sentence begins with וַיְהִי, a consecutive preterite form, the "then" clause usually also begins with a consecutive preterite form verb.

וַיְהִי כְּשָׁמְעִי אֶת־דְּבָרָיו וָאֶכְתֹּב אֹתָם בַּסֵּפֶר

When I heard his words, I wrote them in the book.

---

2. Note the furtive *patakh*, which appears because of the long *o*-vowel before the guttural ע.

Similarly, a temporal sentence with וְהָיָה at the beginning of the "when" clause will usually have a וְקָטַל form at the beginning of the "then" clause.

וְהָיָה כְּשָׁמְעִי אֶת־דְּבָרָיו וְכָתַבְתִּי אֹתָם בַּסֵּפֶר

When I hear his words, I will write them in the book.

Note that in English we do not translate the וַיְהִי or וְהָיָה, and we do not translate the *vav* at the beginning of the "then" clause in either case. In Hebrew, this *vav* is connecting the two clauses, but in English translation it is at most the "then" of the "then" clause and can even be thought of simply as the comma between the two clauses.

17.9. THE "WHEN" CLAUSE OF A TEMPORAL SENTENCE WITHOUT AN INFINITIVE CONSTRUCT

There is another type of temporal sentence in BH that is closer to the English word order. Instead of an infinitive construct, the sentence uses a conjunction like כַּאֲשֶׁר 'when, as' or כִּי 'when', plus a prefix conjugation or suffix conjugation verb. For instance,

| וַיְהִי כַּאֲשֶׁר מָלַכְתִּי עַל־יִשְׂרָאֵל | When I ruled over Israel… |
| וְהָיָה כִּי יִמְלֹךְ הַמֶּלֶךְ עַל־יִשְׂרָאֵל | When the king rules/will rule over Israel… |

17.10. THE INFINITIVE ABSOLUTE AS MORE FREQUENTLY USED

The second infinitive in BH, the infinitive absolute, does not really behave in the same way as the English infinitive at all but rather is usually used as an adverb, to add emphasis to a verb from the same root. The form of the *qal* infinitive absolute is שָׁמוֹר (the *vav mater* is usually written). Other than the possible alternation between *holem* and *holem-vav*, the form is unchangeable.

The infinitive absolute used for emphasis usually comes before the finite verb (prefix conjugation or suffix conjugation) that it is giving emphasis to.

| שָׁמוֹר יִשְׁמֹר אֶת־הַצֹּאן | He will certainly/of course watch the sheep/goats. |
| עָבוֹד עָבַד בַּהֵיכָל | He served diligently in the temple/palace. |

Note that there is a certain amount of flexibility in translation. "Indeed" or "surely" will suffice, but they are not elegant translations.

17.11. THE INFINITIVE ABSOLUTE AS A SUBSTITUTE FOR ANY OTHER VERBAL FORM

The infinitive absolute has another usage that we will discuss here: it can be used to substitute for any other form of a verb, as long as the context is clear. It is a sort of empty vessel with only a verbal meaning; the rest of the contents (gender, number, verb form, etc.) are added as needed. The most common examples of this usage are of the infinitive absolute substituting for an imperative. For example, Exod 20:8 reads זָכוֹר אֶת־יוֹם הַשַּׁבָּת לְקַדְּשׁוֹ 'Remember the day of the Sabbath, to keep it holy'. Although two of the words of this verse are new, the basic idea that the infinitive absolute can substitute for an imperative is clear.

17.12. VOCABULARY FOR LESSON 17

verbs

אָסַר	'to bind, tie up'; pref. conj. irregular but usually יַאְסֹר, יֶאֱסֹר
וְהָיָה	*və-qatal* (3ms) form of the verb 'to be', usually used simply to indicate that what comes after it is future, habitual, or ongoing
וַיְהִי	cons. pret. (3ms) form of the verb 'to be', usually used simply to indicate that what comes after it is past tense
לָכַד	'to capture'; pref. conj. יִלְכֹּד
לָקַח	'to take; receive'; pref. conj. will be learned later
רָדַף	'to pursue, chase; follow'; pref. conj. יִרְדֹּף; dir. obj. usually expressed with אַחֲרֵי: וַיִּרְדֹּף אַחֲרַי '(And) he pursued me'
שָׁפַךְ	'to pour out; to shed (blood)'; pref. conj. יִשְׁפֹּךְ

nouns

אָדָם	'humankind; a male human being; Adam'
אֲדָמָה	'ground, land, soil'; cs. אַדְמַת; pl. very rare
אֱמֶת	'truth' (fem.); with sf. אֲמִתִּי; no pl.; note the *hateph-seghol* in the first syllable: this word is not a segholate.
דָּם	'blood'; cs. דַּם; with sf. דָּמִי; pl. דָּמִים is often used of blood shed in violence; cs. pl. דְּמֵי
חַיִּים	'life(time)'; always pl., although translated into English as sg.; cs. חַיֵּי
שֹׁפֵט	'judge' (usually judicial, but also used in the book of Judges to mean nondynastic charismatic leader); pl. שֹׁפְטִים

pronoun

מָה   'what; what?' (can be used at beginning of a clause as an interroga-
            tive); also written מַה plus doubling of the next consonant and some-
            times מֶה

adverbs

בִּלְתִּי   negative used with inf. cs.; usually seen with preposition לְ: לְבִלְתִּי

כֵּן   'thus, so' (usually refers to something that has already been mentioned)

רַק   'only'

conjunction

כַּאֲשֶׁר   'as; when; since, because'

17.13. EXERCISES FOR LESSON 17

A. Translate from Hebrew to English:

1. יִקְרְאוּ לוֹ הָאָדָם כִּי מֵהָאֲדָמָה הוּא

2. וְהָיָה כְלָכְדָם אֶת־עָרֵיכֶם וְלָקְחוּ אֶת־בָּתֵּיכֶם וְאָסוֹר יַאַסְרוּ אֶת־בְּנֵיכֶם וְאֶת־בְּנוֹתֵיכֶם

3. הֲיִמְלֹךְ עָלֵינוּ הַשֹּׁפֵט בְּחָכְמָה וּבֶאֱמֶת

4. וְהָיָה כַּאֲשֶׁר יִמְצָא אֶת־מַחֲנֵה הַצָּבָא וְנָפַל בְּרַגְלֵי הַגִּבּוֹרִים אֲשֶׁר שָׁם

5. אַל־תִּשְׁפֹּךְ אֶת־דַּם הַצַּדִּיקָה הַזֹּאת כִּי יָדַע יְהוָה אֶת־כָּל־דְּרָכֶיךָ

6. וַיִּרְדְּפוּ הָאֲנָשִׁים אַחֲרֵי הַכֹּהֲנִים הָרְשָׁעִים עַד־רֹאשׁ הָהָר כִּי לָקְחוּ אֶת־תּוֹרַת יְהוָה
   אֶל־הַמָּקוֹם הַהוּא

7. וַיִּקְרָא שָׁאוּל אֶל־בְּנוֹ לְבִלְתִּי עֲזֹב אֶת־חַרְבּוֹ

8. מִי כָמוֹךָ אֱלֹהִים בַּשָּׁמַיִם וּבָאָרֶץ

9. וַיֹּאמֶר יְהוָה אֶל־שָׂרָה לֵאמֹר עַתָּה אִמְרִי־נָא אֶל־הַנָּשִׁים אֲשֶׁר בָּעִיר הַזֹּאת כִּי
   שָׁמַעַתְּ אֶת־קוֹל יְהוָה וְכֵן אָמְרָה

10. וַיְהִי בְּקָבְרוֹ אֶת־אִמּוֹ תַּחַת הָעֵץ אֲשֶׁר אֵצֶל הַנָּהָר הַגָּדוֹל וַיֹּאמֶר אֶל־אֶחָיו לֵאמֹר
    הַיּוֹם שָׁכְבָה אִמֵּנוּ עִם־אֲבוֹתֶיהָ

11. שָׁנָה אַחַת מָלַךְ הַמֶּלֶךְ בִּירוּשָׁלַ͏ִם רַק לֹא שָׁמַע בְּקוֹל יְהוָה אֱלֹהָיו לִשְׁמֹר[3] אֶת מִצְוֺתָיו

12. אַתְּ מַלְכַּת עַמֵּי הַיָּם וְיָשַׁבְתְּ בָּאָרֶץ הַגְּדוֹלָה הַזֹּאת אֲשֶׁר בָּהּ בָּקָר וְצֹאן רַב מְאֹד וְגַם יִזְכֹּר אֹתָךְ אֱלֹהַיִךְ כָּל־יְמֵי חַיַּיִךְ

13. מַה יָּדַעְתָּ אֲשֶׁר לֹא יָדַעְתִּי

B. Translate from English to Hebrew:

　1. Capture Jerusalem! (said to a mixed group)

　2. He came down from the mountain to watch the cattle.

　3. He will surely judge us.

C. Practice reading Gen 22:1–4.

---

3. Translate 'by observing'. Explaining how something is done is another use of the infinitive construct.

יח ◄ **18** ► יח

THE *QAL* PARTICIPLES, THE WORDS יֵשׁ AND אַיִן, AND THE ACCENTS *SOPH PASUQ* AND *ATNAKH*

18.1. THE ACTIVE AND PASSIVE PARTICIPLES GENERALLY

BH has both an active and a passive participle. The active participle (ptcp.) is by far the more common. They are both verbal adjectives, which, like all adjectives, can be "substantivized" and used as a noun. The participle is not a present-tense verb form in BH, as it is in Modern Hebrew, but rather is really a tenseless verb that takes its tense from context. In a past context, the participle is past tense, but in a future context, the same word will be translated into English as a future.

18.2. THE MEANINGS OF THE ACTIVE PARTICIPLE

The BH participle[1] has two major English translations: (1) as the –ing form of the verb that is used as an adjective (which is also called a participle in English): a walk*ing* man, a rul*ing* queen; or (2) as an agent noun, one who does the action of the verb: a walking person = a walker; a ruling person = a ruler.

18.3. THE FORMS OF THE ACTIVE PARTICIPLE

The participle in BH has gender and number but not person.[2] Like all nouns and adjectives, it appears as ms, fs, mp, or fp, and with the same endings that we have

---

1. Since the passive participle is relatively rare, we use the word *participle* (and abbreviation ptcp.) to refer to the active participle. When the passive participle is meant, the word "passive" will always be included.

2. For that reason, the participle in BH is not a "finite" verb.

already learned, with the exception of the most common form of the feminine singular. The paradigm for the *qal* active participle (using the root שׁמר in its meaning 'to guard') is:

THE *QAL* ACTIVE PARTICIPLE

guarding (mp) or	שֹׁמְרִים	[3]שֹׁמֵר	guarding (ms) or
guards (mp)			guard (ms)
guarding (fp) or	שֹׁמְרוֹת	[4]שֹׁמֶרֶת	guarding (fs) or
guards (fp)			guards (fs)

18.4. WORD ORDER WITH THE ACTIVE PARTICIPLE

The subject tends to come before a participle, the opposite word order from the typical verbal sentence (one that begins with a *finite* verb). As was mentioned above, a participle is a verbal adjective or verbal noun. Compare the following:

אִישׁ טוֹב	a good man		אִישׁ הֹלֵךְ	a walking man
הָאִישׁ הַטּוֹב	the good man		הָאִישׁ הַהֹלֵךְ	the walking man
טוֹב הָאִישׁ	The man is good.		הָאִישׁ הֹלֵךְ	The man is walking.

Except for the word order, the final set of two are identical in use.

The following sentences illustrate the determination of tense from context:

וַיֹּאמֶר הַמַּלְאָךְ כִּי הָאִישׁ כֹּתֵב סֵפֶר	The messenger said that the man was writing a book.
נֹאמַר כִּי הָאִשָּׁה כֹּתֶבֶת סֵפֶר	We will say that the woman is writing/will be writing a book.

18.5. THE PARTICIPLE DOES NOT USE THE RELATIVE PRONOUN

In BH, הָאִישׁ הַהֹלֵךְ is both 'the walking man' and 'the man *who is* walking'. אֲשֶׁר is ordinarily *not* used with the participle in BH[5]; what the student should learn for 'the man who is walking' is הָאִישׁ הַהֹלֵךְ, as above, *not* הָאִישׁ אֲשֶׁר הֹלֵךְ.

---

3. In the stative verb, the verbal adjective כָּבֵד functions like a participle.
4. Occasionally, the form is שֹׁמְרָה.
5. There are rare exceptions.

18.6. THE MEANING AND FORMS OF THE PASSIVE PARTICIPLE

There is also a passive participle in BH; unlike the active participle, which is often used as a noun, the passive participle is almost always used as an adjective. Its forms are:

THE *QAL* PASSIVE PARTICIPLE

guarded (mp) or	שְׁמוּרִים	שָׁמוּר	guarded (ms) or
guarded (fp)	שְׁמוּרוֹת	שְׁמוּרָה	guarded (fs)

'The written word' is הַדָּבָר הַכָּתוּב

'The word was/is/will be written' is הַדָּבָר כָּתוּב

'The captured cities' is הֶעָרִים הַלְּכוּדוֹת

'The cities were/are/will be captured' is הֶעָרִים לְכוּדוֹת

The forms of the participle now given, the entire paradigm of the Hebrew word שָׁמַר has been provided. The full paradigm may be found at the very beginning of appendix H as a model for the paradigms of the yet-to-be-given weak verbs.

18.7. FORMS OF POSSESSION USING לְ, יֵשׁ, AND אֵין

BH has no verb 'to have' in the sense of possession. Instead, the preposition לְ can serve to mark possession ('belonging to'). The word לְמֹשֶׁה on the rim of a pot, for instance, would indicate that the pot was owned by someone named Moses.

If tense is not indicated, לְ can be used in combination with יֵשׁ ('there is') or אֵין ('there is not'), to mean 'to have' or 'not to have'. Thus, 'The woman has a horse' is יֵשׁ לָאִשָּׁה סוּס (which can also mean 'had' or 'will have'). 'I do not have a house' is אֵין לִי בַּיִת. These two sentences are *not* to be translated 'There is to the woman a horse' or 'There is not to me a house'. That is the literal, word-for-word Hebrew, but it is awkward English, and these phrases are perfectly normal in Hebrew. Consequently, they should be translated as above: 'The woman has a horse'; 'I do not have a house'.

If tense is indicated in such a sentence, it can be denoted by some form of the verb 'to be'; for instance:

וַיְהִי לְאִשָּׁה סוּס   The woman had a horse.

לֹא הָיָה[6] לִי בַּיִת   I did not have a house.

18.8. THE USE OF אַיִן WITH PRONOMINAL SUFFIXES

The word אַיִן can be used with pronominal suffixes to mean 'I am not' (or 'was not' or 'will not be'), 'he is not', and so on.[7] The paradigm for אַיִן is:

The Word אַיִן with Pronominal Suffixes

אֵינֶנּוּ	אֵינֶנִּי
אֵינְכֶם	אֵינְךָ
—	אֵינֵךְ
אֵינָם	אֵינֶנּוּ
—	אֵינֶנָּה

18.9. ACCENTS: THE *SOPH PASUQ* AND THE *ATNAKH*

Every verse in the Hebrew Bible ends with a mark called סוֹף פָּסוּק 'end of the verse', which looks like this: ׃ . The most important pause within a verse is marked by the accent mark called אַתְנַח, which is printed under the accented syllable of the last word in the first part of the verse: ̭ . In other words, the pause comes *after* the word that has the *atnakh*. From now on, the sentences in the exercises will ordinarily use both these marks.

18.10. VOCABULARY FOR LESSON 18

verbs

נָשָׂא   'to lift, carry, bear'; pref. conj. will be learned later

שָׂרַף   'to burn' (transitive); pref. conj. יִשְׂרֹף (often used along with בָּאֵשׁ 'with fire'; see noun list below)

---

6. הָיָה is the suffix conjugation 3ms of the verb 'to be'.
7. יֵשׁ is also used with suffixes, but much less commonly.

nouns

אֵשׁ   'fire' (fem.); with sf. אִשִׁי

זָהָב   'gold'; cs. זְהַב ; with sf. זְהָבִי

כֶּסֶף   'silver, money'; with sf. כַּסְפִּי

מִזְבֵּחַ   'altar'; cs. מִזְבַּח; with sf. מִזְבְּחִי; pl. מִזְבְּחוֹת

עֹלָה   'whole burnt offering, holocaust'

רוּחַ   'breath, spirit, wind' (fem.); pl. רוּחוֹת

שַׂר   'captain, chief, prince'; pl. שָׂרִים; cs. pl. irreg. שָׂרֵי

adverb

כֹּה   'thus' (usually referring to what follows)

particles

אֵין   'there is not'

יֵשׁ   'there is'

18.11. EXERCISES FOR LESSON 18

A. Translate from Hebrew to English:

1. כֹּה אָמַר[8] יְהוָה תַּעַבְרוּ אֶת־הַנָּהָר לִשְׂרֹף אֶת־הָעִיר הָרְשָׁעָה בָּאֵשׁ:

2. וַיְהִי כְּשָׁמְעֵנוּ אֶת־דִּבְרֵי שַׂר הַצָּבָא וַנִּרְדֹּף אַחֲרֵי שֹׁפְטֵנוּ הַהֹלֵךְ לְפָנֵינוּ:

3. יֵשׁ לִי כֶּסֶף וְאֵין לִי זָהָב:

4. וַיֶּאְסֹר הַכֹּהֵן אֶת־הָאִשָּׁה כִּי לֹא נָשְׂאָה אֶת־בְּנָהּ אֶל־רֹאשׁ הָהָר:

5. זְכוֹר תִּזְכְּרוּ אֶת־אֲבוֹתֵיכֶם:

6. וַיְהִי כַּאֲשֶׁר לָקְחוּ הָאֲנָשִׁים אֶת־עֹלָתָם אֶל־הַמִּזְבֵּחַ וַיִּמְצָאֵם מַלְאַךְ יְהוָה:

7. וַתֶּחֱזַק עָלֵינוּ יַד פַּרְעֹה וְגַם יָדַעְנוּ כִּי נָפְלוּ גִבּוֹרֵינוּ בַּמִּלְחָמָה:

8. וַיִּקְרְאוּ בְּנֵי יִשְׂרָאֵל לֵאלֹהֵיהֶם פְּעָמַיִם לִבְחֹר לָהֶם בְּמַלְכָּה אֲשֶׁר תִּמְלֹךְ עֲלֵיהֶם:

9. לֹא יֵשְׁבוּ עוֹד הַנָּשִׁים הַטּוֹבוֹת בֶּעָרִים הַלְּכֻדוֹת אֲשֶׁר בֵּין יְרוּשָׁלַםִ וּבֵין הַיָּם:

10. עֲמֹד לְפָנַי וַעֲבֹד אֹתִי עַד־הַבֹּקֶר:

---

8. Suffix conjugation אָמַר can be present tense in the context of a messenger delivering a message.

11. לֹא אָכַל שָׁאוּל לֶחֶם עִם צְבָאוֹ כִּי הָיְתָה[9] עָלָיו רוּחַ רָעָה מֵיהֹוָה:

12. אֵלֶּה הַנְּעָרִים הַיֹּרְדִים מִן־הָהָר כִּי עֲזָבוּם שֹׁמְרֵיהֶם:

B. Translate from English to Hebrew:

    1. The woman has a husband (אִישׁ).

    2. The woman doesn't have a husband.

C. Practice reading Gen 22:1–5.

---

9. 'She was'.

19 ◄ יט ► יט

THE DERIVED STEM *NIPHAL* (PART 1) AND THE ACCENT *SILLUQ*

19.1. THE DERIVED STEMS GENERALLY

Until this point, we have consistently referred to verbs as *qal* verbs, the 'simple' stem. Now we will turn to four additional important stems, called "derived" stems because they can often be traced back to the *qal*.[1] For instance, if the *qal* verb means 'to rule', like מָלַךְ, the same root in the passive stem would mean 'to be ruled'; in the causative, 'to make someone rule' (that is, to put someone on the throne); and in the reflexive, 'to rule over oneself' (e.g., one's emotions). This system of understanding the relationships among the various stems is not foolproof, but it is a good shorthand for beginning students.

19.2. THE NAMING OF THE DERIVED STEMS

The derived stems are traditionally named by the 3ms suffix conjugation of the verb פעל 'to do, make', as it would appear in the stem in question. The *qal* is sometimes called the *pa'al* (from פָּעַל, the 3ms suff. conj. of פעל in that stem). The subject of this lesson, the *niphal*, is so called because the 3ms suffix conjugation of פעל in that stem would be נִפְעַל. (In the romanization of the name of the stem, the ע is often ignored.) After the *niphal*, we will learn the *hiphil* (הִפְעִיל), the *piel* (פִּעֵל), and the *hitpael* (הִתְפַּעֵל).

19.3. THE MEANING AND FORMS OF THE *NIPHAL* STEM

The first derived stem we will take up is the *niphal*. The *niphal* has several functions in BH, but the most common is to form passive verbs for the *qal* stem (and

---

1. "Stems" are also frequently referred to by the Hebrew term *binyanim* (בִּנְיָנִים).

for the *hiphil* stem, to be taken up in the lesson 21). The forms of the *niphal* are as follows (using the root שמר again, which in the *niphal* means 'to be guarded, kept; to be careful, to watch out').[2]

THE FORMS OF THE *NIPHAL* STEM

inf. cs.	suff. conj.	cons. pret.	volitives		pref. conj.
הִשָּׁמֵר	נִשְׁמַׂרְתִּי	וָאֶשָּׁמֵר	אֶשָּׁמְרָה	cohort.	אֶשָּׁמֵר
	נִשְׁמַׂרְתָּ	וַתִּשָּׁמֵר	הִשָּׁמֵר	impv.	תִּשָּׁמֵר
inf. abs.	נִשְׁמַרְתְּ	וַתִּשָּׁמְרִי	הִשָּׁמְרִי	impv.	תִּשָּׁמְרִי
נִשְׁמוֹר	נִשְׁמַר	וַיִּשָּׁמֵר/וַיִּשָּׁמֶר	יִשָּׁמֵר	juss.	יִשָּׁמֵר
הִשָּׁמֵר	נִשְׁמְרָה	...	תִּשָּׁמֵר	juss.	תִּשָּׁמֵר
	נִשְׁמַׂרְנוּ		נִשָּׁמְרָה	cohort.	נִשָּׁמֵר
ptcp.	נִשְׁמַרְתֶּם		הִשָּׁמְרוּ	impv.	תִּשָּׁמְרוּ
נִשְׁמָר	נִשְׁמַרְתֶּן		הִשָּׁמַׂרְנָה	impv.	תִּשָּׁמַׂרְנָה
נִשְׁמֶׂרֶת/נִשְׁמָרָה	נִשְׁמְרוּ		יִשָּׁמְרוּ	juss.	יִשָּׁמְרוּ
נִשְׁמָרִים			תִּשָּׁמַׂרְנָה	juss.	תִּשָּׁמַׂרְנָה
נִשְׁמָרוֹת					

Notes to the paradigm (moving from right to left):

19.3.1. Glosses for the *niphal* verbal forms are: pref. conj. = 'I/he/etc. will be guarded'; cohort. = 'may I/we be guarded'; impv. = 'be guarded!'; juss. = 'may he/she be guarded'; cons. pret. = 'and he, etc., was guarded'; suff. conj. = 'I/he/etc. was guarded'; inf. cs. = 'to be guarded'; and ptcp. = 'one who is/was guarded'.

19.3.2. The *niphal*, as its name suggests, includes an *n*-sound in all its forms. In the prefix conjugation, the נ of the *niphal* assimilates to the first root letter after the preformative, so the doubled שׁ in the prefix conjugation is the result of the assimi-

---

2. Most of the sections of the *niphal*, *hiphil*, *piel*, and *hitpael* strong-verb paradigms in the next few lessons will be glossed, as an aid to understanding. There is no simple and short way to gloss the infinitive absolute, however, since it serves with finite verbs for emphasis or substitutes for other verbs, as we have seen. Consequently, no gloss will be provided for the infinitive absolute in any of the paradigms for these verbs.

lation of the נ of the *niphal*. That is, אֶשָּׁמֵר would have earlier been אֶנְשָׁמֵר, but the נ plus silent *shwa* meant that the נ would have been pronounced immediately before the שׁ. In BH, such a situation results in the assimilation of the נ to the next letter. This assimilation can be seen throughout the paradigm, in the imperative, cohortative, consecutive preterite, and infinitive construct.

19.3.3. The prefix conjugation of the *niphal* can be identified both by the doubling of the first root letter and by the vowel pattern *hireq-qamets-tsere* ("i-ah-ay"). In the Bible, we find both אֶ and אָ for the 1cs preformative.

19.3.4. The *metheg*s scattered throughout the paradigm indicate that the *qamets* plus *shwa* combinations in this paradigm are to be pronounced *ah* plus vocal *shwa*.

19.3.5. Note that in the prefix conjugation the 2fp and 3fp have *patakh* instead of *tsere*.

19.3.6. The ה at the beginning of the imperative is unexpected; it must simply be learned.

19.3.7. In the strong verb, the jussive form is the same as the prefix conjugation.

19.3.8. Some consecutive preterites have the accent moved toward the beginning of the word. The two forms mean exactly the same thing.

19.3.9. In the suffix conjugation, the נ of the *niphal* is clear. Once the basic pattern *nish + mar* is absorbed, the suffix conjugation paradigm is easily learned.

19.3.10. The *niphal* infinitive construct looks exactly the same as the ms imperative. It is possible to have the *niphal* infinitive construct with pronominal suffixes, just as it is with the *qal* infinitive construct, and the suffixes are the same (basically, the בִּי ,בְ, בְּךָ endings) and are easily recognized.

19.3.11. Note that the infinitive construct is patterned after the prefix conjugation, while the infinitive absolute is patterned after the suffix conjugation, although we also find the infinitive construct form acting as an infinitive absolute (before a finite verb, to provide emphasis, for example).

19.3.12. The masculine singular *niphal* participle looks almost exactly the same as the 3ms suffix conjugation form, except that the participle has *qamets* where the 3ms suff. conj. has *patakh*, and the *qamets* remains throughout the forms of the participle.[3]

19.4. PASSIVES IN BIBLICAL HEBREW DO NOT EXPRESS AGENT

Passives in BH almost never express the "agent" of the action. For example, in the sentence וַיִּכְתֹּב הַכֹּהֵן אֶת־דִּבְרֵי יְהוָה 'The priest wrote the words of Yahweh', הַכֹּהֵן is

---

3. Where a *niphal* participle and *qal* passive participle both exist for a given root, they will have the same meaning.

the subject of the sentence and the "agent" of the action, the actor. Its passive form in BH would be וַיִּכָּתְבוּ דִּבְרֵי יְהוָה 'The words of Yahweh were written'. The agent is no longer expressed; the phrase 'by the priest' would not be part of the sentence. The words were simply written, without any clue as to who wrote them.

19.5. STRONG VERBS LEARNED TO THIS POINT WITH *NIPHAL* STEMS

What follows is a list of the *niphal* forms of some of the strong verbs we have learned so far; only four of them occur often enough in the Hebrew Bible for us to include them in the vocabulary list below.[4]

root	*qal* meaning	*niphal* meaning	*niphal* pref. conj.	*niphal* cons. pret.	*niphal* suff. conj.
			he will be…	and he was…	he was…
בחר	to choose	to be chosen, choice			נִבְחַר
זכר	to remember	to be remembered	יִזָּכֵר		נִזְכַּר
כרת	to cut (off)	to be cut (off)	יִכָּרֵת		נִכְרַת
כתב	to write	to be written	יִכָּתֵב	וַיִּכָּתֵב	
לכד	to capture	to be captured	יִלָּכֵד	וַיִּלָּכֵד	נִלְכַּד
קבר	to bury	to be buried	יִקָּבֵר	וַיִּקָּבֵר	
שׂרף	to burn	to be burned	יִשָּׂרֵף	וַיִּשָּׂרֵף	
שמר	to guard, keep	to be careful	יִשָּׁמֵר		נִשְׁמַר
שפט	to judge	to be judged; to plead w/ each other	יִשָּׁפֵט		נִשְׁפַּט

---

4. The blank cells in the table represent forms that do not appear in the Hebrew Bible, that is, the root בחר does not occur at all in the prefix conjugation or consecutive preterite of the *niphal*. On the other hand, the fact that a cell is filled in does not mean that that exact word occurs in the Bible but rather simply that the conjugation appears. The word נִבְחַר may not occur, but the suffix conjugation of בחר does occur in the *niphal* stem.

שׁפך	to pour out	to be poured out	יִשָּׁפֵךְ		נִשְׁפַּךְ

19.6. ACCENT: THE *SILLUQ*

The final word in a verse is followed by סוֹף פָּסוּק (:), as we have seen. The accented syllable in that word will be marked by its own accent mark, called סִלּוּק (*silluq*). *Silluq* looks exactly like a *metheg*, but when the context is the last word in a verse, the accent mark is called *silluq*.

19.7. VOCABULARY FOR LESSON 19

> As with the verbs above, we will identify *niphal* verbs according to the 3ms *niphal* suffix conjugation of the root. Thus, נִכְרַת, for instance, will be listed separately from כָּרַת in the glossary, although *niphal* verbs will also be identified in the vocabulary lists as the *niphal* of a given root. It is most useful for the student to keep together, however, all the vocabulary verbs that come from a given root. A vocabulary card might have the root כרת, for instance, and then have separate entries for כרת *qal* and כרת *niphal*; alternatively, the card might have the root כרת, then list the possibilities as כָּרַת and נִכְרַת. The details are up to the student, but it will be easier to learn the vocabulary and to remember the meanings of the various stems if verbs from the same root occur in the same place for the purposes of vocabulary drill.

verbs

נִכְרַת 'to be cut (off)' (*niphal* of כרת); pref. conj. יִכָּרֵת

נִלְחַם 'to fight, do battle with, wage war against' (*niphal* of לחם); 'with/against' can be בְּ, עִם־, אֶת־, עַל־, אֶל־; pref. conj. יִלָּחֵם; cons. pret. 3ms וַיִּלָּחֶם

נִלְכַּד 'to be captured' (*niphal* of לכד); pref. conj. יִלָּכֵד

נִקְבַּר 'to be buried' (*niphal* of קבר); pref. conj. יִקָּבֵר

נִשְׁאַר 'to remain, to be left, to be left over' (*niphal* of שאר); pref. conj. יִשָּׁאֵר

נִשְׁמַר 'to be careful; be guarded' (*niphal* of שמר); pref. conj. יִשָּׁמֵר

noun

אֹיֵב 'enemy'; pl. אֹיְבִים; cs. pl. אֹיְבֵי

נָבִיא 'prophet'; cs. נְבִיא; pl. נְבִיאִים

conjunction and preposition

לְמַעַן   as conj., 'so that, in order that' (followed by the pref. conj., although it is often to be translated into English as 'in order to' + English infinitive);

as prep., 'on account of, for the sake of, for the purpose of';

prep. + inf. cs. = 'in order to'

19.8. EXERCISES FOR LESSON 19

A. Translate from Hebrew to English:

1. וַיֹּאמֶר יְהוָה אֶל־אַבְרָם הִשָּׁמֵר׃

2. נִכְרַתְנוּ מֵאֶרֶץ הַחַיִּים⁵ וְנִכְרַת שְׁמוֹ מֵעַמּוֹ׃

3. וְהָיָה כַּאֲשֶׁר יִלָּחֵם הַגִּבּוֹר בְּאֹיְבֵי יִשְׂרָאֵל וּרְדָפָם עַד־הַיָּם הַגָּדוֹל׃

4. וְלֹא־קָם⁶ נָבִיא עוֹד בְּיִשְׂרָאֵל כְּמֹשֶׁה אֲשֶׁר יְדָעוֹ יְהוָה פָּנִים אֶל־פָּנִים׃ (Deut 34:10)

5. וַיִּלָּחֲמוּ אַנְשֵׁי יְהוּדָה הַנִּשְׁאָרִים בְּאַנְשֵׁי מִצְרַיִם כָּל־הַבֹּקֶר עַד־הַצָּהֳרָיִם׃

6. כְּתָב־נָא אֶת־מִצְוֺת יְהוָה עַל־לֵב הָעָם וְגַם עַל־מִזְבְּחוֹת בֵּית יְהוָה כִּי מִשְׁפְּטֵי אֱלֹהִים הֵנָּה׃

7. וַיִּשְׁכַּב שְׁלֹמֹה עִם־אֲבוֹתָיו וַיִּקָּבֵר בְּעִיר דָּוִד׃ (from 1 Kgs 11:43)

8. וַיְהִי⁷ בַּשָּׁנָה הַהִיא בַּחֹשֶׁךְ הַלַּיְלָה וַיִּשְׂרְפוּ בָאֵשׁ אֶת־הַבָּתִּים אֲשֶׁר אֵצֶל הַהֵיכָל כִּי רְשָׁעִים בְּעֵינֵי אֱלֹהִים הַשֹּׁפְטִים הַיֹּשְׁבִים בָּם׃

9. וַיִּשָּׂא⁸ שָׁאוּל אֶת־עֵינָיו אֶל־הָעִיר הַנִּלְכָּדָה וַיִּשְׁלַח מַלְאָכִים אֶל־מַלְכָּתָהּ לֵאמֹר כֹּה אָמַר הַמֶּלֶךְ שָׁאוּל עִזְבִי אֶת־עִירֵךְ הַיּוֹם׃

---

5. We have learned that this word means 'life', which it does, but it is also the plural of the adjective חַי 'alive, living'.

6. קָם = 'he arose/has arisen'. For the *maqqeph*, see note 1 in lesson 9.

7. This is the 3ms consecutive preterite of the verb 'to be', often used at the beginning of sentences simply to determine the tense in which the rest of the sentence occurs. It is best not to translate the word in such situations.

8. 'He [Saul] lifted up'.

10. וַיֹּאמֶר יְהוָה אֶל־קַ֫יִן⁹ אֵי¹⁰ הֶ֫בֶל¹¹ אָחִ֑יךָ וַיֹּאמֶר לֹא יָדַ֫עְתִּי הֲשֹׁמֵר אָחִי אָנֹֽכִי¹²:

(Gen 4:9)

11. תַּעֲמֹד בַּת הַשַּׂר בְּתוֹךְ הַדֶּ֫רֶךְ לְמַ֫עַן תִּבְחַר בָּאִישׁ אֲשֶׁר יַעַבְדֶ֫נָּה:

12. גְּדוֹלָה רוּחַ הַנָּבִיא מִמָּֽוֶת:

B. Translate from English to Hebrew:

1. The king's horse will be captured.

2. And the king's horse was captured.

3. And the king's horse will be captured.

C. Practice reading Gen 22:1–6.

---

9. A personal name, Cain.

10. 'Where is'.

11. A personal name, Abel.

12. The accent here is on the נ syllable, instead of the final syllable, as expected, because the word is "in pause," a concept that will be explained in one of the exercises in lesson 23.

THE DERIVED STEM *NIPHAL* (PART 2); THE NUMBERS 1–2, THE PARTITIVE מִן, AND THE ACCENT *ZAQEPH*

20.1. THE *NIPHAL* AS REFLEXIVE OR RECIPROCAL

Besides its passive function, the *niphal* can also be used as a reflexive or reciprocal verb (although these meanings are usually expressed by the *hitpael*, to be learned in a later lesson). For instance, נִשְׁמַר can mean 'to be kept, guarded' but more often means 'to guard oneself' = 'to watch out'; נִשְׁפַּט can be 'to be judged' but more often means 'to enter into litigation/controversy with one another'.

20.2. THE *NIPHAL* WITH ACTIVE MEANING

There are some peculiar uses of the *niphal* that are not predictable and must simply be learned. Some *niphals* have no (or almost no) corresponding *qal* verb that is extant in BH. We have already seen two: נִלְחַם 'to fight' (used a few times in the *qal* with the same meaning); נִשְׁאַר 'to remain, be left behind' (used once in the *qal* with the same meaning).

20.3. VARIATIONS OF THE FORM OF *NIPHAL* VERBS LEARNED TO THIS POINT

What follows is a list of the *niphal* forms of more of the verbs we have learned so far that appear in the *niphal* in the Hebrew Bible; four of them occur often enough to warrant inclusion in the vocabulary list below. Note that there are occasional differences in vowel pointing from the paradigm in lesson 19.

root	*qal* meaning	*niphal* meaning	*niphal* pref. conj.	*niphal* cons. pret.	*niphal* suff. conj.
			he will be …	and he was …	he was …
אכל	to eat	to be eaten	יֵאָכֵל	וַיֵּאָכֵל	נֶאֱכַל
אמר	to say	to be said, told	יֵאָמֵר	וַיֵּאָמַר	נֶאֱמַר
לקח	to take	to be taken	יִלָּקַח	וַיִּלָּקַח	נִלְקַח
מצא	to find	to be found, to be	יִמָּצֵא	וַיִּמָּצֵא	נִמְצָא
עזב	to abandon	to be aban-doned	יֵעָזֵב		נֶעֱזַב
קרא	to call	to be called	יִקָּרֵא	וַיִּקָּרֵא	נִקְרָא
שמע	to hear	to be heard, obeyed	יִשָּׁמַע	וַיִּשָּׁמַע	נִשְׁמַע

Note that, since נ assimilates to and doubles the first consonant after the pre-formative in the prefix conjugation (and consecutive preterite, imperative, jussive, cohortative, and infinitive construct), a problem arises when that consonant cannot be doubled, that is, when it is א, ה, ח, ע, or ר. The resolution is compensatory lengthening, as can be seen above with אכל, אמר, and עזב. In the suffix conjugation (and participle and infinitive absolute), *seghol* plus *hateph-seghol* are substituted for *hireq* and silent *shwa*.

20.4. CLUES FOR RECOGNIZING *NIPHAL* VERBS

20.4.1. The suffix conjugation, participle, and infinitive absolute begin with נ; be careful not to confuse *niphal* forms with 1cp prefix conjugation verbs, the "we" forms, which also begin with נ.

20.4.2. The first consonant after the preformative in the prefix conjugation, imperative, jussive, cohortative, consecutive preterite, and infinitive construct contains a *dagesh* (doubling *dagesh*); when doubling is impossible, compensatory lenghthening takes place.

20.4.3. The imperative and infinitive construct begin with ה; they also contain the doubling noted above.

20.4.4. The vowel "melody" in the prefix conjugation, imperative, jussive, cohortative, and consecutive preterite is "i-ah-ay" (or "ay-ah-ay" in I-G verbs).

20.5. RECOGNIZING NUMBERS GENERALLY

Numbers in BH are difficult to produce but easy to recognize. We will focus on recognizing the numbers in this book, and that entails simply knowing one basic form of the numbers from 1 to 10, plus the forms for 20, 30, and so on, and for 100, 200, 1,000, and so on. Armed with those few forms, you can figure out any number.

20.6. THE NUMBERS 1 AND 2

As we have seen, the number 1 is אֶחָד in the masculine and אַחַת in the feminine. These words are usually used like any other adjective, following the words they modify: אִישׁ אֶחָד 'one man'; עִיר אַחַת 'one city'.

The number 2 (like 3–10) occurs in BH in the absolute form and in the construct form. The absolute form can occur *before or after* the noun it modifies; the construct form always comes *before* the noun being counted.[1]

masculine absolute	שְׁנַיִם	masculine construct	שְׁנֵי
feminine absolute	שְׁתַּיִם	feminine construct	שְׁתֵּי

For example, 'two men' can be written in any of the following three ways:

אֲנָשִׁים שְׁנַיִם   שְׁנַיִם אֲנָשִׁים   שְׁנֵי אֲנָשִׁים

Similarly, 'two women':

נָשִׁים שְׁתַּיִם   שְׁתַּיִם נָשִׁים   שְׁתֵּי נָשִׁים

Even when the thing counted is defined, the number (without definite article) can come before or after the noun, although it is far more common for the number to come before. There are also several ways to express 'of' after a number, as in 'one of the men': the number (absolute or construct) can precede the noun, or the absolute form can follow the noun (הָאֲנָשִׁים אֶחָד, אֶחָד הָאֲנָשִׁים); or the number precedes the noun with the word מִן ('of' here) inserted between the number and the noun (אֶחָד מִן־הָאֲנָשִׁים).

---

1. The *shwa* under the שׁ is silent in all four forms of the number 2 in BH (hence the *beged-kephet dagesh* in the ת, because there is no vowel *sound* before the ת). These are the only words in BH that begin with a consonant cluster. They are pronounced shná-yim, shnay (-ay as in English *say*); shtá-yim, shtay.

20.7. THE PARTITIVE מִן

We have just seen the preposition מִן used with the numbers 1 and 2 to mean 'one of' or 'two of'. There is another use of מִן, called "partitive מִן," in which מִן plus a plural or collective noun is translated 'some of (the noun)'. מֵהָאֲנָשִׁים, then, can be translated 'some of the men'. The choice to translate מִן partitively is up to the reader, according to context.

20.8. ACCENT: THE *ZAQEPH*

The largest pause between the beginning of a verse and the *atnakh* and between the *atnakh* and the end of the verse is signaled by the accent mark known as *zaqeph*. *Zaqeph* looks like a colon and falls directly over the accented syllable, as in מֶ֫לֶךְ.

20.9. VOCABULARY FOR LESSON 20

verbs

נֶאֱכַל	'to be eaten' (*niphal* of אכל); pref. conj. יֵאָכֵל
נִמְצָא	'to be found'; with the extended meaning simply 'to be' (*niphal* of מצא); pref. conj. יִמָּצֵא
נִקְרָא	'to be called, named' (*niphal* of קרא); pref. conj. יִקָּרֵא
נִשְׁמַע	'to be heard, obeyed' (*niphal* of שמע); pref. conj. יִשָּׁמַע

numbers

שְׁנַ֫יִם	'two' (masc.); cs. שְׁנֵי
שְׁתַּ֫יִם	'two' (fem.); cs. שְׁתֵּי

20.10. EXERCISES FOR LESSON 20

> From this point onward, it will be helpful if, before translating each sentence, you draw a vertical line after each word with a disjunctive accent. So, in sentence 6, you would draw a line after הֶעָרִים and another after הַיָּם. This will have the effect of dividing the sentence into smaller syntactic units and will make translating much easier.

A. Translate from Hebrew to English:

1. יַאַסְרוּ מֵהָאֲנָשִׁים אֶת־מַלְכְּכֶם׃

2. וְלֹא־יִקָּרֵא עוֹד שִׁמְךָ אַבְרָם וְהָיָה שִׁמְךָ אַבְרָהָם׃ (taken from Gen 17:5)

3. אֵלֶּה שְׁנֵי הַסְּפָרִים² אֲשֶׁר נִשְׁאֲרוּ בְּבֵית אֱלֹהִים:

4. טוֹב הַיַּיִן אֲשֶׁר מֵהָהָר מִן־הַמַּיִם אֲשֶׁר מֵהַשָּׂדֶה:

5. יִשְׁמְעוּ דִּבְרֵי יְהוָה עַד־עוֹלָם:

6. יִלְכְּדוּ אַנְשֵׁי יִשְׂרָאֵל אֶת הֶעָרִים אֲשֶׁר בֵּין הֶהָרִים וּבֵין הַיָּם וְלָקְחוּ אֶת־הַזָּהָב הַנִּמְצָא בַּהֵיכָל שָׁם:

7. בַּיּוֹם הַהוּא נָשְׂאוּ הַנָּשִׁים אֶת־קוֹלוֹתֵיהֶן וַתִּקְרֶאנָה לֵאמֹר מָה הַקּוֹל אֲשֶׁר אֲנַחְנוּ שֹׁמְעוֹת בַּמִּדְבָּר:

8. וַיְהִי בְּהִשָּׁמַע פִּי דָוִד בַּמַּחֲנֶה וַיַּעֲבֹר הָעָם אֶת־נְהַר מִצְרַיִם וַיִּלָּחֶם בְּגִבּוֹרֵי הָאָרֶץ הַגְּדוֹלָה הַהִיא:

9. וַיִּלְכְּדוּ אֶת־הָעִיר הַקְּטַנָּה וַיִּמְצְאוּ אֶת־יֵין הַמָּקוֹם הַזֶּה רַק נֶאֱכַל כָּל־הַלֶּחֶם:

10. יִשְׁפֹּט שְׁמוּאֵל אֶת־הָעָם בְּאַחַת מֵעָרֵי הֶהָרִים:

11. אַל־תִּקְבְּרוּ אֶת־שָׂרַי בָּאָרֶץ הַזֹּאת כִּי תִּקָּבֵר בְּקֶבֶר אַבְרָהָם:

12. בַּיּוֹם הַזֶּה הָלְכוּ כָּל־גִּבּוֹרֵי יִשְׂרָאֵל אֶל־הַמִּלְחָמָה כְּאִישׁ אֶחָד:

B. Translate from English to Hebrew:

  1. one woman

  2. one man

  3. two cities (write it three ways)

  4. the two kings (write it two ways)

C. Practice reading Gen 22:6–7.

---

2. Since ס is a Skin-'em-Levi letter and is followed by *shwa*, it is not doubled after the definite article.

21 ◄ כא

THE DERIVED STEM *HIPHIL* (PART 1)
AND THE ACCENT *REVIA*

21.1. THE MOST COMMON MEANING OF THE *HIPHIL* STEM

The next verb stem we will learn is the *hiphil*. The *hiphil* is first and foremost a causative for *qal* verbs. From מָלַךְ 'he ruled', the *hiphil* is הִמְלִיךְ 'he caused someone to rule' or 'he made someone king/queen'. זָכַר אֶת־יְהוָה 'he remembered Yahweh' becomes in the *hiphil* הִזְכִּיר אֶת־יְהוָה 'he caused (someone) to remember Yahweh' or 'he mentioned Yahweh'.

21.2. THE FORMS OF THE *HIPHIL* STEM

The forms of the *hiphil* verb are shown on the following page (using the root מלך, which, in the *qal* means 'to rule' and in the *hiphil* means 'to make someone king/queen; to enthrone, to cause to rule').

THE FORMS OF THE *HIPHIL* STEM

inf. cs.	suff. conj.	cons. pret.	volitives		pref. conj.
הַמְלִיךְ	הִמְלַכְתִּי	וָאַמְלִיךְ	אַמְלִיכָה	cohort.	אַמְלִיךְ
	הִמְלַכְתָּ	וַתַּמְלֵךְ	הַמְלֵךְ	impv.	תַּמְלִיךְ
inf. abs.	הִמְלַכְתְּ	וַתַּמְלִיכִי	הַמְלִיכִי	impv.	תַּמְלִיכִי
הַמְלֵךְ	הִמְלִיךְ	וַיַּמְלֵךְ	יַמְלֵךְ	juss.	יַמְלִיךְ
	הִמְלִיכָה	…	תַּמְלֵךְ	juss.	תַּמְלִיךְ
ptcp.	הִמְלַכְנוּ		נַמְלִיכָה	cohort.	נַמְלִיךְ
מַמְלִיךְ	הִמְלַכְתֶּם		הַמְלִיכוּ	impv.	תַּמְלִיכוּ
מַמְלִיכָה	הִמְלַכְתֶּן		הַמְלֵכְנָה	impv.	תַּמְלֵכְנָה
מַמְלִיכִים	הִמְלִיכוּ		יַמְלִיכוּ	juss.	יַמְלִיכוּ
מַמְלִיכוֹת			תַּמְלֵכְנָה	juss.	תַּמְלֵכְנָה

Notes to the paradigm (moving from right to left):

21.2.1. Glosses for the *hiphil* verbal forms are: pref. conj. = 'I/he/etc. will enthrone'; cohort. = 'may I/we enthrone'; impv. = 'enthrone!'; juss. = 'may he/she/you enthrone'; cons. pret. = 'and he, etc., enthroned'; suff. conj. = 'I/he/etc. enthroned'; inf. cs. = 'to enthrone'; and ptcp. = 'one who enthrones'.

21.2.2. The prefix conjugation of the *hiphil* can be identified by the *patakh* in the preformative and the accented *hireq gadol* in all but two forms: the 2fp and 3fp have *tsere* before the נָה- ending.

21.2.3. Like the *niphal* imperative, the imperative of the *hiphil* begins with ה. Except for the ms form, the *hiphil* imperative is made by removing the תּ preformative from the second-person prefix conjugation forms and adding ה instead. The ms imperative is irregular and must simply be learned.

21.2.4. Most forms of the *hiphil* are accented on the syllable beginning with the middle root letter (ל in this paradigm), for instance, תַּמְלִיכִי, יַמְלִיךְ. The exceptions are suffix conjugation 2mp and 2fp and participle fs, mp, and fp.

21.2.5. Even in strong verbs, the *hiphil* jussive is different from the prefix conjugation in the 3ms, 3fs, and 2ms, with *tsere* instead of *hireq gadol*. Consequently, the consecutive preterite also has *tsere* and not *hireq gadol* in these three forms. Note that the 2fs jussive, on the other hand, is exactly like the 2fs prefix conjugation.

21.2.6. The suffix conjugation forms begin with ה and have the telltale *hireq gadol* in the third-person forms but *patakh* in first- and second-person forms. Except for the second-person plural of the suffix conjugation, which is always accented on the last syllable, the forms of the suffix conjugation are accented on the syllable beginning with the middle root letter (ל in this paradigm), for instance, הִמְלַכְתִּי, הִמְלִיךְ.

21.2.7. The *hiphil* infinitive construct and participle are both modeled after the prefix conjugation; the infinitive absolute looks exactly like the imperative.

21.3. STRONG VERBS LEARNED TO THIS POINT WITH *HIPHIL* STEMS

What follows is a list of the *hiphil* forms of some of the strong verbs we have learned so far that appear in the *hiphil* in the Hebrew Bible. Most of them occur frequently enough to warrant including them in the vocabulary list below.

Note that III-G verbs have furtive *patakh* before the guttural.

root	*qal* meaning	*hiphil* meaning	*hiphil* pref. conj.	*hiphil* cons. pret.	*hiphil* suff. conj.
			he will cause…	and he did…	he did…
זכר	to remember	to cause to be remembered; to mention	יַזְכִּיר		הִזְכִּיר
כרת	to cut (off)	to cut off, destroy	יַכְרִית	וַיַּכְרֵת	הִכְרִית
מלך	to rule	to make (s.o.) ruler	יַמְלִיךְ	וַיַּמְלֵךְ	הִמְלִיךְ
מצא	to find	to cause to find	יַמְצִיא	וַיַּמְצֵא	הִמְצִיא
שאר	(*niphal*) to be left	to leave, spare	יַשְׁאִיר	וַיַּשְׁאֵר	הִשְׁאִיר
שמע	to hear	to proclaim	יַשְׁמִיעַ	וַיַּשְׁמַע	הִשְׁמִיעַ

21.4. THE *HIPHIL* WITH DOUBLE ACCUSATIVE

Because of its causative nature, the *hiphil* can take a double accusative (that is, two direct objects). For instance, in יַזְכִּיר הַמֶּלֶךְ אֶת־הַכֹּהֵן אֶת־הַמִּצְוֺת 'The king will cause the priest to remember the commandments', יַזְכִּיר is the *hiphil* prefix conjugation 3ms of the root זכר; הַמֶּלֶךְ is the subject; הַכֹּהֵן is the direct object of the 'caused' part of the *hiphil* verb; and הַמִּצְוֺת is the direct object of the 'remember' part of the verb. Both objects take אֶת־.

It is also common to encounter sentences with only one of the possible direct objects, such as יַזְכִּיר הַמֶּלֶךְ אֶת־הַמִּצְוֺת 'The king will cause (someone) to remember the commandments' or 'The king will cause the commandments to be remembered'.[1]

21.5. VERBS WITH *NIPHAL* AND *HIPHIL* STEMS

Besides *qal-hiphil* pairs, where the *hiphil* verb is the causative of the verb from the same root in the *qal* stem, there are many verbs that occur in a *niphal-hiphil* pair. In those cases, the *niphal* is not the passive of any *qal* verb but is rather the passive of the *hiphil* verb. הִשְׁמִיד 'to destroy' is a case in point. The root שמד does not occur in the *qal* in BH, but there is a *niphal* verb נִשְׁמַד that means 'to be destroyed'. So the basic form of the verb, as we have it in BH at least, is the *hiphil* rather than the *qal*, and the *niphal* is the passive of that *hiphil* verb.

21.6. ACCENT: THE *REVIA*

The next disjunctive accent we will learn is called *revia* (pronounced rə-vée-ah). It looks like a small diamond or simply a dot and is placed above the accented syllable of the word in question, for instance, מֶֽלֶךְ.

21.7. VOCABULARY FOR LESSON 21

verbs

הִזְכִּיר[2]   'to cause to remember/be remembered, mention, commemorate, record' (*hiphil* of זכר); pref. conj. יַזְכִּיר

---

1. This use of the passive in the English translation should not be taken to mean that there is anything inherently passive in the use of the *hiphil* here. The issue is translation into English. In a case like this one, where only one of two possible objects is expressed, the second translation above, which uses an English passive, is simply more elegant than the first one (with "someone" in parentheses), and the two sentences mean the same thing.

2. As with *niphal* verbs, we will identify *hiphil* verbs according to the 3ms *hiphil* suffix conjugation of the root. See the box under 19.7.

הִכְרִית   'to cut off, destroy' (*hiphil* of כרת); pref. conj. יַכְרִית; cons. pret. וַיַּכְרֵת

הִמְלִיךְ   'to cause to rule, put someone on the throne, make someone king/queen' (*hiphil* of מלך); pref. conj. יַמְלִיךְ; cons. pret. וַיַּמְלֵךְ

הִשְׁאִיר   'to leave, keep over, spare (someone)' (*hiphil* of שאר); pref. conj. יַשְׁאִיר

הִשְׁכִּים   'to get up early, do something early in the morning' (*hiphil* of שכם); pref. conj. יַשְׁכִּים; cons. pret. וַיַּשְׁכֵּם

הִשְׁלִיךְ   'to throw (down), cast' (*hiphil* of שלך); pref. conj. יַשְׁלִיךְ; cons. pret. וַיַּשְׁלֵךְ

הִשְׁמִיד   'to destroy' (*hiphil* of שמד); pref. conj. יַשְׁמִיד; cons. pret. וַיַּשְׁמֵד

נִשְׁמַד   'to be destroyed' (*niphal* of שמד)

הִשְׁמִיעַ   'to cause (someone) to hear (something); to proclaim' (*hiphil* of שמע); pref. conj. יַשְׁמִיעַ

nouns

כִּסֵּא   'throne, chair'; with sf. [3] כִּסְאִי; pl. כִּסְאוֹת (masc., like the sg.)

נֶפֶשׁ   'the essence of a human being, self, person' (fem.); often translated 'soul', but it should not be thought of in the Greek sense of something separate from the body; with pronominal suffixes, it is the reflexive pronoun: נַפְשִׁי 'myself', נַפְשׁוֹ 'himself', and so on; pl. נְפָשׁוֹת; cs. pl. נַפְשׁוֹת

שָׂרִיד   'survivor'; with sf. שְׂרִידִי; pl. שְׂרִידִים; cs. pl. שְׂרִידֵי

proper noun

יְהוֹשֻׁעַ   'Joshua'

conjunction

אִם   'if'

---

3. Another example of the Skin-'em-Levi rule, as is the plural (see above, lesson 15, note 2).

21.8. EXERCISES FOR LESSON 21

A. Translate from Hebrew to English:

1. וַיַּשְׁמֵד זִמְרִי[4] אֶת כָּל־בֵּית בַּעְשָׁא[5] כִּדְבַר יְהוָה אֲשֶׁר דִּבֶּר[6] אֶל־בַּעְשָׁא בְּיַד[7] יֵהוּא[8] הַנָּבִיא: (1 Kgs 16:12)

2. יַשְׁכִּים אַבְרָהָם בַּבֹּקֶר וְהָלַךְ אֶל־הַמָּקוֹם אֲשֶׁר עָמַד שָׁם לִפְנֵי יְהוָה: (adapted from Gen 19:27)

3. בַּיּוֹם הַהוּא יָשַׁב שְׁלֹמֹה עַל־כִּסֵּא דָוִד אָבִיו כִּי הִמְלִיכוּהוּ אַנְשֵׁי יְרוּשָׁלַ͏ִם:

4. וַתָּבוֹא[9] הָאִשָּׁה אֶל־כָּל־הָעָם בְּחָכְמָתָהּ וַיִּכְרְתוּ אֶת־רֹאשׁ שֶׁבַע[10] בֶּן־בִּכְרִי[11] וַיַּשְׁלִיכוּ[12] אֶל־יוֹאָב[13] ...: (taken from 2 Sam 20:22)

5. וַיִּלָּחֶם אָבִי עֲלֵיכֶם[14] וַיַּשְׁלֵךְ אֶת־נַפְשׁוֹ לָכֶם: (adapted from Judg 9:17)

6. וַיַּשְׁמֵד יְהוֹשֻׁעַ אֶת־כָּל־הָאָרֶץ מִן־הֶהָרִים וְעַד־הָעָרִים וְאֵת כָּל־מַלְכֵיהֶם לֹא הִשְׁאִיר שָׂרִיד: (adapted from Josh 10:40)

7. אִם־תַּכְרִית אֶת־בְּנֵי מָתְנַי אַחֲרַי וְאִם־תַּשְׁמִיד אֶת־שְׁמִי מִבֵּית אָבִי וְיָרַד[15] יְהוָה אֱלֹהַי לְהַשְׁמִיד שִׁמְךָ מֵעַמְּךָ לְעוֹלָם: (adapted from 1 Sam 24:21)

---

4. A personal name, Zimri.

5. A personal name, Ba'asha.

6. 'He spoke'.

7. Literally, 'by the hand of', but the expression is metaphorical; translate 'through' or 'by means of'.

8. A personal name, Jehu.

9. '(And) she came'.

10. A personal name, Sheva.

11. Sheva's patronymic, Bikhri.

12. In BH, if the antecedent of a pronominal direct object has already been mentioned in a sentence, it can be left out. So, you must insert "it" here in your English translation.

13. A personal name, Joab.

14. עַל here means 'on behalf of'. The second half of this sentence is meant metaphorically: translate it literally, then look at the answer.

15. Notice that this clause begins with וְ, sometimes called the "*vav* of apodosis" because it comes at the beginning of the "then"-clause of an "if-then" sentence, and "apodosis" is a technical term for the then-clause. In fact, in any compound sentence with both a subordinate and an independent clause, the independent clause often begins with וְ. One effect of beginning this clause with וְ is that the future-tense verb must be expressed in the *və-qatal* form.

8. וּבְכֹל אֲשֶׁר אָמַ֫רְתִּי אֲלֵיכֶם תִּשָּׁמֵ֑רוּ וְשֵׁם אֱלֹהִים אֲחֵרִים¹⁶ לֹא תַזְכִּ֫ירוּ לֹא יִשָּׁמַע
עַל־פִּ֫יךָ: (Exod 23:13)

9. הַשְׁמִ֫יעוּ בְּכָל־הָאָ֫רֶץ אֶת־דִּבְרֵי הַמֶּ֫לֶךְ אֲשֶׁר אָמַר אֶל־עֲבָדֽוֹ:

10. וְהָיָה אִם לֹא נִשְׁמֹר אֶת־תּוֹרַת יְהֹוָה לְבִלְתִּי עֲבֹד אֶת־אֱלֹהֵי הָעַמִּים וְהֻשְׁמֵד נִשָּׁמֵֽד:

11. בַּשָּׁנָה הַהִיא נָפְלוּ גִבּוֹרִים רַבִּים לְפִי חֶ֫רֶב¹⁷ כִּי לֹא שָׁמְעוּ אֶת־עֲצַת אִישׁ הָאֱלֹהִים¹⁸
אֲשֶׁר אָמַר בְּחָכְמָה וּבֶאֱמֶת:

12. בָּעֶ֫רֶב הַזֶּה יַעֲבֹר הַמַּשְׁמִיד אֶת־הַיַּרְדֵּן וְהָלַךְ אֶל־רֹאשׁ הָהָר וְהִשְׁמִיעַ בְּאָזְנֵי כָּל־
הָעָם אֲשֶׁר שָׁם כִּי הוּא שָׁפַךְ אֶת־דָּמָם מֵהַבֹּ֫קֶר וְעַד־הַלָּ֫יְלָה:

B. Translate from English to Hebrew:

1. They will make Solomon king.

2. (And) they made Solomon king.

C. Practice reading Gen 22:1–7.

---

16. 'Other'.

17. 'At the point of a sword' = 'by/with the sword'.

18. אֱלֹהִים often occurs in the Bible with the definite article, with no obvious effect on the meaning of the word; the two forms are used interchangeably.

כב ◄ **22** ► כב

THE DERIVED STEM *HIPHIL* (PART 2), THE DERIVED STEM *HOPHAL*, THE NUMBERS 3–10, AND THE ACCENT *MUNAKH*

22.1. THE SECONDARY *HIPHIL* MEANING: DENOMINATIVE

Besides *hiphil*s with causative meaning, there are many *hiphil* verbs that are denominative verbs; that is, the meaning of the verb is taken from a noun. In English, we use the word "chair" as both a noun and a verb: "The president chaired the meeting." It is logical, however, that the verbal usage is secondary and comes about because the person in charge of a meeting was seated in a special chair. In BH, for example, the verb הֶאֱזִין 'to hear, listen' is clearly secondary to and derived from the noun אֹזֶן 'ear'.

There are also *hiphil* verbs that never occur in the *qal*. הִשְׁלִיךְ 'to cast, throw down' is one common such verb, and הִשְׁכִּים 'to get up early' is another.

22.2. THE TERTIARY *HIPHIL* MEANING: STATIVE

Finally, the oddest group of *hiphil* verbs is a small group of verbs that can be both causative and *stative* in the *hiphil*. For instance, הֶאֱרִיךְ can mean both 'to lengthen' and 'to be long'.

22.3. MORE STRONG VERBS LEARNED TO THIS POINT WITH *HIPHIL* STEMS

What follows is a list of more *hiphil* forms of strong verbs we have learned so far that appear in the *hiphil* in the Hebrew Bible. Most of them occur frequently enough to warrant including them in the vocabulary list below. Note that there are occasional differences in vowel pointing from the paradigm in lesson 21.

root	*qal* meaning	*hiphil* meaning	*hiphil* pref. conj.	*hiphil* cons. pret.	*hiphil* suff. conj.
			he will be…	and he did…	he did…
אכל	to eat	to cause to eat, feed	יַאֲכִיל	וַיַּאֲכֶל	הֶאֱכִיל
חזק	to be strong	to make strong; to grasp	יַחֲזִיק	וַיַּחֲזֵק	הֶחֱזִיק
עבד	to serve	to cause to serve	יַעֲבִיד	וַיַּעֲבֵד	הֶעֱבִיד
עבר	to cross over	to cause to cross over[1]	יַעֲבִיר	וַיַּעֲבֵר	הֶעֱבִיר
עמד	to stand	to cause to stand[2]	יַעֲמִיד	וַיַּעֲמֵד	הֶעֱמִיד

Note that I-G verbs have *hateph-patakh* in the prefix conjugation and *seghol* and *hateph-seghol* in the suffix conjugation.

22.4. CLUES FOR RECOGNIZING *HIPHIL* VERBS

22.4.1. The suffix conjugation, imperative, and infinitives begin with ה; be careful not to confuse the *hiphil* imperative and infinitives with the suffix conjugation.

22.4.2. The preformatives of the strong verb all have *patakh*, with the exception of the suffix conjugation, which has *hireq* (or *seghol*, if the verb is I-G).

22.4.3. Many of the forms in the paradigm have the telltale *hireq gadol*.

22.5. THE *HOPHAL* STEM

Although some *hiphil* verbs have *niphal* passives, there is an entire stem, the *hophal*, that serves as the passive of *hiphil* verbs. Quite often it is the *hophal* parti-

---

1. *Hiphils* of verbs of motion are common, and there is usually a nicer translation to be found than 'to cause to…'. 'To cause to cross over' can mean 'to carry over', 'to lead over', and so on. The same will be true for other verbs of motion that we will learn fully in a later lesson, such as 'to go', 'to come', 'to go up', and 'to go down'.

2. As with the previous verb, 'to cause to stand' has more elegant translations, such as 'to appoint', 'to set up', and 'to erect'.

ciple that we see, and it is used as an attributive adjective. For instance, בֵּ֫יִת מָשְׁמָד would be a 'destroyed house'. The vowel at the beginning of *hophal* verbs is variable, but in the strong verb it is usually a *qamets* with the value short *o* (hence the *o* of the name *hophal*). The *hophal* is rare enough that it need not be learned well at this point, but the major forms are:

prefix conjugation	יָשְׁמַד	he/it will be destroyed
suffix conjugation	הָשְׁמַד	he/it was destroyed
participle	מָשְׁמָד	destroyed

Note that in the participle, the second *qamets* is long *a*.

22.6. THE NUMBERS 3–10

The numbers 3–10 have the odd quality that the ones that appear to be masculine are used to modify feminine nouns, and the ones that appear to be feminine are used to modify masculine nouns.

THE NUMBERS 3–10

	modifies feminine noun		modifies masculine noun	
	construct	*absolute*	*construct*	*absolute*
three	שְׁלֹשׁ	שָׁלֹשׁ	שְׁלֹ֫שֶׁת	שְׁלֹשָׁה
four	אַרְבַּע	אַרְבַּע	אַרְבַּ֫עַת	אַרְבָּעָה
five	חֲמֵשׁ	חָמֵשׁ	חֲמֵ֫שֶׁת	חֲמִשָּׁה
six	שֵׁשׁ	שֵׁשׁ	שֵׁ֫שֶׁת	שִׁשָּׁה
seven	שְׁבַע	שֶׁ֫בַע	שִׁבְעַת	שִׁבְעָה
eight	שְׁמֹנֶה	שְׁמֹנֶה	שְׁמֹנַת	שְׁמֹנָה
nine	תֵּ֫שַׁע	תֵּ֫שַׁע	תִּשְׁעַת	תִּשְׁעָה
ten	עֶ֫שֶׂר	עֶ֫שֶׂר	עֲשֶׂ֫רֶת	עֲשָׂרָה

Construct forms come before the noun being counted. Absolute forms can come before or after the noun being counted; in both cases, the absolute form is in apposition with the noun. 'Three mares' is שָׁלֹשׁ סוּסוֹת, שָׁלֹשׁ סוּסוֹת, or סוּסוֹת שָׁלֹשׁ.

'The three mares' is שְׁלֹשׁ הַסּוּסוֹת. For 'the seven men' and 'seven of the men', see the explanations in 20.6.

The numbers are generally easy to deal with. You should memorize the absolute forms of the numbers that modify a feminine noun. These are the dictionary forms of these words. Knowing that one form well should make it possible for you to recognize the other three forms of each number.

22.7. ACCENT: THE *MUNAKH*

So far, the accent marks we have learned have all been "disjunctive"; that is, since they signal a pause after the word in question, they also signal a separation (a disjunction) between the word with the accent and the next word. There are also, however, "conjunctive" accents that signal that two or more words are tied together in some way, such as the words in a construct chain. A two-word construct chain is marked with a conjunctive accent on the first word and a disjunctive accent on the second word (to signal that the words in the construct chain are more closely related to each other than they are to the other words in the sentence). The first conjunctive accent we will learn is *munakh*, which is a corner or right angle placed under the accented syllable of the word in question, for instance: מֶלֶךְ.

22.8. VOCABULARY FOR LESSON 22

verbs

הֶאֱזִין   'to hear, listen, give ear' (*hiphil* of אזן); pref. conj. יַאֲזִין

הֶאֱרִיךְ   'to make long, prolong, lengthen; to be long' (*hiphil* of ארך); pref. conj. יַאֲרִיךְ

הֶחֱזִיק   'to make strong; to grasp, seize, take hold of' (*hiphil* of חזק); usually takes obj. with בְּ instead of אֶת; pref. conj. יַחֲזִיק; cons. pret. וַיַּחֲזֵק

הֶחֱרִים   'to ban, exterminate; to devote (to the deity) = to exterminate' (*hiphil* of חרם); pref. conj. יַחֲרִים; cons. pret. וַיַּחֲרֵם

הֶעֱבִיר   'to cause to cross, cause to pass over/through/by; to carry/bring over/through' (*hiphil* of עבר); pref. conj. יַעֲבִיר; cons. pret. וַיַּעֲבֵר

הֶעֱמִיד   'to cause to stand, to erect, set up; to appoint' (*hiphil* of עמד); pref. conj. יַעֲמִיד; cons. pret. וַיַּעֲמֵד

numbers (refer to the chart above for the various forms of these words)

שָׁלֹשׁ   'three'

אַרְבַּע   'four'

חָמֵשׁ	'five'
שֵׁשׁ	'six'
שֶׁבַע	'seven'
שְׁמֹנֶה	'eight'
תֵּשַׁע	'nine'
עֶשֶׂר	'ten'

22.9 EXERCISES FOR LESSON 22

A. Translate from Hebrew to English:

1. וַתָּבֹא³ אֶל־אִישׁ הָאֱלֹהִים אֶל־הָהָר וַתַּחֲזֵק בְּרַגְלָיו ... (taken from 2 Kgs 4:27) :

2. וַיַּעֲבֵר יִשַׁי⁴ שִׁבְעַת בָּנָיו לִפְנֵי שְׁמוּאֵל וַיֹּאמֶר שְׁמוּאֵל אֶל־יִשַׁי לֹא־בָחַר יְהוָה בָּאֵלֶּה: (1 Sam 16:10)

3. וְעַתָּה יְהוָה אֱלֹהֵי יִשְׂרָאֵל שְׁמֹר לְעַבְדְּךָ⁵ דָוִד אָבִי אֵת אֲשֶׁר⁶ דִּבַּרְתָּ⁷ לּוֹ לֵאמֹר לֹא־יִכָּרֵת לְךָ אִישׁ מִלְּפָנַי⁸ יֹשֵׁב עַל־כִּסֵּא יִשְׂרָאֵל רַק אִם־⁹יִשְׁמְרוּ בָנֶיךָ אֶת־דַּרְכָּם לָלֶכֶת¹⁰ לְפָנַי כַּאֲשֶׁר הָלַכְתָּ לְפָנָי: (1 Kgs 8:25)

4. שִׁמְעוּ דְבַר יְהוָה קְצִינֵי¹¹ סְדֹם¹² הַאֲזִינוּ¹³ תּוֹרַת אֱלֹהֵינוּ עַם עֲמֹרָה¹⁴: (Isa 1:10)

5. וְהָיָה אַחֲרֵי אֲשֶׁר¹⁵ הֶחֱרַמְתֶּם אֶת־כָּל־עַמֵּי הָאָרֶץ וַהֲלַכְתֶּם לַעֲמֹד לִפְנֵי יְהוָה אֱלֹהֵיכֶם שָׁלֹשׁ פְּעָמִים בַּשָּׁנָה:

---

3. '(And) she came'.

4. A personal name, Jesse.

5. Translate the ל here as 'for the sake of'.

6. אֵת אֲשֶׁר together mean that the next clause is the direct object of the verb, to be translated something like 'that which'.

7. 'You promised'.

8. A combination of מִן and לִפְנֵי, plus the first-person singular suffix.

9. רַק אִם together = 'if only'.

10. 'To walk'.

11. 'Rulers of'.

12. A place name, Sodom.

13. This verb is used almost exclusively in poetry in the Hebrew Bible, and in poetry we should not expect to find mundane words like אֵת. It will sometimes occur, but its absence is not a problem.

14. A place name, Gomorrah.

15. אַחֲרֵי אֲשֶׁר together = 'after' as a conjunction, beginning a clause.

6. שָׂרְפוּ אֶת־בָּתֵּי הַכֹּהֲנִים הָרָעִים בָּאֵשׁ לְמַעַן תַּאֲרִיכוּ יָמִים עַל־הָאֲדָמָה אֲשֶׁר
נָתַן[16] לָכֶם יְהוָה אֱלֹהֵיכֶם:

7. וַיַּעֲבֹר יְהוֹשֻׁעַ וְכָל־יִשְׂרָאֵל עִמּוֹ מִמַּקֵּדָה[17] לְבְנָה[18] וַיִּלָּחֶם עִם־לִבְנָה: (Josh 10:29)

8. וַיִּלְכְּדוּהָ[19] וַיַּכּוּהָ[20] לְפִי־חֶרֶב וְאֶת־מַלְכָּהּ וְאֶת־כָּל־עָרֶיהָ וְאֶת־כָּל־הַנֶּפֶשׁ אֲשֶׁר־בָּהּ
לֹא־הִשְׁאִיר שָׂרִיד כְּכֹל אֲשֶׁר עָשָׂה[21] לְעֶגְלוֹן[22] וַיַּחֲרֵם[23] אֹתָהּ וְאֶת־כָּל־הַנֶּפֶשׁ
אֲשֶׁר בָּהּ: (Josh 10:37)

9. הֲמָצָאתָ אַרְבָּעָה צַדִּיקִים אֲשֶׁר לְבָבָם יָפֶה וַאֲשֶׁר עֵינֵיהֶם עַל־אֱלֹהֵיהֶם כָּל־הַיּוֹם
וְכָל־הַלַּיְלָה:

10. וַיַּעֲמֵד יְהוָה חֲמֵשֶׁת שֹׁמְרִים לִפְנֵי הַשָּׂדֶה לְמַעַן לֹא יֹאכְלוּ מֵהָעֵץ אֲשֶׁר בְּתוֹךְ
הַשָּׂדֶה לֹא־אָדָם וְלֹא־בָקָר:

11. וַיִּכְרְתוּ כֹּהֲנֵי יְרוּשָׁלַםִ אֶת־רֹאשׁ הַנָּבִיא אֲשֶׁר הִמְלִיךְ אֶת־הַנַּעַר הָרָשָׁע וְזֶה רֹאשׁוֹ
הַמֻּשְׁלָךְ[24] מִן־הָעִיר:

12. מִי הַגִּבּוֹר הַשֹּׁכֵב תַּחַת הַשָּׁמַיִם וְלֹא עָבַד אֶת־עֲבֹדָתוֹ:

B. Translate from English to Hebrew:

1. 'ten men' (three different ways)

2. 'nine women' (two different ways)

3. 'eight houses' (three different ways)

4. 'six fathers' (three different ways)

C. Practice reading Gen 22:1–8.

---

16. 'Has given'.
17. A place name, Maqqedah.
18. '(To) Libnah', a place name.
19. The pronominal suffix refers to a city mentioned in the verse immediately before this one.
20. '(And) they struck it/her down'.
21. 'He did'.
22. 'To Eglon', a place name.
23. '(And) he completely destroyed' or '(and) he put (it) to the ban'.
24. In this particular verb, the *hophal* participle has *qibbuts* in the first syllable.

כג ◄ 23 ► כג

THE DERIVED STEMS *PIEL* AND *PUAL*, THE ORDINAL NUMBERS, AND THE ACCENTS *TIPHKHAH* AND *MERKHAH*

23.1. THE *PIEL* STEM GENERALLY

The *piel* stem is in some ways an easy stem to learn and in some ways difficult. It is easy to identify because its forms are recognizable, but it is the hardest to define with relation to the *qal*. *Piel* verbs often simply have to be learned as words on their own, not as verbs that have some relationship to a *qal* verb.

23.2. THE FORMS OF THE *PIEL* STEM FOR THE STRONG VERB

One of the most common verbs in the Bible appears in the *piel*: דִּבֶּר 'to speak'. We will use דִּבֶּר as the paradigm verb to illustrate the forms of the *piel, even though the* seghol *in the second syllable is unusual for the* piel (see note 23.2.6 below).

THE FORMS OF THE *PIEL* STEM

inf. cs.	suff. conj.	cons. pret.	volitives		pref. conj.
דַּבֵּר	דִּבַּ֫רְתִּי	וָאֲדַבֵּר	אֲדַבְּרָה	cohort.	אֲדַבֵּר
	דִּבַּ֫רְתָּ	וַתְּדַבֵּר	דַּבֵּר	impv.	תְּדַבֵּר
inf. abs.	דִּבַּרְתְּ	וַתְּדַבְּרִי	דַּבְּרִי	impv.	תְּדַבְּרִי
דַּבֵּר	דִּבֶּר	וַיְדַבֵּר	יְדַבֵּר	juss.	יְדַבֵּר
	דִּבְּרָה	...	תְּדַבֵּר	juss.	תְּדַבֵּר
ptcp.	דִּבַּ֫רְנוּ		נְדַבְּרָה	cohort.	נְדַבֵּר
מְדַבֵּר	דִּבַּרְתֶּם		דַּבְּרוּ	impv.	תְּדַבְּרוּ
מְדַבֶּ֫רֶת	דִּבַּרְתֶּן		דַּבֵּ֫רְנָה	impv.	תְּדַבֵּ֫רְנָה
מְדַבְּרִים	דִּבְּרוּ		יְדַבְּרוּ	juss.	יְדַבְּרוּ
מְדַבְּרוֹת			תְּדַבֵּ֫רְנָה	juss.	תְּדַבֵּ֫רְנָה

Notes to the paradigm (moving from right to left):

23.2.1. Glosses for the *piel* verbal forms are: pref. conj. = 'I/he/etc. will speak'; cohort. = 'may I/we speak'; impv. = 'speak!'; juss. = 'may he/she speak'; cons. pret. = 'and he, etc., spoke'; suff. conj. = 'I/he/etc. spoke'; inf. cs. = 'to speak'; and ptcp. = 'speaking; speaker'.

23.2.2. The prefix conjugation of the *piel* can be identified by the doubled middle root consonant (although in דִּבֶּר the middle root consonant is a *beged-kephet* letter, the *dagesh* is the doubling *dagesh*); by the *shwa* of the preformative syllable (*hateph-patakh* in the 1cs); and by the vowel pattern *shwa-patakh-tsere*.

23.2.3. The *piel* imperative can be recognized by the *patakh* in the first syllable, since it is the second-person prefix conjugation form without the preformative.

23.2.4. The *tsere* of the prefix conjugation reduces to *shwa* when the cohortative ending is added.

23.2.5. In strong verbs, the jussive of the *piel* looks the same as the prefix conjugation.

23.2.6. In the consecutive preterite third-person forms, the י is not doubled, as we would expect, because י is one of those letters that tends to lose its doubling when its vowel is *shwa* (see note 2 of lesson 15). (The first-person plural preformative נ, however, which is also a Skin-'em-Levi letter, does not lose its doubling in the *piel* consecutive preterite.)

23.2.7. The 3ms suffix conjugation in this paradigm is דִּבֶּר, but the *seghol* is unusual for a *piel* verb. Usually, the 3ms has either *tsere* or *patakh*, for instance, סִפֵּר 'to narrate', חִזֵּק 'to strengthen', שִׁבַּר 'to shatter', אִבַּד 'to kill'.

23.2.8. Most other forms of the suffix conjugation have *patakh* in the second syllable, except 3fs and 3mp, in which the vowel reduces to *shwa*.

23.2.9. The *piel* infinitive construct looks exactly like the ms imperative.

23.2.10. The infinitive absolute is usually not a separate form in the *piel*; rather, the infinitive construct is used as the infinitive absolute also. Occasionally, a form such as דַּבּוֹר shows up in the text.

23.2.11. As in the *hiphil*, the *piel* participle begins with מ, but in the *piel*, the vowel under the מ is always *shwa*.

23.3. THE FORMS OF THE *PIEL* STEM WITH SECOND GUTTURAL OR *RESH*

As with other stems, the forms of *piel* verbs can be influenced in predictable ways by the presence of a guttural root consonant (presence of furtive *patakh*, tendency to substitute *patakh* for *tsere*). With the *piel*, however, the need to double the middle root consonant makes for special problems if that consonant is a guttural or ר. The two solutions to such a situation that we have seen so far are also evident in the *piel* paradigm. Sometimes compensatory lengthening takes place, as in מֵאֵן 'to refuse' and בֵּרֶךְ or בֵּרֵךְ 'to bless'; sometimes the middle consonant is virtually doubled, as in שִׁחֵת 'to corrupt; to destroy' and מִהַר 'to hurry, to do something quickly'.

23.4. THE MEANINGS OF THE *PIEL* STEM: INTENSIVE

The *piel* is often called the "intensive" stem because in those roots in which both *qal* and *piel* are known, the *piel* can represent an action that seems to be intensified in some way over the *qal* meaning. For instance, *qal* שָׁלַח means 'to send', while *piel* שִׁלַּח means 'to send away, let go', as in 'Let my people go' in Exodus: שַׁלַּח אֶת־עַמִּי.

The intensifying sometimes comes in the form of multiplying the objects of a verb or the results of verbal action. For instance, *qal* בָּקַע means 'to divide', whereas *piel* בִּקַּע can mean 'to chop up (wood), tear into pieces'.

23.5. THE MEANINGS OF THE *PIEL* STEM: TRANSITIVE

One of the more common *qal-piel* pairings is a root that is stative in the *qal* but transitive in the *piel*. We have learned that חזק in the *qal* means 'to be strong' and that the *hiphil* of this root means 'to make strong, to strengthen' or 'to grasp'. There is also a *piel* verb from this root, חִזֵּק, and its meaning is the same as one of the *hiphil* meanings: 'to strengthen'. It is not uncommon in such roots to have both *piel* and *hiphil* forms of the transitive meaning of the verb. Another example of such a *qal-piel* pairing is גָּדַל *qal* 'to be great' and גִּדֵּל or גָּדַל *piel* 'to magnify, glorify, praise someone or something', that is, to make it great or declare it great.

גָּדַל יְהוָה	Yahweh is great.
גִּדֵּל הַכֹּהֵן אֶת־יְהוָה	The priest glorified/praised Yahweh.

A similar *qal-piel* pairing consists of verbs that are intransitive in the *qal* and transitive in the *piel*: *qal* אָבַד means 'to die', and *piel* אִבַּד means 'to kill'.

23.6. THE MEANINGS OF THE *PIEL* STEM: DENOMINATIVE

Piel verbs can also be denominative (see lesson 20.5). Our paradigm word דִּבֶּר 'to speak' is denominative from דָּבָר 'word'. The *piel* verb סִפֵּר 'to narrate, tell a story, recount' seems to be related to the noun סֵפֶר rather than the *qal* verb סָפַר, which means 'to count'. There is a rare *qal* verb בָּרַךְ 'to kneel' and a noun בְּרָכָה 'blessing'. The *piel* verb בֵּרַךְ 'to bless' seems to be related to the noun rather than the *qal* verb, and so it would be an example of a denominative verb.[1]

23.7. THE MEANINGS OF THE *PIEL* STEM: UNCLASSIFIED

Finally, some *piel* verbs are impossible to classify with our present state of knowledge. מִהַר 'to hurry' is one, as are בִּקֵּשׁ 'to seek' and גֵּרֵשׁ 'to banish, drive away'.

23.8. CLUES FOR RECOGNIZING *PIEL* VERBS

23.8.1. The middle root letter is doubled in *piel* verbs.

23.8.2. The preformatives have *shwa* or a *hateph*-vowel.

23.8.3. As in the *hiphil*, the participle begins with מ, but the vowel here is *shwa*.

23.8.4. The first vowel of the suffix conjugation is usually *hireq*, sometimes *tsere* when the second root letter cannot be doubled.

23.8.5. The difference between the suffix conjugation 3ms, on the one hand, and the imperative and infinitives, on the other, is usually simply the *hireq* in the first syllable of the suffix conjugation and the *patakh* in the first syllable of the others.

23.9. THE *PUAL* STEM

There is a paradigm that expresses the passive of *piel* verbs, called the *pual*. An example is שֻׁלַּח 'he was let go, sent away'. Like the *hophal*, the *pual* occurs frequently as a participle used as an adjective: מְשֻׁלָּח 'one who is sent away'; מְבֹרָךְ 'one

---

1. There is, however, a common *qal* passive participle of this root, בָּרוּךְ 'blessed', but no *active* equivalent in the *qal*.

who is blessed' (note the compensatory lengthening of *qibbuts* to *holem* before the nondoubling ר). The *pual* is rare enough that it need not be learned at this point, but the major forms are:

prefix conjugation	יְדֻבַּר	It will be spoken
suffix conjugation	דֻּבַּר	It was spoken
participle	מְדֻבָּר	spoken

23.10. ACCENTS: THE *TIPHKHAH* AND THE *MERKHAH*

Tiphkhah and *merkhah* are a disjunctive and conjunctive accent, respectively. They often occur together, marking a two-word unit like a construct chain. Both accent marks are diagonal lines placed under the accented syllable of a word, but they go in opposite directions. *Merkhah* under the word דָּבָר looks like this: דָּבָ֥ר; *tiphkhah* under the same word looks like this: דָּבָ֖ר. Both accent marks within a construct chain look like this: דְּבַ֥ר הַמֶּ֖לֶךְ.[2]

23.11. VOCABULARY FOR LESSON 23

verbs

> Since few of the verbs we have seen so far occur in the *piel* stem, we will dispense with the kind of chart that was used for the *niphal* and *hiphil* verbs. *Piel* verbs will simply be given as vocabulary items.

אָבַד	'to die'; pref. conj. יֹאבַד
אִבַּד	'to kill, destroy' (*piel* of אבד); pref. conj. יְאַבֵּד
בִּקֵּשׁ	'to seek' (*piel* of בקשׁ); pref. conj. יְבַקֵּשׁ
בֵּרֵךְ	'to bless' (*piel* of ברך); sometimes בֵּרַךְ; pref. conj. יְבָרֵךְ; cons. pret. 3ms וַיְבָרֶךְ
בָּרוּךְ	'blessed' (*qal* passive ptcp. of ברך)
גָּדַל	'to be great, large; to grow up'; pref. conj. יִגְדַּל

---

2. It should be pointed out that in this book accent marks in nonbiblical exercise sentences do not follow all the complications of the placement of accents in the Hebrew Bible. What is important at this point is to recognize accent marks, to distinguish between disjunctive accents and conjunctive accents, and to allow those distinctions to guide the syntax of the translation.

גִּדֵּל   'to magnify, praise; to bring up (children)' (also גִּדַּל; *piel* of גדל); pref. conj. יְגַדֵּל

דִּבֵּר   'to speak' (*piel* of דבר); pref. conj. יְדַבֵּר

חִזֵּק   'to strengthen; harden (the heart)' (*piel* of חזק); pref. conj. יְחַזֵּק

לָמַד   'to learn'; pref. conj. יִלְמַד [3]

לִמֵּד   'to teach' (*piel* of למד); pref. conj. יְלַמֵּד

מֵאֵן   'to refuse' (*piel* of מאן); pref. conj. יְמָאֵן

מִהַר   'to hurry, do something quickly' (*piel* of מהר); pref. conj. יְמַהֵר

סִפֵּר   'to narrate, tell a story, recount' (*piel* of ספר); pref. conj. יְסַפֵּר

שָׁבַר   'to break'; pref. conj. יִשְׁבֹּר

שִׁבֵּר   'to break (into pieces), shatter' (*piel* of שבר); pref. conj. יְשַׁבֵּר

שִׁחֵת   'to corrupt; destroy' (*piel* of שחת)

שִׁלַּח   'to send away, let go' (*piel* of שלח); pref. conj. יְשַׁלַּח

noun

בְּרָכָה   'blessing'; cs. בִּרְכַּת; pl. בְּרָכוֹת; cs. pl. בִּרְכוֹת

adjectives/numbers

> The ordinal numbers in BH generally have a specific form, with *hireq gadol* between the second and third root consonants and again at the end of the word. Ordinal numbers function like any other adjective.

'3rd'   שְׁלִישִׁי masc. and שְׁלִישִׁית fem.

'4th'   רְבִיעִי masc. and רְבִיעִית fem. (without the א that appears at the beginning of אַרְבַּע)

'5th'   חֲמִישִׁי masc. and חֲמִישִׁית fem.

'6th'   שִׁשִּׁי masc. and שִׁשִּׁית fem. (note no *hireq gadol* between the *shin*s)

'7th'   שְׁבִיעִי masc. and שְׁבִיעִית fem.

'8th'   שְׁמִינִי masc. and שְׁמִינִית fem.

'9th'   תְּשִׁיעִי masc. and תְּשִׁיעִית fem.

'10th'   עֲשִׂירִי masc. and עֲשִׂירִית fem.

---

3. Like שכב, למד has a prefix conjugation with *patakh* for no obvious reason.

'2nd'   slightly different: שֵׁנִי masc. and שֵׁנִית fem.

'1st'   does not follow this pattern; is usually רִאשׁוֹן/רִאשׁוֹנָה

23.12. EXERCISES FOR LESSON 23

A. Translate from Hebrew to English:

1. וַיִּשְׁכֵּם שְׁלֹמֹה בַּבֹּקֶר וַיִּקְרָא לְכָל־עֲבָדָיו וַיְדַבֵּר אֶת־כָּל־הַדְּבָרִים הָאֵלֶּה בְּאָזְנֵיהֶם:

2. וַיְחַזֵּק אֱלֹהֵי יִשְׂרָאֵל אֶת־לֵב פַּרְעֹה וְלֹא שִׁלַּח אֶת־הָעָם:

3. וְהָיָה אִם יִשְׁמְרוּ בָנֶיךָ אֶת־בְּרִיתִי וּבֵרַכְתִּים[4] וְלִמַּדְתִּים אֶת־דְּרָכִי:

4. וַיְהִי בְּשַׁחֵת אֱלֹהִים אֶת־עָרֵי הָאָרֶץ הָרְשָׁעָה הַהִיא וַיִּזְכֹּר אֶת־אַבְרָהָם כִּי גָדַל אַבְרָהָם בָּאָרֶץ הַהִיא:

5. יְבָרֶכְךָ יְהוָה וְיִשְׁמְרֶךָ[5]:

6. כֹּה אָמַר יְהוָה מַהֵר לְסַפֵּר אֶת אֲשֶׁר נִמְצָא בְּמַחֲנֵה הָאֹיְבִים:

7. וַיִּשְׁמַע הַשֹּׁפֵט הָרָע אֶת־הַדָּבָר הַזֶּה וַיְבַקֵּשׁ לְאַבֵּד אֶת־הַנָּבִיא[6]:

8. וַיְדַבֵּר יְהוָה אֶל־הָעָם וַיֹּאמֶר מֵאֲנוּ אֲבוֹתֵיכֶם לִשְׁמֹעַ בְּקוֹלִי וְגַם־אַתֶּם מֵאַנְתֶּם:

9. וַיֹּאמֶר דָּוִד לְאִשְׁתּוֹ בָּרוּךְ יְהוָה אֱלֹהֵי יִשְׂרָאֵל אֲשֶׁר שְׁלָחֵךְ לִי הַיּוֹם הַזֶּה:

10. יְלַמֵּד כָּל־הָעָם אֶת־הַבְּרָכָה הַזֹּאת יְהִי[7] שֵׁם יְהוָה מְבֹרָךְ מֵעַתָּה וְעַד־עוֹלָם:

(last section taken from Ps 113:2)

11. וַיְהִי אַחֲרֵי מוֹת שָׁאוּל וַיֹּאבְדוּ גַּם־שְׁלֹשֶׁת בְּנֵי שָׁאוּל כִּי לֹא נִשְׁאַר לָהֶם צָבָא:

12. גִּדֵּל אֶת־אֱלֹהִים הַמְשַׁבֵּר אֶת־הֶהָרִים וְהַשֹּׁבֵר אֶת־הַחֹשֶׁךְ בְּאוֹרוֹ:

---

4. Note again that, like temporal sentences, conditional sentences ("if-then" sentences) begin their second clauses with a *və-qatal* or consecutive preterite verb, depending on context.

5. The *seghol* here and the retracted accent are something we have not yet seen, but in fact, words that have heavy pauses, like *silluq* or *atnakh*, are said to be "in pause" and sometimes undergo changes of accent and vowels. Such "pausal" forms will be pointed out when we come to them.

6. A sentence like this one might be translated as an "unmarked" temporal sentence. Take, as an example, the sentence "God spoke and I acted." This sentence could also mean, "When God spoke, I acted," and could be so translated, if that meaning fits the context.

7. We have seen this word briefly before; it is the 3ms jussive of the verb 'to be'.

B. Translating English to Hebrew

    1. the sixth woman

    2. the eighth day

    3. the fourth tree

    4. the second Torah

    5. the fifth daughter

    6. the first son

    7. the third holocaust offering

    8. the tenth altar

    9. the seventh house

    10. the ninth captain

C. Practice reading Gen 22:1–8 from *BHS*, taking care to follow the syntax dictated by the accent marks that you have learned so far. It can be useful to photocopy Gen 22 from *BHS* and then to draw vertical lines on the photocopied sheets after each of the disjunctive accents that we have learned. While there are disjunctives that we have not learned that will influence the Masoretic syntax as well, for the most part the pieces between each set of vertical lines can be translated together, and the disjunctive accents themselves often signal a break in the syntax, something like a comma or semicolon in English.

24

כד ◄ ► כד

THE DERIVED STEM *HITPAEL* AND THE PARSING OF VERBS

24.1. THE MEANINGS OF THE *HITPAEL* STEM

The last of the major verb stems in BH is the *hitpael*. The *hitpael* has the following common meanings.

24.1.1. Reflexive, as in הִתְחַזֵּק 'to strengthen oneself'; also indirect reflexive, to do something for one's own benefit, as in הִתְפַּלֵּל 'to pray, to intercede for someone', including for oneself.

24.1.2. Reciprocal, as in הִתְרָאָה 'to look at each other" (from רָאָה 'to see').[1]

24.1.3. Iterative, to do something over and over, as in הִתְהַלֵּךְ 'to walk back and forth, to wander around, to pace'.

24.1.4. Denominative, as in הִתְנַבֵּא 'to prophesy' (from נָבִיא).

24.1.5. To pretend to do something, as in Amnon's pretending to be ill so as to fool Tamar into tending to him, הִתְחַלָּה, from the root חלה 'to be ill'.[1]

24.2. THE FORMS OF THE *HITPAEL* STEM

The paradigm of the *hitpael* will be illustrated using the root הלך.

---

1. This is a weak verb that we have not yet studied, but it is the best example of this meaning.

THE FORMS OF THE *HITPAEL* STEM

inf. cs.	suff. conj.	cons. pret.	volitives		pref. conj.
הִתְהַלֵּךְ	הִתְהַלַּכְתִּי	וָאֶתְהַלֵּךְ	אֶתְהַלְכָה	cohort.	אֶתְהַלֵּךְ
	הִתְהַלַּכְתָּ	וַתִּתְהַלֵּךְ	הִתְהַלֵּךְ	impv.	תִּתְהַלֵּךְ
inf. abs.	הִתְהַלַּכְתְּ	וַתִּתְהַלְכִי	הִתְהַלְכִי	impv.	תִּתְהַלְכִי
הִתְהַלֵּךְ	הִתְהַלֵּךְ	וַיִּתְהַלֵּךְ	יִתְהַלֵּךְ	juss.	יִתְהַלֵּךְ
	הִתְהַלְכָה	...	תִּתְהַלֵּךְ	juss.	תִּתְהַלֵּךְ
	הִתְהַלַּכְנוּ		נִתְהַלְכָה	cohort.	נִתְהַלֵּךְ
ptcp.	הִתְהַלַּכְתֶּם		הִתְהַלְכוּ	impv.	תִּתְהַלְכוּ
מִתְהַלֵּךְ	הִתְהַלַּכְתֶּן		הִתְהַלֵּכְנָה	impv.	תִּתְהַלֵּכְנָה
מִתְהַלֶּכֶת	הִתְהַלְכוּ		יִתְהַלְכוּ	juss.	יִתְהַלְכוּ
מִתְהַלְכִים			תִּתְהַלֵּכְנָה	juss.	תִּתְהַלֵּכְנָה
מִתְהַלְכוֹת					

Notes to the paradigm and clues for identifying *hitpael*s:

24.2.1. Glosses for the *hitpael* verbal forms are: pref. conj. = 'I/he/etc. will pace'; cohort. = 'may I/we pace'; impv. = 'pace!'; juss. = 'may he/she pace'; cons. pret. = 'and he, etc., paced'; suff. conj. = 'I/he/etc. paced'; inf. cs. = 'to pace'; and ptcp. = 'pacing; pacer'.

24.2.2. The *hitpael* can be recognized in most circumstances by the extra syllable תְ- (pronounced *it*). In some cases, however, the form changes for phonological reasons. For instance, when the first root consonant is ד, ז (1x), ט, sometimes נ, and ת (4x), the telltale ת of the Hitpael assimilates to that consonant, for instance, הִנַּשֵּׂא (< הִתְנַשֵּׂא) 'to lift oneself up'. Such assimilation is sporadic: הִתְנַשֵּׂא also occurs.

The most striking of these changes is "metathesis" (mə-tá-thə-sis), the switching around of two consonants. When the first root consonant is one of the sibilants ס, צ, שׂ, or שׁ, the ת of the *hitpael* and the sibilant of the root switch places. There are, however, only about thirty instances of *hitpael* verbs beginning with one of these sibilants in the Bible, so at this point a few examples will suffice to demonstrate the point. From the root שׁמר, we expect הִתְשַׁמֵּר in the *hitpael*, but in fact what we see is הִשְׁתַּמֵּר, still recognizable if this change is kept in mind, and the word still has an extra ת. When צ is the first root consonant, not only does it switch places with the ת, but the "emphatic" nature of צ affects the ת, so that the ת also becomes "emphatic"; that is, it becomes ט (see lesson 5.2 for צ as an emphatic consonant and lesson 3.6 for ט), as in הִצְטַדֵּק from the root צדק.

24.2.3. Another mark of the *hitpael* is the doubled middle root consonant. This doubling tips us off that the *hitpael* was originally the reflexive/reciprocal stem of the *piel*, but by the time we get to BH it has become the all-purpose reflexive/recip-rocal stem.[2] A root that is II-G or has ר in the second position will exhibit either compensatory lengthening of the preceding vowel, as in הִתְבָּרֵךְ 'to bless oneself, receive blessing (for oneself)', or virtual doubling, as in הִתְנַחֵם 'to comfort oneself, be comforted'.

24.2.4. Sometimes the final vowel is *patakh* instead of *tsere*, as with the *piel*: הִתְחַזֵּק is also written הִתְחַזַּק.

24.2.5. It should be noted that Skin-'em-Levi consonants (see note 2 of lesson 15), like ל in this paradigm, retain the doubling *dagesh*, even when followed by vocal *shwa*.

24.3. THE ART OF PARSING

Parsing is the process of explaining the form of a verb completely, and it is tradi-tionally done in a fixed list of categories: stem, verb form, person, number, gender, root, plus any extra prefixes or suffixes that occur. Although it is not necessary to the process, it is also helpful to remember the basic meaning of the root and to figure out the meaning of the verb in question after the parsing has been com-pleted. A few examples follow.

word	stem	form	person, gender, number	root	prefix/ suffix	word meaning
נָשָׂאתִי	*qal*	suff. conj.	1cs	נשׂא		I carried.
וַיְדַבֵּר	*piel*	cons. pret.	3ms	דבר		(And) he spoke.

---

2. Except for a few rare "*t*-forms" that seem to relate to *qal* and one frozen verb form to be taken up in a later lesson.

לְהַשְׁמִיד	*hiphil*	inf. cs.		שמד	prep. לְ	to destroy
אֶשְׁלָחֲךָ	*qal*	pref. conj.	1cs	שלח	2ms obj. sf.	I will send you (m).
מַשְׁמִידִים	*hiphil*	ptcp.	mp	שמד		destroyers (m)
כְּתֹב	*qal* *qal*	impv. inf. cs.	ms	כתב כתב		Write! to write[3]

24.3.1. The וַ of the consecutive preterite (and the וְ of the *və-qatal* form) are not considered extra prefixes because they are included in the definition of consecutive preterite and *və-qatal*.

24.3.2. Similarly, the תִי of נָשָׂאתִי is not an extra suffix because it is part of the definition of the suffix conjugation 1cs.

24.3.3. Since infinitives have no person, number, or gender, those boxes are left blank. Similarly, participles have gender and number but do not have person, so that element is omitted when parsing a participle.

24.3.4. Finally, all imperatives are second person, so filling in the person box is redundant for imperatives.

24.4. VOCABULARY FOR LESSON 24

verbs

הִתְהַלֵּךְ	'to walk around, walk back and forth' (*hitpael* of הלך); pref. conj. יִתְהַלֵּךְ
הִתְחַזֵּק	'to strengthen oneself, gather power to oneself' (*hitpael* of חזק); pref. conj. יִתְחַזֵּק
הִתְנַבֵּא	'to prophesy' (*hitpael* of נבא; see נִבָּא below; the two forms seem to be interchangeable); pref. conj. יִתְנַבֵּא
הִתְפַּלֵּל	'to pray, to intercede' (for oneself or for others) (*hitpael* of פלל; see תְּפִלָּה below); pref. conj. יִתְפַּלֵּל
הִתְקַדֵּשׁ	'to sanctify/consecrate oneself (ritually)' (*hitpael* of קדש; see קָדֵשׁ and קָדוֹשׁ below); pref. conj., only 3mp attested: יִתְקַדְּשׁוּ

---

3. כְּתֹב could be either an imperative or an infinitive construct; the correct choice would depend on the context.

נָבָא   'to prophesy' (*niphal* of נבא; see הִתְנַבֵּא above; the two forms seem to be interchangeable); pref. conj. יִנָּבֵא

קִדֵּשׁ   'to sanctify, make holy, consecrate, celebrate as holy' (*piel* of קדשׁ; see הִתְקַדֵּשׁ above and קָדוֹשׁ below); pref. conj. יְקַדֵּשׁ

nouns

חֵן   'grace, favor'; with sf. חִנִּי; note the idiom: X מָצָא חֵן בְּעֵינֵי (literally, 'to find favor in the eyes of X'; idiomatically, 'if I have found favor in your eyes' means 'if I am acceptable to you' or even 'if you have come to like me/approve of me/trust me/care about me'

חֶסֶד   'loyalty, faithfulness'; with sf. חַסְדִּי; often used of both Yahweh and human beings in a covenant context; implies obligation on both sides of a covenant, treaty, agreement

שַׁבָּת   'Sabbath' (fem.); from a root that means 'to cease'

תְּפִלָּה   'prayer'; cs. תְּפִלַּת; with sf. תְּפִלָּתִי (see הִתְפַּלֵּל above)

adjective

קָדוֹשׁ   'holy' (*qamets* reduces in fs, mp, and fp)

adverbs

אַיֵּה   'where?'

אֵיפֹה   'where?'

conjunctions

לָכֵן   'therefore'

עַל־כֵּן   'therefore'

24.5. EXERCISES FOR LESSON 24

A. Translate from Hebrew to English:

1.   וַיִּתְחַזֵּק שְׁלֹמֹה בֶן־דָּוִד עַל־הָאָרֶץ וַיהוָה אֱלֹהָיו עִמּוֹ:

2.   וַיִּתְקַדְּשׁוּ הַכֹּהֲנִים לְלַמֵּד אֶת־הָעָם לִשְׁמֹר אֶת־מִצְוֹת יְהוָה אֱלֹהֵיהֶם:

3.   וַיַּעַבְרוּ אַבְרָהָם וּבְנוֹ עַד־הֶהָרִים וַיְבַקַּע[4] אַבְרָהָם שָׁם עֲצֵי[5] עֹלָה:

4.   אֵיפֹה נִקְבְּרָה שָׂרָה:

---

4. 'And he chopped up'.
5. The plural עֵצִים generally means 'pieces of wood, sticks'.

5. ‏וַיְסַפְּרוּ לְשַׂר הַצָּבָא וַיֹּאמְרוּ אֵלָיו הָלַכְנוּ אֶל־הָעִיר הַקְּדוֹשָׁה אֲשֶׁר שְׁלַחְתָּנוּ
‏אֵלֶיהָ וְלֹא מָצָאנוּ אֶת־הַכֶּסֶף וְאֶת־הַזָּהָב:

6. ‏וַיִּשְׁמְעוּ אֶת־קוֹל יְהוָה אֱלֹהִים מִתְהַלֵּךְ בַּגָּן⁶ לְרוּחַ הַיּוֹם⁷ וַיִּתְחַבֵּא⁸ הָאָדָם וְאִשְׁתּוֹ
‏מִפְּנֵי⁹ יְהוָה אֱלֹהִים בְּתוֹךְ עֵץ¹⁰ הַגָּן: (Gen 3:8)

7. ‏וַיְדַבֵּר מֶלֶךְ יִשְׂרָאֵל אֶל־מֶלֶךְ יְהוּדָה וַיֹּאמֶר אֵלָיו יֵשׁ אִישׁ אֶחָד מְבַקֵּשׁ¹¹ אֶת־יְהוָה
‏וְלֹא יִתְנַבֵּא עָלַי טוֹב כִּי אִם¹² רָע¹³: (adapted from 1 Kgs 22:8)

8. ‏אִם מָצָאתִי חֵן בְּעֵינֶיךָ תִּתְפַּלֵּל־נָא¹⁴ בַּעֲדִי¹⁵ וְתִשְׁמְרֵנִי תְּפַלֵּתְךָ מֵאֹיְבָי:

Note that ‏וְתִשְׁמְרֵנִי in number 8 is not consecutive preterite but rather simply ‏ו 'and'
plus the prefix conjugation (plus suffix). In standard BH, a verb that needs to express
both 'and' and future tense would be written as a *və-qatal* form, so ‏ו plus prefix conjugation must be something other than that. In fact, simple ‏ו plus prefix conjugation
often means something like 'so that', and that is the translation you should use here.

---

9. ‏יֵשׁ בְּרִית בֵּינֵינוּ וּבֵין עַמֶּךָ לָכֵן אַל־תְּגָרְשֵׁינוּ¹⁶ מֵאַרְצֶךָ וְנַעֲבֹד אֹתְךָ בְּחֶסֶד:

10. ‏זָכוֹר¹⁷ אֶת־יוֹם הַשַּׁבָּת לְקַדְּשׁוֹ: (Exod 20:8)

---

6. 'In the garden'; ‏גַּן = 'garden'.

7. In ‏לְרוּחַ הַיּוֹם, ‏לְ = 'at', and the whole phrase describes a time of day.

8. 'And they hid themselves' (note the reflexive *hitpael*).

9. 'From'.

10. ‏עֵץ is being used as a collective here: 'trees, forest'.

11. I.e., by means of divination.

12. ‏כִּי אִם = 'but rather'.

13. The long vowel appears because the word is "in pause."

14. As sometimes happens, the prefix conjugation here is being used as the equivalent of the imperative. Note the ‏נָא־ at the end. This verb could also be translated as an *indirect* imperative, 'May you…', but this is somewhat awkward in English.

15. 'For me, on my behalf'.

16. The verb means 'to banish, send away'.

17. We learned in lesson 17 that an infinitive absolute can substitute for any other verb form; here it is substituting for an imperative.

11. וַיִּפְשַׁט[18] שָׁאוּל אֶת־בְּגָדָיו[19] וַיִּתְנַבֵּא גַם־הוּא לִפְנֵי שְׁמוּאֵל וַיִּפֹּל[20] עָרֹם[21] כָּל־הַיּוֹם הַהוּא וְכָל־הַלָּיְלָה[22] עַל־כֵּן יֹאמְרוּ הֲגַם שָׁאוּל בַּנְּבִיאִים:

(adapted from 1 Sam 19:24)

B. Parse all the verbs in exercises A2, 3, 5, 7, 9, and 10, above.

C. Practice reading Gen 22:7–9 from *BHS*, taking care to follow the syntax dictated by the accent marks that you have learned so far.

---

18. 'He stripped off'.
19. 'His clothes'.
20. 'And he fell down'.
21. 'Naked'.
22. The usual spelling of this word is לַיְלָה, with *patakh* in the first syllable; it is spelled with *qamets* here because the word is written over the *atnakh* and is "in pause" (see note 5 in lesson 23).

THIRD-WEAK VERBS

25.1. THIRD-WEAK VERBS GENERALLY

Up to this point, all the verbs we have examined through all the stems have been "strong" verbs, that is, verbs with three obvious root consonants. Our next assignment is to learn the "weak" verbs. Weak verbs are verbs that have lost one of their three root consonants, almost always because historically that consonant was a ו or a י, which tend to be lost in certain positions in the verb paradigms. Some of the most common verbs in BH are weak verbs. Our task for the last few lessons will be to parse these verbs, that is, to figure out the root, stem, and form that is before us. We will begin with verbs whose *third* root consonant was originally ו or י, because among the weak verbs they are the easiest to identify. These verbs are called third-weak verbs (III-weak).[1]

25.2. FORM OF THE THIRD-WEAK VERB IN THE *QAL*, *NIPHAL*, *HIPHIL*, AND *PIEL*

We will see that the III-weak verbs differ from the strong verb in predictable ways that span all the stems. Therefore, we will examine the *qal*, *niphal*, *hiphil*, and *piel* of the III-weak verbs all at the same time, pointing out the differences that are particular to III-weak verbs.[2] The paradigm root we will use is גָּלָה. We will begin with the *qal* paradigm of גָּלָה 'to uncover; to remove' (with the specialized meaning 'to go into exile').

---

1. Also called third-ה verbs (III-*he*, III-ה) or *lamed*-ה (*lamed-he*, ל״ה, where ״ is the symbol in Hebrew that indicates the unit is an abbreviation; for the use of ל to indicate the third root letter, see the explanation in lesson 19.2, above), because the 3ms in the suffix conjugation and prefix conjugation ends in ה.

2. The *hitpael* is excluded here because it is easily reconstructed from the *piel*, with the addition of the various prefixes: -הָת, -יָת, -מָת, and so on.

THE *QAL* FORMS OF THE THIRD-WEAK VERBS

inf. cs.	suff. conj.	cons. pret.	volitives		pref. conj.
גְּלוֹת	גָּלִיתִי	וָאֶגֶל/וָאֶגְלֶה	אֶגְלֶה	cohort.	אֶגְלֶה
	גָּלִיתָ	וַתִּגֶל	גְּלֵה	impv.	תִּגְלֶה
inf. abs.	גָּלִית	וַתִּגְלִי	גְּלִי	impv.	תִּגְלִי
גָּלֹה	גָּלָה	וַיִּגֶל	יְגֶל	juss.	יִגְלֶה
	גָּלְתָה	...	תִּגֶל	juss.	תִּגְלֶה
ptcp.	גָּלִינוּ		נִגְלֶה	cohort.	נִגְלֶה
גֹּלֶה	גְּלִיתֶם		גְּלוּ	impv.	תִּגְלוּ
גֹּלָה	גְּלִיתֶן		גְּלֶינָה	impv.	תִּגְלֶינָה
גֹּלִים	גָּלוּ		יִגְלוּ	juss.	יִגְלוּ
גֹּלוֹת			תִּגְלֶינָה	juss.	תִּגְלֶינָה
גָּלוּי passive					

Notes to the paradigm:

25.2.1. Five of the forms in the prefix conjugation column end in ◌ֶה. The ה here is a *mater lectionis* and not a root letter. The *seghol* is the result of the loss of the third root consonant, *yod* or *vav*.

25.2.2. The 2fs, 2mp, and 3mp in the prefix conjugation are exactly the same as those forms in the strong verb, except that the third root consonant is simply missing.

25.2.3. The 2fp and 3fp prefix conjugation begin and end exactly the same way as the strong verb. The "weakness" occurs precisely between the second root consonant and the ending, that is, where the third root consonant would have been.

25.2.4. With the exception of the ms, the imperative forms follow the usual pattern: simply remove the preformative of the second-person forms. Note that the ms imperative is unusual, in that it ends in a *tsere* rather than a *seghol*.

25.2.5. There is no special form for the cohortative in III-weak verbs.

25.2.6. The jussive and consecutive preterite require more extensive comment and will be taken up below.

25.2.7. In the first and second persons, the suffix conjugation has a telltale *hireq gadol* as the vowel of the second syllable (and in some stems this alternates with *tsere-yod*). The usual suffix conjugation endings come immediately after this long vowel.

25.2.8. The 3ms of the suffix conjugation starts out the same way as that of the strong verb, but after the second root letter, there is only a vowel plus ה *mater* where the third root consonant would have been. The *patakh* of the strong verb is compensatorily lengthened to *qamets*.

25.2.9. The 3fs of the suffix conjugation in all stems and roots originally ended in ת-, and that feminine ת reappears in the suffix conjugation 3fs of the III-weak verbs. What is unusual is that the ordinary ה ָ - ending of the suffix conjugation 3fs is *also* present in this form, so that the 3fs suffix conjugation of III-weak verbs is *doubly* feminine: we see the usual feminine ending after the older feminine ending. Note that a root that ends in ת as an actual root letter would look exactly the same in the suffix conjugation 3fs: גָּלְתָה can be from a root גָּלָה or from a root גָּלַת. (Since III-weak roots are much more common than III-ת roots, III-weak should be the first choice.)

25.2.10. The infinitive construct of III-weak verbs is generally easy to spot, since it ends in וֹת-. The only possible confusion is with the feminine plural ending on nouns and adjectives, but context will usually make clear whether the word is a noun or adjective, on the one hand, or a verb, on the other.

25.2.11. The infinitive absolute is rare, but when it occurs, it is exactly the same as that of the strong verb, except that the final root letter is missing, and the word ends in a ה *mater lectionis*.

25.2.12. The participles of III-weak verbs begin the same way as their strong verb counterparts. Except for the ms, the endings are also familiar; there is simply a third root consonant missing. The ms participle of III-weak verbs ends in ה ֶ - consistently throughout the stems.

25.2.13. The *qal* passive participle of III-weak verbs has been included because it is not easy to predict.

25.3. SIMILARITY OF THE MOST COMMON FORMS OF THE THIRD-WEAK VERBS

The paradigms for the *qal*, *niphal*, *hiphil*, and *piel* of גלה are gathered together in the next two pages, so that they can be compared. It will become clear how similar the III-weak verbs are from stem to stem. The endings (plus the middle consonant ל) are presented in color in appendix H, so that the similarities will be obvious as one compares, for instance, the prefix conjugation in each of the four stems (*qal*, *niphal*, *hiphil*, and *piel*). Furthermore, when the derived stem paradigms are studied closely in conjunction with the *qal* paradigm, it will also be clear that almost all of the notes included after the *qal* paradigm are equally applicable to these other paradigms.

THE *QAL* FORMS OF THE THIRD-WEAK VERBS

inf. cs.	suff. conj.	cons. pret.	volitives		pref. conj.
גְּלוֹת	גָּלִיתִי	וָאֶגֶל/וָאֶגְלֶה	אֶגְלֶה	cohort.	אֶגְלֶה
	גָּלִיתָ	וַתִּגֶל	גְּלֵה	impv.	תִּגְלֶה
inf. abs.	גָּלִית	וַתִּגְלִי	גְּלִי	impv.	תִּגְלִי
גָּלֹה	גָּלָה	וַיִּגֶל	יִגֶל	juss.	יִגְלֶה
	גָּלְתָה	...	תִּגֶל	juss.	תִּגְלֶה
ptcp.	גָּלִינוּ		נִגְלֶה	cohort.	נִגְלֶה
גֹּלֶה	גְּלִיתֶם		גְּלוּ	impv.	תִּגְלוּ
גֹּלָה	גְּלִיתֶן		גְּלֶינָה	impv.	תִּגְלֶינָה
גֹּלִים	גָּלוּ		יִגְלוּ	juss.	יִגְלוּ
גֹּלוֹת			תִּגְלֶינָה	juss.	תִּגְלֶינָה

THE *NIPHAL* FORMS OF THE THIRD-WEAK VERBS

inf. cs.	suff. conj.	cons. pret.	volitives		pref. conj.
הִגָּלוֹת	נִגְלֵיתִי	וָאֶגָּל	אֶגָּלֶה	cohort.	אֶגָּלֶה
	נִגְלֵיתָ	וַתִּגָּל	הִגָּלֶה	impv.	תִּגָּלֶה
inf. abs.	נִגְלֵית	וַתִּגָּלִי	הִגָּלִי	impv.	תִּגָּלִי
נִגְלֹה	נִגְלָה	וַיִּגָּל	יִגָּל	juss.	יִגָּלֶה
	נִגְלְתָה	...	תִּגָּל	juss.	תִּגָּלֶה
ptcp.	נִגְלֵינוּ		נִגָּלֶה	cohort.	נִגָּלֶה
נִגְלֶה	נִגְלֵיתֶם		הִגָּלוּ	impv.	תִּגָּלוּ
נִגְלָה	נִגְלֵיתֶן		הִגָּלֶינָה	impv.	תִּגָּלֶינָה
נִגְלִים	נִגְלוּ		יִגָּלוּ	juss.	יִגָּלוּ
נִגְלוֹת			תִּגָּלֶינָה	juss.	תִּגָּלֶינָה

THE *HIPHIL* FORMS OF THE THIRD-WEAK VERBS

inf. cs.	suff. conj.	cons. pret.	volitives		pref. conj.
הַגְלוֹת	הִגְלֵיתִי/הִגְלֵתִי	וָאַגְל/וָאַגְלֶה	אַגְלֶה	cohort.	אַגְלֶה
	הִגְלֵיתָ	וַתֶּגֶל	הַגְלֵה	impv.	תַּגְלֶה
inf. abs.	הִגְלֵית/הִגְלֵיתְ	וַתַּגְלִי	הַגְלִי	impv.	תַּגְלִי
הַגְלֵה	הִגְלָה	וַיֶּגֶל	יֶגֶל	juss.	יַגְלֶה
	הִגְלְתָה	...	תֶּגֶל	juss.	תַּגְלֶה
ptcp.	הִגְלֵינוּ		נַגְלֶה	cohort.	נַגְלֶה
מַגְלֶה	הִגְלִיתֶם		הַגְלוּ	impv.	תַּגְלוּ
מַגְלָה	הִגְלִיתֶן		הַגְלֶינָה	impv.	תַּגְלֶינָה
מַגְלִים	הִגְלוּ		יַגְלוּ	juss.	יַגְלוּ
מַגְלוֹת			תַּגְלֶינָה	juss.	תַּגְלֶינָה

THE *PIEL* FORMS OF THE THIRD-WEAK VERBS

inf. cs.	suff. conj.	cons. pret.	volitives		pref. conj.
גְּלוֹת	גִּלִּיתִי/גִּלֵּיתִי	וָאַגַל/וָאֲגַלֶּה	אֲגַלֶּה	cohort.	אֲגַלֶּה
	גִּלִּיתָ	וַתְּגַל	גַּלֵּה	impv.	תְּגַלֶּה
inf. abs.	גִּלִּית	וַתְּגַלִּי	גַּלִּי	impv.	תְּגַלִּי
גַּלֵּה/גַּלֹּה	גִּלָּה	וַיְגַל	יְגַל	juss.	יְגַלֶּה
	גִּלְּתָה	...	תְּגַל	juss.	תְּגַלֶּה
ptcp.	גִּלִּינוּ		נְגַלֶּה	cohort.	נְגַלֶּה
מְגַלֶּה	גִּלִּיתֶם		גַּלוּ	impv.	תְּגַלוּ
מְגַלָּה	גִּלִּיתֶן		גַּלֶּינָה	impv.	תְּגַלֶּינָה
מְגַלִּים	גִּלוּ		יְגַלוּ	juss.	יְגַלוּ
מְגַלּוֹת			תְּגַלֶּינָה	juss.	תְּגַלֶּינָה

25.4. JUSSIVE AND CONSECUTIVE PRETERITE FORMS OF THE THIRD-WEAK VERBS

The jussive, and therefore the consecutive preterite forms, deserve comment. We noted before (lesson 15.1) that in verbs where the jussive and prefix conjugation forms are different, the consecutive preterite reflects the jussive form rather than the prefix conjugation form. We have seen this in the *hiphil*: prefix conjugation יַשְׁמִיד, jussive יַשְׁמֵד, consecutive preterite וַיַּשְׁמֵד. The III-weak verbs are another example: *qal* prefix conjugation יִגְלֶה, jussive יִגֶל, consecutive preterite וַיִּגֶל. The jussive and consecutive preterite make the loss of the third root consonant obvious, since there is not even a vowel plus *mater* to mark it. These jussive/consecutive preterite forms are the norm for the five forms of the paradigm that end in ה ֶ-: in 1cs, 2ms, 3ms, 3fs, and 1cp. For the other five forms, the jussive and therefore consecutive preterite reflect the prefix conjugation form. The question for the beginning student is how to recognize that this consecutive preterite reflects a III-weak verb, as opposed to any other weak verb. The key is to observe the preformative.

The Use of Appendix D for Finding the Root of Consecutive Preterites

The chart of "Clues for Finding the Root of Consecutive Preterites" (appendix D) gives all the common possibilities for weak-verb consecutive preterites, sorted according to their preformatives. (The 3ms is used throughout, but the chart is helpful for any of the five prefix conjugation forms mentioned above.) We see in the first line of the chart that a weak consecutive preterite (i.e., one with a root letter missing) that begins with an *accented* יַ (like וַיִּגֶל) virtually always means that the verb is a *qal* consecutive preterite from a root that is III-weak. The second line of the chart shows another form of the III-weak consecutive preterite: sometimes the jussive is only one syllable, with a rare consonant cluster at the end, such as יֵשְׁתְּ 'may he drink' from שָׁתָה 'to drink', with consecutive preterite [3]וַיֵּשְׁתְּ '(and) he drank'. The third row of the chart shows a fairly rare form of the III-weak *qal* consecutive preterite, a consecutive preterite with accented יַ for the preformative, plus a second syllable, like וַיִּפֶן 'and he turned' from פָּנָה 'to turn'.

The *niphal* jussive (and therefore consecutive preterite) from the III-weak verbs is the prefix conjugation form without the ה ֶ- ending for the five forms that end in ה ֶ-, and simply the prefix conjugation form for the other five forms (2fs, 2mp, 2fp, 3mp, 3fp). (Refer to the charts above or to the color charts on pages 280–81 in appendix H.) For example, the *niphal* prefix conjugation 3ms of the root גלה is

---

3. Note that the יַ syllable here is *accented*, though it is not marked, since it is the final syllable in the word.

יִגְלֶה; the consecutive preterite is וַיִּגֶל. The *hiphil* consecutive preterite for the five forms with the הֶ - ending looks very much like the *qal* consecutive preterite of such forms, with one important difference: the accented preformative has a *seghol* instead of *hireq* or *tsere*: וַיֶּגֶל '(and) he took (someone) into exile'. (Again, refer to the charts.) The accented *seghol* in the preformative is a clear giveaway that the form is *hiphil*. The *piel* consecutive preterite in the five forms that end in הֶ - is, again, the prefix conjugation without the ending (יְגַלֶּה > יְגַל), but since words in BH cannot end in a doubled consonant, we lose the doubling as well, giving us יְגַל. This means that one of the sure marks of a *piel*, the doubled middle root letter, disappears. Note, however, that the *shwa* under the preformative is still there. The extant forms of the weak verb consecutive preterite will be noted in the vocabulary lists.

25.5. FORMS OF THE THIRD-WEAK VERB WITH FIRST OR SECOND GUTTURALS

When one of the root consonants of a III-weak verb is a guttural, the resulting forms look like a combination of strong verbs with guttural root letters and the endings for III-weak verbs. For instance, עָלָה means 'to go up', and מָחָה means 'to wipe out'. What follows are the *qal*, *niphal*, and *hiphil* paradigms of עָלָה and the *qal* paradigm of מָחָה.

THE *QAL* FORMS OF THE THIRD-WEAK VERBS WITH FIRST-GUTTURAL

inf. cs.	suff. conj.	cons. pret.	volitives		pref. conj.
עֲלוֹת	עָלִיתִי	וָאֶעֱלֶה/וָאֹעַל	אֶעֱלֶה	cohort.	אֶעֱלֶה
	עָלִיתָ	וַתַּעַל	עֲלֵה	impv.	תַּעֲלֶה
inf. abs.	עָלִית	וַתַּעֲלִי	עֲלִי	impv.	תַּעֲלִי
עָלֹה	עָלָה	וַיַּעַל	יַעַל	juss.	יַעֲלֶה
	עָלְתָה	…	תַּעַל	juss.	תַּעֲלֶה
ptcp.	עָלִינוּ		נַעֲלֶה	cohort.	נַעֲלֶה
עֹלֶה	עֲלִיתֶם		עֲלוּ	impv.	תַּעֲלוּ
עֹלָה	עֲלִיתֶן		עֲלֶינָה	impv.	תַּעֲלֶינָה
עֹלִים	עָלוּ		יַעֲלוּ	juss.	יַעֲלוּ
עֹלוֹת			תַּעֲלֶינָה	juss.	תַּעֲלֶינָה
passive עָלוּי					

THE *NIPHAL* FORMS OF THE THIRD-WEAK VERBS WITH FIRST-GUTTURAL

inf. cs.	suff. conj.	cons. pret.	volitives		pref. conj.
הֵעָלוֹת	נַעֲלֵיתִי		אֵעָלֶה	cohort.	אֵעָלֶה
	נַעֲלֵיתָ	וַתֵּעָל	הֵעָלֵה	impv.	תֵּעָלֶה
inf. abs.	נַעֲלֵית	וַתֵּעָלִי	הֵעָלִי	impv.	תֵּעָלִי
נַעֲלֹה	נַעֲלָה	וַיֵּעָל	יֵעָל	juss.	יֵעָלֶה
	נֶעֶלְתָה	…	תֵּעָל	juss.	תֵּעָלֶה
ptcp.	נַעֲלֵינוּ		נֵעָלֶה	cohort.	נֵעָלֶה
נַעֲלֶה	נַעֲלֵיתֶם		הֵעָלוּ	impv.	תֵּעָלוּ
נַעֲלָה	נַעֲלֵיתֶן		הֵעָלֶינָה	impv.	תֵּעָלֶינָה
נַעֲלִים	נַעֲלוּ		יֵעָלוּ	juss.	יֵעָלוּ
נַעֲלוֹת			תֵּעָלֶינָה	juss.	תֵּעָלֶינָה

THE *HIPHIL* FORMS OF THE THIRD-WEAK VERBS WITH FIRST-GUTTURAL

inf. cs.	suff. conj.	cons. pret.	volitives		pref. conj.
הַעֲלוֹת	הֶעֱלֵיתִי	וָאַֽעַל/וָאַעֲלֶה	אַעֲלֶה	cohort.	אַעֲלֶה
	הֶעֱלֵיתָ	וַתַּֽעַל	הַעֲלֵה	impv.	תַּעֲלֶה
inf. abs.	הֶעֱלֵית	וַתַּעֲלִי	הַעֲלִי	impv.	תַּעֲלִי
הַעֲלֵה	הֶעֱלָה	וַיַּֽעַל	יַֽעַל	juss.	יַעֲלֶה
	הֶעֶלְתָה	...	תַּֽעַל	juss.	תַּעֲלֶה
ptcp.	הֶעֱלִינוּ		נַעֲלֶה	cohort.	נַעֲלֶה
מַעֲלֶה	הֶעֱלִיתֶם		הַעֲלוּ	impv.	תַּעֲלוּ
מַעֲלָה	הֶעֱלִיתֶן		הַעֲלֶֽינָה	impv.	תַּעֲלֶֽינָה
מַעֲלִים	הֶעֱלוּ		יַעֲלוּ	juss.	יַעֲלוּ
מַעֲלוֹת			תַּעֲלֶֽינָה	juss.	תַּעֲלֶֽינָה
hophal הָעֳלָה					

THE *QAL* FORMS OF THE THIRD-WEAK VERBS WITH SECOND-GUTTURAL

inf. cs.	suff. conj.	cons. pret.	volitives		pref. conj.
מְחוֹת	מָחִיתִי	וָאֶֽמַח/וָאֶמְחֶה	אֶמְחֶה	cohort.	אֶמְחֶה
	מָחִיתָ	וַתִּֽמַח	מְחֵה	impv.	תִּמְחֶה
inf. abs.	מָחִית	וַתִּמְחִי	מְחִי	impv.	תִּמְחִי
מָחֹה	מָחֲתָה	וַיִּֽמַח	יִֽמַח	juss.	יִמְחֶה
	מָחֲתָה	...	תִּֽמַח	juss.	תִּמְחֶה
ptcp.	מָחִינוּ		נִמְחֶה	cohort.	נִמְחֶה
מֹחֶה	מְחִיתֶם		מְחוּ	impv.	תִּמְחוּ
מֹחָה	מְחִיתֶן		מְחֶֽינָה	impv.	תִּמְחֶֽינָה
מֹחִים	מָחוּ		יִמְחוּ	juss.	יִמְחוּ
מֹחוֹת			תִּמְחֶֽינָה	juss.	תִּמְחֶֽינָה
passive מָחוּי					

Notes to the paradigms:

25.5.1. The *qal* and *hiphil* of first-guttural verbs are exactly the same in a number of forms, including the prefix conjugation and consecutive preterite.

25.5.2. Jussives and consecutive preterites like יֵמַח and וַיִּמַח have *patakh*s in the final syllable because of the guttural.

25.5.3. In the suffix conjugation, the first-guttural and third-weak verbs show two different paradigms. We have used the one for עלה because it is such a common verb, but other verbs of the same type show *seghol* then *hateph-seghol* at the beginning, such as נֶחֱלֵתִי from חלה 'to be sick'.

25.5.4. The *hophal* form (found in the lower left corner of the *hiphil* paradigm above) is unusual because it has a *holem* rather than the short-o *qamets* that we would expect in the first syllable.

25.6. UNUSUAL DEVIATIONS FROM THE FORM OF THIRD-WEAK VERBS

There are a few very common III-weak *qal* consecutive preterites that are different from the paradigms above, specifically:

וַיַּרְא '(and) he saw', from רָאָה 'to see' (only the 3ms follows this form; other extant forms are וָאֵרֶא and וַתֵּרֶא)

וַיְהִי '(and) he/it was', from הָיָה 'to be'; jussive יְהִי, תְּהִי

וַיְחִי '(and) he lived', from חָיָה 'to live'; jussive יְחִי; easily confused with הָיָה above

25.7. VOCABULARY FOR LESSON 25

verbs

בָּנָה   'to build, rebuild'; pref. conj. יִבְנֶה; cons. pret. וַיִּבֶן

       niphal נִבְנָה, יִבָּנֶה 'to be built, rebuilt'

גָּלָה   'to uncover; remove, depart; go into exile'; pref. conj. יִגְלֶה; cons. pret. וַיִּגֶל; 'to uncover the ears of someone' = to reveal to someone

       niphal נִגְלָה 'to be uncovered' ; pref. conj. יִגָּלֶה

       hiphil הִגְלָה 'to carry into exile'; pref. conj. יַגְלֶה; cons. pret. וַיֶּגֶל

       piel גִּלָּה 'to uncover, expose, disclose'; pref. conj. יְגַלֶּה; cons. pret. וַיְגַל

הָיָה   'to be, become'; pref. conj. יִהְיֶה; cons. pret. וַיְהִי; impv. הֱיֵה ; note הָיָה + לְ = 'to become'

       niphal נִהְיָה 'to occur, come to pass, become; be done, finished'

הִשְׁקָה   'to give someone something to drink, to water (animals)' (*hiphil* of שׁקה); pref. conj. יַשְׁקֶה; cons. pret. וַיַּשְׁקְ; see שָׁתָה below

חָיָה   'to live'; pref. conj. יִחְיֶה; cons. pret. וַיְחִי; impv. חֲיֵה

     hiphil הֶחֱיָה 'to preserve alive, let live; to revive, restore'

     piel חִיָּה, 'to preserve alive, let live; to revive, restore'; pref. conj. יְחַיֶּה

חָנָה   'to encamp'; pref. conj. יַחֲנֶה; cons. pret. וַיִּחַן

מָחָה   'to wipe out, blot out, obliterate, exterminate'; pref. conj. יִמְחֶה; cons. pret. וַיִּמַח

עָלָה   'to go up'; pref. conj. יַעֲלֶה; cons. pret. וַיַּעַל

     niphal נַעֲלָה, 'to be brought up, taken up, away'; pref. conj. יֵעָלֶה

     hiphil הֶעֱלָה, 'to bring up, send up, take away; to offer (a sacrifice)'; pref. conj. יַעֲלֶה; cons. pret. וַיַּעַל

עָנָה   'to answer, reply, respond, be responsive'; pref. conj. יַעֲנֶה; cons. pret. וַיַּעַן

עָשָׂה   'to do, make; prepare'; pref. conj. יַעֲשֶׂה; cons. pret. וַיַּעַשׂ

     niphal נַעֲשָׂה, 'to be done, be made'; pref. conj. יֵעָשֶׂה

צִוָּה[4]   'to command, order, appoint, commission' (*piel* of צוה); pref. conj. יְצַוֶּה; cons. pret. וַיְצַו

רָאָה   'to see, look at, perceive, consider'; pref. conj. יִרְאֶה; cons. pret. וַיַּרְא; וָאֵרֶא ;וַתֵּרֶא

     niphal נִרְאָה, 'to appear; to be seen, to be visible'; pref. conj. יֵרָאֶה; cons. pret. וַיֵּרָא

     hiphil הֶרְאָה, 'to show, to cause to see; to allow to see'; pref. conj. יַרְאֶה; cons. pret. וַיַּרְא

רָבָה   'to multiply, be(come) many, be(come) great'; pref. conj. יִרְבֶּה; cons. pret. וַתֵּרֶב ;וַיִּרֶב

     hiphil הִרְבָּה, 'to do something a lot, greatly; to make great'; pref. conj. יַרְבֶּה; cons. pret. וַיֶּרֶב; inf. abs. הַרְבֵּה is very common as an adverb or adjective: 'greatly, much; many'

שָׁתָה   'to drink'; pref. conj. יִשְׁתֶּה; cons. pret. וַיֵּשְׁתְּ

     hiphil is from another root, שׁקה: see הִשְׁקָה above

---

4. Note that the medial ו in this verb is actually a consonant.

proper noun

יוֹסֵף   personal name, 'Joseph'

25.8. EXERCISES FOR LESSON 25

A. Translate from Hebrew to English:

1. ‏וַיַּרְא הַשֹּׁפֵט אֶת־אִישׁ אֱלֹהִים וַיַּעַשׂ לוֹ לֶחֶם:

2. ‏וַיַּרְא אֵלֶיהָ מַלְאַךְ יְהוָה וַיֹּאמֶר אֵלֶיהָ אַיֵּה הָלָכְתְּ וַתַּעַן וַתֹּאמַר⁵ חָנִיתִי בִּשְׂדֵה אָבִי:

3. ‏וַיֶּגֶל הַצָּבָא אֶת־הָעָם וְלֹא נַעֲלָה הָעָם עוֹד מִמִּצְרָיִם:

4. ‏וַיִּשְׁלַח מֹשֶׁה אֶת־כֹּהֲנֵי בְנֵי יִשְׂרָאֵל וַיַּעֲלוּ עֹלוֹת לַיהוָה:

5. ‏וַיְצַו מֹשֶׁה אֶת־בְּנֵי יִשְׂרָאֵל וְכֵן עָשׂוּ:

6. ‏וַיַּשְׁקְ הַנַּעַר אֶת־הַצֹּאן וַיֵּשְׁתְּ הַצֹּאן מַיִם הַרְבֵּה מְאֹד:

7. ‏אִם מָצָאתִי חֵן בְּעֵינֶיךָ הַחֲיֵה אֶת־נַפְשִׁי:

8. ‏וַיֹּאמֶר אֲלֵהֶם יוֹסֵף בַּיּוֹם הַשְּׁלִישִׁי זֹאת עֲשׂוּ וִחְיוּ: (part of Gen 42:18)

9. ‏מָה הָרָעָה הַזֹּאת אֲשֶׁר נִהְיְתָה בָּכֶם: (taken from Judg 20:12)

10. ‏הֲיָדַעְתָּ כִּי תֵעָשֶׂה לִּי הָרָעָה הַזֹּאת וְלֹא גָּלִיתָ אֶת־אָזְנִי:

11. ‏וַיְגַל יְהוָה אֶת־עֵינֵי בִלְעָם⁶ וַיַּרְא בִלְעָם אֶת־מַלְאַךְ יְהוָה: (part of Num 22:31)

12. ‏וְהָיָה כִּי יִרְאוּ אֹתָךְ הַמִּצְרִים⁷ וְאָמְרוּ אִשְׁתּוֹ זֹאת וְהָרְגוּ⁸ אֹתִי וְאֹתָךְ יְחַיּוּ:

(Gen 12:12)

13. ‏וַיֹּאמֶר יְהוָה אֶל־אַבְרָם לֶךְ־לְךָ⁹ מֵאַרְצְךָ אֶל־הָאָרֶץ אֲשֶׁר אַרְאֶךָ:

(part of Gen 12:1)

---

5. It is often the case that there is a distinction in the biblical text between וַיֹּאמֶר and וַתֹּאמֶר, on the one hand, and וַתֹּאמַר and וַיֹּאמַר, on the other, so that וַתֹּאמַר or וַיֹּאמַר indicates that what follows is a direct quote. That distinction in meaning, however, is not made consistently.

6. A personal name, Balaam.

7. 'The Egyptians'.

8. 'They will kill'.

9. 'Go' (imperative).

14. וַיִּבֶן שָׁם מִזְבֵּחַ לַיהוָה וַיֹּאמֶר אֵלָיו יְהוָֹה פְּרוּ [10] וּרְבוּ עַל־פְּנֵי הָאֲדָמָה:

15. וַיַּעַל אַבְרָם מִמִּצְרַיִם הוּא וְאִשְׁתּוֹ וְכָל־אֲשֶׁר־לוֹ: (part of Gen 13:1)

16. וַיֹּאמֶר יְהוָֹה אֶמְחֶה אֶת־הָאָדָם אֲשֶׁר בָּרָאתִי [11] מֵעַל פְּנֵי הָאֲדָמָה ... כִּי נִחַמְתִּי [12] כִּי עֲשִׂיתִם: (part of Gen 6:7)

17. וְהָיָה כְּהִבָּנוֹת בֵּית יְהוָֹה וְנִגְלְתָה רוּחַ אֱלֹהֵינוּ:

18. וִהְיִיתֶם לִי לְעָם וְאָנֹכִי אֶהְיֶה לָכֶם לֵאלֹהִים: (Jer 30:22)

B. Parse all the verbs in exercises A7 and 17, above.

C. Go through Gen 22:1–19 and identify every verb that you think is III-weak.

---

10. 'Be fruitful' (imperative).
11. 'I created'.
12. 'I regret, I am sorry'.

First-*Nun* Verbs and לָקַח; the Verb הִשְׁתַּחֲוָה

26.1. First-*nun* verbs generally

First-נ verbs (I-נ, also referred to as פ"ן "pe-*nun*" verbs) are not weak verbs in the usual sense, that is, those that lost an original ו or י root letter, but in several places in the paradigms I-נ verbs *do* lose the נ, either because it assimilates or because it simply drops out. I-נ verbs are identified by the doubling of the first consonant after a preformative. Many *niphal* forms are identified in the same way, and in both cases it is because a נ has assimilated. We will focus below on distinguishing between *niphal* verbs and I- נ verbs.

26.2. Two types of first-*nun* verbs

In the *piel*, I-נ verbs are normal (there is no place in the *piel* paradigm where נ as the first root letter occurs directly before another consonant without an intervening vowel). In the *qal*, *niphal*, *hiphil*, and *hophal*, however, there are specific forms that predictably lose the נ. In the *qal*, furthermore, there are two categories of I-נ verbs: type 1—those that lose the נ only in those places where it assimilates to the next consonant; and type 2—those that have special forms of the *qal* infinitive construct and imperative, in addition to the regular cases of assimilation mentioned under type 1. We begin with type 1.

26.3. Type 1 first-*nun* verbs

We have seen before that there is a split within the *qal* verb between those that have *holem* in the prefix conjugation and those that have *patakh* or even *qamets* (in the case of the III-א verbs). So we have יִשְׁמֹר 'he will guard', with *holem*, versus יִשְׁמַע 'he will hear' and יִמְצָא 'he will find', with *patakh* and *qamets*, respectively. I-נ verbs exhibit this same split, and generally type 1 I-נ verbs are those that have *holem* in the prefix conjugation. The most frequently-occurring type 1 I-נ verb is נָפַל 'to fall', and it will be the paradigm verb for type 1.

THE *QAL* FORMS OF THE TYPE 1 FIRST-*NUN* VERBS

inf. cs.	suff. conj.	cons. pret.	volitives		pref. conj.
נְפֹל	נָפַלְתִּי	וָאֶפֹּל	אֶפְּלָה	cohort.	אֶפֹּל
	נָפַלְתָּ	וַתִּפֹּל	נְפֹל	impv.	תִּפֹּל
inf. abs.	נָפַלְתְּ	וַתִּפְּלִי	נִפְלִי	impv.	תִּפְּלִי
נָפוֹל	נָפַל	וַיִּפֹּל	יִפֹּל	juss.	יִפֹּל
	נָפְלָה	…	תִּפֹּל	juss.	תִּפֹּל
ptcp.	נָפַלְנוּ		נִפְלָה	cohort.	נִפֹּל
נֹפֵל	נְפַלְתֶּם		נִפְלוּ	impv.	תִּפְּלוּ
נֹפֶלֶת	נְפַלְתֶּן		נְפֹלְנָה	impv.	תִּפֹּלְנָה
נֹפְלִים	נָפְלוּ		יִפְּלוּ	juss.	יִפְּלוּ
נֹפְלוֹת			תִּפֹּלְנָה	juss.	תִּפֹּלְנָה

Notes to the paradigm:

26.3.1. In Type 1 I-נ verbs, the forms that are affected by the assimilation of the נ are the prefix conjugation, cohortative, jussive, and consecutive preterite. Note that there is no visible נ in any of these forms and that instead the second root letter appears with a doubling *dagesh*.

26.3.2. These I-נ verbs can be distinguished from *niphal* verbs in two ways: (1) by their vowel patterns—there is no typical *niphal hireq-qamets-tsere* ("i-ah-ay") in the prefix conjugation and the other forms dependent on it; and (2) unlike *niphal* verbs, the suffix conjugation, infinitive absolute, and participle of I-נ verbs do not begin with נ.

26.4. TYPE 2 FIRST-*NUN* VERBS

Type 2 I-נ verbs are typically those with *patakh* in the prefix conjugation.[1] We will use נָגַע 'to touch' to illustrate type 2. (Note that נָגַע is also III-G.)

---

1. The most common type 2, נָתַן, which will be discussed below, has *tsere* instead of *patakh*.

THE *QAL* FORMS OF THE TYPE 2 FIRST-*NUN* VERBS

inf. cs.	suff. conj.	cons. pret.	volitives		pref. conj.
גֶּ֫עַת	נָגַ֫עְתִּי	וָאֶגַּע	אֶגְּעָה	cohort.	אֶגַּע
	נָגַ֫עְתָּ	וַתִּגַּע	גַּע	impv.	תִּגַּע
inf. abs.	נָגַ֫עְתְּ	וַתִּגְּעִי	גְּעִי	impv.	תִּגְּעִי
נָגוֹעַ	נָגַע	וַיִּגַּע	יִגַּע	juss.	יִגַּע
	נָגְעָה	…	תִּגַּע	juss.	תִּגַּע
ptcp.	נָגַ֫עְנוּ		נִגְּעָה	cohort.	נִגַּע
נֹגֵעַ	נְגַעְתֶּם		גְּעוּ	impv.	תִּגְּעוּ
נֹגַ֫עַת	נְגַעְתֶּן		גַּ֫עְנָה	impv.	תִּגַּ֫עְנָה
נֹגְעִים	נָגְעוּ		יִגְּעוּ	juss.	יִגְּעוּ
נֹגְעוֹת			תִּגַּ֫עְנָה	juss.	תִּגַּ֫עְנָה

Notes to the paradigm:

26.4.1. The first difference one notices between this paradigm and the נָפַל paradigm above is, of course, the *patakh* in the place of *holem*.

26.4.2. The imperative, however, is something new. The imperative of the type 2 I-נ verbs loses the נ altogether. The only way to recognize this form as coming from a I-נ verb is to know that this is a possibility for two-consonant imperatives.

26.4.3. The only other unusual form in this paradigm is the infinitive construct. The infinitive construct of type 2 I-נ verbs loses the initial consonant of the root but adds a ת at the end, as if to compensate. The resulting form looks like a segholate noun and behaves like a segholate noun when pronominal suffixes are added to it. In the case of נֶגַע, the ע of the root attracts *patakh*s to itself, but in other roots we see *seghol*s, such as גֶּשֶׁת from the root נגשׁ. Again, the only way to recognize that this kind of infinitive construct can come from a I-נ verb is to know that such a form is typical of

> **The Preposition לְ Appended to Words Accented on the First Syllable**
>
> When the preposition לְ is added to any infinitive construct that has the shape of a segholate noun and is accented on the first syllable (like גֶּ֫שֶׁת above), the vowel of לְ becomes *qamets*: לָגֶ֫שֶׁת. In fact, לְ often becomes לָ when it is attached to a word that is accented on the first syllable.

I-נ verbs. Context will, of course, help to identify the word as a verb. Forms necessary for the classification of I-נ verbs will be given in the vocabulary lists.

26.5. THE *QAL* FORMS OF THE TYPE 2 FIRST-*NUN* VERB נָשָׂא

The common verb נָשָׂא 'to lift, carry' is a type 2 I-נ verb. Its forms are very much like the paradigm just above, with the following exceptions: (1) at the end of a word, the א quiesces, and the *patakh* lengthens to *qamets*; and (2) the infinitive construct is שְׂאֵת or שֵׂאת.

26.6. THE *QAL* FORMS OF THE TYPE 2 FIRST-*NUN* VERB נָטָה

The common verb נָטָה 'to stretch out, extend' is both I- and III-weak. Most of the paradigm is still straightforward, but such verbs nearly disappear in the consecutive preterite. For נָטָה, the 3ms consecutive preterite is וַיֵּט, and it should be learned as a word in itself so that it need not be analyzed every time it is encountered.

26.7. THE *QAL* FORMS OF THE TYPE 2 FIRST-*NUN* VERB נָתַן

The most common I-נ verb is נָתַן "to give." It has a slightly different paradigm because it has *tsere* rather than *holem* or *patakh* in the prefix conjugation. It is also different from other verbs because the *second* נ in the root *also* assimilates whenever possible. Its paradigm is given below.

THE *QAL* FORMS OF THE VERB נָתַן

inf. cs.	suff. conj.	cons. pret.	volitives		pref. conj.
תֵּת	נָתַ֫תִּי	וָאֶתֵּן	אֶתְּנָה	cohort.	אֶתֵּן
תִּתִּי	נָתַ֫תָּ	וַתִּתֵּן	תֵּן	impv.	תִּתֵּן
inf. abs.	נָתַתְּ	וַתִּתְּנִי	תְּנִי	impv.	תִּתְּנִי
נָתוֹן	נָתַן	וַיִּתֵּן	יִתֵּן	juss.	יִתֵּן
	נָתְנָה	…	תִּתֵּן	juss.	תִּתֵּן
ptcp.	נָתַ֫נּוּ		נִתְּנָה	cohort.	נִתֵּן
נֹתֵן	נְתַתֶּם		תְּנוּ	impv.	תִּתְּנוּ
נֹתֶ֫נֶת	נְתַתֶּן		תֵּ֫נָּה	impv.	תִּתֵּ֫נָּה
נְתֻנִים	נָתְנוּ		יִתְּנוּ	juss.	יִתְּנוּ
נְתֻנוֹת			תִּתֵּ֫נָּה	juss.	תִּתֵּ֫נָּה

Notes to the paradigm:

26.7.1. The doubling *dagesh* in the ת identifies the forms of the prefix conjugation as from a I-נ verb. The *tsere* between the ת and the ן is new.

26.7.2. Like other type 2 I-נ verbs, נָתַן loses the initial נ in the imperative and infinitive construct. The infinitive construct looks very little like נָתַן, but it is actually much the same as גֶּ֫עַת. גֶּ֫עַת started out as something like גֶּעְתְּ, and picked up the extra *patakh* to help in pronunciation. תֵּת, on the other hand, started out as something like תֶּנְתְּ, with the initial נ lost and a final ת added. Then the נ (which was the *second* נ of נָתַן) assimilated to the added ת, giving us תֵּתּ. But a doubled consonant at the end of a Hebrew word is very unusual, so the second ת lost the *dagesh*. (The *dagesh* remains when ת is "protected" by a pronominal suffix, as in תִּתִּי 'my giving'.)

26.7.3. We have just seen that the second נ of נָתַן assimilates to the following consonant whenever there is no vowel between the two consonants. That fact makes the suffix conjugation of נָתַן more difficult to recognize. In all of the first- and second-person suffix conjugation forms, the original second נ is evident only in the doubling of the ת or נ to which it has assimilated.

26.8. THE MIXING OF TYPE 1 AND TYPE 2 FORMS

It should be pointed out that the two types of I-נ verbs outlined above are rarely as separate as they may seem. There is a lot of mixing of types, so that besides גֶּ֫עַת, נָגַע also has an infinitive construct נְגֹעַ, a perfectly normal form. נָטַע 'to plant' has יִטַּע for the prefix conjugation, but the only imperative attested is נִטְעוּ, perfectly normal. It has an infinitive construct נְטֹעַ that occurs four times in the Bible and an infinitive construct טַ֫עַת that occurs once. The two types above, then, should be seen to point to possibilities rather than totally separate ways of dealing with I-נ verbs.

26.9. THE VERB לָקַח

The *qal* verb לָקַח 'to take' is normal only in the suffix conjugation, infinitive absolute, and participle. It behaves like a type 2 I-נ verb in the *qal* prefix conjugation, consecutive preterite, imperative, and infinitive construct. A partial paradigm of the extant forms follows:

THE *QAL* FORMS OF THE VERB לקח

inf. cs.	cons. pret.	volitives		pref. conj.
קַחַת, קַחְתִּי				אֶקַּח
	וָתִּקַּח	קַח	impv.	תִּקַּח
		קְחִי	impv.	תִּקְחִי
	וַיִּקַּח			יִקַּח
	וַתִּקַּח			תִּקַּח
				נִקַּח
		קְחוּ	impv.	תִּקְחוּ
				יִקְחוּ

26.10. THE *NIPHAL* FORMS OF THE FIRST-*NUN* VERBS

The *niphal* of I-נ verbs will be illustrated using the root נצב, which in the *niphal* means 'to stand, be stationed, station oneself'.

THE *NIPHAL* FORMS OF THE FIRST-*NUN* VERBS

inf. cs.	suff. conj.	cons. pret.	volitives		pref. conj.
הִנָּצֵב	נִצַּבְתִּי	וָאֶנָּצֵב	אֶנָּצְבָה	cohort.	אֶנָּצֵב
	נִצַּבְתָּ	וַתִּנָּצֵב	הִנָּצֵב	impv.	תִּנָּצֵב
inf. abs.	נִצַּבְתְּ	וַתִּנָּצְבִי	הִנָּצְבִי	impv.	תִּנָּצְבִי
נִצּוֹב	נִצַּב	וַיִּנָּצֵב	יִנָּצֵב	juss.	יִנָּצֵב
	נִצְּבָה	...	תִּנָּצֵב	juss.	תִּנָּצֵב
ptcp.	נִצַּבְנוּ		נִנָּצְבָה	cohort.	נִנָּצֵב
נִצָּב	נִצַּבְתֶּם		הִנָּצְבוּ	impv.	תִּנָּצְבוּ
נִצֶּבֶת/נִצָּבָה	נִצַּבְתֶּן		הִנָּצַבְנָה	impv.	תִּנָּצַבְנָה
נִצָּבִים	נִצְּבוּ		יִנָּצְבוּ	juss.	יִנָּצְבוּ
נִצָּבוֹת			תִּנָּצַבְנָה	juss.	תִּנָּצַבְנָה

Notes to the paradigm:

26.10.1. The prefix conjugation and the forms built on it are not a problem. The preformative is the clue that the form is prefix conjugation or prefix conjugation–like, and the three root letters are clear after the preformative, as is the typical *hireq-qamets-tsere* pattern.

26.10.2. The suffix conjugation, however, is ambiguous: a *piel* suffix conjugation from the root נצב would look exactly the same, with the exception of 3ms נִצֵּב instead of נִצַּב, and as we have seen, even that form could be a *piel* also. In such cases, context and a dictionary are needed in order to make a decision. The context will perhaps demand a *niphal* verb, or a dictionary may provide the information that the root exists only in the *niphal* or in the *piel*.

26.10.3. The infinitive absolute of the *niphal* varies so much (and is so rare) that there is no true model.

26.10.4. The participle here cannot be confused with any other I-נ participle. The telltale *qamets* that distinguishes the *niphal* participle from the *niphal* suffix conjugation is evident; besides, the *piel* participle begins with מְ.

26.11. THE *HIPHIL* FORMS OF THE FIRST-*NUN* VERBS

The *hiphil* paradigm of I-נ verbs will be illustrated with הִגִּיד 'to tell', a common *hiphil* verb.

THE *HIPHIL* AND *HOPHAL* FORMS OF THE FIRST-*NUN* VERBS

inf. cs.	suff. conj.	cons. pret.	volitives		pref. conj.
הַגִּיד	הִגַּדְתִּי	וָאַגִּיד	אַגִּידָה	cohort.	אַגִּיד
	הִגַּדְתָּ	וַתַּגֵּד	הַגֵּד	impv.	תַּגִּיד
inf. abs.	הִגַּדְתְּ	וַתַּגִּידִי	הַגִּידִי	impv.	תַּגִּידִי
הַגֵּד	הִגִּיד	וַיַּגֵּד	יַגֵּד	juss.	יַגִּיד
	הִגִּידָה	...	תַּגֵּד	juss.	תַּגִּיד
ptcp.	הִגַּדְנוּ		נַגִּידָה	cohort.	נַגִּיד
מַגִּיד	הִגַּדְתֶּם		הַגִּידוּ	impv.	תַּגִּידוּ
מַגִּידָה	הִגַּדְתֶּן		הַגֵּדְנָה	impv.	תַּגֵּדְנָה
מַגִּידִים	הִגִּידוּ		יַגִּידוּ	juss.	יַגִּידוּ
מַגִּידוֹת			תַּגֵּדְנָה	juss.	תַּגֵּדְנָה
hophal הֻגַּד, יֻגַּד					

This verb is so common that it is generally easy to spot: any verb with a *gimel* with *dagesh* plus *dalet* will usually be הִגִּיד.

26.12. THE *HIPHIL* FORMS OF THE FIRST-*NUN*, THIRD-WEAK VERB נכה

Another very common verb, which is I-נ and III-weak, occurs almost exclusively in the *hiphil*: הִכָּה 'to strike down; to kill' from the root נכה. (This is the 'smite' verb in King James English.) The *hiphil* 3ms consecutive preterite of this verb is וַיַּךְ. It should be learned as a word in itself; it is extremely common in certain parts of the Bible.

26.13. THE RARE STEM *HISHTAPHEL*

There is a very rare verb type in BH known as the *hishtaphel*. It occurs with just one root, the III-weak חוה, to make הִשְׁתַּחֲוָה 'to bow down, prostrate oneself'.[2] This

2. People have also suggested that this verb is an odd kind of *hitpael* and that the שׁ is part of the

verb is fairly common in the Bible and should be recognized. The attested forms are as follows:

THE *HISHTAPHEL* FORMS OF THE VERB חָוָה

inf. cs.	suff. conj.	cons. pret.	impv.	pref. conj.
הִשְׁתַּחֲוֹת	הִשְׁתַּחֲוֵיתִי	וָאֶשְׁתַּחֲוֶה		אֶשְׁתַּחֲוֶה
	הִשְׁתַּחֲוֵיתָ			תִּשְׁתַּחֲוֶה
			הִשְׁתַּחֲוִי	
	הִשְׁתַּחֲוָה	וַיִּשְׁתַּחוּ		יִשְׁתַּחֲוֶה
		וַתִּשְׁתַּחוּ		
ptcp.				נִשְׁתַּחֲוֶה
מִשְׁתַּחֲוֶה	הִשְׁתַּחֲוִיתֶם		הִשְׁתַּחֲווּ	תִּשְׁתַּחֲווּ
מִשְׁתַּחֲוִים	הִשְׁתַּחֲווּ	וַיִּשְׁתַּחֲווּ		יִשְׁתַּחֲווּ
		וַתִּשְׁתַּחֲוֶינָה		

Notes to the paradigm:

26.13.1. Most of the forms of הִשְׁתַּחֲוָה are a combination of the *hishtaphel* properties and III-weak properties of the root. Note that ו as the middle root letter is pronounced as a consonant throughout the paradigm, except for the third-person singular consecutive preterites. (Another verb with a consonantal ו is צִוָּה 'to command'.)

26.13.2. The only real difficulty in this paradigm comes with the 3ms and 3fs consecutive preterites. In these cases, the accent of the consecutive preterite retracts, and the middle root letter ו becomes a vowel וּ *shureq*. The וּ also marks the plural, of course, but plural forms in וּ throughout this paradigm have the root letter consonantal ו preceding the vowel וּ, so two וs in a row.

---

root, but we know that חוה is the correct root and *hishtaphel* the correct stem because the same word occurs in Ugaritic, where it is written out in such a way as to leave no ambiguity.

26.14. VOCABULARY FOR LESSON 26

verbs

הִגִּיד   'to tell' (*hiphil* of נגד); pref. conj. יַגִּיד; cons. pret. וַיַּגֵּד; the person who is told something is usually preceded by the preposition לְ

hophal* הֻגַּד 'to be told'; /pref. conj. יֻגַּד (note the short *u*-vowel of the preformative, which is typical of I-נ verbs)

הִכָּה   'to strike down; attack; kill' (*hiphil* of נכה); pref. conj. יַכֶּה; cons. pret. וַיַּךְ; sometimes ambiguous whether the striking down has indeed killed the person in question

הִשְׁתַּחֲוָה   'to bow down, prostrate oneself' (*hishtaphel* of חוה); pref. conj. יִשְׁתַּחֲוֶה; cons. pret. 3ms וַיִּשְׁתַּחוּ

לָקַח   'to take'; pref. conj. יִקַּח; impv. קַח; like type 2 I-נ

נָגַע   'to touch; reach'; pref. conj. יִגַּע, type 2; usually takes its direct object with בְּ rather than אֵת

נִגַּשׁ   'to approach, come near'; an unusual verb (root נגשׁ) whose suff. conj. appears as a *niphal*, נִגַּשׁ, but whose type 2 pref. conj. appears as a *qal*, יִגַּשׁ, inf. cs. גֶּשֶׁת , גִּשְׁתִּי

hiphil* הִגִּישׁ 'to bring near'; pref. conj. יַגִּישׁ; cons. pret. וַיַּגֵּשׁ

נָטָה   'to stretch out, extend' (usually transitive); 'to turn, bend' (usually intransitive); 'to pitch (a tent)'; pref. conj. יִטֶּה; cons. pret. וַיֵּט; type 1

hiphil* הִטָּה 'to turn, turn aside' (transitive); pref. conj. יַטֶּה; cons. pret. וַיֵּט

נָסַע   'to set out, depart; to travel, march; to strike (take down) a tent'; pref. conj. יִסַּע, type 2

נָפַל   'to fall'; pref. conj. יִפֹּל, type 1

hiphil* הִפִּיל 'to cause to fall; to drop; cast; overthrow'; pref. conj. יַפִּיל; cons. pret. וַיַּפֵּל

נִצַּב   'to stand, take one's stand'; also 'to stand' = 'be stationed, in charge' (*niphal* of נצב); pref. conj. יִנָּצֵב

hiphil* הִצִּיב 'to station, set; erect, set up'; pref. conj. יַצִּיב; cons. pret. וַיַּצֵּב

נָשָׂא   ‘to lift, carry, bear’; pref. conj. יִשָּׂא; inf. cs. שְׂאֵת/שֵׂאת; type 2

niphal נִשָּׂא ‘to be lifted up, carried, taken away; be exalted’; pref. conj. יִנָּשֵׂא

נָתַן   ‘to give; put, set; permit, allow’; in the ‘permit’ sense, usually followed by an inf. cs. of another verb; pref. conj. יִתֵּן; impv. תֵּן; inf. cs. תִּתִּי,תֵּת; type 2

noun

קֹדֶשׁ   ‘holiness’; with sf. קָדְשִׁי; pl. [3] קָדָשִׁים; often used in construct chains that substitute for noun + adjective: הַר קָדְשׁוֹ ‘the mountain of his holiness’ = ‘his holy mountain’

26.15. EXERCISES FOR LESSON 26

A. Translate from Hebrew to English:

1. וַיַּגֵּד הַמֶּלֶךְ לְעַמּוֹ כִּי יִשְׂאוּ [4] אֶת־קוֹלָם אֶל־הַשָּׁמַיִם:

2. וַיִּתְפַּלֵּל הַנָּבִיא אֶל־יְהוָֹה וַיְדַבֵּר אֵלָיו תֶּן־נָא לָנוּ אֶת־בִּרְכָתְךָ לַמִּלְחָמָה:

3. וַיָּדֶן הַשֹּׁפֵט אֶת אֹיְבֵי יִשְׂרָאֵל וַיִּשְׁתַּחוּ לַיהוָה אֱלֹהָיו:

4. אַל־תִּגַּע בְּהַר קָדְשִׁי כִּי נָפוֹל תִּפֹּל:

5. וַיֵּט מֹשֶׁה יָדוֹ [5] עַל־הַיָּם וַיֵּט יְהוָה אֶת־מֵי הַיָּם וַיִּסְעוּ [6] הָעָם לַעֲבֹר:

6. וַיִּשְׁלַח שָׁאוּל מַלְאָכִים לָקַחַת אֶת־דָּוִד וַיַּרְא אֶת־לַהֲקַת [7] הַנְּבִיאִים נִבְּאִים [8]

וּשְׁמוּאֵל עֹמֵד נִצָּב עֲלֵיהֶם וַתְּהִי [9] עַל־מַלְאֲכֵי שָׁאוּל רוּחַ אֱלֹהִים וַיִּתְנַבְּאוּ גַם־הֵמָּה: [10]

(1 Sam 19:20)

---

3. Often written simply קְדָשִׁים, with the first *qamets* = short *o*. The plurals of segholates with *holem* in the first syllable often have *hateph-qamets* in the first syllable instead of simple *shwa*.

4. (a) Since שׂ is a Skin-ʾem-Levi letter, the doubling that is the result of the assimilation of the נ in this root has been dropped. (b) There is no other way to express modal ‘should, could, would’ in BH except to use the pref. conj. , or its equivalent, the *və-qatal* form.

5. See note 6 in lesson 12.

6. Since ס is a Skin-ʾem-Levi letter, the doubling that is the result of the assimilation of the נ in this root has been dropped.

7. ‘The group/company’.

8. We would expect a *qamets* instead of the *shwa* under the ב.

9. This word can mean ‘came’, especially in the context of prophecy.

10. הֵמָּה is a long form of הֵם.

7.   (1 Sam 27:4) ¹⁴:עֹוד לְבַקְשֹׁו¹³ וְלֹא יָסַף¹² דָּוִד גַּת¹¹ וַיֻּגַּד לְשָׁאוּל כִּי בָרַח

8.   (Gen 33:20) :וַיַּצֶּב־שָׁם¹⁵ מִזְבֵּחַ וַיִּקְרָא־לֹו¹⁶ אֵל¹⁷ אֱלֹהֵי יִשְׂרָאֵל

9.   וְאֶל־מֹשֶׁה אָמַר¹⁸ עֲלֵה אֶל־יְהוָה אַתָּה וְאַהֲרֹן¹⁹ נָדָב וַאֲבִיהוּא וְשִׁבְעִים²⁰ מִזִּקְנֵי²¹

> An imperative plus a *və-qatal* form is very often the equivalent of two imperatives: in sentence 9, עֲלֵה followed later by וְהִשְׁתַּחֲוִיתֶם, therefore, means 'go up … and bow down'.

יִשְׂרָאֵל וְהִשְׁתַּחֲוִיתֶם מֵרָחֹק²² וְנִגַּשׁ מֹשֶׁה לְבַדֹּו²³

אֶל־יְהוָה וְהֵם²⁴ לֹא יִגָּשׁוּ²⁵ וְהָעָם לֹא יַעֲלוּ עִמֹּו:

(Exod 24:1–2)

10.   שְׂאוּ שְׁעָרִים²⁶ רָאשֵׁיכֶם וְהִנָּשְׂאוּ פִּתְחֵי²⁷ עֹולָם וְיָבֹוא²⁸ מֶלֶךְ הַכָּבֹוד²⁹ (Ps 24:7)

---

11. The verb means 'to flee'.

12. 'To Gath' (a place name).

13. The verb means 'to continue' here.

14. Note the lack of an expected *dagesh* in the ק, a result of the Skin-'em-Levi process.

15. Because וַיַּצֶּב here is connected to שָׁם by a *maqqeph*, it loses the accent that would normally fall on the צֶב syllable; words connected by *maqqeph* go together to make just one word for the purposes of accentuation. The loss of the accent makes צֶב an unaccented, closed syllable; it cannot, therefore, have a long vowel. The solution is to change the vowel to *seghol*, a short vowel.

16. Although it may seem a strange translation, קְרָא לֹו here = שְׁמֹו קְרָא.

17. This word simply means 'god'; it is the singular of the more common אֱלֹהִים. It is used both as a common noun and as a proper name of a deity El, known throughout the ancient Near East. In the Hebrew Bible, Yahweh is often referred to as El.

18. The 'he' who is speaking here is Yahweh, even though he refers to himself in the third person.

19. This word and the next two are personal names: Aaron, Nadav, and Avihu.

20. 'Seventy'.

21. Remember that the adjective זָקֵן can also be read as the noun 'elder'.

22. 'From afar'.

23. 'Alone, by himself'.

24. 'They' are the four named men; later in the sentence 'the people' refers to the rest of Israel, waiting at the foot of Mount Sinai.

25. We expect יִגְּשׁוּ, with *shwa* under the ג and the accent on the final syllable. This word is "in pause," however, and as often happens in pause, the accent has shifted, and the *shwa* has become a full vowel.

26. This word is vocative here, 'O gates'; i.e., it is the gates that are being addressed.

27. 'Doors of'.

28. 'So that he may enter/come in'.

29. 'Glory'.

11. וַיֹּאמֶר הַגֵּשׁ לִי וְאֹכְלָה³⁰ מִצֵּיד³¹ בְּנִי לְמַעַן תְּבָרֶכְךָ נַפְשִׁי וַיַּגֶּשׁ־לֹוֹ³² וַיֹּאכַל וַיָּבֵא³³
לֹו יַיִן וַיֵּשְׁתְּ: (adapted from Gen 27:25)

12. וַיִּקַּח הַכֹּהֵן אֶת הַלֶּחֶם הַטּוֹב אֲשֶׁר לֹא נֶאֱכַל וַיִּתֵּן אֹתוֹ לַצַּדִּיקִים:

13. וַיֹּאמֶר מִי הִגִּיד לְךָ כִּי עֵירֹם³⁴ אַתָּה הֲמִן־הָעֵץ אֲשֶׁר צִוִּיתִיךָ לְבִלְתִּי אֲכָל־מִמֶּנּוּ³⁵
אָכָלְתָּ: (adapted from Gen 3:11)

B. Parse all the verbs in exercises A7, 9, and 11, above. (Leave out וַיָּבֵא in 11.)

C. Go through Gen 22:1–19 and find every verb that you think is I-נ, לקח, or
הִשְׁתַּחֲוָה. (Note: הִשְׁתַּחֲוָה is actually a III-weak verb.)

---

30. ן plus the cohortative = 'so that'. See the boxed explanation in the exercises of lesson 24.
31. צַיִד = 'game', i.e., meat from the hunt.
32. Remember that if the antecedent of a pronominal direct object has already been mentioned in a sentence, it can be left out. So, you must insert 'it' here in your English translation.
33. 'And he brought'.
34. 'Naked'.
35. ־אֲכָל here is the same as אֲכֹל without the *maqqeph*. See ־וַיֵּצֶב in sentence 8, above.

FIRST-WEAK VERBS, INCLUDING THE VERB
הָלַךְ; THE VERB יכל

27.1. THE FIRST-WEAK VERBS GENERALLY

We learned in lesson 25 that weak verbs are verbs that once had ו or י as a root letter and the ו or י has fallen out. In this lesson, we will study verbs that once *began* with ו or י but that have lost that initial root letter and have adapted the strong verbal patterns to compensate for the loss.

Finding out which verbs originally began with ו and which originally began with י can be a problem, however. BH has virtually no words left that begin with ו (the word 'and' is an obvious exception); instead, at some point, initial ו changed to י in almost every case. That means that all I-weak verbs in Biblical Hebrew *look like* I-י verbs. Luckily for us, however, some of the languages that Hebrew is closely related to (such as Arabic) never lost the initial ו, so when BH roots have cognates in these other languages, we can find out from the cognate language whether what looks like a I-י root in BH was *originally* I-י or *originally* I-ו.

For instance, we learned the verbs יָרַד and יָשַׁב in lesson 16. When we look at the same roots in Arabic, we discover that both of these roots begin with ו rather than י. That means that they would have been וָרַד and וָשַׁב, respectively, in the precursors of Hebrew as well. It is important to know what the original first root letter was, because there are two paradigms of I-weak verbs, which we will call type 1 and type 2, and it turns out in almost every case that the type 2 paradigm applies to verbs that were originally I-ו. The type 1 paradigm applies to verbs that were originally I-י, but these verbs are incredibly rare in BH. Type 1 is in reality a mixed group with original I-ו verbs along with original I-י verbs. We will begin with the type 2 original I- ו verbs, since they are by far the more common.

> **The Suffix Conjugation of the First-Weak Verbs**
>
> The *qal* suffix conjugation of I-weak verbs is perfectly normal, as are the infinitive absolute and the participle. All other *qal* verbal forms of the I-weak verbs, however, have patterns that reflect the loss of the initial root letter, and we will concentrate on those forms.

27.2. THE *QAL* FORMS OF THE TYPE 2 FIRST-WEAK VERBS

The *qal* paradigm of the type 2 I-weak verbs will be illustrated using the verb יָשַׁב 'to sit, dwell'.

THE *QAL* FORMS OF THE TYPE 2 FIRST-WEAK VERB

inf. cs.	suff. conj.	cons. pret.	volitives		pref. conj.
שֶׁבֶת	יָשַׁבְתִּי	וָאֵשֵׁב	אֵשְׁבָה	cohort.	אֵשֵׁב
שִׁבְתִּי	יָשַׁבְתָּ	וַתֵּשֶׁב	שֵׁב	impv.	תֵּשֵׁב
inf. abs.	יָשַׁבְתְּ	וַתֵּשְׁבִי	שְׁבִי	impv.	תֵּשְׁבִי
יָשׁוֹב	יָשַׁב	וַיֵּשֶׁב	יֵשֵׁב	juss.	יֵשֵׁב
	יָשְׁבָה	…	תֵּשֵׁב	juss.	תֵּשֵׁב
ptcp.	יָשַׁבְנוּ		נֵשְׁבָה	cohort.	נֵשֵׁב
יֹשֵׁב	יְשַׁבְתֶּם		שְׁבוּ	impv.	תֵּשְׁבוּ
יֹשֶׁבֶת	יְשַׁבְתֶּן		שֵׁבְנָה	impv.	תֵּשַׁבְנָה
יֹשְׁבִים	יָשְׁבוּ		יֵשְׁבוּ	juss.	יֵשְׁבוּ
יֹשְׁבוֹת			תֵּשֵׁבְנָה	juss.	תֵּשַׁבְנָה

Notes to the paradigm:

27.2.1. When there is a *tsere* in the preformative syllable of a prefix conjugation, it usually means that something is being compensated for: for instance, we saw in the *niphal* prefix conjugation that, when the first root consonant is a guttural or ר and therefore cannot be doubled, the preformative vowel *hireq* is usually lengthened to *tsere*, to compensate for the loss of doubling. In the case of the *qal* prefix conjugation of I-weak verbs above, the lengthening to *tsere* is compensating for the loss of the first root consonant altogether.

27.2.2. The pattern of two *tsere*s, or a *tsere* plus a *seghol*, is ordinarily going to indicate a I-weak verb in the *qal*. While there are some III-weak verbs that also have the *tsere* plus *seghol* pattern in the consecutive preterite (as is indicated on the Clues for Consecutive Preterites chart), the majority of verbs with this pattern are I-weak. (An example of a III-weak verb with this pattern is וַתֵּפֶן 'and she turned', from the root פנה. Although one's first thought is that this must be a I-weak verb, there is no root יפן in BH. As the chart indicates, the next choice would be III-weak.)

27.2.3. The retraction of the accent to the preformative syllable in the consecutive preterite leaves an unaccented closed syllable שֵׁב-. Such a syllable should have a short vowel rather than a long vowel, so the *tsere* becomes *seghol*:

יֵשֵׁב prefix conjugation > (וַיֵּשֵׁב) > וַיֵּשֶׁב consecutive preterite

27.2.4. Like the I-נ type 2 verbs, type 2 I-weak verbs lose the first root consonant entirely in the imperative. Another way to look at it is that the imperative is simply the prefix conjugation without the preformative. While I-נ type 2 verbs generally have *patakh* or *qamets* in the imperative, type 2 I-weak imperatives have *tsere*, unless a guttural root consonant is involved. (Compare סַע and שָׂא from נסע and נשא, respectively, to שֵׁב and רֵד from ישב and ירד, although דַע from ידע shows the influence of the guttural root letter on a I-weak imperative.)

27.2.5. Like the I-נ type 2 verbs, type 2 I-weak verbs lose the first root consonant in the infinitive construct and compensate for that by adding a ת at the end, with the result being a kind of segholate noun, with its accent on the first syllable: here, שֶׁבֶת; with ל, לָשֶׁבֶת (as was pointed out at the end of lesson 26.4).

27.3. THE *QAL* FORMS OF THE TYPE 2 FIRST-WEAK, THIRD-GUTTURAL VERB

Because it is also III-G, the common type 2 verb יָדַע 'to know' has *tsere* plus *patakh* in the prefix conjugation: אֵדַע, תֵּדַע, יֵדַע, and so on. The imperative is דַע, דְּעִי, and so on, and the infinitive construct is דַּעַת, with suffix דְּעְתִּי.

27.4. THE *NIPHAL* AND *HIPHIL* FORMS OF THE TYPE 2 FIRST-WEAK VERB

Whereas in the *qal*, I-weak verbs all look as if they are I-י, in the *niphal* and *hiphil* almost all look as if they are I-ו. The ו is consonantal in the prefix conjugation and its dependents, and they are perfectly regular, and the ו reappears in the form of the vowel *holem-vav* in the suffix conjugation and its dependents.

THE *NIPHAL* FORMS OF THE TYPE 2 FIRST-WEAK VERB

inf. cs.	suff. conj.	cons. pret.	volitives		pref. conj.
הִוָּשֵׁב	נוֹשַׁבְתִּי	וָאִוָּשֵׁב	אִוָּשְׁבָה	cohort.	אִוָּשֵׁב
	נוֹשַׁבְתָּ	וַתִּוָּשֵׁב	הִוָּשֵׁב	impv.	תִּוָּשֵׁב
	נוֹשַׁבְתְּ	וַתִּוָּשְׁבִי	הִוָּשְׁבִי	impv.	תִּוָּשְׁבִי
	נוֹשַׁב	וַיִּוָּשֵׁב	יִוָּשֵׁב	juss.	יִוָּשֵׁב
	נוֹשְׁבָה	...	תִּוָּשֵׁב	juss.	תִּוָּשֵׁב
ptcp.	נוֹשַׁבְנוּ		נִוָּשְׁבָה	cohort.	נִוָּשֵׁב
נוֹשָׁב	נוֹשַׁבְתֶּם		הִוָּשְׁבוּ	impv.	תִּוָּשְׁבוּ
נוֹשֶׁבֶת	נוֹשַׁבְתֶּן		הִוָּשַׁבְנָה	impv.	תִּוָּשַׁבְנָה
נוֹשָׁבִים	נוֹשְׁבוּ		יִוָּשְׁבוּ	juss.	יִוָּשְׁבוּ
נוֹשָׁבוֹת			תִּוָּשַׁבְנָה	juss.	תִּוָּשַׁבְנָה

THE *HIPHIL* FORMS OF THE TYPE 2 FIRST-WEAK VERB

inf. cs.	suff. conj.	cons. pret.	volitives		pref. conj.
הוֹשִׁיב	הוֹשַׁבְתִּי	וָאוֹצִיא/וָאֹלֵךְ	אוֹשִׁיבָה	cohort.	אוֹשִׁיב
	הוֹשַׁבְתָּ	וַתּוֹשֶׁב	הוֹשֵׁב	impv.	תּוֹשִׁיב
inf. abs.	הוֹשַׁבְתְּ	וַתּוֹשִׁיבִי	הוֹשִׁיבִי	impv.	תּוֹשִׁיבִי
הוֹשֵׁב	הוֹשִׁיב	וַיּוֹשֶׁב	יוֹשֵׁב	juss.	יוֹשִׁיב
	הוֹשִׁיבָה	...	תּוֹשֵׁב	juss.	תּוֹשִׁיב
ptcp.	הוֹשַׁבְנוּ		נוֹשִׁיבָה	cohort.	נוֹשִׁיב
מוֹשִׁיב	הוֹשַׁבְתֶּם		הוֹשִׁיבוּ	impv.	תּוֹשִׁיבוּ
מוֹשֶׁבֶת	הוֹשַׁבְתֶּן		הוֹשֵׁבְנָה	impv.	תּוֹשֵׁבְנָה
מוֹשִׁיבִים	הוֹשִׁיבוּ		יוֹשִׁיבוּ	juss.	יוֹשִׁיבוּ
מוֹשִׁיבוֹת			תּוֹשֵׁבְנָה	juss.	תּוֹשֵׁבְנָה

Notes to the *niphal* paradigm:

27.4.1. As was noted above, the prefix conjugation, imperative, cohortative, jussive, consecutive preterite, and infinitive construct are exactly like the strong verb.

27.4.2. The suffix conjugation and participle substitute *holem-vav* for the initial root consonant.

27.4.3. There is no extant infinitive absolute.

Notes to the *hiphil* paradigm:

27.4.4. In every form, the *hiphil* of I-weak verbs has simply substituted *holem-vav* for the first root consonant.

27.4.5. The singular consecutive preterite forms (except 1cs and 2fs) plus 1cp retract the accent and shorten the *tsere* to *seghol,* as in וַיּ֫וֹשֶׁב.

The paradigms for *qal, niphal,* and *hiphil* of ישׁב are gathered together in appendix H (pp. 282–83). It will become clear how similar the type 2 I-weak verbs are from stem to stem. The similarities are presented in color in appendix H, so that they will be obvious. Furthermore, when the derived stem paradigms are studied closely in conjunction with the *qal* paradigm, it will also be clear that almost all of the notes included after the *qal* paradigm are equally applicable to these other paradigms.

27.5. THE *PIEL* FORMS OF THE TYPE 2 FIRST-WEAK VERBS

In the *piel,* I-weak verbs (both type 1 and type 2) are exactly like the strong verbs.

27.6. THE QAL FORMS OF THE TYPE 1 FIRST-WEAK VERBS

We now turn to the type 1 I-weak verbs, a much smaller group of verbs, many of which were originally I-י. Many verbs have features of both type 1 and type 2 paradigms, but still there are some characteristics that can be seen that are specific to the *qal* of type 1. The type 1 prefix conjugation typically retains the initial י, except now as part of a *hireq gadol,* and ends in *patakh,* instead of the *tsere* that is typical of type 2. יִיטַב, for instance, the prefix conjugation of the root יטב 'to be good; to go well', is typical.

There is no type 1 verb that occurs with typical type 1 forms in all four verb forms we are concerned with: suffix conjugation; prefix conjugation; imperative; and infinitive construct. A paradigm is difficult to produce with forms from a single root, but the verb ירשׁ 'to inherit' occurs in most forms of the *qal* prefix conjugation, reproduced below:

THE *QAL* PREFIX CONJUGATION FORMS OF A TYPE 1 FIRST-WEAK VERB

אִירַשׁ

תִּירַשׁ

תִּירְשִׁי

יִירַשׁ

תִּירַשׁ

נִירַשׁ

תִּירְשׁוּ

יִירְשׁוּ

The imperative and infinitive construct of ירשׁ are, unfortunately, of the type 2 variety (רְשׁוּ ,רֵשׁ; and רֶשֶׁת). The only other type 1 imperative that is at all common is יְרָא 'fear! be afraid!', but the *qamets* in יְרָא is simply there because of the following א. For יטב , therefore, we would expect יְטַב as the masculine singular imperative. We would also expect יְטֹב for the infinitive construct; there is one example, with a different verb, יְבֹשׁ. The suffix conjugation of these verbs is normal, as is the participle. This partial information is all that can be reconstructed or used about these type 1 verbs in the *qal*.

In the *niphal*, these type 1 verbs have the same form as the type 2 verbs. This is true as well in the *hiphil*, with a few exceptions. יטב in the *hiphil* retains its type 1 quality. The suffix conjugation is הֵיטִיב, and the prefix conjugation is תֵּיטִיב ,יֵיטִיב, and so on. The imperative and infinitive construct are הֵיטִיב, and the infinitive absolute is הֵיטֵיב. The meaning of the *hiphil* is 'to do well, or to do something well; to make good, right'.

27.7. THE VERB הָלַךְ

The *qal* verb הָלַךְ 'to go, walk' looks like a first-ה verb only in the suffix conjugation, infinitive absolute, and participle. All other forms of this verb in the *qal*, and all the forms of the *hiphil*, behave like a type 2 I-weak verb. A partial *qal* paradigm follows:

THE *QAL* FORMS OF THE VERB הלך

inf. cs.	cons. pret.	volitives		pref. conj.
לֶכֶת, לֶכְתִּי				אֵלֵךְ
	וַתֵּלֶךְ	לֵךְ	impv.	תֵּלֵךְ
		לְכִי	impv.	תֵּלְכִי
	וַיֵּלֶךְ			יֵלֵךְ
	וַתֵּלֶךְ			תֵּלֵךְ
				נֵלֵךְ
		לְכוּ	impv.	תֵּלְכוּ
		לֵכְנָה	impv.	תֵּלַכְנָה
				יֵלְכוּ
				תֵּלַכְנָה

The suffix conjugation *hiphil* of הלך is הוֹלִיךְ; the prefix conjugation is אוֹלִיךְ, תּוֹלִיךְ, יוֹלִיךְ, and so on; and the consecutive preterite 3ms is וַיּוֹלֶךְ.

We have seen the *hitpael* of this root (lesson 24); the *piel* of this root is normal: 3ms prefix conjugation יְהַלֵּךְ, for instance.

27.8. THE VERB יכל

The root יכל 'to be able' is a I-weak verb, but its forms do not fit into either type 1 or type 2 I-weak verbs. A partial paradigm that includes the extant forms of יכל follows:

THE *QAL* FORMS OF THE VERB יכל

inf. cs.	suff. conj.		pref. conj.
יְכֹלֶת	יָכֹלְתִּי		אוּכַל
	יָכֹלְתָּ		תּוּכַל
			תּוּכְלִי
	יָכֹל		יוּכַל
	יָכְלָה		תּוּכַל
			נוּכַל
			תּוּכְלוּ
	יָכְלוּ		יוּכְלוּ

27.9. VOCABULARY FOR LESSON 27

verbs

הוֹשִׁיעַ   'to save, deliver' (*hiphil* of יָשַׁע); pref. conj. יוֹשִׁיעַ; cons. pret. וַיּוֹשַׁע

הָלַךְ   'to go, walk'; type 2, pref. conj. יֵלֵךְ, cons. pret. וַיֵּלֶךְ, impv. לֵךְ, Inf. cs. לֶכְתִּי, לֶכֶת

hiphil הוֹלִיךְ 'to lead, bring'; pref. conj. יוֹלִיךְ; cons. pret. וַיּוֹלֶךְ

piel הִלֵּךְ 'to go' (largely in poetry); pref. conj. יְהַלֵּךְ

hitpael הִתְהַלֵּךְ 'to walk around' (lesson 24); pref. conj. יִתְהַלֵּךְ

יטב   'to be good, go well'; type 1, pref. conj. יִיטַב

hiphil הֵיטִיב 'to do well, do something well; to make good, right'; pref. conj. יֵיטִיב

יָכֹל   'to be able'; 'can' plus inf. cs. of another verb; 'to prevail over'; pref. conj. יוּכַל

יָלַד   'to bear a child' (rarely, of males, 'to beget'); type 2, pref. conj. יֵלֵד, cons. pret.וַיֵּלֶד, inf. cs. לֵדֶת, לִדְתִּי

     niphal נוֹלַד 'to be born'; pref. conj. יִוָּלֵד

     hiphil הוֹלִיד 'to beget, father'; pref. conj. יוֹלִיד; cons. pret. וַיּוֹלֶד

     piel 'to deliver', usually in the form מְיַלֶּדֶת 'midwife'

יָסַף   'to increase' (trans. and intrans.); type 2, impv. mp סְפוּ

     hiphil הוֹסִיף 'to add'; pref. conj. יוֹסִיף; cons. pret. וַיּוֹסֶף

> While הוֹסִיף does mean 'to add', it is more commonly used with a second verb, with the meaning 'to do again', i.e., to do again the action of the second verb: וַיּוֹסֶף לְדַבֵּר or וַיּוֹסֶף וַיְדַבֵּר both mean '(and) he spoke again'.

יָצָא   'to go out, leave' (usually followed by מִן); type 2, pref. conj. יֵצֵא, cons. pret. וַיֵּצֵא, impv. צֵא, inf. cs. צֵאת

     hiphil הוֹצִיא 'to bring out, lead out'; pref. conj. יוֹצִיא; cons. pret. וַיּוֹצֵא

יָרֵא   'to be afraid of, fear, revere'; type 1, pref. conj.יִירָא, inf. cs. יִרְאָה [1]

     niphal נוֹרָא 'to inspire fear, awe, respect; to be dreadful'

יָרַד   'to go down'; type 2, pref. conj. יֵרֵד, cons. pret. וַיֵּרֶד, impv. רֵד, inf. cs. רֶדֶת, רִדְתִּי

     hiphil הוֹרִיד 'to bring down, lead down'; pref. conj. יוֹרִיד; cons. pret. וַיּוֹרֶד

יָרַשׁ   'to take possession of, dispossess, inherit'; type 1, pref. conj. יִירַשׁ, impv.רֵשׁ, inf. cs. רֶשֶׁת, רִשְׁתִּי

     hiphil הוֹרִישׁ 'to cause to possess, inherit'; pref. conj. יוֹרִישׁ; cons. pret. וַיּוֹרֶשׁ

יָשַׁב   'to sit; to dwell, inhabit'; type 2, pref. conj. יֵשֵׁב, cons. pret. וַיֵּשֶׁב, impv. שֵׁב, inf. cs. שֶׁבֶת, שִׁבְתִּי

     niphal נוֹשַׁב 'to be inhabited, inhabitable'

     hiphil הוֹשִׁיב 'to settle something somewhere; to set, place'; cons. pret. וַיּוֹשֶׁב

proper noun

   יִצְחָק   personal name, 'Isaac'

---

1. יִרְאָה is a noun meaning 'fear', but it is also used as the *qal* infinitive construct of יָרֵא.

adverbs

לָמָּה   'why?'

פֹּה   'here'

preposition

בְּקֶרֶב   'in the midst of'; with sf. בְּקִרְבִּי

27.10. EXERCISES FOR LESSON 27

A. Translate from Hebrew to English:

1.   לֹא יָכֹלְתִּי לָרֶדֶת מִן־הַהֵיכָל׃

2.   לָמָּה הוֹסַפְתֶּם לָצֵאת מֵהָעִיר² וַתֵּלְכוּ אֶל־הֶהָרִים׃

3.   כִּי³ תִּשְׁמֹר אֶת־כָּל־הַמִּצְוָה הַזֹּאת לַעֲשֹׂתָהּ⁴ אֲשֶׁר אָנֹכִי מְצַוְּךָ הַיּוֹם לְאַהֲבָה⁵ אֶת־יְהוָה אֱלֹהֶיךָ וְלָלֶכֶת בִּדְרָכָיו כָּל־הַיָּמִים וְיָסַפְתָּ לְךָ עוֹד שָׁלֹשׁ עָרִים עַל⁶ הַשָּׁלֹשׁ הָאֵלֶּה׃ (Deut 19:9)

4.   יוֹרִשְׁךָ אֱלֹהֶיךָ הַנּוֹרָא אֶת־אַרְצָם׃

5.   וַיּוֹשֶׁב הַמֶּלֶךְ דָּוִד אֶת־אָבִיו וְאֶת־אִמּוֹ בְּבֵית בְּנוֹ׃

6.   אָנֹכִי יְהוָה אֱלֹהֶיךָ אֲשֶׁר הוֹצֵאתִיךָ מֵאֶרֶץ מִצְרַיִם מִבֵּית עֲבָדִים׃ (Exod 20:2)

7.   אַל־תֵּלְכִי שָׁם שְׁבִי פֹּה׃

8.   וַיִּהְיוּ יְמֵי אָדָם⁷ אַחֲרֵי הוֹלִידוֹ אֶת־שֵׁת⁸ שְׁמֹנֶה⁸ מֵאוֹת⁹ שָׁנָה⁹ וַיּוֹלֶד¹⁰ בָּנִים וּבָנוֹת׃

(Gen 5:4)

---

2. מִן + יָצָא = 'to leave'.

3. Translate 'if' here.

4. This word must be translated along with the main verb תִּשְׁמֹר, and it adds emphasis to the main verb. Taken together, they mean something like 'to be careful to do something'.

5. אַהֲבָה serves as the infinitive construct of the verb אהב 'to love'.

6. Here this preposition means 'in addition to'; cf. English 'over and above'.

7. In this passage, this is the personal name Adam.

8. A personal name, Seth.

9. The plural of 'hundred'; singular מֵאָה.

10. After the word for 'hundred', the thing counted is commonly in the singular.

9. וַיֹּאמֶר מֶלֶךְ מִצְרַיִם לַמְיַלְּדֹת[11] הָעִבְרִיֹּת[12] אֲשֶׁר שֵׁם הָאַחַת שִׁפְרָה[13] וְשֵׁם הַשֵּׁנִית פּוּעָה[14]: (Exod 1:15)

In verse 16, Pharaoh tells them to kill the male babies. Then, verse 17:

וַתִּירֶאןָ[15] הַמְיַלְּדֹת אֶת־הָאֱלֹהִים וְלֹא עָשׂוּ כַּאֲשֶׁר דִּבֶּר אֲלֵיהֶן מֶלֶךְ מִצְרָיִם וַתְּחַיֶּין אֶת־הַיְלָדִים[16]:

10. אָנֹכִי הֶעֱלֵיתִי אֶתְכֶם מֵאֶרֶץ מִצְרַיִם וָאוֹלֵךְ אֶתְכֶם בַּמִּדְבָּר אַרְבָּעִים[17] שָׁנָה לָרֶשֶׁת אֶת־אֶרֶץ הָאֱמֹרִי[18]: (Amos 2:10)

11. וַיִּיטַב הַדָּבָר בְּעֵינֵי פַרְעֹה וּבְעֵינֵי כָּל־עֲבָדָיו: (Gen 41:37)

12. וַיַּעֲזֹב דָּוִד אֶת־צֹאן אָבִיו וַיִּסַּע לָגֶשֶׁת אֶל־הַפְּלִשְׁתִּי[19]:

13. וַיִּקְרָא אַבְרָהָם אֶת־שֶׁם־בְּנוֹ הַנּוֹלַד־לוֹ אֲשֶׁר יָלְדָה לּוֹ שָׂרָה יִצְחָק: (Gen 21:3)

14. וְהָיָה אִם יֵיטִיב הָעָם הַנּוֹשֵׁב עַל־הָהָר הַהוּא לִשְׁמֹר אֶת־מִצְוֹת אֱלֹהֵיהֶם וְהוֹרִיד יְהוָה אֶת־הָעָם מִשָּׁם וְהוֹלִיךְ אֹתָם אֶל־אֶרֶץ יָפָה:

15. אִם־אֵלֵךְ בְּקֶרֶב צָרָה[20] תְּחַיֵּנִי עַל אַף[21] אֹיְבַי תִּשְׁלַח יָדֶךָ[22] וְתוֹשִׁיעֵנִי[23] יְמִינֶךָ[24]: (Ps 138:7)

---

11. Note the feminine plural without the *vav mater* under the final *holem*.
12. 'Hebrew'.
13. A personal name, Shiphrah.
14. A personal name, Puah.
15. This is the same as the paradigm form, except for the lack of a final *mater*: ןָ- and נָה- are the same thing.
16. '(Male) children'; singular יֶלֶד.
17. 'Forty'.
18. 'The Amorite(s)'.
19. 'The Philistine'.
20. 'Trouble'.
21. 'Anger'.
22. This is the pausal form of יָדְךָ.
23. וְ + prefix conjugation in prose would probably carry the nuance of purpose: 'so that'. This is poetry, however, and וְ + prefix conjugation is not unusual in poetry. It is to be translated simply 'and…'.
24. 'Your right hand'.

B. Parse all the verbs in exercises exercises A3, 8, and 9, above.

C. Go through Gen 22:1–19 and find all the verbs that you think are I-weak verbs (including הלך).

כח ◄ **28** ► כח

MIDDLE-WEAK VERBS AND LOCATIVE ה

28.1. MIDDLE-WEAK ("HOLLOW") VERBS GENERALLY

The next group of weak verbs we will study are the middle-weak verbs, also called hollow verbs or II-weak verbs. The hollow verbs are verbs that originally had a ו or a י as the middle root consonant. Predictably, there are two types of middle-weak verbs, the ones that were originally II-ו and the ones that were originally II-י.

As we have seen, the *qal* suffix conjugation forms of the III-weak verbs sometimes end in הָ- and sometimes have a *hireq gadol* before the suffix conjugation endings. The prefix conjugation forms either end in ה ֶ - or lose all trace of the third root consonant.

The I-נ and I-weak verbs are normal in the *qal* suffix conjugation. In the *qal* prefix conjugation, I-נ verbs double the root consonant that comes right after the preformative (i.e., יִפֹּל); I-weak verbs lose the first root consonant altogether and compensate by lengthening the *hireq* of the preformative to *tsere* or *hireq gadol* (i.e., יֵשֵׁב or יִירָא).

The middle-weak verbs have ways of dealing with the loss of the middle consonant that are different from those of any of the weak verbs that have come before, and that is good, since it allows us to identify the II-weak verbs easily.

28.2. THE *QAL* FORMS OF THE MIDDLE-WEAK *VAV* VERBS

We will begin with the II-ו verbs, and we will use the verb קוּם 'to arise, stand up' as our paradigm verb.

THE *QAL* FORMS OF THE MIDDLE-WEAK *VAV* VERB

inf. cs.	suff. conj.	cons. pret.	volitives		pref. conj.
קוּם	קַ֫מְתִּי	וָאָ֫קוּם	אָק֫וּמָה	cohort.	אָקוּם
	קַ֫מְתָּ	וַתָּ֫קָם	קוּם	impv.	תָּקוּם
inf. abs.	קַמְתְּ	וַתָּק֫וּמִי	ק֫וּמִי	impv.	תָּק֫וּמִי
קוֹם	קָם	וַיָּ֫קָם	יָקֹם	juss.	יָקוּם
	קָ֫מָה	...	תָּקֹם	juss.	תָּקוּם
ptcp.	קַ֫מְנוּ		נָק֫וּמָה	cohort.	נָקוּם
קָם	קַמְתֶּם		ק֫וּמוּ	impv.	תָּק֫וּמוּ
קָמָה	קַמְתֶּן		קֹ֫מְנָה	impv.	תְּקוּמֶ֫ינָה
קָמִים	קָ֫מוּ		יָק֫וּמוּ	juss.	יָק֫וּמוּ
קָמוֹת		תָּקֹ֫מְנָה/תְּקוּמֶ֫ינָה		juss.	תָּקֹ֫מְנָה/תְּקוּמֶ֫ינָה

Notes to the paradigm:

28.2.1. Most of the *qal* prefix conjugation forms of middle-weak verbs indicate in some way the original middle consonant that has been lost. In the II-ו verbs, the *shureq* substitutes for the lost middle consonant, conveniently leaving a visible *vav*, even if only a *mater*. The exceptions are the two feminine plurals, and even they have a *holem* vowel that, if it is reminiscent of any consonant, is reminiscent of a *vav*. Note also the consistent *qamets* in the preformative.

28.2.2. The *qal* imperative is predictable from the prefix conjugation and is also easy to recognize as from a root קוּם.

28.2.3. The *qal* jussive is very much like the prefix conjugation, but the second vowel is *holem* instead of *shureq*.

28.2.4. The *qal* consecutive preterite is the jussive with the accent retracted. Once the accent moves off the last syllable קֹם, that syllable becomes impossible because it is closed and unaccented, with a long vowel. It needs a short vowel, and the short vowel that corresponds to *holem* is *qamets* as short *o*. So the consecutive preterite is pronounced vay-yá-qom (the last syllable is pronounced the same as English "comb").

28.2.5. Note that the infinitive construct is the same as the imperative, and the ms participle is the same as the suffix conjugation 3ms. Context will almost always make the difference obvious. Furthermore, in standard BH, participles that take a subject, whether that subject is a noun or a pronoun ("she is watching"; "the king was writing"), almost always have that subject expressed, and the subject more often than not *precedes* the participle, whereas the subjects of suffix conjugation verbs, when expressed, tend to *follow* the verb.

28.2.6. The fs participle and suffix conjugation 3fs are distinguished by their accent: קָמָה versus קָ֫מָה.

28.2.7. The suffix conjugation 3cp is distinguished from the same form in the III-weak verbs, again, by accent. For example, the verb רוּץ means 'to run', and the verb רָצָה means 'to be pleased with, to accept'. רָ֫צוּ is 'they ran', and רָצוּ is 'they accepted'.

28.2.8. Notice, in fact, that with a few exceptions the accent throughout this paradigm tends to fall on the syllable that begins with the first root letter, here ק. The exceptions are several forms in the consecutive preterite and most of the participle, the fp forms of the prefix conjugation, and the 2mp and 2fp forms of the suffix conjugation. The same is true for almost all the middle-weak paradigms; knowing about the accentuation of middle-weak verbs can be very useful in determining the root of a new verb.

28.3. The *qal* forms of the middle-weak *yod* verbs

The *qal* of the II-י verbs is very similar, except that where there is an indication of the lost middle consonant, we find *hireq gadol* instead of *shureq*. We will illustrate with the verb שִׂים 'to put, set'.[1]

---

1. Because there are a few forms of שִׂים that look as though they are from a II-ו root, the Brown-Driver-Briggs dictionary lists this most common II-י verb alphabetically as שׂוּם. The forms of this verb in BH are overwhelmingly II-י, however, and we will consider it such.

THE *QAL* FORMS OF THE MIDDLE-WEAK *YOD* VERB

inf. cs.	suff. conj.	cons. pret.	volitives		pref. conj.
שׂוּם	שַׂמְתִּי	...	אָשִׂימָה	cohort.	אָשִׂים
שִׂים	שַׂמְתָּ	וַתָּשֶׂם	שִׂים	impv.	תָּשִׂים
inf. abs.	שַׂמְתְּ	וַתָּשִׂימִי	שִׂימִי	impv.	תָּשִׂימִי
שׂוֹם	שָׂם	וַיָּשֶׂם	יָשֵׂם	juss.	יָשִׂים
	שָׂמָה	...	תָּשֵׂם	juss.	תָּשִׂים
ptcp.	שַׂמְנוּ		נָשִׂימָה	cohort.	נָשִׂים
שָׂם	שַׂמְתֶּם		שִׂימוּ	impv.	תָּשִׂימוּ
שָׂמָה	שַׂמְתֶּן		שֵׂמְנָה	impv.	תְּשֵׂמְנָה
שָׂמִים	שָׂמוּ		יָשִׂימוּ	juss.	יָשִׂימוּ
שָׂמוֹת			תְּשֵׂמְנָה	juss.	תְּשֵׂמְנָה

Notes to the paradigm:

28.3.1. Most of the *qal* prefix conjugation forms of middle-weak verbs indicate in some way the original middle consonant that has been lost. In the II-י verbs, the *hireq gadol* substitutes for the lost middle consonant, conveniently leaving a visible *yod*, even if only a *mater*. The exceptions are the two feminine plurals, and even they have a *tsere* vowel that, if it is reminiscent of any consonant, is reminiscent of a *yod*. Note also the consistent *qamets* in the preformative.

28.3.2. The *qal* imperative is predictable from the prefix conjugation and is also easy to recognize as from a root שִׂים.

28.3.3. The *qal* jussive is very much like the prefix conjugation, but the second vowel is *tsere* instead of *hireq gadol*.

28.3.4. The *qal* consecutive preterite is based on the jussive, with the accent retracted in the 2ms, 3ms, and 3fs forms. Once the accent moves off the last syllable שֵׂם, that syllable becomes impossible because it is closed and unaccented, with a long vowel. It needs a short vowel, and the short vowel that corresponds to *tsere* is *seghol*. So the consecutive preterite is pronounced vay-yá-sem.

28.3.5. Note that the suffix conjugation of II-י roots looks the same as the suffix conjugation of II-ו roots.

28.3.6. Note that the infinitive construct is the same as the imperative, but context will almost always make the difference obvious. It is more difficult to distinguish between the ms participle and the suffix conjugation 3ms (but see the comments above in 28.2.5). The fs participle and suffix conjugation 3fs are distinguished only by their accent.

28.4. The *Qal* forms of the verb בּוֹא

There is one other kind of middle-weak verb that is II-וֹ, but has וֹ between the first and third root consonants instead of וּ. בּוֹא 'to enter, come' is by far the most common verb of this type.

THE *QAL* FORMS OF THE MIDDLE-WEAK VERB בּוֹא

inf. cs.	suff. conj.	cons. pret.	volitives		pref. conj.
בּוֹא	בָּאתִי	וָאָבוֹא	אָבוֹאָה	cohort.	אָבוֹא
	בָּאתָ	וַתָּבֹא	בּוֹא	impv.	תָּבוֹא
inf. abs.	בָּאת	וַתָּבֹאִי	בּוֹאִי	impv.	תָּבוֹאִי
בּוֹא	בָּא	וַיָּבֹא	יָבֹא	juss.	יָבוֹא
	בָּאָה	…	תָּבֹא	juss.	תָּבוֹא
ptcp.	בָּאנוּ		נָבוֹאָה	cohort.	נָבוֹא
בָּא	בָּאתֶם		בּוֹאוּ	impv.	תָּבוֹאוּ
בָּאָה	בָּאתֶן		בּוֹאנָה	impv.	תָּבוֹאנָה
בָּאִים	בָּאוּ		יָבוֹאוּ	juss.	יָבוֹאוּ
בָּאוֹת			תָּבוֹאנָה	juss.	תָּבוֹאנָה

Notes to the paradigm:

28.4.1. Throughout the paradigm, these forms can be spelled with simple *holem* instead of *holem-vav*, which makes it harder to identify the verb as II-וֹ.

28.4.2. Unlike the II-וּ verbs with *shureq* between the first and third root consonants, the consecutive preterite of this verb does not retract the accent to the preformative, so the *holem* remains. (Compare וַיָּבֹא to וַיָּקָם.)

28.4.3. Because בּוֹא in particular is III-א, the various forms reflect the quiescence of א whenever it is at the end of a syllable, as was true with קָרָא, for instance.

28.5. THE *NIPHAL* AND *HIPHIL* FORMS OF THE MIDDLE-WEAK VERBS GENERALLY

In the *niphal* and *hiphil* of the middle-weak verbs, there is no distinction between those verbs that were originally II-ו and those that were originally II-י. Both behave the same way. At the end of the following discussion of the *niphal* and *hiphil* individually, the paradigms for *qal*, *niphal*, and *hiphil* of II-ו and II-י verbs are presented together; comparison will make clear how similar the middle-weak verbs are from stem to stem.

28.6. THE *NIPHAL* FORMS OF THE MIDDLE-WEAK VERBS

We will illustrate the *niphal* with the verb כּוּן, which in the *niphal* means 'to be established; to prepare, be ready' (neither קוּם nor שִׂים occurs in the *niphal* in BH).

THE *NIPHAL* FORMS OF THE MIDDLE-WEAK VERB

inf. cs.	suff. conj.	cons. pret.	volitives		pref. conj.
הִכּוֹן	נְכוּנֹ֫תִי	וָאֶכּוֹן	אֶכּוֹנָה	cohort.	אֶכּוֹן
	נְכוּנֹ֫ותָ	וַתִּכּוֹן	הִכּוֹן	impv.	תִּכּוֹן
inf. abs.	נְכוּנֹות	וַתִּכֹּ֫ונִי	הִכֹּ֫ונִי	impv.	תִּכֹּ֫ונִי
הִכּוֹן	נָכוֹן	וַיִּכּוֹן	יִכּוֹן	juss.	יִכּוֹן
	נָכֹ֫ונָה	…	תִּכּוֹן	juss.	תִּכּוֹן
ptcp.	נְכֹ֫ונוּ		נִכֹּ֫ונָה	cohort.	נִכּוֹן
נָכוֹן	נְכוּנֹתֶם		הִכֹּ֫ונוּ	impv.	תִּכֹּ֫ונוּ
נְכוֹנָה	נְכוּנֹתֶן			impv.	
נְכוֹנִים	נָכֹ֫ונוּ		יִכֹּ֫ונוּ	juss.	יִכֹּ֫ונוּ
נְכוֹנוֹת				juss.	

Notes to the paradigm:

28.6.1. Instead of יִכָּוֵן, which is what we would expect if כּוּן were a strong verb, the middle -כָּוֵ- has become simply כֹ.

28.6.2. As was mentioned above (28.4.1), in almost every form these verbs can be spelled with simple *holem* without the *vav mater*, and the middle-weak classification is harder to see when that happens.

28.6.3. The suffix conjugation third-person forms are not hard to identify, but the preformative vowel *qamets* should be noticed. The first- and second-person forms, however, have a new feature.

Alternative Endings to the Suffix Conjugation

Besides the suffix conjugation endings we have learned (תִּי-, תָ-, and so on), there is *another slightly different set of endings with an extra -ô- syllable* that is sometimes used especially for weak verbs (perhaps to fill them out). תִּי- becomes וֹתִי-; תָ- becomes וֹתָ-, etc. The vowels of the first two syllables in the words change somewhat, but that does not make the form less identifiable; it is simply necessary to know that the ending that can be removed as a part of analyzing a verb can include -ô- on the front of the ending (often simply *holem*, without the *vav mater*).

28.7. THE *HIPHIL* FORMS OF THE MIDDLE-WEAK VERBS

The *hiphil* of middle-weak verbs will be illustrated using the verb קוּם, which in the *hiphil* means 'to raise, set up, erect; set, station'.

THE *HIPHIL* FORMS OF THE MIDDLE-WEAK VERB

inf. cs.	suff. conj.	cons. pret.	volitives		pref. conj.
הָקִים	הֲקִימֹׁתִי	וָאָקִים	אָקִֽימָה	cohort.	אָקִים
	הֲקִימֹׁתָ	וַתָּקֶם	הָקֵם	impv.	תָּקִים
inf. abs.	הֲקִימֹות	וַתָּקִֽימִי	הָקִֽימִי	impv.	תָּקִֽימִי
הָקֵם	הֵקִים	וַיָּֽקֶם	יָקֶם/יָקֵם	juss.	יָקִים
	הֵקִֽימָה	…	תָּקֶם/תָּקֵם	juss.	תָּקִים
ptcp.	הֲקִימֹׁנוּ		נָקִֽימָה	cohort.	נָקִים
מֵקִים	הֲקִימֹׁתֶם		הָקִֽימוּ	impv.	תָּקִֽימוּ
מְקִימָה	הֲקִימֹׁתֶן		הָקֵֽמְנָה	impv.	תָּקֵֽמְנָה
מְקִימִים	הֵקִֽימוּ		יָקִֽימוּ	juss.	יָקִֽימוּ
מְקִימֹות			תָּקֵֽמְנָה/תָּקִימֶֽינָה	juss.	תָּקֵֽמְנָה/תָּקִימֶֽינָה

There is an alternative, less common paradigm for the suffix conjugation. The more typical paradigm is presented on the left below, the alternate paradigm on the right.[2]

הֲקִימֹ֫תִי	הֲקִמֹ֫תִי
הֲקִימֹ֫תָ	הֲקִמֹ֫תָ
הֲקִימֹת	הֲקִמֹת
הֵקִים	הֵקִים
הֵקִ֫ימָה	הֵקִ֫ימָה
הֲקִימֹ֫נוּ	הֲקִמֹ֫נוּ
הֲקִימֹתֶם	
הֲקִימֹתֶן	
הֵקִ֫ימוּ	הֵקִ֫ימוּ

Notes to the paradigm:

28.7.1. The *hiphil* prefix conjugation of any middle-weak verb looks exactly like the *qal* of a II-י verb. The same is true for the jussive and consecutive preterite forms. (The feminine plural prefix conjugation forms in the *hiphil* are a problem, however. They should both be of the form תְּקֵ֫מְנָה; they are rare, however, and the forms we find in the Bible are a mixture of the expected and unexpected.)

28.7.2. The imperative ms can be recognized as the *hiphil* imperative of a middle-weak verb by a process of elimination: the ה suggests *hiphil* (possibly *niphal*), and there is nothing odd about the beginning or the end of the rest of the word. Middle-weak verb *hiphil* is a good guess.

28.7.3. Both forms of the suffix conjugation are common and should be recognized. The third-person forms are the same for both, with the *hireq gadol* as a clue to the stem, and the *tsere* under the ה because the loss of a root letter has left this unaccented syllable open. The differences come in the first- and second-person forms, where in the first paradigm, we see another instance of the וֹתִי ֗-, וֹתָ ֗- longer suffix conjugation endings (as in the *niphal*, above). The second paradigm is more

---

2. It is difficult to know what the 2mp and 2fp would look like in a verb such as קום: the forms we have are הֲבֵאתֶם from בוא, which is unusual because of the א, and הֲמִתֶּם/ן from מות, which is unusual because its root letter ת assimilates with the ת of the suffix conjugation verbal ending.

what we would expect, with the *patakh* before the third root consonant, and the הָ, as above, the product of the open-syllable preformative.

28.7.4. The ms participle is a bit surprising, with the *tsere* under the מ instead of an *a*-vowel.

> Since the *piel* is the stem that doubles the middle root letter, there is no place for a *piel* in the middle-weak verbs: there is nothing to double.[3] The same is true for the *hitpael*. Instead, the middle-weak verbs have a special form that functions as a *piel* and one that functions as a *hitpael*, which will be taken up in the next lesson.

28.8. A SUMMARY OF THE FORMS OF THE MIDDLE-WEAK VERBS

The paradigms for *qal* of קוּם and שִׂים, the *niphal* of כּוּן, and *hiphil* of קוּם are gathered together on pages 284–85 of appendix H, so that they can be compared. (There is no one root in BH that occurs at all frequently in all three stems.) The first consonants plus vowels are presented in color, again so that the similarities will be obvious. The *qal* of קוּם and the *niphal* of כּוּן are presented together on one page, since both feature וּ and וֹ vowels prominently; the *qal* of שִׂים and the *hiphil* of קוּם are together on another page, because the *qal* of II-י verbs shares some forms with the *hiphil* of any middle-weak verb. It should be noted that all these forms are similar in that the middle "weakness" of the verb shows up as a vowel of some sort, written between the first and last root consonants.

28.9. THE LOCATIVE ה

An *unaccented* הָ- ending on a noun of place (common or proper) implies motion to or toward that place. אַרְצָה, for instance, means 'to the ground' or 'to the land of'; הָהָרָה means 'to the mountain';[4] יְרוּשָׁלַמָה means 'to Jerusalem'. This ending is referred to as "locative ה" or "directive ה."

Note the difference between this ending and the feminine singular הָ- ending: the fs

> Note also that לַיְלָה 'night' contains an unaccented הָ- ending. While לַיְלָה has nothing to do with place, it is a noun of time, and time and place are both adverbial functions; it is possible, then, that the הָ- ending on לַיְלָה is related to locative ה.

---

3. In later BH, we find artificial forms such as קִיֵּם as the piel of קוּם, but these are rare.

4. This form, like the usual form of יְרוּשָׁלַם, is pointed by the Masoretes as if there were a י between the ל and the ם. It has an extra *shwa* written to the right of the ם, because the Masoretes were pronouncing יְרוּשָׁלַיְמָה.

ending is *accented*. Locative ה is one of the few things that can come between two parts of a construct chain. So, 'to the land of Canaan' is אַ֫רְצָה כְּנַ֫עַן.

28.10. VOCABULARY FOR LESSON 28

> **The "Naming" of the Middle-Weak Verbs**
>
> Note that middle-weak verbs are "named" by their infinitive construct forms, rather than the 3ms suffix conjugation form that is the norm for the rest of the verb. So when we speak of the verb with the root שוב, we say שׁוּב.

verbs

בּוֹא   'to enter, come (in, to)'; pref. conj. יָבוֹא; cons. pret. וַיָּבֹא

     hiphil הֵבִיא 'to bring, lead in/to'; pref. conj. יָבִיא; cons. pret. וַיָּבֵא

בִּין   'to perceive, understand'; pref. conj. יָבִין; cons. pret. וַיָּ֫בֶן

     niphal, esp. ptcp. נָבוֹן 'intelligent'

     hiphil הֵבִין 'to understand; to cause understanding, teach'; pref. conj. יָבִין; cons. pret. וַיָּ֫בֶן

     The pref. conj. and cons. pret. of *qal* and *hiphil* are identical; when the meaning is 'to understand', a verb could be considered either *qal* or *hiphil*.

בָּכָה   'to weep, cry'; pref. conj. יִבְכֶּה; cons. pret. וַיֵּבְךְ

הֵכִין   'to establish, set up; make ready, prepare' (*hiphil* of כון; see נָכוֹן below); pref. conj. יָכִין; cons. pret. וַיָּ֫כֶן

מוּת   'to die'; pref. conj. יָמוּת; cons. pret. וַיָּ֫מָת; suff. conj. 3ms מֵת; מֵת also = ptcp./verbal adjective 'dead'; note that the ת of the root assimilates to the ת of the suff. conj. paradigm endings (מַ֫תָּה, מַ֫תִּי, and so on)

     hiphil הֵמִית 'to kill'; pref. conj. יָמִית; cons. pret. וַיָּ֫מֶת; the ת also assimilates in the *hiphil* suff. conj. (הֵמַ֫תָּה, הֵמַ֫תִּי, and so on)

     hophal הוּמַת 'to be killed, put to death'; pref. conj. יוּמַת; often used in law codes with *qal* inf. abs.: מוֹת יוּמַת 'he will surely be put to death'

נָכוֹן   'to be ready, prepared; to be established, set up' (*niphal* of כון); pref. conj. יִכּוֹן; see הֵכִין above

סוּר   'turn aside; depart'; pref. conj. יָסוּר; cons. pret. וַיָּסַר (the final vowel of this form is *patakh* because of the following ר)

hiphil הֵסִיר 'to remove, take away'; pref. conj. יָסִיר; cons. pret. in the *hiphil* is also וַיָּסַר, because of the final ר

קוּם   'to arise, stand up'; pref. conj. יָקוּם; cons. pret. וַיָּקָם

hiphil הֵקִים 'to raise, set up, erect'; pref. conj. יָקִים; cons. pret. וַיָּקֶם

שִׂים   'to put, place, set'; pref. conj. יָשִׂים; cons. pret. וַיָּשֶׂם

שׁוּב   'to return (intrans.), turn back, come back'; pref. conj. יָשׁוּב; cons. pret. וַיָּשָׁב

hiphil הֵשִׁיב 'to bring back, put back, give back'; pref. conj. יָשִׁיב; cons. pret. וַיָּשֶׁב

> Like הוֹסִיף in lesson 27, שׁוּב is commonly used with a second verb with the meaning 'to do again', i.e., to do again the action of the second verb; thus, וַיָּשָׁב וַיָּבוֹא can mean 'he entered again'.

nouns

אֶבֶן   'stone' (fem.); with sf. אַבְנִי; pl. אֲבָנִים; cs. pl. אַבְנֵי

כְּלִי   'article; utensil, vessel (temple); armor (military)'; cs. is the same; pl. כֵּלִים; cs. pl. כְּלֵי

מִשְׁפָּחָה   'clan; family'; cs. מִשְׁפַּחַת; with sf. מִשְׁפַּחְתִּי; pl. מִשְׁפָּחוֹת; cs. pl. מִשְׁפְּחוֹת

proper noun

כְּנַעַן   place name, 'Canaan'

adverbial ending

ָה -   locative ה, added to common and proper nouns of place, to imply motion to or toward that place

28.11. EXERCISES FOR LESSON 28

A. Translate from Hebrew to English:

1.   וַיָּקָם הַכֹּהֵן וַיָּסַר אֶת־כְּלֵי בֵית יְהֹוָה׃

2.   וַתָּשָׁב הַמַּלְכָּה אֶל־מִשְׁפַּחְתָּהּ וַתִּבֶן אֶת־בְּנָהּ לַמֶּלֶךְ׃

3.   הַאֲכִילוּ אֶת־הַבָּקָר וְהַשְׁקוּ אֹתָם לְמַעַן יֶחֱזְקוּ וְגָדְלוּ וְהַאֲרִיכוּ קַרְנֵיהֶם׃[5]

---

5. 'Their horns'.

4. ‏וַיָּקֶם יְהוֹשֻׁעַ אֶת־אַבְנֵי הַבְּרִית הַגְּדוֹלוֹת בְּתוֹךְ הַנָּהָר:‏

5. ‏וַיִּשָּׂא דָוִד וְהָעָם אֲשֶׁר אִתּוֹ אֶת־קוֹלָם וַיִּבְכּוּ עַד אֲשֶׁר אֵין־בָּהֶם כֹּחַ⁶ לִבְכּוֹת:‏

(1 Sam 30:4)

6. ‏וַיֹּאמֶר הַמֶּלֶךְ קְחוּ לִי חָרֶב⁷ וַיָּבִאוּ הַחֶרֶב⁸ לִפְנֵי הַמֶּלֶךְ: (1 Kgs 3:24)‏

7. ‏וְיִגְדַּל⁹ שִׁמְךָ עַד־עוֹלָם לֵאמֹר¹⁰ יְהוָה צְבָאוֹת¹¹ אֱלֹהִים עַל־יִשְׂרָאֵל וּבֵית עַבְדְּךָ דָוִד
יִהְיֶה נָכוֹן לְפָנֶיךָ: (2 Sam 7:26)‏

8. ‏וַיֹּאמֶר מֹשֶׁה אָסוּר לִרְאוֹת אֶת־הַדָּבָר הַנּוֹרָא:‏

9. ‏אֱלֹהִים הֵבִין דַּרְכָּהּ וְהוּא יָדַע אֶת־מְקוֹמָהּ:‏

(Job 28:23; Job is talking about חָכְמָה in this short poetic line.)

10. ‏וַיֹּסֶף יְהוָה קְרֹא שְׁמוּאֵל בַּשְּׁלִישִׁית וַיָּקֶם וַיֵּלֶךְ אֶל־עֵלִי¹² וַיֹּאמֶר הִנְנִי¹³ כִּי קָרָאתָ
לִי וַיָּבֶן עֵלִי כִּי יְהוָה קֹרֵא לַנָּעַר: (1 Sam 3:8)‏

11. ‏וַתָּבֹא¹⁴ בַת־שֶׁבַע¹⁵ אֶל־הַמֶּלֶךְ שְׁלֹמֹה לְדַבֶּר־לוֹ¹⁶ עַל־אֲדֹנִיָּהוּ¹⁷ וַיָּקָם הַמֶּלֶךְ
לִקְרָאתָהּ¹⁸ וַיִּשְׁתַּחוּ לָהּ וַיֵּשֶׁב עַל־כִּסְאוֹ וַיָּשֶׂם כִּסֵּא לְאֵם הַמֶּלֶךְ וַתֵּשֶׁב לִימִינוֹ¹⁹:‏

(1 Kgs 2:19)

---

6. ‘Strength’.

7. This word is in pause; hence the *qamets*.

8. We expect אֵת here, but it is not in this passage.

9. Note that this verb is *not* the consecutive preterite. Rather, the וְ at the beginning suggests connection with an earlier imperative and should be translated ‘so that’.

10. The לֵאמֹר is a little awkward here but makes good sense if you treat it as a colon.

11. This two-word phrase is usually translated ‘Yahweh of hosts’.

12. A personal name, Eli.

13. ‘Here I am’.

14. Note that this word is written “defectively,” i.e., without the expected *mater* for the *holem*.

15. A personal name, Bathsheba.

16. There is often a *maqqeph* between words in the Hebrew Bible for no obvious semantic reason. The effect is to make two (or more) words into one accentual unit. See note 1 in lesson 9.

17. אֲדֹנִיָּהוּ is a personal name, Adonijah; עַל־ here means ‘about’.

18. ‘To meet her’.

19. ‘On his right/at his right hand’.

12. וַיִּקַּח אֲבִימֶ֫לֶךְ[20] צֹאן וּבָקָר וַעֲבָדִים וּשְׁפָחֹת[21] וַיִּתֵּן[22] לְאַבְרָהָם וַיָּ֫שֶׁב לֹו אֵת שָׂרָה אִשְׁתֹּו: (Gen 20:14)

13. וַיָּ֫שָׁב[23] וַיִּ֫בֶן אֶת־הַבָּמֹות[24] אֲשֶׁר אִבַּד חִזְקִיָּ֫הוּ[25] אָבִיו וַיָּ֫קֶם מִזְבְּחֹת לַבַּ֫עַל[26] וַיַּ֫עַשׂ אֲשֵׁרָה[27] כַּאֲשֶׁר עָשָׂה אַחְאָב[28] מֶ֫לֶךְ יִשְׂרָאֵל וַיִּשְׁתַּ֫חוּ לְכָל־צְבָא הַשָּׁמַ֫יִם[29] וַיַּעֲבֹד אֹתָם: (2 Kgs 21:3)

14. אִם יָמִית אִישׁ אֶת־אָחִיו מֹות יוּמָת:

15. וַיִּקַּח אַבְרָם אֶת־שָׂרַי אִשְׁתֹּו וְאֶת־לֹוט[30] בֶּן־אָחִיו ... וַיֵּצְאוּ לָלֶ֫כֶת אַ֫רְצָה כְּנַ֫עַן וַיָּבֹ֫אוּ אַ֫רְצָה כְּנָ֫עַן: (part of Gen 12:5)

B. Parse all the verbs in exercises exercises A3, 10, and 13, above.

C. List all the verbs in Gen 22:1–19 that you think are middle-weak verbs.

---

20. A personal name, Abimelech.

21. Note that this feminine plural is written without the *vav mater* for the *holem*. The word means 'female servants'.

22. The direct object 'them' is understood in Hebrew but must be added in English.

23. The 'he' in this passage is King Manasseh of Judah. Remember the special usage of שׁוּב explained in the vocabulary list.

24. A בָּמָה is some sort of open-air sanctuary, usually translated 'high place'.

25. A personal name, Hezekiah.

26. 'The Baal', the god Baal; Baal's name is usually accompanied by a definite article in the Hebrew Bible (or is defined in some other way). The word בַּעַל means 'lord'.

27. 'An Asherah', i.e., some cultic representation of the goddess Asherah (most probably a tree).

28. A personal name, Ahab.

29. 'The host of heaven', i.e., gods, understood to make up a heavenly army.

30. A personal name, Lot.

29 ◄ כט

THE DERIVED STEMS *POLEL*, *POLAL*, AND *HITPOLEL*, THE WORD הִנֵּה, AND THE FORMS OF OATHS

29.1. THE DERIVED STEMS *POLEL*, *POLAL*, AND *HITPOLEL* GENERALLY

We learned in the previous lesson that middle-weak verbs ordinarily do not appear in the *piel*, *pual*, or *hitpael* for the reason that there is no middle root consonant to double in that set of verbs. Instead, the middle-weak verbs have separate stems that function in the same way as the *piel*, *pual*, and *hitpael*; they are called the *polel*, *polal*, and *hitpolel*.

29.2. THE FORMS OF THE *POLEL*

As the name implies, the *polel*'s pattern repeats the third root consonant, as a way to compensate for the lack of a middle root consonant. The vowel pattern is also distinctive. Note that the vowel pattern of the 3ms suffix conjugation of the *polel* (רוֹמֵם) looks like that of the *qal* participle of the strong verb (שֹׁמֵר). The *polel* is usually written with *holem-vav* and the *qal* participle with simple *holem*, but it is still possible to confuse the two. There are rare *polel*s from common middle-weak roots, such as קוֹמֵם 'to raise' from קום and מוֹתֵת 'to kill' from מות, but only a very few occur often enough to justify putting them in the vocabulary list below. We will demonstrate the *polel* with the verb רוֹמֵם 'to raise, lift up; exalt', from the root רום 'to be high, exalted'.

THE *POLEL* FORMS OF THE MIDDLE-WEAK VERB

inf. cs.	suff. conj.	cons. pret.	volitives		pref. conj.
רוֹמֵם	רוֹמַ֫מְתִּי	וָאֲרוֹמֵם	אֲרוֹמְמָה	cohort.	אֲרוֹמֵם
	רוֹמַ֫מְתָּ	וַתְּרוֹמֵם	רוֹמֵם	impv.	תְּרוֹמֵם
	רוֹמַמְתְּ	וַתְּרוֹמְמִי	רוֹמְמִי	impv.	תְּרוֹמְמִי
	רוֹמֵם	וַיְרוֹמֵם	יְרוֹמֵם	juss.	יְרוֹמֵם
	רוֹמְמָה	...	תְּרוֹמֵם	juss.	תְּרוֹמֵם
ptcp.	רוֹמַ֫מְנוּ		נְרוֹמְמָה	cohort.	נְרוֹמֵם
מְרוֹמֵם	רוֹמַמְתֶּם		רוֹמְמוּ	impv.	תְּרוֹמְמוּ
מְרוֹמֶ֫מֶת	רוֹמַמְתֶּן		רוֹמֵ֫מְנָה	impv.	תְּרוֹמֵ֫מְנָה
מְרוֹמְמִים	רוֹמְמוּ		יְרוֹמְמוּ	juss.	יְרוֹמְמוּ
מְרוֹמְמוֹת			תְּרוֹמֵ֫מְנָה	juss.	תְּרוֹמֵ֫מְנָה

Notes to the paradigm:

29.2.1. The preformative vowel of the *polel* is *shwa* (or *hateph-patakh*), as it is in the *piel*.

29.2.2. The full *holem-vav* is written more than half the time, but there are many cases where the vowel is simply *holem*, as in רֹמֵם.

29.2.3. 3ms is the only place in the suffix conjugation where the *tsere* indicated by the name *polel* actually appears. The same is true of the *piel*.

29.2.4. There is no attested infinitive absolute of the *polel*.

29.3. THE FORMS OF THE *POLAL*

Just as the *piel* has a passive counterpart in the *pual*, so the *polel* has a passive counterpart in the *polal* (רוֹמַם). It is extremely rare, but it is worth noting that the suffix conjugation of the *polal* is exactly like that of the *polel*, with the exception of the 3ms.

29.4. THE FORMS OF THE *HITPOLEL*

The *hitpolel* (הִתְרוֹמֵם) is the middle-weak equivalent of the *hitpael* in other verbs and carries all the same meanings. Its paradigm is exactly the same as the *polel*'s, with יִתְ instead of יְ in the prefix conjugation, cohortative, jussive, and consecutive preterite; הִתְ added to the beginning of the imperative, suffix conjugation, and infinitive construct; and מִתְ instead of מְ in the participle.

29.5. THE WORD הִנֵּה

The BH word הִנֵּה, King James's 'behold', is often the cause of consternation among beginning students. 'Behold' is simply not used any longer in any register of modern English, so we must find a way of translating the word that has some meaning in our own language. הִנֵּה seems to function in four related ways in BH.

29.5.1. הִנֵּה is used as a "presentation particle":

Here is the book.	הִנֵּה הַסֵּפֶר
There is your daughter.	הִנֵּה בִּתֶּךָ

It can be used this way with pronouns to mean 'Here I am', 'Here it is'; the pronouns are expressed as pronominal suffixes.

THE WORD הִנֵּה WITH PRONOMINAL SUFFIXES

Here we are.	הִנְנוּ/הִנֶּנּוּ	הִנְנִי/הִנֶּנִּי	Here I am.
Here/there you are.	הִנְּכֶם	הִנְּךָ	Here/there you are.
		הִנָּךְ	Here/there you are.
Here/there they are.	הִנָּם	הִנּוֹ	Here/there he/it is.

Note the following examples:

הִנֵּה אֱלֹהֵיכֶם	*Here* is your God.
וְעַתָּה הִנֵּה אִשְׁתְּךָ קַח וָלֵךְ	Now, *here* is your wife; take (her) and go!

29.5.2. הִנֵּה stresses the "here-and-nowness" of a situation: to indicate that something has 'just' happened or is happening right now or is just about to happen; to imply that something is happening here, in this place. Pronominal suffixes can also be used on הִנֵּה in this kind of situation.

הִנְּךָ מְבַקֵּשׁ לָלֶכֶת אֶל־אַרְצֶךָ	*Now you* are seeking to go to your country.
הִנָּם אֹכְלִים וְשֹׁתִים לִפְנֵי בֶּן־הַמֶּלֶךְ	*They are now* eating and drinking in the presence of the king's son.
הִנֵּה שָׁמַעְתִּי אָבִיךָ מְדַבֵּר אֶל־אָחִיךָ	I have *just* heard your father speaking to your brother.

29.5.3. In a more general way, הִנֵּה "sets up" a situation that is then to be acted upon. As such, it is often followed by an imperative (look back at the 'Here is your wife' sentence under 29.5.1 above).

הִנֵּה עַבְדְּךָ עֲשֵׂה לּוֹ הַטּוֹב בְּעֵינֶיךָ	*Here* is your servant. Do to him whatever seems good in your eyes.
וָאֹמַר הִנְנִי שְׁלָחֵנִי	And I said, "*Here I am*. Send me!"

29.5.4. הִנֵּה is sometimes best translated 'while' or 'that'.

וַיַּעַל אֵלָיו וְהִנֵּה יֹשֵׁב עַל־רֹאשׁ הָהָר	And he went up to him, *while* he was sitting on the top of the mountain.[1]
לֵךְ אֶל־פַּרְעֹה בַּבֹּקֶר וְהִנֵּה יֹצֵא אֶל־הַמַּיִם	Go to Pharaoh in the morning, *while* he is going out to the water.
וַיִּשָּׂא הָאִישׁ עֵינָיו וַיַּרְא וְהִנֵּה אָחִיו בָּא[2]	The man lifted up his eyes, and he saw *that* his brother was coming.

29.6. FORMS OF OATHS

There is a form that is generally followed for oaths in BH. They may begin with a verb that has to do with oath-taking, such as the *niphal* or *hiphil* of שבע, נִשְׁבַּע 'to take an oath' or הִשְׁבִּיעַ 'to make someone swear', plus a phrase such as חַי יְהוָה (or חַי־יְהוָה) 'as Yahweh lives'.

The next element is usually אִם or אִם לֹא, with counterintuitive meanings. אִם in an oath is a strong negative; that is, someone swears that she or he will absolutely *not* do something; while אִם לֹא is a strong *positive*; that is, someone swears that he or she absolutely *will* do something.

> This odd usage is usually explained by assuming that the middle part of the oath is missing. So, for instance, a full oath might be: "I swear, as Yahweh lives, *that you can strike me down*, if (אִם) I ever betray you." Now, if we leave out the phrase in italics, we must translate the אִם clause negatively: "I swear, as Yahweh lives, that I will not (אִם) ever betray you." The same sort of logic turns אִם לֹא (often אִם־לֹא , with *maqqeph*) into a positive.

---

1. In this sentence and the one following (from 2 Kgs 1:9 and Exod 7:15, respectively), the subject pronoun, which would ordinarily be required with a participle, is left out after הִנֵּה. (i.e., we would expect וְהִנֵּה הוּא יֹשֵׁב ...) This omission perhaps occurs because הִנֵּה is felt to imply the pronoun; in context, furthermore, the subject has just been mentioned, so the meaning is clear.

2. This combination of the verb ראה plus וְהִנֵּה is common and should almost always be translated as above: 'someone *saw that*...'.

חַי־יְהֹוָה אִם־אֶעֱשֶׂה אֶת־הַדָּבָר הַזֶּה

As Yahweh lives, I will not do this thing.

וַיִּשָּׁבַע מֹשֶׁה לֵאמֹר אִם־לֹא הָאָרֶץ הַזֹּאת תִּהְיֶה לָכֶם עַד־עוֹלָם

Moses swore: "Surely this land will be yours forever."

Another kind of oath is begun with some variant of these words:

כֹּה יַעֲשֶׂה יְהֹוָה לִי וְכֹה יוֹסִיף

Thus may Yahweh do to me and even more so.

This phrase is often followed by a normal אִם 'if' or אִם־לֹא 'if … not' clause. Exactly what punishment the phrase refers to need not be stated; it is understood that the oath-taker is willing to have something very bad happen to her or him if she or he does or does not do what is sworn to.

29.7. VOCABULARY FOR LESSON 29

verbs

הִצִּיל 'to deliver, rescue, save (from battle or trouble, and from sin); to take away' (*hiphil* of נצל); pref. conj. יַצִּיל; cons. pret. וַיַּצֵּל (There is a passive *niphal* of this verb, נִצַּל, but it is fairly rare.)

הִשְׁבִּיעַ 'to cause someone to swear/take an oath' (*hiphil* of שבע; see נִשְׁבַּע below); pref. conj. יַשְׁבִּיעַ; cons. pret. וַיַּשְׁבַּע

הִתְבּוֹנֵן 'to pay close attention to, consider' (*hitpolel* of בין); pref. conj. יִתְבּוֹנֵן

חָרָה literally 'to burn, become hot', but generally used in an impersonal construction with לְ to mean 'to get angry'; the verb is unchangeable in this construction: חָרָה לוֹ 'he got angry' (that is, 'it got hot for him'); חָרָה לִי 'I got angry' ('it got hot for me'). The verb is the same, and person is expressed by the suffix on לְ; pref. conj. is rare; cons. pret. וַיִּחַר

כּוֹנֵן 'to set up, establish' (*polel* of כון); pref. conj. יְכוֹנֵן

נִשְׁבַּע 'to swear, take an oath' (*niphal* of שבע); pref. conj. יִשָּׁבַע; cons. pret. both וַיִּשָּׁבַע and וַיִּשָּׁבַע; see הִשְׁבִּיעַ above

רום 'to be high, exalted'; pref. conj. יָרוּם; cons pret. וַיָּרָם

hiphil הֵרִים 'to raise, lift; set up, erect; exalt; remove; offer'; pref. conj. יָרִים; cons. pret. וַיָּרֶם

polel רוֹמֵם 'to lift up; exalt, extol'; pref. conj. יְרוֹמֵם (a poetic form)

שָׁאַל   'to ask; to consult' (in divination); pref. conj. יִשְׁאַל

nouns

אֹהֶל   'tent'; with sf. אָהֳלִי (pronounced o-ho-lee); pl. אֹהָלִים/אֹהָלִים; cs. pl. אָהֳלֵי; pl. with sf. אֹהָלַי

אַף   'nose; anger'; with sf. אַפִּי; used with חָרָה (see above) in a variant of the חָרָה לְ construction: חָרָה אַפּוֹ 'he got angry' (literally, 'his nose got hot'); חָרָה אַפִּי 'I got angry' ('my nose got hot'); in the dual, אַפַּיִם 'face'; du. with sf. אַפִּי

גּוֹי   'nation, people'; pl. גּוֹים (note only one י); cs. pl. גּוֹיֵי

מוֹעֵד   'appointed time, season; appointed place, meeting' (from the root יעד); with sf. מוֹעֲדִי; pl. מוֹעֲדִים; the אֹהֶל מוֹעֵד 'tent of meeting' is the tabernacle in the wilderness where Yahweh appears to Moses

נְאֻם   'utterance'; esp. in prophetic literature, in phrases like נְאֻם יְהוָה 'utterance of Yahweh' literally, but similar in meaning to כֹּה אָמַר יְהוָה 'thus says Yahweh'

שָׁלוֹם   'peace, welfare, well-being'; cs. sg. שְׁלוֹם; שָׁאַל לְשָׁלוֹם means to ask someone (with לְ plus the person) how they are, as in שָׁאַל לָהּ לְשָׁלוֹם 'he asked her how she was' or הֲשָׁלוֹם אַתָּה 'How are you?' 'Are you well?' (can be used with any form of 'you')

conjunction

אוֹ   'or'

particle

הִנֵּה   See discussion above.

29.8 EXERCISES FOR LESSON 29

A. Translate from Hebrew to English:

1.   וַיַּעֲמֹד דָּוִד לִפְנֵי הַפְּלִשְׁתִּי³ וַיִּקַּח אֶת־חַרְבּוֹ וַיְמֹתֵת אֹתוֹ וַיִּכְרֹת אֶת־רֹאשׁוֹ:

2.   וַיִּחַר אַף מֹשֶׁה וַיַּשְׁלֵךְ מִיָּדָיו אֶת־הַלּוּחֹת⁴ וַיְשַׁבֵּר אֹתָם:

---

3. 'The Philistine'.
4. 'The tablets'.

3. וַיֹּאמֶר אֲלֵהֶם רְאוּבֵן⁵ אַל־תִּשְׁפְּכוּ־דָם הַשְׁלִיכוּ אֹתוֹ אֶל־הַבּוֹר⁶ הַזֶּה אֲשֶׁר בַּמִּדְבָּר
   וְיָד⁷ אַל־תִּשְׁלְחוּ־בוֹ לְמַעַן⁸ הַצִּיל אֹתוֹ מִיָּדָם לַהֲשִׁיבוֹ אֶל־אָבִיו:

   (Gen 37:22; Reuben is speaking of Joseph here)

4. כֹּה יַעֲשֶׂה־לִּי אֱלֹהִים וְכֹה יֹסִיף⁹ כִּי אִם־¹⁰לִפְנֵי בוֹא־הַשֶּׁמֶשׁ¹¹ אֶטְעַם¹² לֶחֶם אוֹ
   כָל־מְאוּמָה¹³:

   (part of 2 Sam 3:35; David is mourning the death of his general Abner)

5. וַיִּשְׁאַל לָהֶם לְשָׁלוֹם וַיֹּאמֶר הֲשָׁלוֹם אֲבִיכֶם הַזָּקֵן:

6. גַּדְּלוּ לַיהוָה¹⁴ אִתִּי וּנְרוֹמְמָה¹⁵ שְׁמוֹ יַחְדָּו¹⁶: (Ps 34:4)

7. לָכֵן הִנֵּה־יָמִים בָּאִים נְאֻם־יְהוָה וְלֹא־יֵאָמֵר¹⁷ עוֹד חַי־יְהוָה אֲשֶׁר הֶעֱלָה אֶת־בְּנֵי
   יִשְׂרָאֵל מֵאֶרֶץ מִצְרָיִם: כִּי אִם־¹⁸חַי־יְהוָה אֲשֶׁר הֶעֱלָה אֶת־בְּנֵי יִשְׂרָאֵל מֵאֶרֶץ
   צָפוֹן¹⁹ ...: (Jer 16:14 plus a clause from 16:15)

8. וַיְדַבֵּר יְהוָה לַנָּבִיא עַל־הַכֹּהֲנִים²⁰ וַיֹּאמֶר וְהָיָה בְּבוֹאָם אֶל־אֹהֶל מוֹעֵד אוֹ בְּגִשְׁתָּם
   אֶל־הַמִּזְבֵּחַ וְלֹא²¹ יָמוּתוּ:

---

5. A personal name, Reuben.

6. בּוֹר means 'pit'.

7. Read וְ as 'but' here.

8. The quotation ends with בוֹ; the לְמַעַן phrase explains why Reuben spoke up. '(He said all this) in order to…'.

9. This verb is written defectively; it is missing the *vav mater* for the *holem*.

10. Translate כִּי אִם here simply as 'if'.

11. הַשֶּׁמֶשׁ is 'the sun', and when the sun 'goes in', it sets.

12. The verb טעם means 'to taste'.

13. 'Anything at all'.

14. לְ here is functioning much the same as אֶת.

15. In order to translate this word correctly, see the explanation in the box at lesson 24.5, exercise A.8.

16. 'Together'.

17. This is the *niphal* prefix conjugation of the root אמר.

18. כִּי אִם = 'but rather'.

19. 'The north'.

20. עַל = 'about' here.

21. You should interpret the וְ on this word as a comma.

9. ‏וַיִּשְׁמַ֣ע שָׁא֔וּל בְּק֖וֹל יְהוֹנָתָ֑ן²² וַיִּשָּׁבַ֣ע שָׁא֔וּל חַי־יְהוָ֖ה אִם־יוּמָ֥ת דָּוִֽד׃

10. ‏אַל־תִּזְכְּר֖וּ רִאשֹׁנ֑וֹת²³ וְקַדְמֹנִיּ֖וֹת²⁴ אַל־תִּתְבֹּנָֽנוּ׃ (Isa 43:18)

11. ‏ה֥וּא יִבְנֶה־בַּ֖יִת לִשְׁמִ֑י וְכֹנַנְתִּ֛י אֶת־כִּסֵּ֥א מַמְלַכְתּ֖וֹ²⁵ עַד־עוֹלָֽם׃ (2 Sam 7:13)

12. ‏כֹּֽה־אָמַ֞ר אֲדֹנָ֣י²⁶ יְהוִ֗ה הִנֵּ֨ה אֶשָּׂ֤א אֶל־גּוֹיִם֙ יָדִ֔י וְאֶל־עַמִּ֖ים אָרִ֣ים נִסִּ֑י²⁷ וְהֵבִ֤יאוּ בָנַ֙יִךְ֙²⁹ בְּחֹ֔צֶן²⁸ וּבְנֹתַ֖יִךְ עַל־כָּתֵ֥ף³⁰ תִּנָּשֶֽׂאנָה³¹ (Isa 49:22)

13. ‏מִ֥י חָזָ֖ק מֵאֱלֹהֵ֑ינוּ הָאֹסֵ֣ר אֶת־הָרָעִ֔ים וְהַמַּשְׁלִ֖יךְ אֹתָ֥ם בַּיָּֽם׃

14. ‏אִם־לֹ֤א תִירָא֙ יְהוָ֣ה אֱלֹהֶ֔יךָ יִרְדְּפ֤וּ אַחֲרֶ֙יךָ֙ אַנְשֵׁ֣י הָעִ֔יר עַד־אֲשֶׁ֥ר תֵּצֵ֖א מֵאַרְצָ֑ם וְשָׂרְפ֤וּ אֶת־בֵּיתְךָ֙ בָּאֵ֔שׁ וְגַ֖ם תִּכָּרֵ֥ת מֵעַמָּֽךְ׃

15. ‏וַֽיְהִ֧י הַמַּבּ֛וּל³² אַרְבָּעִ֥ים³³ י֖וֹם עַל־הָאָ֑רֶץ וַיִּרְבּ֣וּ הַמַּ֗יִם וַיִּשְׂאוּ֙ אֶת־הַתֵּבָ֔ה³⁴ וַתָּ֖רָם מֵעַ֥ל³⁵ הָאָֽרֶץ׃ (Gen 7:17)

16. ‏וַיַּשְׁבַּ֣ע אַבְרָהָ֗ם אֶת־עַבְדּוֹ֙ הַנִּבֹּ֔ון לִמְצֹ֥א אִשָּׁ֖ה לִבְנ֑וֹ וּלְהַזְכִּ֛יר שֵׁ֥ם אַבְרָהָ֖ם כָּל־יְמֵ֥י חַיָּֽיו׃

---

22. Jonathan, Saul's son.
23. 'First things'.
24. 'Ancient things'.
25. 'His kingdom'.
26. 'My lord'. This is the term that is usually substituted for Yahweh in the Masoretic Text. When אֲדֹנָי and יהוה occur together in a text, יהוה is vocalized יֱהוִה and pronounced "Elohim."
27. 'My sign'.
28. The feminine 'you' here is Jerusalem.
29. 'Bosom'. This is poetry, so some explanatory words may need to be added in this passage. One might translate 'in (their) bosom', for instance.
30. 'Shoulder'.
31. This is the *niphal* of נשׂא.
32. 'The flood, the deluge'.
33. "forty" (plus the thing counted in the singular)
34. 'The ark' (Noah's boat).
35. Translate simply 'above'.

30

Geminate Verbs and the Numbers above Ten

30.1. Geminate verbs generally

The last category of verbs to be taken up here is the geminate verbs. Geminate verbs are those that have the same consonant as the second and third root letters, for instance, סָבַב 'to turn around; to surround' (like Gemini, "the twins"). These verbs can be difficult to identify, but they are, fortunately, fairly rare.

> A Note on the Paradigms for the Geminate Verbs
>
> The paradigms for geminate verbs are given below, for completeness, but most beginning students simply memorize the root consonants of the most common geminate verbs, and when they come across a verb they do not know but that contains those root consonants, they know to consider the possibility that the root is geminate when they are trying to decide where to look it up in the dictionary. The most common geminate verbs in BH are given in the vocabulary for this lesson.

30.2. The difficulties associated with distinguishing geminate verbs

The geminate verbs are uncommon, and in certain forms they look exactly like those forms in another, more common, category of verbs (for instance, the *qal* consecutive preterite of סָבַב is וַיָּסָב, indistinguishable from the *qal* consecutive preterite of a II-ו verb). Consequently, geminate verbs were often reanalyzed by ancient speakers as some other category of verb, and we find "biforms"; that is, some forms of a given verb are typical of the geminate category, while other forms appear to be from another category altogether. For instance, the geminate verb שָׁדַד 'to ruin' has the normal forms of a geminate verb, but there is one example of the prefix conjugation 3ms of this verb that is written יְשׁוּד, as if from a II-ו verb.

(There is no root שׁוד in BH.) So when a weak verb cannot be found in dictionaries under the category that it *should* be, it is always a good idea to look up the verb as if it were a geminate, before deciding that the initial parsing was simply wrong.

Even more confusing, the *niphal* suffix conjugation 3ms of סָבַב is נָסַב, which looks exactly like a *qal* suffix conjugation 3ms of a root נסב (which does not exist in BH). It should come as no surprise, then, that besides the regular *qal* prefix conjugation of סָבַב, there is a whole other *qal* prefix conjugation that looks something like a I-נ paradigm. That prefix conjugation paradigm will also be presented below.

Stative geminate verbs (see 13.2) can also have a slightly different paradigm from nonstative geminate verbs, and that paradigm will be presented below also.

30.3. THE REGULAR NONSTATIVE QAL FORMS FOR GEMINATE VERBS

The regular nonstative geminate *qal* paradigm will be illustrated using the verb סָבַב 'to turn around (intrans.); to surround (trans.)'.

THE REGULAR QAL FORMS OF THE GEMINATE VERB

inf. cs.	suff. conj.	cons. pret.	volitives		pref. conj.
סֹב	סַבֹּ֫ותִי	…			אָסֹב
סְבִּי	סַבֹּ֫ות	…	סֹב	impv.	תָּסֹב
inf. abs.	סַבֹּות	…	סֹ֫בִּי	impv.	תָּסֹ֫בִּי
סָבֹוב	סָבַב	וַיָּ֫סָב	יָסֹב	juss.	יָסֹב
	סֶבְבָה	…	תָּסֹב	juss.	תָּסֹב
ptcp.	סַבֹּונוּ			cohort.[1]	נָסֹב
סֹבֵב	סַבֹּותֶם		סֹ֫בּוּ	impv.	תָּסֹ֫בּוּ
סֹבְבָה	סַבֹּותֶן		סֻבֶּ֫ינָה	impv.	תְּסֻבֶּ֫ינָה
סֹבְבִים	סָבְבוּ	וַיָּסֹ֫בּוּ	יָסֹ֫בּוּ	juss.	יָסֹ֫בּוּ
סֹבְבֹות			תְּסֻבֶּ֫ינָה	juss.	תְּסֻבֶּ֫ינָה

---

1. There are only two occurrences of the *qal* cohortative of geminate verbs, both plural and both in forms that are influenced by other verb types and so not appropriate for the paradigm presented here: נָבְלָה 'let us confuse', from בלל; and נִדְמֶה 'let us perish', from דמם.

Notes to the paradigm:

30.3.1. The *qal* prefix conjugation forms that also have suffixes (2fs, 2mp, 2fp, 3mp, 3fp) indicate that the verb is geminate because the second root letter is doubled. The other five *qal* prefix conjugation forms look exactly like the jussive of II-weak verbs.

30.3.2. The *qal* imperative forms are identifiable: three have a doubled second root letter, and the ms has a *holem*, unlike any other weak *qal* imperative, with the exception of בּוֹא.

30.3.3. As noted above, the *qal* consecutive preterite of geminate verbs can look exactly like the *qal* consecutive preterite of II-weak verbs.

30.3.4. The *qal* suffix conjugation of geminate verbs is fairly easy to identify. In the first and second persons, they have a doubled second root letter, and they have the longer suffix conjugation endings that we have seen before: וֹתִי ׳-, וֹתָ ׳-, and so on. The third-person forms actually have all three root letters. The *qal* infinitive absolute and participle are also normal.

30.3.5. The *qal* infinitive construct of geminate verbs looks exactly like the *qal* imperative, unless suffixes are added. The infinitive construct has *qibbuts* before a doubled second root letter, instead of the *holem* of the imperative.

30.4. THE REGULAR STATIVE *QAL* FORMS FOR GEMINATE VERBS

THE REGULAR *QAL* FORMS OF THE STATIVE GEMINATE VERB

suff. conj.	cons. pret.	volitives		pref. conj.
קַלּוֹתִי	וָאֵקַל			אֵקַל
קַלּוֹתָ	וַתֵּקַל			תֵּקַל
קַלּוֹת	וַתֵּקַלִּי			תֵּקַלִּי
קַל	וַיֵּקַל	יֵקַל	juss.	יֵקַל
קָלָּה	…	תֵּקַל	juss.	תֵּקַל
קַלּוֹנוּ				נֵקַל
קַלּוֹתֶם				תֵּקַלּוּ
קַלּוֹתֶן				תְּקַלֶּינָה
קַלּוּ		יֵקַלּוּ	juss.	יֵקַלּוּ
		תְּקַלֶּינָה	juss.	תְּקַלֶּינָה

The *qal* stative geminate verb paradigm is illustrated with the root קלל 'to be disrespected, not respected; to be thought little of'. The only differences between the stative and nonstative paradigms occur in the prefix conjugation (and jussive and consecutive preterite) and suffix conjugation, so only those forms are given.
Notes to the paradigm:

30.4.1. In the five forms that have no suffix, the *qal* geminate stative prefix conjugation is much like the strong verb stative prefix conjugation (יִכְבַּד), except that there is one root letter missing, and the preformative *hireq* lengthens to *tsere* in compensation. In the other five forms, the doubled second root consonant gives away the geminate root.

30.4.2. The *qal* geminate stative suffix conjugation is the same as the nonstative suffix conjugation in the first and second persons. In 3fs and 3cp, the doubled root letter identifies the verb as geminate. The 3ms gives no clue to the fact that it comes from a geminate root; the form should simply be learned.

30.5. THE ALTERNATIVE *QAL* FORMS FOR GEMINATE VERBS

Finally, here is the alternative *qal* prefix conjugation paradigm (which can be confused with I-נ), both stative (קלל) and nonstative forms (סבב).

THE ALTERNATIVE PREFIX CONJUGATION FOR THE REGULAR AND STATIVE GEMINATE VERB

pref. conj. stative	pref. conj. nonstative
אֵקַל	אָסֹב
תֵּקַל	תָּסֹב
תֵּקַלִּי	תָּסֹבִּי
יֵקַל	יָסֹב
תֵּקַל	תָּסֹב
נֵקַל	נָסֹב
תֵּקַלּוּ	תָּסֹבּוּ
תֵּקַלְנָה	תָּסֹבְנָה
יֵקַלּוּ	יָסֹבּוּ
תֵּקַלְנָה	תָּסֹבְנָה

Note to the paradigm:

The five forms without any suffix are indistinguishable from a *qal* I-נ verb. The feminine plural could also be confused with *qal* I-נ verbs. The remaining three forms (2fs, 2mp, and 3mp) have a doubled second root letter and are accented differently from I- נ verbs.

30.6. THE *NIPHAL* AND *HIPHIL* FORMS FOR GEMINATE VERBS

For completeness, the *niphal* and *hiphil* paradigms of geminate verbs are presented next, but it should be remembered (see the box at the beginning of the lesson) that the geminates are the rarest weak verb forms, so while the paradigms and notes that follow should be examined, it is not necessary for the beginning student to be as familiar with the geminates as with the other weak verbs.

THE *NIPHAL* FORMS OF THE GEMINATE VERB

inf. cs.	suff. conj.	cons. pret.	volitives		pref. conj.
הִסֵּב	נְסַבּוֹתִי	וָאֶחַל		cohort.[2]	אֶסַּב
	נְסַבּוֹת		הִסַּב	impv.	תִּסַּב
inf. abs.	נְסַבּוֹת		הִסַּּבִּי	impv.	תִּסַּּבִּי
הִסּוֹב	נָסַב/נָמֵס		יִסַּב	juss.	יִסַּב
	נָסַבָּה		תִּסַּב	juss.	תִּסַּב
ptcp.	נְסַבּוֹנוּ				נִסַּב
נָסָב	נְסַבּוֹתֶם		הִסַּּבּוּ	impv.	תִּסַּּבּוּ
נְסַבָּה	נְסַבּוֹתֶן		הִסַּבֶּינָה	impv.	תִּסַּבֶּינָה
נְסַבִּים	נָסַבּוּ		יִסַּּבּוּ	juss.	יִסַּּבּוּ
נְסַבּוֹת			תִּסַּבֶּינָה	juss.	תִּסַּבֶּינָה

Notes to the paradigm:

30.6.1. The prefix conjugation, jussive, and consecutive preterite of the *niphal* geminate verb can be confused with the alternative prefix conjugation of the *qal* stative geminate paradigm.

---

2. Only one such form exists in the Hebrew Bible: אַל־אֵחָתָּה 'let me not be dismayed' from חתת.

30.6.2. The imperative has the הֲ- prefix of the *niphal* imperative.

30.6.3. The first- and second-person forms of the suffix conjugation of the *niphal* geminate verb are simply the regular suffix conjugation of the *qal*, with the addition of נ. The third-person forms are exactly the same as verbs I-נ and can be identified as geminate only if it is remembered that this confusion occurs. (נָמֵס is the *niphal* 3ms for verbs that are stative in form but not in meaning.)

30.6.4. The infinitives construct and absolute have the הֲ- prefix of the *niphal*.

30.6.5. The fp, mp, and fp participle are identifiable by the doubled second root letter. The ms participle must simply be learned.

THE *HIPHIL* FORMS OF THE GEMINATE VERB

inf. cs.	suff. conj.	cons. pret.	volitives		pref. conj.
הָסֵב	הֲסִבֹּ֫תִי				אָסֵב
	הֲסִבֹּ֫ת		הָסֵב	impv.	תָּסֵב
inf. abs.	הֲסִבֹּ֫ות		הָסֵ֫בִּי	impv.	תָּסֵ֫בִּי
הָסֵב	הֵסֵב/הֵסַב	וַיָּ֫סֵב/וַיָּ֫חֶל	יָסֵב	juss.	יָסֵב/יַסֵב
	הֵסֵ֫בָּה	וַתָּ֫חֶל	תָּסֵב	juss.	תָּסֵב
ptcp.	הֲסִבֹּ֫ונוּ		נָסֵ֫בָּה	cohort.[3]	נָסֵב
מֵסֵב	הֲסִבֹּותֶם		הָסֵ֫בּוּ	impv.	תָּסֵ֫בּוּ
מְסִבָּה	הֲסִבֹּותֶן		הֲסִבֶּ֫ינָה	impv.	תְּסִבֶּ֫ינָה
מְסִבִּים	הֵסֵ֫בּוּ	וַיָּסֵ֫בּוּ	יָסֵ֫בּוּ/יַסֵ֫בּוּ	juss.	יָסֵ֫בּוּ/יַסֵ֫בּוּ
מְסִבּות			תְּסִבֶּ֫ינָה	juss.	תְּסִבֶּ֫ינָה

Notes to the paradigm:

30.6.6. In the prefix conjugation, the two forms to the left of slashes follow the I-נ type paradigm. The five forms without suffixes look exactly like the jussive of the *hiphil* II-weak verbs. Also, the jussive and consecutive preterite of the *hiphil*

---

3. While the plural cohortative נָסֵ֫בָּה actually exists, the only singular *hiphil* cohortative from a geminate root is one occurrence of אֵלִ֫ילָה 'let me wail/lament', from the root ילל, which occurs only in the *hiphil* in BH.

geminate verbs look exactly like the jussive and consecutive preterite of the *hiphil* of II-weak verbs.

30.6.7. Note the *hateph-patakh* under the ה of the suffix conjugation, first and second persons, as well as the longer וֹתִי ֫-, וֹתָ ֫- endings.

30.6.8. The suffix conjugation 3fs and 3mp forms of these verbs have the doubled second root letter. The 3ms form must simply be learned.

30.6.9. The infinitive construct of these forms is exactly the same as the infinitive absolute, and they are both exactly the same as the *hiphil* infinitive absolute of II-weak verbs.

30.6.10. The fs, mp, and fp participles have the doubled second root letter. The ms participle must simply be learned.

> Note that the *piel* and *hitpael* of the geminate verbs are perfectly normal.

The paradigms for *qal*, *niphal*, and *hiphil* geminate verbs are gathered together on pages 286–88 in appendix H so that they may be compared. The portions in color on these three pages show in the prefix conjugation, the imperative, the jussive, the suffix conjugation, and the infinitive construct those instances where a dagesh represents the geminated second and third consonants of the root. Those doubled consonants and the vowel that follows each instance have been highlighted.

30.7. THE NUMBERS 11 AND 12

So far, we have studied the numbers from 1 to 10 in BH. The numbers 11 and 12 occur in two forms each: besides the usual numbers for 1 and 10, 11 has one form that uses the word עַשְׁתֵּי plus 10; 12 has both שְׁנֵי and שְׁנֵים before 10. There are slightly different words for 10, as well, עֶשְׂרֵה and עָשָׂר. (Like 1 and 2, 11 and 12 do *not* use a masculine-looking form to modify a feminine noun and vice versa.)

THE NUMBERS 11 AND 12

modifies feminine noun	modifies masculine noun	
אַחַת עֶשְׂרֵה	אַחַד עָשָׂר	11
עַשְׁתֵּי עֶשְׂרֵה	עַשְׁתֵּי עָשָׂר	11
שְׁתֵּי עֶשְׂרֵה	שְׁנֵי עָשָׂר	12
שְׁתֵּים עֶשְׂרֵה	שְׁנֵים עָשָׂר	12

30.8. THE NUMBERS 13–19

The numbers 13–19 use the same words for 10 as 11 and 12 do, and, like the numbers 3–9, the masculine-looking form of the unit modifies feminine nouns and vice versa.

THE NUMBERS 13–19

modifies feminine noun	modifies masculine noun	
שְׁלֹשׁ עֶשְׂרֵה	שְׁלֹשָׁה עָשָׂר	13
אַרְבַּע עֶשְׂרֵה	אַרְבָּעָה עָשָׂר	14
חֲמֵשׁ עֶשְׂרֵה	חֲמִשָּׁה עָשָׂר	15
שֵׁשׁ עֶשְׂרֵה	שִׁשָּׁה עָשָׂר	16
שְׁבַע עֶשְׂרֵה	שִׁבְעָה עָשָׂר	17
שְׁמֹנֶה עֶשְׂרֵה	שְׁמֹנָה עָשָׂר	18
תְּשַׁע עֶשְׂרֵה	תִּשְׁעָה עָשָׂר	19

30.9. THE DECADE NUMBERS

In BH, 20 is the plural of 10: עֶשְׂרִים. The other decades, 30, 40, and so on, are the plurals of 3, 4, and so on. They are: שְׁלֹשִׁים, אַרְבָּעִים, חֲמִשִּׁים, שִׁשִּׁים, שִׁבְעִים, שְׁמֹנִים, תִּשְׁעִים.

30.9.1. When these multiples of ten are used, the thing counted is usually in the singular.

30.9.2. The decades plus units (24, 76, etc.) appear as follows

| 4 and 20 | אַרְבָּעָה/אַרְבַּע וְעֶשְׂרִים | or | 20 and 4 | עֶשְׂרִים וְאַרְבָּעָה/אַרְבַּע |
| 6 and 70 | שִׁשָּׁה/שֵׁשׁ וְשִׁבְעִים | or | 70 and 6 | שִׁבְעִים וְשִׁשָּׁה/שֵׁשׁ |

For example, '24 men' is written עֶשְׂרִים וְאַרְבָּעָה אִישׁ; '76 women', שֵׁשׁ וְשִׁבְעִים אִשָּׁה.

30.10. THE NUMBERS 100, 1,000, AND 10,000

In BH, 100 is מֵאָה (construct מְאַת); 200 is מָאתַיִם; and 300 is שְׁלֹשׁ מֵאוֹת. The number 1,000 is אֶלֶף; 2,000 is אַלְפַּיִם; and 3,000 is שְׁלֹשֶׁת אֲלָפִים. Finally, 10,000 is רְבָבָה.

30.11. THE NUMBERS TO COMMIT TO MEMORY

In the end, what should be memorized about BH numbers is the following:

The Crucial Numbers to Memorize	
the basic form of each number 1–10	the decades as plurals
the ordinals	מֵאָה (= 100)
עַשְׁתֵּי (in some forms of 11)	אֶלֶף (= 1000)
עֶשְׂרִים (=20)	רְבָבָה (= 10,000)

30.12. VOCABULARY FOR LESSON 30

numbers: Memorize the set of numerals listed in 30.11 above.

verbs

אָהֵב   'to love'; pref. conj. varies, 3ms יֶאֱהַב, 1cs אֹהַב; אַהֲבָה 'love' (see below) is used as inf. cs.; ptcp. אֹהֵב 'lover' can also mean 'friend'

אָסַף   'to gather'; to remove; pref. conj. יֶאֱסֹף

   niphal נֶאֱסַף 'to assemble, be gathered; to be removed'; pref. conj. יֵאָסֵף; cons. pret. 3ms וַיֵּאָסֶף

אָרַר   'to curse'; pref. conj. יָאֹר; suff. conj. 1cs אָרוֹתִי (the *qamets* under the א compensates for inability to double the ר); used esp. in the passive ptcp. form אָרוּר 'cursed'

הָלַל   'to praise' (*piel* of הלל); pref. conj. יְהַלֵּל; note the impv. הַלְלוּ־יָהּ 'Praise Yahweh!' (with *maqqeph* or written as one word)

חָטָא   'to sin; to incur guilt'; pref. conj. יֶחֱטָא

hiphil הֶחֱטִיא 'to cause to sin'; pref. conj. יַחֲטִיא

חִלֵּל   'to defile, pollute' (*piel* of חלל); pref. conj. יְחַלֵּל

hiphil הֵחֵל 'to begin; to do something for the first time'; pref. conj. יָחֵל; cons. pret. וַיָּחֶל

סָבַב   'to turn around; to surround'; pref. conj. יָסֹב or יִסֹּב; cons. pret. וַיָּסָב or וַיִּסֹּב

פָּקַד   'to pay attention to, take care of; to visit; to punish; to muster; to appoint'; pref. conj. יִפְקֹד

קָלַל   'to be small, light, fast; to be disrespected, not respected; to be thought little of'; suff. conj. 3ms קַל, 1cs קַלּוֹתִי; pref. conj. יֵקַל; cons. pret. וַיֵּקַל

piel קִלֵּל 'to curse'; pref. conj. יְקַלֵּל

רעע   'to be evil, bad; to be troubling'; suff. conj. 3ms רַע; pref. conj. יֵרַע; cons. pret. וַיֵּרַע

hiphil הֵרַע 'to act wickedly; to treat badly, injure, hurt, do harm'; pref. conj. יָרַע/יָרֵעַ; cons. pret. וַיָּרַע/וַיָּרֵעַ

nouns

אַהֲבָה   'love'; cs. אַהֲבַת; also used as inf. cs. of the verb אהב above; as such, can be translated '(to) love' and 'loving' (as a noun, e.g., 'my loving him')

אָרוֹן   'ark' (of the covenant; not Noah's ark); with def. art. הָאָרוֹן

בָּשָׂר   'flesh'; cs. בְּשַׂר; with sf. בְּשָׂרִי; pl. very rare

חֹדֶשׁ   'month; new moon'; with sf. חָדְשִׁי; pl. חֳדָשִׁים; cs. pl. חָדְשֵׁי

חַטָּאת   'sin; sin offering' (fem.); cs. חַטַּאת; pl. חַטָּאוֹת; cs. pl. is spelled oddly, חַטֹּאות

מַעֲשֶׂה   'deed, work'; cs. מַעֲשֵׂה; with sf. מַעֲשֵׂהוּ; pl. מַעֲשִׂים (root עשה)

עֵת   'time' (fem.); with sf. עִתִּי; pl. rare

proper nouns

אַהֲרֹן   personal name, 'Aaron', brother of Moses

יַעֲקֹב   personal name, 'Jacob'

רָחֵל   personal name, 'Rachel'

adverb/preposition

סָבִיב   'round about, all around'

30.13. EXERCISES FOR LESSON 30

A. Which numbers are represented?

7. עֶשְׂרִים וְאַרְבָּעָה		1. אֶחָד וְעֶשְׂרִים	
8. שֶׁבַע עֶשְׂרֵה		2. שֶׁבַע וְשִׁבְעִים	
9. תִּשְׁעִים וּשְׁמֹנָה		3. מֵאָה וַחֲמִשִּׁים	
10. תְּשַׁע מֵאוֹת וּשְׁלֹשִׁים		4. אַרְבָּעִים אֶלֶף	
11. שְׁנַיִם וּשְׁלֹשִׁים אֶלֶף וּמָאתַיִם		5. שְׁתַּיִם וּשְׁמֹנִים	
12. שִׁבְעָה וְשִׁשִּׁים אֶלֶף וַחֲמֵשׁ מֵאוֹת וַחֲמִשִּׁים		6. שְׁבַע מֵאוֹת	

B. Translate from Hebrew to English:

1. עַל־כֵּן יַעֲזֹב אִישׁ אֶת־אָבִיו וְאֶת־אִמּוֹ וְדָבַק⁴ בְּאִשְׁתּוֹ וְהָיוּ לְבָשָׂר אֶחָד: (Gen 2:24)

2. הִנֵּה אֲרוֹן הַבְּרִית אֲדוֹן⁵ כָּל־הָאָרֶץ עֹבֵר לִפְנֵיכֶם בַּיַּרְדֵּן: (Josh 3:11)

3. מִיּוֹם אֶחָד לַחֹדֶשׁ⁶ הַשְּׁבִיעִי הֵחֵלּוּ לְהַעֲלוֹת עֹלוֹת לַיהוָה:.... (part of Ezra 3:6)

4. וַיֶּאֱהַב יַעֲקֹב אֶת־רָחֵל וַיֹּאמֶר אֶעֱבָדְךָ⁷ שֶׁבַע שָׁנִים בְּרָחֵל⁸ בִּתְּךָ הַקְּטַנָּה⁹:
   (Gen 29:18)

5. וַיַּעֲבֹד יַעֲקֹב בְּרָחֵל שֶׁבַע שָׁנִים וַיִּהְיוּ בְעֵינָיו כְּיָמִים אֲחָדִים¹⁰ בְּאַהֲבָתוֹ אֹתָהּ:
   (Gen 29:20)

---

4. 'And cling to' (including the following בְּ); this is the word that was traditionally translated 'cleave to'.

5. 'The lord of'.

6. לְ here = 'of, belonging to'.

7. The 'you' here is Rachel's father, Laban.

8. One of the meanings of the preposition בְּ is 'in exchange for'.

9. 'Small', when used of siblings or offspring, means 'youngest'; here it is 'younger', since there are only two daughters.

10. 'Several, a few'.

6. וַיְהִי בְּבוֹאָם¹¹ בְּשׁוּב דָּוִד מֵהַכּוֹת אֶת־הַפְּלִשְׁתִּי¹² וַתֵּצֶאנָה הַנָּשִׁים מִכָּל־עָרֵי

   יִשְׂרָאֵל ... לִקְרַאת¹³ שָׁאוּל הַמֶּלֶךְ ...: וַתַּעֲנֶינָה¹⁴ הַנָּשִׁים הַמְשַׂחֲקוֹת¹⁵ וַתֹּאמַרְן

   הִכָּה שָׁאוּל בַּאֲלָפָיו וְדָוִד בְּרִבְבֹתָיו: וַיִּחַר לְשָׁאוּל מְאֹד וַיֵּרַע בְּעֵינָיו הַדָּבָר הַזֶּה

   וַיֹּאמֶר נָתְנוּ לְדָוִד רְבָבוֹת וְלִי נָתְנוּ הָאֲלָפִים וְעוֹד לוֹ¹⁶ אַךְ¹⁷ הַמְּלוּכָה¹⁸:

   (adapted from 1 Sam 18:6-8)

7. וַיְכַל¹⁹ יַעֲקֹב לְצַוֺּת אֶת־בָּנָיו וַיֶּאֱסֹף רַגְלָיו אֶל־הַמִּטָּה²⁰ וַיִּגְוַע²¹ וַיֵּאָסֶף אֶל־עַמָּיו:

   (Gen 49:33)

8. וַתָּבֹא הָעִיר בַּמָּצוֹר²² עַד עַשְׁתֵּי עֶשְׂרֵה שָׁנָה לַמֶּלֶךְ צִדְקִיָּהוּ²³: (2 Kgs 25:2)

9. וַיָּבֹא²⁴ וַיֹּאכַל וַיֵּשְׁתְּ וַיֹּאמֶר פִּקְדוּ־נָא אֶת־הָאֲרוּרָה הַזֹּאת וְקִבְרוּהָ כִּי בַת־

   מֶלֶךְ הִיא: (2 Kgs 9:34)

10. הַלְלוּיָהּ הוֹדוּ²⁵ לַיהוָה כִּי־טוֹב²⁶ כִּי לְעוֹלָם חַסְדּוֹ: (Ps 106:1)

---

11. 'They' are Saul and David and the army. They are coming back from battling the Philistines.
12. 'The Philistine'.
13. 'To meet'.
14. This is not the root ענה that means 'to respond' but rather a different ענה (ענה IV in BDB), which means 'to sing'.
15. The verb means 'to celebrate'.
16. These two words are a question here: literally, 'still for him' or 'still his'; in context, 'What more for him?'/'What more can he have?'
17. 'Except'.
18. 'The kingdom'.
19. 'He finished', the *piel* of כלה.
20. 'To the bed'.
21. Another verb for 'to die', often translated 'to breathe one's last'.
22. Translate 'under siege'.
23. A personal name, Zedekiah.
24. The 'he' is King Jehu, and the woman is Queen Jezebel, whom Jehu has just had killed. Jezebel was the daughter of King Ittobaal of Tyre (not Sidon).
25. 'Give thanks'.
26. טוב is not only an adjective; it can also be a 3ms suffix conjugation verb 'to be good'.

11. אֲבָרֲכָה²⁷ מְבָרֲכֶיךָ וּמְקַלֶּלְךָ²⁸ אָאֹר וְנִבְרְכוּ בְךָ כֹּל מִשְׁפְּחֹת הָאֲדָמָה:

(adapted from Gen 12:3)

12. וַיְשַׁלַּח אֶת־הַיּוֹנָה²⁹ מֵאִתּוֹ³⁰ לִרְאוֹת הֲקַלּוּ³¹ הַמַּיִם מֵעַל³² פְּנֵי הָאֲדָמָה:

(Gen 8:8)

13. וְיִתֵּן³³ אֶת־יִשְׂרָאֵל בִּגְלַל³⁴ חַטֹּאות יָרָבְעָם³⁵ אֲשֶׁר חָטָא³⁶ וַאֲשֶׁר הֶחֱטִיא אֶת־יִשְׂרָאֵל:

(1 Kgs 14:16)

14. וַעֲבַדְתֶּם־שָׁם אֱלֹהִים מַעֲשֵׂה יְדֵי אָדָם עֵץ וָאֶבֶן אֲשֶׁר לֹא־יִרְאוּן³⁷ וְלֹא יִשְׁמְעוּן
וְלֹא יֹאכְלוּן וְלֹא יְרִיחֻן³⁸: (Deut 4:28)

15. וְהָיָה בָּעֵת הַהִיא אֲחַפֵּשׂ אֶת־יְרוּשָׁלַםִ בַּנֵּרוֹת³⁹ וּפָקַדְתִּי⁴⁰ עַל־הָאֲנָשִׁים הָאֹמְרִים
בִּלְבָבָם לֹא־יֵיטִיב יְהֹוָה וְלֹא יָרֵעַ: (adapted from Zeph 1:12)

---

27. The cohortative often substitutes for a simply prefix conjugation verb, so if the volitive meaning makes no sense, it can always be translated as a simple future.

28. This word is singular in the biblical text, even though its companion word is plural.

29. 'The dove'.

30. מֵאֵת, including with suffixes as we find it here in מֵאִתּוֹ, is simply another way of saying 'from', so מֵאִתּוֹ is simply 'from him(self)'.

31. הֲ here introduces an *indirect* question; translate 'whether'.

32. This word is to be translated as a double preposition, exactly as it appears: 'from upon'.

33. Note the prefix conjugation with regular וְ, connecting this thought to what came before. Translate 'so that he (Yahweh) will give Israel up…'.

34. 'Because of'.

35. A personal name, Jeroboam, first king of northern Israel.

36. Note the word חַטֹּאות, from the root חטא, used as direct object of the verb חָטָא in the *qal* and in the *hiphil*. This word is called a "cognate accusative," and this combination of verbs and objects from the same root is a common usage in Hebrew prose.

37. The final ן- on this 3mp prefix conjugation and the three that follow it sometimes occurs on 3mp and 2mp prefix conjugation forms. It is left over from an older form of the verb and is known as "paragogic *nun*," which simply describes it as a *nun* that appears along with something else.

38. The root ריח means 'to smell' (trans. = to smell something); note that the verb is written defectively, without the *vav mater* for the *shureq* between the ח and the ן, so the Masoretes had to use the vowel *qibbuts* to represent the *u*-vowel.

39. 'With lamps'.

40. With עַל here = 'to punish'.

16. וְלֹא־תִשָּׁבְעוּ בִשְׁמִי לַשֶּׁקֶר[41] וְחִלַּלְתָּ[42] אֶת־שֵׁם אֱלֹהֶיךָ אֲנִי יְהוָה: (Lev 19:12)

17. וַיִּשְׁחַט[43] אֶת־הָעֹלָה וַיַּמְצִאוּ[44] בְּנֵי אַהֲרֹן אֵלָיו אֶת־הַדָּם וַיִּזְרְקֵהוּ[45] עַל־הַמִּזְבֵּחַ סָבִיב:

(Lev 9:12)

---

41. 'Falsely'.

42. The variation between singular and plural within the same sentence is not unusual and is explained by a variety of proposals, none of which need be learned at this introductory level.

43. 'He slaughtered'; the 'he' is Aaron.

44. This is the *hiphil* of מצא 'to find' (written defectively), and here it means 'to present'.

45. 'And he sprinkled it'.

◄ APPENDIX A ►
THE CONSONANTS OF BIBLICAL HEBREW

The chart on the following three pages provides a single reference source for the Hebrew consonants, including their names, how they are pronounced, whether or not they may appear with a *dagesh*, and how they should be transliterated. In addition, the chart provides a handwritten form for each consonant as well as the order in which the lines making up a consonant should be written, moving from right to left.

letter	name	pronunciation	drawn model	order of drawing	drawing hints	dagesh	transliteration
א	*aleph*	glottal stop or zero					ʾ
ב	*bet*	*b* as in *bat* / *v* as in *vat*			horizontal line extends to right	(dagesh form)	b
ג	*gimel*	*g* as in *get* / *g* as in *get*			a very thin letter	(dagesh form)	g
ד	*dalet*	*d* as in *dog* / *d* as in *dog*			horizontal line extends to right of vertical	(dagesh form)	d
ה	*he*	*h* as in *hat* or zero			small vertical does not touch top horizontal	(*mappiq*)	h
ו	*vav*	*v* as in *vat* or zero				(dagesh form)	w
ז	*zayin*	*z* as in *zebra*				(dagesh form)	z
ח	*khet*	*kh* as in *Bach*, *loch*			left vertical does touch top horizontal		ḥ
ט	*tet*	*t* as in *top*				(dagesh form)	ṭ

transliteration	dagesh	drawing hints	order of drawing	drawn model	pronunciation	name	letter
y		written above line (as in וַיִּ)			y as in yet or zero	yod	
k	כּ	a backwards "C"			k as in kid	kaph	
		extends below line (as in גֶךְ)			כ, ך kh as in Bach, loch	final kaph	
l	לּ	higher than others (as in כְּלַב)			l as in lid	lamed	
m	מּ				m as in map	mem	
		right shoulder is rounded				final mem	
n	נּ	a very thin letter			n as in not	nun	
		a very thin letter, extends below line (as in מִן)				final nun	
s	סּ	completely rounded			s as in sit	samekh	
ʿ					glottal stop	ayin	

translit-eration	dagesh	drawing hints	order of drawing	drawn model	pronunciation	name	letter
p	פּ				פ p as in *pit*	pe	פ
		extends below line (as in סוף)			ף, ף f as in *fit*	final pe	ף
ṣ	צ				ts as in *hits*	tsade	צ
		extends below line (as in חמץ)				final tsade	ץ
q	קּ	extends below line (as in קרד)			k as in *kid*	qoph	ק
r		rounded, no sharp angles			r as in *red*; or a French velar r	resh	ר
ś	שׂ	dot over left arm			s as in *sip*	sin	שׂ
š	שׁ	dot over right arm			sh as in *ship*	shin	שׁ
t	תּ	"foot" on left leg			ת t as in *top* ת t as in *top*	tav	ת

◄ APPENDIX B ►

TRANSLITERATION OF HEBREW VOWELS

The transliteration of Hebrew vowels is summarized here. The location of the discussion of each is noted by lesson and section (e.g., 3.4).

SHORT VOWELS

patakh	*a* (2.6)
hireq	*i* (2.6)
seghol	*e* (2.6)
qibbuts	*u* (2.6)
qamets	*o* (when *qamets* is a short vowel) (11.8)

LONG VOWELS

qamets	*ā* (when *qamets* is a long vowel) (3.5)
tsere	*ē* (3.5)
holem	*ō* (3.5)

IRREDUCIBLY LONG VOWELS

hireq gadol	*î* (4.5)
tsere-yod	*ê* (4.5)
shureq	*û* (4.5)
holem-vav	*ô* (and occasionally simple *holem ō*) (4.5)
hireq	*ī*, when *hireq gadol* is expected but the word is written defectively, i.e., without the expected *yod mater* (4.5)
qibbuts	*ū*, when *shureq* is expected but the word is written defectively, i.e., without the expected *vav mater* (4.5)

Diphthongs

îv (5.5)
êv, ēv (5.5)
âv, āv, av (5.5)
āy, ay (5.5)
ôy, ōy (5.5)
ûy, uy (5.5)

Reduced Vowels

shwa   ə (6.6)
hateph-patakh   ă (6.6)
hateph-seghol   ĕ (6.6)
hateph-qamets   ŏ (6.6)

◄ Appendix C ►

Genesis 22:1–19

1 וַיְהִי אַחַר הַדְּבָרִים הָאֵלֶּה

וְהָאֱלֹהִים נִסָּה אֶת־אַבְרָהָם

וַיֹּאמֶר אֵלָיו אַבְרָהָם

וַיֹּאמֶר הִנֵּנִי׃

2 וַיֹּאמֶר קַח־נָא אֶת־בִּנְךָ אֶת־יְחִידְךָ אֲשֶׁר־אָהַבְתָּ אֶת־יִצְחָק

וְלֶךְ־לְךָ אֶל־אֶרֶץ הַמֹּרִיָּה

וְהַעֲלֵהוּ שָׁם לְעֹלָה עַל אַחַד הֶהָרִים

אֲשֶׁר אֹמַר אֵלֶיךָ׃

3 וַיַּשְׁכֵּם אַבְרָהָם בַּבֹּקֶר

וַיַּחֲבֹשׁ אֶת־חֲמֹרוֹ

וַיִּקַּח אֶת־שְׁנֵי נְעָרָיו אִתּוֹ וְאֵת יִצְחָק בְּנוֹ

וַיְבַקַּע עֲצֵי עֹלָה

וַיָּקָם

וַיֵּלֶךְ אֶל־הַמָּקוֹם אֲשֶׁר־אָמַר־לוֹ הָאֱלֹהִים׃

4 בַּיּוֹם הַשְּׁלִישִׁי

וַיִּשָּׂא אַבְרָהָם אֶת־עֵינָיו

וַיַּרְא אֶת־הַמָּקוֹם מֵרָחֹק׃

5 וַיֹּאמֶר אַבְרָהָם אֶל־נְעָרָיו

שְׁבוּ־לָכֶם פֹּה עִם־הַחֲמוֹר

וַאֲנִי וְהַנַּעַר נֵלְכָה עַד־כֹּה

וְנִשְׁתַּחֲוֶה

וְנָשׁוּבָה אֲלֵיכֶם:

6 וַיִּקַּח אַבְרָהָם אֶת־עֲצֵי הָעֹלָה

וַיָּשֶׂם עַל־יִצְחָק בְּנוֹ

וַיִּקַּח בְּיָדוֹ אֶת־הָאֵשׁ וְאֶת־הַמַּאֲכֶלֶת

וַיֵּלְכוּ שְׁנֵיהֶם יַחְדָּו:

7 וַיֹּאמֶר יִצְחָק אֶל־אַבְרָהָם אָבִיו

וַיֹּאמֶר אָבִי

וַיֹּאמֶר הִנֶּנִּי בְנִי

וַיֹּאמֶר הִנֵּה הָאֵשׁ וְהָעֵצִים

וְאַיֵּה הַשֶּׂה לְעֹלָה:

8 וַיֹּאמֶר אַבְרָהָם

אֱלֹהִים יִרְאֶה־לּוֹ הַשֶּׂה לְעֹלָה בְּנִי

וַיֵּלְכוּ שְׁנֵיהֶם יַחְדָּו:

9 וַיָּבֹאוּ אֶל־הַמָּקוֹם

אֲשֶׁר אָמַר־לוֹ הָאֱלֹהִים

וַיִּבֶן שָׁם אַבְרָהָם אֶת־הַמִּזְבֵּחַ

וַיַּעֲרֹךְ אֶת־הָעֵצִים

וַיַּעֲקֹד אֶת־יִצְחָק בְּנוֹ

וַיָּשֶׂם אֹתוֹ עַל־הַמִּזְבֵּחַ מִמַּעַל לָעֵצִים:

10 וַיִּשְׁלַח אַבְרָהָם אֶת־יָדוֹ

וַיִּקַּח אֶת־הַמַּאֲכֶלֶת לִשְׁחֹט אֶת־בְּנוֹ:

11 וַיִּקְרָ֨א אֵלָ֜יו מַלְאַ֤ךְ יְהוָה֙ מִן־הַשָּׁמַ֔יִם

וַיֹּ֖אמֶר אַבְרָהָ֣ם ׀ אַבְרָהָ֑ם

וַיֹּ֖אמֶר הִנֵּֽנִי׃

12 וַיֹּ֗אמֶר אַל־תִּשְׁלַ֤ח יָֽדְךָ֙ אֶל־הַנַּ֔עַר

וְאַל־תַּ֥עַשׂ ל֖וֹ מְא֑וּמָה

כִּ֣י ׀ עַתָּ֣ה יָדַ֗עְתִּי כִּֽי־יְרֵ֤א אֱלֹהִים֙ אַ֔תָּה

וְלֹ֥א חָשַׂ֛כְתָּ אֶת־בִּנְךָ֥ אֶת־יְחִֽידְךָ֖ מִמֶּֽנִּי׃

13 וַיִּשָּׂ֨א אַבְרָהָ֜ם אֶת־עֵינָ֗יו

וַיַּרְא֙ וְהִנֵּה־אַ֔יִל אַחַ֕ר נֶאֱחַ֥ז בַּסְּבַ֖ךְ בְּקַרְנָ֑יו

וַיֵּ֤לֶךְ אַבְרָהָם֙

וַיִּקַּ֣ח אֶת־הָאַ֔יִל

וַיַּעֲלֵ֥הוּ לְעֹלָ֖ה תַּ֥חַת בְּנֽוֹ׃

14 וַיִּקְרָ֧א אַבְרָהָ֛ם שֵֽׁם־הַמָּק֥וֹם הַה֖וּא יְהוָ֣ה ׀ יִרְאֶ֑ה

אֲשֶׁר֙ יֵאָמֵ֣ר הַיּ֔וֹם

בְּהַ֥ר יְהוָ֖ה יֵרָאֶֽה׃

15 וַיִּקְרָ֛א מַלְאַ֥ךְ יְהוָ֖ה אֶל־אַבְרָהָ֑ם שֵׁנִ֖ית מִן־הַשָּׁמָֽיִם׃

16 וַיֹּ֕אמֶר בִּ֥י נִשְׁבַּ֖עְתִּי נְאֻם־יְהוָ֑ה

כִּ֗י יַ֚עַן אֲשֶׁ֤ר עָשִׂ֙יתָ֙ אֶת־הַדָּבָ֣ר הַזֶּ֔ה

וְלֹ֥א חָשַׂ֖כְתָּ אֶת־בִּנְךָ֥ אֶת־יְחִידֶֽךָ׃

17 כִּֽי־בָרֵ֣ךְ אֲבָרֶכְךָ֗

וְהַרְבָּ֨ה אַרְבֶּ֤ה אֶֽת־זַרְעֲךָ֙ כְּכוֹכְבֵ֣י הַשָּׁמַ֔יִם וְכַח֕וֹל אֲשֶׁ֖ר עַל־שְׂפַ֣ת הַיָּ֑ם

וְיִרַ֣שׁ זַרְעֲךָ֔ אֵ֖ת שַׁ֥עַר אֹיְבָֽיו׃

18 וְהִתְבָּרֲכ֣וּ בְזַרְעֲךָ֔ כֹּ֖ל גּוֹיֵ֣י הָאָ֑רֶץ

עֵ֕קֶב אֲשֶׁ֥ר שָׁמַ֖עְתָּ בְּקֹלִֽי׃

19 וַיָּ֤שָׁב אַבְרָהָם֙ אֶל־נְעָרָ֔יו

וַיָּקֻמוּ

וַיֵּלְכוּ יַחְדָּו אֶל־בְּאֵר שָׁבַע

וַיֵּשֶׁב אַבְרָהָם בִּבְאֵר שָׁבַע:

◄ Appendix D ►

Clues for Finding the Root of Weak Consecutive Preterites

This appendix consists of two different aids that are designed to assist the student in finding the root (and occasionally the stem) of the 3ms consecutive preterite forms of weak verbs. The first aid is a chart, and the second aid is a set of questions and directions. Each aid depends on the fact that the presence or absence of the accent on the preformative plus the vowel used with it are often the only clues necessary to determine, especially in the *qal*, the root of the verb.

When using the first aid, the information about the preformative that the student should look for is found in the column at the far left of the chart. The possibilities for the root (and occasionally the stem) are marked with an "X" in the row to the right of the correct preformative pattern. Thus if one finds the performative to be accented ' + ָ plus the following syllable with ָ , the root will be the *hiphil* of a III-weak verb.

The second aid uses a tree structure to ascertain the possible root or stem of a weak verb in the 3ms consecutive preterite. When using the second aid, the student should begin with question 1 about the preformative pattern of the 3ms verb and answer each of the questions to which she or he is pointed in turn. Each answer either leads to another question or describes the possibilities for the root (or stem) represented by the consecutive preterite. It is quite possible that the answer is ultimately a "problem." In this case the beginning student must either look up the word in a dictionary under every possible root or, more likely, consult the instructor.

Clue	qal III-weak	qal I-ו	qal I-'	qal II-ו	qal II-'	qal gem.	hiphil	niphal
accented ◌ (root בנה)	X							
accented ◌ + cons. cluster (all one syllable) (וַיַּשְׁתְּ root שתה)	X							
accented ◌ + syllable with ◌ָ or ◌ֶ (וַיִּגֶל root גלה)	rarely		X (first choice)					
accented ◌ + syllable with ◌ָ (o) (וַיָּשָׁב root שוב; וַיָּסָב root סבב)				X (first choice)		maybe		
accented ◌ + syllable with ◌ֵ (וַיָּשֶׁת root שית)					X		II-weak; geminate	
dagesh in first root cons., no retract. accent (וַיִּפֹּל root נפל; וַיִּסֹב root סבב)		X				maybe		X
accented ◌ + syllable with ◌ֶ (וַיִּבֶן root בנה)							III-weak	
accented ◌ִי + syllable with ◌ֶ (וַיֹּסֶף root יסף)							I-ו	
accented ◌ + syllable with ◌ַ	X, I-G						X, I-G, III-weak	
unaccented ◌ (possibly qal I-G)							X	

This set of instructions provides help in finding the root of weak verbs of consecutive preterites (including some roots with gutturals) in the 3ms, the 2ms, and possibly the 1cs and 1cp forms.

1. accented preformative syllable?

   no: go to #12
   yes: proceed to #2

2. preformative vowel *hireq*? וִֽ

   no: go to #3
   yes: III-weak

3. preformative vowel *tsere*? וֵֽ

   no: go to #6
   yes: proceed to #4

4. followed by consonant cluster (i.e., two consonants, both with silent *shewa*: וַיֵּ֫שְׁתְּ)

   no: go to #5
   yes: III-weak

5. followed by followed by a syllable with *seghol* or *patakh*? וַיֵּ֫שֶׁב

   no: problem
   yes: most probably I-weak; possibly III-weak

6. preformative vowel *qamets*? וָֽ

   no: go to #9
   yes: proceed to #7

7. followed by syllable with *qamets* (= o)?

   no: go to #8
   yes: II-weak, specifically II-ו; could be geminate

8. followed by syllable with *seghol*?

   no: problem
   yes: either *qal* II-י or *hiphil* II-weak or geminate

9. preformative vowel *seghol*? וֶֽ

   no: go to #10
   yes: *hiphil* III-weak

10. preformative vowel *holem-vav*? וַיֹּ

    no: go to #11
    yes: *hiphil* I-י

11. preformative vowel *patakh*? וַֽ

    no: problem
    yes: either *qal* or *hiphil* I-G and III-weak

12. unaccented preformative syllable?

    no: go to #1
    yes: proceed to #13

13. *dagesh* in first root consonant?

    no: go to #14
    yes: could be *niphal*; could be I-נ; could be geminate, paradigm 2

14. preformative vowel *patakh*? וַֽיַּ

    no: problem
    yes: either *qal* I-guttural or *hiphil*

◄ Appendix E ►

Accents and Other Special Markings

There are more than thirty-one accents, some with slight variations, and a dozen or so other special markings found in the Masoretic Text. The uses of the various accents differ somewhat between the majority of the books and the three books, Job, Psalms, and Proverbs. The following accents and special markings are discussed in this book.

atnakh	This accent, used in all books, marks a major division within a verse. See 18.9.
merkhah	This conjunctive accent, used in all books, marks the first word linked to another that is marked with a disjunctive accent (frequently in the twenty-one books, with the disjunctive accent *tiphkhah*). See 23.10.
munakh	This accent, used in all books, marks the first word linked to another. See 22.7.
revia	This accent, used in all books, marks units within the *zaqeph* subordinated unit. See 21.6.
silluq	This accent, used in all books, marks the last accented syllable in a verse. See 19.6.
soph pasuq	This special marking announces the end of a verse. See 18.9.
tiphkhah	This disjunctive accent, not used in the three books, marks a following word linked to another that is usually marked with the conjunctive accent *merkhah*. See 23.10.
zaqeph	This accent, not used in the three books, marks the units subordinate to the *atnakh*. See 20.9.

◄ APPENDIX F ►

WORDLIST, ENGLISH TO HEBREW

Note: "v" alone = a *qal* verb. Verbs are identified by 3ms suffix conjugation, except for *qal* II-weak verbs (listed by inf. cs.) and some geminate verbs (listed by root). The right-hand column lists the lesson where the Hebrew vocabulary is located.

Aaron	proper n	אַהֲרֹן	30
abandon	v	עָזַב	15
above, over, on	prep	עַל-	9
Abraham	proper n	אַבְרָהָם	11
Abram	proper n	אַבְרָם	11
act wickedly; do harm	v *hiphil* (רעע)	הֵרַע	30
add; do something again	v *hiphil* (יסף)	הוֹסִיף	27
Adonai, Yahweh, the LORD	proper n	יְהוָה	12
advice, counsel	n	עֵצָה	11
affair, word, thing, matter	n	דָּבָר	8
after	prep	אַחֲרֵי/אַחַר	9
again, still	adv	עוֹד	14
all, each, every, entire	particle	כֹּל	14
also	adv	גַּם	16
altar	n	מִזְבֵּחַ	18
and, but	conj	וְ	8
angel, messenger	n	מַלְאָךְ	13
anger; nose	n	אַף	29

answer, respond	v	עָנָה	25
appear	v niphal (ראה)	נִרְאָה	25
appoint; set up; cause to stand	v hiphil (עמד)	הֶעֱמִיד	22
appoint; visit; punish; muster	v	פָּקַד	30
appointed time, place; season	n	מוֹעֵד	29
approach	v niphal (נגש)	נִגַּשׁ	26
arise, stand up	v	קוּם	28/14
ark (box, not boat)	n	אֲרוֹן	30
army	n	צָבָא	13
article, utensil, vessel	n	כְּלִי	28
as, like	prep	כְּ	9
as; for, to	prep	לְ	9
as, when	conj	כַּאֲשֶׁר	17
ask	v	שָׁאַל	29
assemble, be gathered	v niphal (אסף)	נֶאֱסַף	30
at, in; with (instrumental)	prep	בְּ	9
bad, evil, troublesome	adj	רַע	5/8
battle, war	n	מִלְחָמָה	14
be	v	הָיָה	25/14/17
be, be found	v niphal (מצא)	נִמְצָא	20
be able	v	יָכֹל	27
be afraid	v	יָרֵא	27
be angry, used impersonally	v	חָרָה	29
be born	v niphal (ילד)	נוֹלַד	27
be brought up	v niphal (עלה)	נַעֲלָה	25
be built	v niphal (בנה)	נִבְנָה	25
be buried	v niphal (קבר)	נִקְבַּר	19
be called	v niphal (קרא)	נִקְרָא	20
be captured	v niphal (לכד)	נִלְכַּד	19
be careful	v niphal (שמר)	נִשְׁמַר	19
be cut (off)	v niphal (כרת)	נִכְרַת	19
be delivered	v niphal (נצל)	נִצַּל	29

be destroyed	v niphal (שמד)	נִשְׁמַד	21
be disrespected, small	v	קלל	30
be done, made	v niphal (עשׂה)	נַעֲשָׂה	25
be eaten	v niphal (אכל)	נֶאֱכַל	20
be evil	v	רעע	30
be found, be	v niphal (מצא)	נִמְצָא	20
be gathered, assemble	v niphal (אסף)	נֶאֱסַף	30
be good, go well	v	יָטַב	27
be great, large	v	גָּדֵל	23
be heard	v niphal (שמע)	נִשְׁמַע	20
be high	v	רוּם	29
be inhabited, inhabitable	v niphal (ישׁב)	נוֹשַׁב	27
be large, great	v	גָּדֵל	23
be left over, survive, remain	v niphal (שׁאר)	נִשְׁאַר	19
be lifted	v niphal (נשׂא)	נִשָּׂא	26
be long; prolong, lengthen	v hiphil (ארך)	הֶאֱרִיךְ	22
be made, done	v niphal (עשׂה)	נַעֲשָׂה	25
be prepared	v niphal (כון)	נָכוֹן	28
be put to death	v hophal (מות)	הוּמַת	28
be small, disrespected	v	קלל	30
be strong	v	חָזַק	13
be told	v hophal (נגד)	הֻגַּד	26
be uncovered	v niphal (גלה)	נִגְלָה	25
bear, lift, carry	v	נָשָׂא	18/26
bear a child	v	יָלַד	27
beautiful, handsome	adj	יָפֶה	8
because, since	conj	כִּי	13
become many, multiply	v	רָבָה	25
before, in front of	prep	לִפְנֵי	10
beget, father	v hiphil (ילד)	הוֹלִיד	27
begin	v hiphil (חלל)	הֵחֵל	30
between	prep	בֵּין	16

big, great, large	adj	גָּדוֹל	7
bind, tie up	v	אָסַר	17
bless	v piel (ברך)	בֵּרֵךְ/בֵּרַךְ	23
blessed	v qal pass ptcp	בָּרוּךְ	23
blessing	n	בְּרָכָה	23
blood	n	דָּם	17
book	n	סֵפֶר	12
bow down	v hishtaphel (חוה)	הִשְׁתַּחֲוָה	26
boy, servant, young man	n	נַעַר	12
bread, food	n	לֶחֶם	13
break	v	שָׁבַר	23
breath, spirit, wind	n	רוּחַ	18
bring, lead	v hiphil (הלך)	הוֹלִיךְ	27
bring back	v hiphil (שוב)	הֵשִׁיב	28
bring down	v hiphil (ירד)	הוֹרִיד	27
bring in	v hiphil (בוא)	הֵבִיא	28
bring near	v hiphil (נגש)	הִגִּישׁ	26
bring out	v hiphil (יצא)	הוֹצִיא	27
bring up; sacrifice	v hiphil (עלה)	הֶעֱלָה	25
brother	n	אָח	3/10
build	v	בָּנָה	25/14
burn	v	שָׂרַף	18
bury	v	קָבַר	15
but, and	conj	וְ	8
call, name	v	קָרָא	13
camp	n	מַחֲנֶה	13
Canaan	proper n	כְּנַעַן	28
captain, chief, prince	n	שַׂר	18
capture	v	לָכַד	17
carry, bear, lift	v	נָשָׂא	18/26
carry into exile	v hiphil (גלה)	הִגְלָה	25
carry over; cause to cross over	v hiphil (עבר)	הֶעֱבִיר	22

cast, throw, throw down	v *hiphil* (שלך)	הִשְׁלִיךְ	21
cattle	n	בָּקָר	12
cause someone to swear	v *hiphil* (שבע)	הִשְׁבִּיעַ	29
cause to cross over; carry over	v *hiphil* (עבר)	הֶעֱבִיר	22
cause to fall	v *hiphil* (נפל)	הִפִּיל	26
cause to hear, proclaim	v *hiphil* (שמע)	הִשְׁמִיעַ	21
cause to possess	v *hiphil* (ירש)	הוֹרִישׁ	27
cause to remember; mention	v *hiphil* (זכר)	הִזְכִּיר	21
cause to sin	v *hiphil* (חטא)	הֶחֱטִיא	30
cause to stand; appoint; set up	v *hiphil* (עמד)	הֶעֱמִיד	22
(cause to) understand	v *hiphil* (בין)	הֵבִין	28
chair, throne	n	כִּסֵּא	21
chief, prince, captain	n	שַׂר	18
choose	v	בָּחַר	13
cities	n	עָרִים	8
city	n	עִיר	8
clan, family	n	מִשְׁפָּחָה	28
come, enter	v	בּוֹא	28
come back, return (intrans.)	v	שׁוּב	28
command	v *piel* (צוה)	צִוָּה	25
commandment	n	מִצְוָה	12
consider	v *hitpael* (בין)	הִתְבּוֹנֵן	29
corrupt; destroy	v *piel* (שחת)	שִׁחֵת	23
counsel, advice	n	עֵצָה	11
country, land	n	אֶרֶץ	8
cousin	n	אָח	3/10
covenant	n	בְּרִית	12
criminal, evil	adj	רָשָׁע	11
cross (over)	v	עָבַר	15
cry, weep	v	בָּכָה	28
curse	v	אָרַר	30
curse	v *piel* (קלל)	קִלֵּל	30

cut off, destroy	v hiphil (כרת)	הִכְרִית	21
cut, make (a covenant)	v	כָּרַת	12
darkness	n	חֹשֶׁךְ	10
daughter	n	בַּת	10
David	proper n	דָּוִד	9
day	n	יוֹם	4/10
death	n	מָוֶת	10
deed, work	n	מַעֲשֶׂה	30
defile	v piel (חלל)	חִלֵּל	30
deliver	v hiphil (נצל)	הִצִּיל	29
deliver, save	v hiphil (ישע)	הוֹשִׁיעַ	27
depart; turn aside	v	סוּר	28
destroy; corrupt	v piel (שחת)	שִׁחֵת	23
destroy, cut off	v hiphil (כרת)	הִכְרִית	21
destroy	v hiphil (שמד)	הִשְׁמִיד	21
destroy	v piel (אבד)	אִבַּד	23
die	v	אָבַד	23
die	v	מוּת	28
direct object marker	particle	אֶת־/אֵת	12
disclose	v piel (גלה)	גִּלָּה	25
do battle, wage war, fight	v niphal (לחם)	נִלְחַם	19
do harm; act wickedly	v hiphil (רעע)	הֵרַע	30
do something a lot	v hiphil (רבה)	הִרְבָּה	25
do something again; add	v hiphil (יסף)	הוֹסִיף	27
do something early in the morning	v hiphil (שכם)	הִשְׁכִּים	21
do something quickly, hurry	v piel (מהר)	מִהַר	23
do well, do something well	v hiphil (יטב)	הֵיטִיב	27
do, make	v	עָשָׂה	25
drink	v	שָׁתָה	25
dwell; sit	v	יָשַׁב	16/27
each, every, entire, all	particle	כֹּל	14
ear	n	אֹזֶן	11

eat	v	אָכַל	13
Egypt	proper n	מִצְרַיִם	16
eight	adj (number)	שְׁמֹנֶה	22
eighth	adj (ord. number)	שְׁמִינִי	23
eighty	adj (number)	שְׁמֹנִים	30
elder; old	n; adj	זָקֵן	7
eleven	adj (number)	עַשְׁתֵּי + ten	30
encamp	v	חָנָה	25
enemy	n	אֹיֵב	19
enter, come	v	בּוֹא	28
enthrone, make s.o. king/queen	v *hiphil* (מלך)	הִמְלִיךְ	21
entire, all, each, every	particle	כֹּל	14
establish; prepare	v *hiphil* (כון)	הֵכִין	28
establish, set up	v *polel* (כון)	כּוֹנֵן	29
eternity	n	עוֹלָם	14
evening	n	עֶרֶב	15
every, entire, all, each	particle	כֹּל	14
evil, bad, troublesome	adj	רַע	5/8
evil, criminal	adj	רָשָׁע	11
exalt	v *hiphil* (רום)	הֵרִים	29
exterminate	v *hiphil* (חרם)	הֶחֱרִים	22
eye; spring	n	עַיִן	11
face	n	פָּנִים	10
faithfulness, loyalty	n	חֶסֶד	24
fall	v	נָפַל	16/26
family, clan	n	מִשְׁפָּחָה	28
father	n	אָב	3/10
father, beget	v *hiphil* (ילד)	הוֹלִיד	27
favor, grace	n	חֵן	24
field	n	שָׂדֶה	9
fifth	adj (ord. number)	חֲמִישִׁי	23
fifty	adj; number	חֲמִשִּׁים	30

fight, do battle, wage war	v *niphal* (לחם)	נִלְחַם	19
find	v	מָצָא	15
fire	n	אֵשׁ	18
first	adj	רִאשׁוֹן	23
first (f); one	adj (number)	אַחַת	15
first (m); one	adj (number)	אֶחָד	15
five	adj; number	חָמֵשׁ	22
flesh	n	בָּשָׂר	30
follow, pursue	v	רָדַף	17
food, bread	n	לֶחֶם	13
foot	n	רֶגֶל	11
for, to; as	prep	לְ	9
forty	adj (number)	אַרְבָּעִים	30
four	adj (number)	אַרְבַּע	22
fourth	adj (number)	רְבִיעִי	23
from (+ comparative, partitive)	prep	מִן	9
gather	v	אָסַף	30
give	v	נָתַן	26
give drink to	v *hiphil* (שקה)	הִשְׁקָה	25
go, walk	v	הָלַךְ	16/27
go	v *piel* (הלך)	הִלֵּךְ	27
go down	v	יָרַד	16/27
go into exile; uncover	v	גָּלָה	25
go out, leave	v	יָצָא	27
go up	v	עָלָה	25
go well, be good	v	יָטַב	27
goats/sheep	n	צֹאן	12
God	proper n	אֱלֹהִים	12
gold	n	זָהָב	18
good	adj	טוֹב	7
grace, favor	n	חֵן	24
grasp; make strong	v *hiphil* (חזק)	הֶחֱזִיק	22

grave	n	קֶבֶר	15
great, large, big	adj	גָּדוֹל	7
ground, land, soil	n	אֲדָמָה	17
guard, watch; keep, observe	v	שָׁמַר	12
hand	n	יָד	3/11
handsome, beautiful	adj	יָפֶה	8
he, it	pron	הוּא	4/7
head	n	רֹאשׁ	8
hear, listen	v *hiphil* (אזן)	הֶאֱזִין	22
hear; obey	v	שָׁמַע	13
heart; mind	n	לֵב	15
heart; mind	n	לֵבָב	15
heaven(s)	n	שָׁמַיִם	11
here	adv	פֹּה	27
here is (presentation particle)	particle	הִנֵּה	29
holiness	n	קֹדֶשׁ	26
holocaust, whole burnt offering	n	עֹלָה	18
holy	adj	קָדוֹשׁ	24
horse	n	סוּס	5/7
house	n	בַּיִת	9
houses	n	בָּתִּים	9
human being; humankind, man	n	אָדָם	17
hundred	adj (number)	מֵאָה	30
hurry, do something quickly	v *piel* (מהר)	מִהַר	23
I	pron	אֲנִי	7
I	pron	אָנֹכִי	7
if	conj	אִם	21
in, at; with (instrumental)	prep	בְּ	9
in front of, in the presence of	prep	לִפְנֵי	10
in order to, in order that	conj	לְמַעַן	19
in the eyes of	prep	בְּעֵינֵי	11
in the middle/midst of	prep	בְּתוֹךְ	16

English	Part of speech	Hebrew	Lesson
in the midst of	prep	בְּקֶרֶב	27
in the opinion of	prep	בְּעֵינֵי	11
increase	v	יָסַף	27
inspire fear, awe	v niphal (יָרֵא)	נוֹרָא	27
instead of; under	prep	תַּחַת	9
instruction, law; Torah	n	תּוֹרָה	11
intelligent	v niphal ptcp (בין)	נָבוֹן	28
interrogative	particle	הֲ	14
Isaac	proper n	יִצְחָק	27
Israel	proper n	יִשְׂרָאֵל	10
it	pron	הוּא, הִיא	4/7
Jacob	proper n	יַעֲקֹב	30
Jerusalem	proper n	יְרוּשָׁלַ‍ם	11
Jordan	proper n	יַרְדֵּן	15
Joseph	proper n	יוֹסֵף	25
Joshua	proper n	יְהוֹשֻׁעַ	21
journey; road, way	n	דֶּרֶךְ	9
Judah	proper n	יְהוּדָה	9
judge	n	שֹׁפֵט	17
judge	v	שָׁפַט	12
judgment, justice	n	מִשְׁפָּט	12
keep, observe; guard, watch	v	שָׁמַר	12
kill	v piel (אבד)	אִבֵּד	23
kill	v hiphil (מות)	הֵמִית	28
king	n	מֶלֶךְ	8
kinsman	n	אָב	3/10
kinsman	n	אָח	3/10
know	v	יָדַע	16
labor, work, service	n	עֲבֹדָה	14
land, country	n	אֶרֶץ	8
land, soil, ground	n	אֲדָמָה	17
large, big, great	adj	גָּדוֹל	7

law, instruction; Torah	n	תּוֹרָה	11
lead, bring	v *hiphil* (הלך)	הוֹלִיךְ	27
learn	v	לָמַד	23
leave, go out	v	יָצָא	27
leave behind, spare	v *hiphil* (שאר)	הִשְׁאִיר	21
lengthen, prolong; be long	v *hiphil* (ארך)	הֶאֱרִיךְ	22
let go, send away	v *piel* (שלח)	שִׁלַּח	23
let live, preserve alive	v *hiphil* (חיה)	הֶחֱיָה	25
let live, preserve alive	v *piel*	חִיָּה	25
lie down	v	שָׁכַב	15
life	n	חַיִּים	16
lift	v *hiphil* (רום)	הֵרִים	29
lift up	v *polel* (רום)	רוֹמֵם	29
lift, carry, bear	v	נָשָׂא	18/26
light	n	אוֹר	10
like, as	prep	כְּ	9
listen, hear	v *hiphil* (אזן)	הֶאֱזִין	22
live	v	חָיָה	25
live (= dwell, inhabit)	v	יָשַׁב	16/27
loins	n	מָתְנַיִם	11
the Lord, Adonai, Yahweh	proper n	יְהוָה	12
love	n	אַהֲבָה	30
love	v	אָהֵב	30
loyalty, faithfulness	n	חֶסֶד	24
magnify; praise	v *piel* (גדל)	גִּדֵּל	23
make, do	v	עָשָׂה	25
make (a covenant), cut	v	כָּרַת	12
make s.o. king/queen, enthrone	v *hiphil* (מלך)	הִמְלִיךְ	21
make strong; grasp	v *hiphil* (חזק)	הֶחֱזִיק	22
man (male human being)	n	אִישׁ	8
man, humankind; human being	n	אָדָם	17
many, much	adj	רַב	16

matter, affair, word, thing	n	דָּבָר	8
men	n	אֲנָשִׁים	8
mention; cause to remember	v *hiphil* (זכר)	הִזְכִּיר	21
messenger, angel	n	מַלְאָךְ	13
midwife	v *piel* fs ptcp	מְיַלֶּדֶת	27
mighty man, warrior, soldier	n	גִּבּוֹר	13
mind; heart	n	לֵב	15
mind; heart	n	לֵבָב	15
money, silver	n	כֶּסֶף	18
month, new moon	n	חֹדֶשׁ	30
morning	n	בֹּקֶר	15
Moses	proper n	מֹשֶׁה	9
mother	n	אֵם	8
mountain	n	הַר	5/8
mouth	n	פֶּה	13
much, many	adj	רַב	16
multiply, become many	v	רָבָה	25
muster; appoint; visit; punish	v	פָּקַד	30
name	n	שֵׁם	5/10
name, call	v	קָרָא	13
narrate, tell a story	v *piel* (ספר)	סִפֵּר	23
nation; (a) nation, people; people (coll.)	n	עַם	8
nation; (a) nation, people; (a) people (usually but not always, non-Hebrew)	n	גּוֹי	29
near, next to	prep	אֵצֶל	9
negative for Inf cs	adv	(לְ)בִלְתִּי	17
new moon, month	n	חֹדֶשׁ	30
night	n	לַיְלָה	11
nine	adj (number)	תֵּשַׁע	22
ninety	adj (number)	תִּשְׁעִים	30

ninth	adj (ord. number)	תְּשִׁיעִי	23
noon	n	צָהֳרִים	11
nose; anger	n	אַף	29
not	adv	אַל-	14
not	adv	לֹא	12
now	adv	עַתָּה	16
obey; hear	v	שָׁמַע	13
observe, keep; guard, watch	v	שָׁמַר	12
occur	v niphal (היה)	נִהְיָה	25
occurrence	n	פַּעַם	11
offer	v hiphil (רום)	הֵרִים	29
old; elder	adj; n	זָקֵן	7
on, above, over	prep	עַל-	9
one; first (f)	adj (number)	אַחַת	15
one; first (m)	adj (number)	אֶחָד	15
only	adv	רַק	17
or	conj	אוֹ	29
over, on, above	prep	עַל-	9
palace, temple	n	הֵיכָל	8
peace; welfare	n	שָׁלוֹם	29
people (coll.); (a) people, nation	n	עַם	8
people; (a) people, nation; (a) nation (usually, but not always, non-Hebrew)	n	גּוֹי	29
perceive, understand	v	בִּין	28
person, self, soul,	n	נֶפֶשׁ	21
Pharaoh	proper n	פַּרְעֹה	14
place	n	מָקוֹם	8
place, put	v	שִׂים	28
place, set; settle someone	v hiphil (ישב)	הוֹשִׁיב	27
pour out, shed (blood)	v	שָׁפַךְ	17
praise	v piel (הלל)	הִלֵּל	30

praise; magnify	v *piel* (גדל)	גִּדֵּל	23
pray	v *hitpael* (פלל)	הִתְפַּלֵּל	24
prayer	n	תְּפִלָּה	24
prepare; establish	v *hiphil* (כון)	הֵכִין	28
presentation particle: here is	particle	הִנֵּה	29
preserve alive, let live	v *hiphil* (חיה)	הֶחֱיָה	25
preserve alive, let live	v *piel*	חִיָּה	25
priest	n	כֹּהֵן	12
prince, captain, chief	n	שַׂר	18
proclaim, cause to hear	v *hiphil* (שמע)	הִשְׁמִיעַ	21
prolong, lengthen; be long	v *hiphil* (ארך)	הֶאֱרִיךְ	22
prophesy	v *hitpael* (נבא)	הִתְנַבֵּא	24
prophesy	v *niphal* (נבא)	נִבָּא	24
prophet	n	נָבִיא	19
punish; muster; appoint; visit	v	פָּקַד	30
pursue, follow	v	רָדַף	17
put, place	v	שִׂים	28
queen	n	מַלְכָּה	8
Rachel	proper n	רָחֵל	30
raise, set up	v *hiphil* (קום)	הֵקִים	28
raise, set up	v *hiphil* (רום)	הֵרִים	29
receive, take	v	לָקַח	17/26
refuse	v *piel* (מאן)	מֵאֵן	23
reign, rule	v	מָלַךְ	12
remain, be left over, survive	v *niphal* (שאר)	נִשְׁאַר	19
remember	v	זָכַר	12
remove	v *hiphil* (סור)	הֵסִיר	28
remove	v *hiphil* (רום)	הֵרִים	29
respond, answer	v	עָנָה	25
return (intrans.), come back	v	שׁוּב	28
righteous	adj	צַדִּיק	13
river	n	נָהָר	9

road, way; journey	n	דֶּרֶךְ	9
round about	adv/prep	סָבִיב	30
rule, reign	v	מָלַךְ	12
Sabbath	n	שַׁבָּת	24
sacrifice; bring up	v *hiphil* (עלה)	הֶעֱלָה	25
Samuel	proper n	שְׁמוּאֵל	16
sanctify	v *piel* (קדש)	קִדֵּשׁ	24
sanctify oneself	v *hitpael* (קדש)	הִתְקַדֵּשׁ	24
Sarah	proper n	שָׂרָה	13
Sarai	proper n	שָׂרַי	13
Saul	proper n	שָׁאוּל	15
save, deliver	v *hiphil* (ישע)	הוֹשִׁיעַ	27
say	v	אָמַר	13
'saying' (intro direct speech)	particle	לֵאמֹר	13
sea	n	יָם	16
season, appointed time, place	n	מוֹעֵד	29
second	adj (number)	שֵׁנִי	23
see	v	רָאָה	25
seek	v *piel* (בקש)	בִּקֵּשׁ	23
seek favor	v *hitpael* (חנן)	הִתְחַנֵּן	24
self, soul, person	n	נֶפֶשׁ	21
send	v	שָׁלַח	14
send away, let go	v *piel* (שלח)	שִׁלַּח	23
servant, slave	n	עֶבֶד	8
servant, young man, boy	n	נַעַר	12
serve, work	v	עָבַד	14
service, labor, work	n	עֲבֹדָה	14
set, place; settle someone	v *hiphil* (ישב)	הוֹשִׁיב	27
set out	v	נָסַע	26
set up; cause to stand; appoint	v *hiphil* (עמד)	הֶעֱמִיד	22
set up, station	v *hiphil* (נצב)	הִצִּיב	26
set up, raise	v *hiphil* (קום)	הֵקִים	28

set up, raise	v hiphil (רום)	הֵרִים	29
set up, establish	v polel (כון)	כּוֹנֵן	29
settle someone; set, place	v hiphil (ישב)	הוֹשִׁיב	27
seven	adj (number)	שֶׁבַע	22
seventh	adj (ord. number)	שְׁבִיעִי	23
seventy	adj (number)	שִׁבְעִים	30
shatter	v piel (שבר)	שִׁבֵּר	23
she, it	pron	הִיא	4/7
shed (blood), pour out	v	שָׁפַךְ	17
sheep/goats	n	צֹאן	12
show	v hiphil (ראה)	הֶרְאָה	25
silver, money	n	כֶּסֶף	18
sin	v	חָטָא	30
sin, sin offering	n	חַטָּאת	30
since (purpose, not time), because	conj	כִּי	13
sit; dwell	v	יָשַׁב	16/27
six	adj (number)	שֵׁשׁ	22
sixth	adj (ord. number)	שִׁשִּׁי	23
sixty	adj (number)	שִׁשִּׁים	30
sky	n	שָׁמַיִם	11
slave, servant	n	עֶבֶד	8
small	adj	קָטֹן	7
small	adj	קָטָן	7
so, thus (of something already mentioned)	adv	כֵּן	15
so, thus (refers to what follows)	adv	כֹּה	18
soil, ground, land	n	אֲדָמָה	17
Solomon	proper n	שְׁלֹמֹה	11
son	n	בֵּן	4/10
soldier, mighty man, warrior	n	גִּבּוֹר	13
soul, person, self	n	נֶפֶשׁ	21
sound, voice	n	קוֹל	8

spare, leave behind	v hiphil (שאר)	הִשְׁאִיר	21
speak	v piel (דבר)	דִּבֶּר	23
spirit, wind, breath	n	רוּחַ	18
spring; eye	n	עַיִן	11
stand	v	עָמַד	13
stand up, arise	v	קוּם	28/14
station, set up	v hiphil (נצב)	הִצִּיב	26
still, again	adv	עוֹד	14
stone	n	אֶבֶן	28
strengthen	v piel (חזק)	חִזֵּק	23
strengthen oneself	v hitpael (חזק)	הִתְחַזֵּק	24
stretch out (usu. intrans.)	v	נָטָה	26
strike down	v hiphil (נכה)	הִכָּה	26
surround, turn around	v	סָבַב	30
survive, remain, be left over	v niphal (שאר)	נִשְׁאַר	19
survivor	n	שָׂרִיד	21
swear	v niphal (שבע)	נִשְׁבַּע	29
sword	n	חֶרֶב	8
take one's stand	v niphal (נצב)	נִצַּב	26
take possession of	v	יָרַשׁ	27
take, receive	v	לָקַח	17/26
teach	v piel (למד)	לִמֵּד	23
tell	v hiphil (נגד)	הִגִּיד	26
tell a story, narrate	v piel (ספר)	סִפֵּר	23
temple, palace	n	הֵיכָל	8
ten	adj (number)	עֶשֶׂר	22
ten thousand	adj (number)	רְבָבָה	30
tent	n	אֹהֶל	29
tenth	adj (ord. number)	עֲשִׂירִי	23
that (f)	demonstr adj	הַהִיא	10
that (m)	demonstr adj	הַהוּא	10
that (after verbs of perception)	conj	כִּי	13

the (definite article)	particle	הַ + doubling	8
there	adv	שָׁם	9
there is	particle	יֵשׁ	18
there is not	particle	אֵין	18
therefore	conj	לָכֵן	24
therefore	conj	עַל־כֵּן	24
these	demonstr adj	אֵלֶּה	10
they (f)	pron	הֵנָּה	7
they (m)	pron	הֵם	7
thing, matter, affair, word	n	דָּבָר	8
third	adj (number)	שְׁלִישִׁי	23
thirty	adj (number)	שְׁלֹשִׁים	30
this (f)	demonstr adj	זֹאת	10
this (m)	demonstr adj	זֶה	10
those (f)	demonstr adj	הָהֵנָּה	10
those (m)	demonstr adj	הָהֵם	10
thousand	adj (number)	אֶלֶף	30
three	adj (number)	שָׁלֹשׁ	22
throne, chair	n	כִּסֵּא	21
throw, throw down, cast	v hiphil (שׁלך)	הִשְׁלִיךְ	21
thus, so (of something already) mentioned)	adv	כֵּן	15
thus, so (refers to what follows)	adv	כֹּה	18
tie up, bind	v	אָסַר	17
time	n	עֵת	30
to	prep	אֶל־	9
to, for; as	prep	לְ	9
today	adv	הַיּוֹם	14
Torah; instruction, law	n	תּוֹרָה	11
touch	v	נָגַע	26
tree	n	עֵץ	9
troublesome, bad, evil	adj	רַע	5/8

WORDLIST, ENGLISH TO HEBREW

truth	n	אֱמֶת	17
turn (trans.)	v *hiphil* (נטה)	הִטָּה	26
turn around, surround	v	סָבַב	30
turn aside; depart	v	סוּר	28
twenty	adj (number)	עֶשְׂרִים	30
two (f)	adj (number)	שְׁתַּיִם	20
two (m)	adj (number)	שְׁנַיִם	20
uncover; go into exile	v	גָּלָה	25
under; instead of	prep	תַּחַת	9
understand, perceive	v	בִּין	28
until, up to	prep	עַד	13
utensil, vessel, article	n	כְּלִי	28
utterance	n	נְאֻם	29
very	adv	מְאֹד	7
vessel, article, utensil	n	כְּלִי	28
visit; punish; muster; appoint	v	פָּקַד	30
voice, sound	n	קוֹל	8
volitive particle	particle	נָא/־נָא	14
wage war, fight, do battle	v *niphal* (לחם)	נִלְחַם	19
walk around	v *hitpael* (הלך)	הִתְהַלֵּךְ	24
walk, go	v	הָלַךְ	16/27
war, battle	n	מִלְחָמָה	14
warrior, soldier, mighty man	n	גִּבּוֹר	13
watch, guard; keep, observe	v	שָׁמַר	12
water(s)	n	מַיִם	11
way, road; journey	n	דֶּרֶךְ	9
we	pron	אֲנַחְנוּ	7
weep, cry	v	בָּכָה	28
welfare; peace	n	שָׁלוֹם	29
what, what?	pron	מָה	17
when, as	conj	כַּאֲשֶׁר	17
where, where?	adv	אַיֵּה	24

where, where?	adv	אֵיפֹה	24
which, who	rel pron/conj	אֲשֶׁר	9
who, who?	pron	מִי	13
whole burnt offering, holocaust	n	עֹלָה	18
why?	adv	לָמָּה	27
wilderness	n	מִדְבָּר	13
wind, breath, spirit	n	רוּחַ	18
wine	n	יַיִן	10
wipe out	v	מָחָה	25
wisdom	n	חָכְמָה	11
with	prep	אֶת־/אֵת	9
with	prep	עִם	9
with (instrumental); at, in	prep	בְּ	9
woman	n	אִשָּׁה	8
women	n	נָשִׁים	8
word, thing, matter, affair	n	דָּבָר	8
work, service, labor	n	עֲבֹדָה	14
work, serve	v	עָבַד	14
work, deed	n	מַעֲשֶׂה	30
write	v	כָּתַב	12
Yahweh, the LORD, Adonai	proper n	יְהוָה	12
year	n	שָׁנָה	11
you (fp)	pron	אַתֵּנָה	7
you (fs)	pron	אַתְּ	7
you (mp)	pron	אַתֶּם	7
you (ms)	pron	אַתָּ(ה)	7
young man, boy, servant	n	נַעַר	12

◄ Appendix G ►

Wordlist, Hebrew to English

Note: "v" alone = a *qal* verb. Verbs are identified by 3ms suffix conjugation, except for *qal* II-weak verbs (listed by inf. cs.) and some geminate verbs (listed by root). The right-hand column lists the lesson where the Hebrew vocabulary is located.

אָב	n	father, kinsman	3/10
אָבַד	v	to die (see also אִבֵּד)	23
אִבֵּד	v *piel* (אבד)	to kill, destroy	23
אֶבֶן	n	stone	28
אַבְרָהָם	proper n	Abraham	11
אַבְרָם	proper n	Abram	11
אָדָם	n	human being; humankind, man	17
אֲדָמָה	n	ground, land, soil	17
אָהֵב	v	to love	30
אַהֲבָה	n	love	30
אֹהֶל	n	tent	29
אַהֲרֹן	proper n	Aaron	30
אוֹ	conj	or	29
אוֹר	n	light	10
אֹזֶן	n	ear	11
אזן	verbal root	see הֶאֱזִין	
אָח	n	brother, kinsman, cousin	3/10
אֶחָד	adj (number)	one; first (m)	15

-263-

אַחֲרֵי/אַחַר	prep	after	9
אַחַת	adj (number)	one; first (f)	15
אֹיֵב	n	enemy	19
אַיֵּה	adv	where, where?	24
אֵין	particle	there is not	18
אֵיפֹה	adv	where, where?	24
אִישׁ	n	man (male human being)	8
אָכַל	v	to eat (see also נֶאֱכַל)	13
אֶל-	prep	to	9
אַל-	adv	not	14
אֵלֶּה	demonstr adj	these	10
אֱלֹהִים	proper n	God	12
אֶלֶף	adj (number)	thousand	30
אֵם	n	mother	8
אִם	conj	if	21
אָמַר	v	to say	13
אֱמֶת	n	truth	17
אֲנַחְנוּ	pron	we	7
אֲנִי	pron	I	7
אָנֹכִי	pron	I	7
אֲנָשִׁים	n	men	8
אָסַף	v	to gather	30
אָסַר	v	to bind, tie up	17
ארך	verbal root	see הֶאֱרִיךְ	
אַף	n	nose; anger	29
אֵצֶל	prep	near, next to	9
אַרְבַּע	adj (number)	four	22
אַרְבָּעִים	adj (number)	forty	30
אָרוֹן	n	ark (box, not boat)	30
אֶרֶץ	n	land, country	8
אָרַר	v	to curse	30
אֵשׁ	n	fire	18

אִשָּׁה	n	woman	8
אֲשֶׁר	rel pron/conj	which, who	9
אַתְּ	pron	you (fs)	7
אַתָּ(ה)	pron	you (ms)	7
אֶת־/אֵת	prep	with	9
אֶת־/אֵת	dir. obj. marker	אֶת־/אֵת	12
אַתֶּם	pron	you (mp)	7
אַתֵּנָה	pron	you (fp)	7
בְּ	prep	in, at; with (instrumental)	9
בּוֹא	v	to enter, come (see also הֵבִיא)	28
בָּחַר	v	to choose	13
בִּין	v	to perceive, understand (see also נָבוֹן, הִתְבּוֹנֵן, הֵבִין)	28
בֵּין	prep	between	16
בַּיִת	n	house	9
בָּכָה	v	to weep, cry	28
בִּלְתִּי	adv	negative for inf cs	17
בֵּן	n	son	4/10
בָּנָה	v	to build (see also נִבְנָה)	14/25
בְּעֵינֵי	prep	in the eyes of, in the opinion of	11
בָּקָר	n	cattle	12
בֹּקֶר	n	morning	15
בְּקֶרֶב	prep	in the midst of	27
בקש	verbal root	see בִּקֵּשׁ	
בִּקֵּשׁ	v piel (בקש)	to seek	23
בְּרִית	n	covenant	12
בָּרוּךְ	v qal pass ptcp (ברך)	blessed	23
ברך	verbal root	see בֵּרֵךְ, בָּרוּךְ	
בֵּרֵךְ/בֵּרַךְ	v piel (ברך)	to bless	23
בְּרָכָה	n	blessing	23
בָּשָׂר	n	flesh	30
בְּתוֹךְ	prep	in the middle/midst of	16

בַּת	n	daughter	10
בָּתִּים	n	houses	9
גִּבּוֹר	n	warrior, soldier, mighty man	13
גָּדוֹל	adj	great, large, big	7
גָּדַל	v	to be great, large (see also גִּדֵּל)	23
גִּדֵּל	v *piel* (גדל)	to magnify; praise	23
גּוֹי	n	(a) nation, people (usually, but not always, non-Hebrew)	29
גָּלָה	v	to uncover; go into exile (see also גָּלָה, הִגְלָה, נִגְלָה)	25
גִּלָּה	v *piel* (גלה)	to disclose	25
גַּם	adv	also	16
דבר	verbal root	see דִּבֶּר	
דָּבָר	n	word, thing, matter, affair	8
דִּבֶּר	v *piel* (דבר)	to speak	23
דָּוִד	proper n	David	9
דָּם	n	blood	17
דֶּרֶךְ	n	way, road; journey	9
הַ + doubling	particle	definite article 'the'	8
הֲ	particle	interrogative	14
הֶאֱזִין	v *hiphil* (אזן)	to hear, listen	22
הֶאֱרִיךְ	v *hiphil* (ארך)	to lengthen, prolong; to be long	22
הֵבִיא	v *hiphil* (בוא)	to bring in	28
הֵבִין	v *hiphil* (בין)	to (cause to) understand	28
הֻגַּד	v *hophal* (נגד)	to be told	26
הִגִּיד	v *hiphil* (נגד)	to tell	26
הִגִּישׁ	v *hiphil* (נגש)	to bring near	26
הִגְלָה	v *hiphil* (גלה)	to carry into exile	25
הַהוּא	demonstr adj	that (m)	10
הַהִיא	demonstr adj	that (f)	10
הָהֵם	demonstr adj	those (m)	10
הָהֵנָּה	demonstr adj	those (f)	10

הוּא	pron	he, it	4/7
הוֹלִיד	v *hiphil* (ילד)	to father, beget	27
הוֹלִיךְ	v *hiphil* (הלך)	to lead, bring	27
הוּמַת	v *hophal* (מות)	to be put to death	28
הוֹסִיף	v *hiphil* (יסף)	to add; to do something again	27
הוֹצִיא	v *hiphil* (יצא)	to bring out	27
הוֹרִיד	v *hiphil* (ירד)	to bring down	27
הוֹרִישׁ	v *hiphil* (ירשׁ)	to cause to possess	27
הוֹשִׁיב	v *hiphil* (ישׁב)	to settle someone; to set, place	27
הוֹשִׁיעַ	v *hiphil* (ישׁע)	to save, deliver	27
הִזְכִּיר	v *hiphil* (זכר)	to cause to remember, to mention	21
הֶחֱזִיק	v *hiphil* (חזק)	to make strong; grasp	22
הֶחֱטִיא	v *hiphil* (חטא)	to cause to sin	30
הֶחֱיָה	v *hiphil* (חיה)	to preserve alive, let live	25
הֵחֵל	v *hiphil* (חלל)	to begin	30
הֶחֱרִים	v *hiphil* (חרם)	to exterminate	22
הִטָּה	v *hiphil* (נטה)	to turn (trans.)	26
הִיא	pron	she, it	4/7
הָיָה	v	to be (see also נִהְיָה)	14/17/25
הַיּוֹם	adv	today	14
הֵיטִיב	v *hiphil* (יטב)	to do well, do something well	27
הֵיכָל	n	palace, temple	8
הִכָּה	v *hiphil* (נכה)	to strike down	26
הֵכִין	v *hiphil* (כון)	to establish; to prepare	28
הִכְרִית	v *hiphil* (כרת)	to cut off, destroy	21
הָלַךְ	v	to walk, go (see also הוֹלִיךְ, (הִתְהַלֵּךְ, הִלֵּךְ)	16/27
הִלֵּךְ	v *piel* (הלך)	to go	27
הלל	verbal root	see הִלֵּל	
הִלֵּל	v *piel* (הלל)	to praise	30
הֵם	pron	they (m)	7
הֵמִית	v *hiphil* (מות)	to kill	28

הִמְלִיךְ	v *hiphil* (מלך)	to make s.o. king/queen, enthrone	21
הִנֵּה	particle	presentation particle: here is	29
הֵנָּה	pron	they (f)	7
הֵסִיר	v *hiphil* (סור)	to remove	28
הֶעֱבִיר	v *hiphil* (עבר)	to cause to cross over; to carry over	22
הֶעֱלָה	v *hiphil* (עלה)	to bring up, sacrifice	25
הֶעֱמִיד	v *hiphil* (עמד)	to cause to stand; to appoint; to set up	22
הִפִּיל	v *hiphil* (נפל)	to cause to fall	26
הִצִּיב	v *hiphil* (נצב)	to station, set up	26
הִצִּיל	v *hiphil* (נצל)	to deliver	29
הֵקִים	v *hiphil* (קום)	to raise, set up	28
הַר	n	mountain	5/8
הֶרְאָה	v *hiphil* (ראה)	to show	25
הִרְבָּה	v *hiphil* (רבה)	to do something a lot	25
הֵרִים	v *hiphil* (רום)	to raise, lift; set up; exalt; remove; offer	29
הֵרַע	v *hiphil* (רעע)	to act wickedly; to do harm	30
הִשְׁאִיר	v *hiphil* (שאר)	to leave behind, to spare	21
הִשְׁבִּיעַ	v *hiphil* (שבע)	to cause s.o. to swear	29
הֵשִׁיב	v *hiphil* (שוב)	to bring back	28
הִשְׁכִּים	v *hiphil* (שכם)	to do s.th. early in the morning	21
הִשְׁלִיךְ	v *hiphil* (שלך)	to cast, throw, throw down	21
הִשְׁמִיד	v *hiphil*(שמד)	to destroy	21
הִשְׁמִיעַ	v *hiphil* (שמע)	to cause to hear, to proclaim	21
הִשְׁקָה	v *hiphil* (שקה)	to give drink to	25
הִשְׁתַּחֲוָה	v *hishtaphel* (חוה)	to bow down	26
הִתְבּוֹנֵן	v *hitpael* (בין)	to consider	29
הִתְהַלֵּךְ	v *hitpael* (הלך)	to walk around	24
הִתְחַזֵּק	v *hitpael* (חזק)	to strengthen oneself	24
הִתְחַנֵּן	v *hitpael* (חנן)	to seek favor	24
הִתְנַבֵּא	v *hitpael* (נבא)	to prophesy	24
הִתְפַּלֵּל	v *hitpael* (פלל)	to pray	24
הִתְקַדֵּשׁ	v *hitpael* (קדש)	to sanctify oneself	24

וְ	conj	and, but	8
זֹאת	demonstr adj	this (f)	10
זֶה	demonstr adj	this (m)	10
זָהָב	n	gold	18
זָכַר	v	to remember (see also הִזְכִּיר)	12
זָקֵן	adj; n	old; elder	7
חֹדֶשׁ	n	month, new moon	30
חוה	verbal root	see הִשְׁתַּחֲוָה	
חָזַק	v	to be strong (see also הֶחֱזִיק, חִזֵּק, הִתְחַזֵּק)	13
חִזֵּק	v *piel* (חזק)	to strengthen	23
חָטָא	v	to sin (see also הֶחֱטִיא)	30
חַטָּאת	n	sin, sin offering	30
חָיָה	v	to live (see also חִיָּה, הֶחֱיָה)	25
חִיָּה	v *piel* (חיה)	to preserve alive, let live	25
חַיִּים	n	life	16
חָכְמָה	n	wisdom	11
חלל	verbal root	see חִלֵּל, הֵחֵל	
חִלֵּל	v *piel* (חלל)	to defile	30
חֲמִישִׁי	adj (ord. number)	fifth	23
חָמֵשׁ	adj/number	five	22
חֲמִשִּׁים	adj/number	fifty	30
חֵן	n	favor, grace	24
חָנָה	v	to encamp	25
חנן	verbal root	see הִתְחַנֵּן	
חֶסֶד	n	faithfulness, loyalty	24
חֶרֶב	n	sword	8
חָרָה	v	used impersonally, to be(come) angry	29
חרם	verbal root	see הֶחֱרִים	
חֹשֶׁךְ	n	darkness	10
טוֹב	adj	good	7
יָד	n	hand	3/11

יָדַע	v	to know	16
יְהוּדָה	proper n	Judah	9
יְהוָה	proper n	Yahweh, the LORD, Adonai	12
יְהוֹשֻׁעַ	proper n	Joshua	21
יוֹם	n	day	4/10
יוֹסֵף	proper n	Joseph	25
יָטַב	v	to be good, go well (see also הֵיטִיב)	27
יַיִן	n	wine	10
יָכֹל	v	to be able	27
יָלַד	v	to bear a child (see immediately below; also נוֹלַד, הוֹלִיד)	27
ילד *piel*	v	midwife מְיַלֶּדֶת (fs *piel* ptcp)	27
יָם	n	sea	16
יָסַף	v	to increase (see also הוֹסִיף)	27
יַעֲקֹב	proper n	Jacob	30
יָפֶה	adj	beautiful, handsome	8
יָצָא	v	to go out, leave (see also הוֹצִיא)	27
יִצְחָק	proper n	Isaac	27
יָרֵא	v	to be afraid (see also נוֹרָא)	27
יָרַד	v	to go down (see also הוֹרִיד)	16/27
יַרְדֵּן	proper n	Jordan	15
יְרוּשָׁלַםִ	proper n	Jerusalem	11
יָרַשׁ	v	to take possession of (see also הוֹרִישׁ)	27
ישׁע	verbal root	see הוֹשִׁיעַ	
יִשְׂרָאֵל	proper n	Israel	10
יֵשׁ	particle	there is	18
יָשַׁב	v	to sit; dwell, live (inhabit) (see also נוֹשַׁב, הוֹשִׁיב)	16/27
כְּ	prep	like, as	9
כַּאֲשֶׁר	conj	when, as	17
כֹּה	adv	thus, so; refers to what follows	18
כֹּהֵן	n	priest	12

Hebrew	Type	English	Ref
כון	verbal root	see נָכוֹן ,כּוֹנֵן ,הֵכִין	
כּוֹנֵן	v *polel* (כון)	to set up, establish	29
כִּי	conj	because, since; that	13
כֹּל	particle	all, each, every, entire	14
כְּלִי	n	article, utensil, vessel	28
כֵּן	adv	thus, so; refers to something already mentioned	15
כְּנַעַן	proper n	Canaan	28
כִּסֵּא	n	chair, throne	21
כֶּסֶף	n	silver, money	18
כָּרַת	v	to cut, make (a covenant) (see also נִכְרַת ,הִכְרִית)	12
כָּתַב	v	to write	12
לְ	prep	to, for; as	9
לֹא	adv	not	12
לֵאמֹר	particle	introduces direct speech	13
לֵב	n	heart, mind	15
לֵבָב	n	heart, mind	15
לְבִלְתִּי	adv	negative for the inf cs	17
לחם	verbal root	see נִלְחַם	
לֶחֶם	n	bread, food	13
לַיְלָה	n	night	11
לָכַד	v	to capture (see also נִלְכַּד)	17
לָכֵן	conj	therefore	24
לָמָּה	adv	why?	27
לָמַד	v	to learn (see also לִמַּד)	23
לִמַּד	v *piel* (למד)	to teach	23
לְמַעַן	conj	in order to, in order that	19
לִפְנֵי	prep	before, in front of, in the presence of	10
לָקַח	v	to take, receive	17/26
מְאֹד	adv	very	7
מֵאָה	adj (number)	hundred	30

מאן	verbal root	see מֵאֵן	
מֵאֵן	v *piel* (מאן)	to refuse	23
מִדְבָּר	n	wilderness	13
מָה	pron	what, what?	17
מהר	verbal root	see מִהַר	
מִהַר	v *piel* (מהר)	to hurry, do something quickly	23
מוֹעֵד	n	appointed time, place; season	29
מָוֶת	n	death	10
מות	v	to die (see also הֵמִית, הוּמַת)	28
מִזְבֵּחַ	n	altar	18
מָחָה	v	to wipe out	25
מַחֲנֶה	n	camp	13
מִי	pron	who, who?	13
מְיַלֶּדֶת	v *piel* fs ptcp (ילד)	midwife	27
מַיִם	n	water(s)	11
מַלְאָךְ	n	messenger, angel	13
מִלְחָמָה	n	battle, war	14
מֶלֶךְ	n	king	8
מָלַךְ	v	to rule, reign (see also הִמְלִיךְ)	12
מַלְכָּה	n	queen	8
מִן	prep	from; comparative	9
מַעֲשֶׂה	n	deed, work	30
מָצָא	v	to find (see also נִמְצָא)	15
מִצְוָה	n	commandment	12
מִצְרַיִם	proper n	Egypt	16
מָקוֹם	n	place	8
מֹשֶׁה	proper n	Moses	9
מִשְׁפָּחָה	n	clan, family	28
מִשְׁפָּט	n	judgment, justice	12
מָתְנַיִם	n	waist (loins)	11
־נָא/נָא	particle	volitive particle	14
נֶאֱכַל	v *niphal* (אכל)	to be eaten	20

נְאֻם	n	utterance	29
נֶאֱסַף	v *niphal* (אסף)	to assemble, be gathered	30
נבא	verbal root	see נִבָּא, הִתְנַבֵּא	
נִבָּא	v *niphal* (נבא)	to prophesy	24
נָבוֹן	v *niphal* (בין)	intelligent (*niphal* ptcp)	28
נָבִיא	n	prophet	19
נִבְנָה	v *niphal* (בנה)	to be built	25
נגד	verbal root	see הִגִּיד, הֻגַּד	
נִגְלָה	v *niphal* (גלה)	to be uncovered	25
נָגַע	v	to touch	26
נגש	verbal root	see הִגִּישׁ, נִגַּשׁ	
נִגַּשׁ	v *niphal* (נגש)	to approach	26
נִהְיָה	v *niphal* (היה)	to occur	25
נָהָר	n	river	9
נוֹלַד	v *niphal* (ילד)	to be born	27
נוֹרָא	v *niphal* (ירא)	to inspire fear, awe	27
נוֹשַׁב	v *niphal* (ישב)	to be inhabited, inhabitable	27
נָטָה	v	to stretch out (usually intransitive) (see also הִטָּה)	26
נכה	verbal root	see הִכָּה	
נָכוֹן	v *niphal* (כון)	to be prepared	28
נִכְרַת	v *niphal* (כרת)	to be cut (off)	19
נִלְחַם	v *niphal* (לחם)	to fight, do battle, wage war	19
נִלְכַּד	v *niphal* (לכד)	to be captured	19
נִלְקַח	v *niphal* (לקח)	to be taken	19
נִמְחָה	v *niphal* (מחה)	to be wiped out	25
נִמְצָא	v *niphal* (מצא)	to be found, to be	20
נָסַע	v	to set out	26
נַעֲלָה	v *niphal* (עלה)	to be brought up	25
נַעַר	n	young man (unmarried), boy, servant	12
נַעֲשָׂה	v *niphal* (עשה)	to be done, made	25
נָפַל	v	to fall (see also הִפִּיל)	16/26

נֶפֶשׁ	n	soul, person, self	21
נצב	verbal root	see הִצִּיב ,נִצַּב	
נִצַּב	v *niphal* (נצב)	to take one's stand	26
נצל	verbal root	see הִצִּיל ,נִצַּל	
נִצַּל	v *niphal* (נצל)	to be delivered	29
נִקְבַּר	v *niphal* (קבר)	to be buried	19
נִקְרָא	v *niphal* (קרא)	to be called	20
נִרְאָה	v *niphal* (ראה)	to appear	25
נָשָׂא	v	to lift, carry, bear (see also נִשָּׂא)	18/26
נִשָּׂא	v *niphal* (נשא)	to be lifted	26
נִשְׁאַר	v *niphal* (שאר)	to remain, be left over, survive	19
נִשְׁבַּע	v *niphal* (שבע)	to swear	29
נָשִׁים	n	women	8
נִשְׁמַד	v *niphal* (שמד)	to be destroyed	21
נִשְׁמַע	v *niphal* (שמע)	to be heard	20
נִשְׁמַר	v *niphal* (שמר)	to be careful	19
נָתַן	v	to give	26
סָבַב	v	to turn around, surround	30
סָבִיב	adv/prep	round about	30
סוּס	n	horse	5/7
סוּר	v	to turn aside; to depart (see also הֵסִיר)	28
ספר	verbal root	see סֵפֶר	
סֵפֶר	n	book	12
סִפֵּר	v *piel* (ספר)	to narrate, tell a story	23
עֶבֶד	n	servant, slave	8
עָבַד	v	to serve, work	14
עֲבֹדָה	n	work, service, labor	14
עָבַר	v	to cross (over) (see also הֶעֱבִיר)	15
עַד	prep	until, up to	13
עוֹד	adv	again, still	14
עוֹלָם	n	eternity	14
עָזַב	v	to abandon	15

עַיִן	n	eye; spring	11
עִיר	n	city	8
עַל־	prep	on, above, over	9
עָלָה	v	to go up (see also נַעֲלָה, הֶעֱלָה)	25
עֹלָה	n	whole burnt offering, holocaust	18
עַל־כֵּן	conj	therefore	24
עַם	n	(a) people, nation; people (coll.)	8
עִם	prep	with	9
עָמַד	v	to stand (see also הֶעֱמִיד)	13
עָנָה	v	to answer, respond	25
עֵץ	n	tree	9
עֵצָה	n	advice, counsel	11
עֶרֶב	n	evening	15
עָרִים	n	cities	8
עָשָׂה	v	to do, make (see also נַעֲשָׂה)	25
עֲשִׂירִי	adj (ord. number)	tenth	23
עֶשֶׂר	adj (number)	ten	22
עֶשְׂרִים	adj (number)	twenty	30
עַשְׁתֵּי	adj (number)	part of the phrase for the no. eleven	30
עֵת	n	time	30
עַתָּה	adv	now	16
פֶּה	n	mouth	13
פֹּה	adv	here	27
פלל	verbal root	see הִתְפַּלֵּל	
פָּנִים	n	face	10
פַּעַם	n	occurrence	11
פָּקַד	v	to visit; punish; muster; appoint	30
פַּרְעֹה	proper n	Pharaoh	14
צֹאן	n	sheep/goats	12
צָבָא	n	army	13
צַדִּיק	adj	righteous	13
צָהֳרַיִם	n	noon	11

צוה	verbal root	see צִוָּה	
צִוָּה	v *piel* (צוה)	to command	25
קֶבֶר	n	grave	15
קָבַר	v	to bury (see also נִקְבַּר)	15
קָדוֹשׁ	adj	holy	24
קדשׁ	verbal root	see קִדֵּשׁ, הִתְקַדֵּשׁ	
קִדֵּשׁ	v *piel* (קדשׁ)	to sanctify	24
קֹדֶשׁ	n	holiness	26
קוֹל	n	voice, sound	8
קוּם	v	to arise, stand up (see also הֵקִים)	14/28
קָטֹן	adj	small	7
קָטָן	adj	small	7
קלל	v (*qal*) (geminate stative: sc 3ms קַל)	to be small, disrespected (see also קִלֵּל)	30
קִלֵּל	v *piel* (קלל)	to curse	30
קָרָא	v	to call, name (see also נִקְרָא)	13
רָאָה	v	to see (see also נִרְאָה, הֶרְאָה)	25
רֹאשׁ	n	head	8
רִאשׁוֹן	adj	first	23
רַב	adj	many, much	16
רְבָבָה	adj (number)	ten thousand	30
רָבָה	v	to multiply, become many (see also הִרְבָּה)	25
רְבִיעִי	adj (number)	fourth	23
רֶגֶל	n	foot	11
רָדַף	v	to pursue, follow	17
רוּחַ	n	breath, spirit, wind	18
רוּם	v	to be high (see also רוֹמֵם, הֵרִים)	29
רוֹמֵם	v *polel* (רום)	to lift up	29
רָחֵל	proper n	Rachel	30
רַע	adj	bad, evil, troublesome	5/8

רעע	v (*qal*) (geminate stative: sc 3ms רַע)	to be evil (see also הֵרַע)	30
רַק	adv	only	17
רָשָׁע	adj	evil, criminal	11
שָׂדֶה	n	field	9
שִׂים (שׂום in BDB)	v	to put, place	28
שַׂר	n	captain, chief, prince	18
שָׂרָה	proper n	Sarah	13
שָׂרַי	proper n	Sarai	13
שָׂרִיד	n	survivor	21
שָׂרַף	v	to burn	18
שָׁאוּל	proper n	Saul	15
שָׁאַל	v	to ask	29
שאר	verbal root	see נִשְׁאַר, הִשְׁאִיר	
שְׁבִיעִי	adj (ord. number)	seventh	23
שבע	verbal root	see נִשְׁבַּע, הִשְׁבִּיעַ	
שֶׁבַע	adj (number)	seven	22
שִׁבְעִים	adj (number)	seventy	30
שָׁבַר	v	to break (see also שִׁבֵּר)	23
שִׁבֵּר	v *piel* (שבר)	to shatter	23
שַׁבָּת	n	Sabbath	24
שׁוּב	v	to return, come back (see also הֵשִׁיב)	28
שחת	verbal root	see שִׁחֵת	
שִׁחֵת	v *piel* (שחת)	to corrupt; destroy	23
שָׁכַב	v	to lie down	15
שכם	verbal root	see הִשְׁכִּים	
שָׁלוֹם	n	peace; welfare	29
שָׁלַח	v	to send (see also שִׁלַּח)	14
שִׁלַּח	v *piel* (שלח)	to send away, let go	23
שְׁלִישִׁי	adj (number)	third	23
שלך	verbal root	see הִשְׁלִיךְ	

שְׁלֹמֹה	proper n	Solomon	11
שָׁלֹשׁ	adj (number)	three	22
שְׁלֹשִׁים	adj (number)	thirty	30
שֵׁם	n	name	5/10
שָׁם	adv	there	9
שׁמד	verbal root	see נִשְׁמַד, הִשְׁמִיד	
שְׁמוּאֵל	proper n	Samuel	16
שָׁמַיִם	n	heaven(s)	11
שְׁמִינִי	adj (ord. number)	eighth	23
שְׁמֹנֶה	adj (number)	eight	22
שְׁמֹנִים	adj (number)	eighty	30
שָׁמַע	v	to hear, obey (see also נִשְׁמַע, הִשְׁמִיעַ)	13
שָׁמַר	v	to watch, guard; keep, observe (see also נִשְׁמַר)	12
שָׁנָה	n	year	11
שֵׁנִי	adj (number)	second	23
שְׁנַיִם	adj (number)	two (m)	20
שָׁפַט	v	to judge	12
שֹׁפֵט	n	judge	17
שָׁפַךְ	v	to pour out, shed (blood)	17
שׁקה	verbal root	see הִשְׁקָה	
שֵׁשׁ	adj (number)	six	22
שִׁשִּׁי	adj (ord. number)	sixth	23
שִׁשִּׁים	adj (number)	sixty	30
שָׁתָה	v	to drink (see הִשְׁקָה)	25
שְׁתַּיִם	adj (number)	two (f)	20
תּוֹרָה	n	instruction, law; Torah	11
תַּחַת	prep	under; instead of	9
תְּפִלָּה	n	prayer	24
תְּשִׁיעִי	adj (ord. number)	ninth	23
תֵּשַׁע	adj (number)	nine	22
תִּשְׁעִים	adj (number)	ninety	30

APPENDIX H

VERBAL PARADIGMS

The paradigms found in this appendix repeat those found in the lessons of this grammar with the added benefit that portions of many of the words in the paradigms are found in color the better to emphasize features helpful to remembering key aspects of each paradigm, as each of the weak roots (III-weak, I-weak, II-weak, and geminate) share some similarities across the *qal*, *niphal*, *hiphil* (and sometimes the *piel*) stems. For further explanation of the use of colors, see page 288.

THE *QAL* FORMS OF THE STRONG VERB

inf. cs.	suff. conj.	cons. pret.	volitives		pref. conj.
שְׁמֹר	שָׁמַרְתִּי	וָאֶשְׁמֹר	אֶשְׁמְרָה	cohort.	אֶשְׁמֹר
	שָׁמַרְתָּ	וַתִּשְׁמֹר	שְׁמֹר	impv.	תִּשְׁמֹר
inf. abs.	שָׁמַרְתְּ	וַתִּשְׁמְרִי	שִׁמְרִי	impv.	תִּשְׁמְרִי
שָׁמוֹר	שָׁמַר	וַיִּשְׁמֹר	יִשְׁמֹר	juss.	יִשְׁמֹר
	שָׁמְרָה	…	תִּשְׁמֹר	juss.	תִּשְׁמֹר
ptcp.	שָׁמַרְנוּ		נִשְׁמְרָה	cohort.	נִשְׁמֹר
שֹׁמֵר	שְׁמַרְתֶּם		שִׁמְרוּ	impv.	תִּשְׁמְרוּ
שֹׁמֶרֶת	שְׁמַרְתֶּן		שְׁמֹרְנָה	impv.	תִּשְׁמֹרְנָה
שֹׁמְרִים	שָׁמְרוּ		יִשְׁמְרוּ	juss.	יִשְׁמְרוּ
שֹׁמְרוֹת			תִּשְׁמֹרְנָה	juss.	תִּשְׁמֹרְנָה

THE *QAL* FORMS OF THE THIRD-WEAK VERBS

inf. cs.	suff. conj.	cons. pret.	volitives		pref. conj.
	גָּלִיתִי	וָאֵגֶל/וָאֶגְלֶה	אֶגְלֶה	cohort.	אֶגְלֶה
גְּלוֹת	גָּלִיתָ	וַתִּגֶל	גְּלֵה	impv.	תִּגְלֶה
inf. abs.	גָּלִית	וַתִּגְלִי	גְּלִי	impv.	תִּגְלִי
גָּלֹה	גָּלָה	וַיִּגֶל	יִגֶל	juss.	יִגְלֶה
	גָּלְתָה	...	תִּגֶל	juss.	תִּגְלֶה
ptcp.	גָּלִינוּ		נִגְלֶה	cohort.	נִגְלֶה
גֹּלֶה	גְּלִיתֶם		גְּלוּ	impv.	תִּגְלוּ
גֹּלָה	גְּלִיתֶן		גְּלֶינָה	impv.	תִּגְלֶינָה
גֹּלִים	גָּלוּ		יִגְלוּ	juss.	יִגְלוּ
גֹּלוֹת			תִּגְלֶינָה	juss.	תִּגְלֶינָה

THE *NIPHAL* FORMS OF THE THIRD-WEAK VERBS

inf. cs.	suff. conj.	cons. pret.	volitives		pref. conj.
	נִגְלֵיתִי	וָאֶגָּל	אֶגָּלֶה	cohort.	אֶגָּלֶה
הִגָּלוֹת	נִגְלֵיתָ	וַתִּגָּל	הִגָּלֶה	impv.	תִּגָּלֶה
inf. abs.	נִגְלֵית	וַתִּגָּלִי	הִגָּלִי	impv.	תִּגָּלִי
נִגְלֹה	נִגְלָה	וַיִּגָּל	יִגָּל	juss.	יִגָּלֶה
	נִגְלְתָה	...	תִּגָּל	juss.	תִּגָּלֶה
ptcp.	נִגְלֵינוּ		נִגָּלֶה	cohort.	נִגָּלֶה
נִגְלֶה	נִגְלֵיתֶם		הִגָּלוּ	impv.	תִּגָּלוּ
נִגְלָה	נִגְלֵיתֶן		הִגָּלֶינָה	impv.	תִּגָּלֶינָה
נִגְלִים	נִגְלוּ		יִגָּלוּ	juss.	יִגָּלוּ
נִגְלוֹת			תִּגָּלֶינָה	juss.	תִּגָּלֶינָה

THE *HIPHIL* FORMS OF THE THIRD-WEAK VERBS

inf. cs.	suff. conj.	cons. pret.	volitives		pref. conj.
הַגְלוֹת	הִגְלֵיתִי/הִגְלֵיתִי	וָאַגֵל/וָאַגְלֶה	אַגְלֶה	cohort.	אַגְלֶה
	הִגְלֵיתָ	וַתֶּגֶל	הַגְלֵה	impv.	תַּגְלֶה
inf. abs.	הִגְלֵית/הִגְלִית	וַתַּגְלִי	הַגְלִי	impv.	תַּגְלִי
הַגְלֵה	הִגְלָה	וַיֶּגֶל	יֶגֶל	juss.	יַגְלֶה
	הִגְלְתָה	...	תֶּגֶל	juss.	תַּגְלֶה
ptcp.	הִגְלִינוּ		נַגְלֶה	cohort.	נַגְלֶה
מַגְלֶה	הִגְלֵיתֶם		הַגְלוּ	impv.	תַּגְלוּ
מַגְלֶה	הִגְלֵיתֶן		הַגְלֶינָה	impv.	תַּגְלֶינָה
מַגְלִים	הִגְלוּ		יַגְלוּ	juss.	יַגְלוּ
מַגְלוֹת			תַּגְלֶינָה	juss.	תַּגְלֶינָה

THE *PIEL* FORMS OF THE THIRD-WEAK VERBS

inf. cs.	suff. conj.	cons. pret.	volitives		pref. conj.
גַּלּוֹת	גִּלֵּיתִי/גִּלִּיתִי	וָאַגַל/וָאַגַלֶּה	אַגַלֶּה	cohort.	אֲגַלֶּה
	גִּלֵּיתָ	וַתְּגַל	גַּלֵּה	impv.	תְּגַלֶּה
inf. abs.	גַּלֵּית	וַתְּגַלִּי	גַּלִּי	impv.	תְּגַלִּי
גַּלֵּה/גַּלֹה	גִּלָּה	וַיְגַל	יְגַל	juss.	יְגַלֶּה
	גִּלְּתָה	...	תְּגַל	juss.	תְּגַלֶּה
ptcp.	גִּלִּינוּ		נְגַלֶּה	cohort.	נְגַלֶּה
מְגַלֶּה	גִּלִּיתֶם		גַּלּוּ	impv.	תְּגַלּוּ
מְגַלֶּה	גִּלִּיתֶן		גַּלֶּינָה	impv.	תְּגַלֶּינָה
מְגַלִּים	גִּלּוּ		יְגַלּוּ	juss.	יְגַלּוּ
מְגַלּוֹת			תְּגַלֶּינָה	juss.	תְּגַלֶּינָה

THE *QAL* FORMS OF THE TYPE 2 FIRST-WEAK VERB

inf. cs.	suff. conj.	cons. pret.	volitives		pref. conj.
שֶׁבֶת	יָשַׁבְתִּי	וָאֵשֵׁב	אֵשְׁבָה	cohort.	אֵשֵׁב
שִׁבְתִּי	יָשַׁבְתָּ	וַתֵּשֵׁב	שֵׁב	impv.	תֵּשֵׁב
inf. abs.	יָשַׁבְתְּ	וַתֵּשְׁבִי	שְׁבִי	impv.	תֵּשְׁבִי
יָשׁוֹב	יָשַׁב	וַיֵּשֵׁב	יֵשֵׁב	juss.	יֵשֵׁב
	יָשְׁבָה	…	תֵּשֵׁב	juss.	תֵּשֵׁב
ptcp.	יָשַׁבְנוּ		נֵשְׁבָה	cohort.	נֵשֵׁב
יֹשֵׁב	יְשַׁבְתֶּם		שְׁבוּ	impv.	תֵּשְׁבוּ
יֹשֶׁבֶת	יְשַׁבְתֶּן		שֵׁבְנָה	impv.	תֵּשַׁבְנָה
יֹשְׁבִים	יָשְׁבוּ		יֵשְׁבוּ	juss.	יֵשְׁבוּ
יֹשְׁבוֹת			תֵּשַׁבְנָה	juss.	תֵּשַׁבְנָה

THE *NIPHAL* FORMS OF THE TYPE 2 FIRST-WEAK VERB

inf. cs.	suff. conj.	cons. pret.	volitives		pref. conj.
הִוָּשֵׁב	נוֹשַׁבְתִּי	וָאִוָּשֵׁב	אִוָּשְׁבָה	cohort.	אִוָּשֵׁב
	נוֹשַׁבְתָּ	וַתִּוָּשֵׁב	הִוָּשֵׁב	impv.	תִּוָּשֵׁב
	נוֹשַׁבְתְּ	וַתִּוָּשְׁבִי	הִוָּשְׁבִי	impv.	תִּוָּשְׁבִי
	נוֹשַׁב	וַיִּוָּשֵׁב	יִוָּשֵׁב	juss.	יִוָּשֵׁב
	נוֹשְׁבָה	…	תִּוָּשֵׁב	juss.	תִּוָּשֵׁב
ptcp.	נוֹשַׁבְנוּ		נִוָּשְׁבָה	cohort.	נִוָּשֵׁב
נוֹשָׁב	נוֹשַׁבְתֶּם		הִוָּשְׁבוּ	impv.	תִּוָּשְׁבוּ
נוֹשֶׁבֶת	נוֹשַׁבְתֶּן		הִוָּשַׁבְנָה	impv.	תִּוָּשַׁבְנָה
נוֹשָׁבִים	נוֹשְׁבוּ		יִוָּשְׁבוּ	juss.	יִוָּשְׁבוּ
נוֹשָׁבוֹת			תִּוָּשַׁבְנָה	juss.	תִּוָּשַׁבְנָה

THE *HIPHIL* FORMS OF THE TYPE 2 FIRST-WEAK VERB

inf. cs.	suff. conj.	cons. pret.	volitives		pref. conj.
הוֹשִׁיב	הוֹשַׁבְתִּי	וָאוֹצֵא/וָאֵלֵךְ	אוֹשִׁיבָה	cohort.	אוֹשִׁיב
	הוֹשַׁבְתָּ	וַתּוֹשֶׁב	הוֹשֵׁב	impv.	תּוֹשִׁיב
inf. abs.	הוֹשַׁבְתְּ	וַתּוֹשִׁיבִי	הוֹשִׁיבִי	impv.	תּוֹשִׁיבִי
הוֹשֵׁב	הוֹשִׁיב	וַיּוֹשֶׁב	יוֹשֵׁב	juss.	יוֹשִׁיב
	הוֹשִׁיבָה	...	תּוֹשֵׁב	juss.	תּוֹשִׁיב
ptcp.	הוֹשַׁבְנוּ		נוֹשִׁיבָה	cohort.	נוֹשִׁיב
מוֹשִׁיב	הוֹשַׁבְתֶּם		הוֹשִׁיבוּ	impv.	תּוֹשִׁיבוּ
מוֹשֶׁבֶת	הוֹשַׁבְתֶּן		הוֹשֵׁבְנָה	impv.	תּוֹשֵׁבְנָה
מוֹשִׁיבִים	הוֹשִׁיבוּ		יוֹשִׁיבוּ	juss.	יוֹשִׁיבוּ
מוֹשִׁיבוֹת			תּוֹשֵׁבְנָה	juss.	תּוֹשֵׁבְנָה

THE *QAL* FORMS OF THE MIDDLE-WEAK *VAV* VERB

inf. cs.	suff. conj.	cons. pret.	volitives		pref. conj.
קום	קַמְתִּי	וָאָקוּם	אָקוּמָה	cohort.	אָקוּם
	קַמְתָּ	וַתָּקָם	קוּם	impv.	תָּקוּם
inf. abs.	קַמְתְּ	וַתָּקוּמִי	קוּמִי	impv.	תָּקוּמִי
קוֹם	קָם	וַיָּקָם	יָקֹם	juss.	יָקוּם
	קָמָה	...	תָּקֹם	juss.	תָּקוּם
ptcp.	קַמְנוּ		נָקוּמָה	cohort.	נָקוּם
קָם	קַמְתֶּם		קוּמוּ	impv.	תָּקוּמוּ
קָמָה	קַמְתֶּן		קֹמְנָה	impv.	תְּקוּמֶינָה
קָמִים	קָמוּ		יָקוּמוּ	juss.	יָקוּמוּ
קָמוֹת			תָּקֹמְנָה/תְּקוּמֶינָה	juss.	תָּקֹמְנָה/תְּקוּמֶינָה

THE *NIPHAL* FORMS OF THE MIDDLE-WEAK VERB

inf. cs.	suff. conj.	cons. pret.	volitives		pref. conj.
הִכּוֹן	נְכוּנוֹתִי	וָאֶכּוֹן	אֶכּוֹנָה	cohort.	אֶכּוֹן
	נְכוּנוֹתָ	וַתִּכּוֹן	הִכּוֹן	impv.	תִּכּוֹן
inf. abs.	נְכוּנוֹת	וַתִּכּוֹנִי	הִכּוֹנִי	impv.	תִּכּוֹנִי
הִכּוֹן	נָכוֹן	וַיִּכּוֹן	יִכּוֹן	juss.	יִכּוֹן
	נָכוֹנָה	...	תִּכּוֹן	juss.	תִּכּוֹן
ptcp.	נְכוּנוֹנוּ		נִכּוֹנָה	cohort.	נִכּוֹן
נָכוֹן	נְכוּנוֹתֶם		הִכּוֹנוּ	impv.	תִּכּוֹנוּ
נְכוֹנָה	נְכוּנוֹתֶן			impv.	
נְכוֹנִים	נָכוֹנוּ		יִכּוֹנוּ	juss.	יִכּוֹנוּ
נְכוֹנוֹת				juss.	

THE *QAL* FORMS OF THE MIDDLE-WEAK *YOD* VERB

inf. cs.	suff. conj.	cons. pret.	volitives		pref. conj.
שִׂים/שׂוּם	שַׂמְתִּי	...	אָשִׂימָה	cohort.	אָשִׂים
	שַׂמְתָּ	וַתָּשֶׂם	שִׂים	impv.	תָּשִׂים
inf. abs.	שַׂמְתְּ	וַתָּשִׂימִי	שִׂימִי	impv.	תָּשִׂימִי
שׂוֹם	שָׂם	וַיָּשֶׂם	יָשֵׂם	juss.	יָשִׂים
	שָׂמָה	...	תָּשֵׂם	juss.	תָּשִׂים
ptcp.	שַׂמְנוּ		נָשִׂימָה	cohort.	נָשִׂים
שָׂם	שַׂמְתֶּם		שִׂימוּ	impv.	תָּשִׂימוּ
שָׂמָה	שַׂמְתֶּן		שֵׂמְנָה	impv.	תְּשֵׂמְנָה
שָׂמִים	שָׂמוּ		יָשִׂימוּ	juss.	יָשִׂימוּ
שָׂמוֹת			תְּשֵׂמְנָה	juss.	תְּשֵׂמְנָה

THE *HIPHIL* FORMS OF THE MIDDLE-WEAK VERB

inf. cs.	suff. conj.	cons. pret.	volitives		pref. conj.
הָקִים	הֲקִימֹתִי	וָאָקֶם	אָקִימָה	cohort.	אָקִים
	הֲקִימֹתָ	וַתָּקֶם	הָקֵם	impv.	תָּקִים
inf. abs.	הֲקִימֹת	וַתָּקִימִי	הָקִימִי	impv.	תָּקִימִי
הָקֵם	הֵקִים	וַיָּקֶם	יָקֶם/יָקֵם	juss.	יָקִים
	הֵקִימָה	...	תָּקֵם/תָּקֶם	juss.	תָּקִים
ptcp.	הֲקִימֹנוּ		נָקִימָה	cohort.	נָקִים
מֵקִים	הֲקִימֹתֶם		הָקִימוּ	impv.	תָּקִימוּ
מְקִימָה	הֲקִימֹתֶן		הָקֵמְנָה	impv.	תָּקֵמְנָה
מְקִימִים	הֵקִימוּ		יָקִימוּ	juss.	יָקִימוּ
מְקִימוֹת		תָּקֵמְנָה/תְּקִימֶינָה		juss.	תָּקֵמְנָה/תְּקִימֶינָה

APPENDIX H

THE REGULAR *QAL* FORMS OF THE GEMINATE VERB

inf. cs.	suff. conj.	cons. pret.	volitives		pref. conj.
סֹב	סַבֹּ֫ותִי	...			אָסֹב
סְבִּי	סַבֹּ֫ות	...	סֹב	impv.	תָּסֹב
inf. abs.	סַבֹּות	...	סֹ֫בִּי	impv.	תָּסֹ֫בִּי
סָבֹוב	סָבַב	וַיָּ֫סָב	יָסֹב	juss.	יָסֹב
	סָבְבָה	...	תָּסֹב	juss.	תָּסֹב
ptcp.	סַבֹּ֫ונוּ				נָסֹב
סֹבֵב	סַבֹּותֶם		סֹ֫בּוּ	impv.	תָּסֹ֫בּוּ
סֹבְבָה	סַבֹותֶן		סֻבֶּ֫ינָה	impv.	תְּסֻבֶּ֫ינָה
סֹבְבִים	סָבְבוּ	וַיָּסֹ֫בּוּ	יָסֹ֫בּוּ	juss.	יָסֹ֫בּוּ
סֹבְבֹות			תְּסֻבֶּ֫ינָה	juss.	תְּסֻבֶּ֫ינָה

THE REGULAR *QAL* FORMS OF THE STATIVE GEMINATE VERB

suff. conj.	cons. pret.	volitives		pref. conj.
קַלֹּ֫ותִי	וָאֵקַל			אֵקַל
קַלֹּ֫ות	וַתֵּקַל			תֵּקַל
קַלֹּות	וַתֵּקַ֫לִּי			תֵּקַ֫לִּי
קַל	וַיֵּקַל	יֵקַל	juss.	יֵקַל
קַ֫לָּה	...	תֵּקַל	juss.	תֵּקַל
קַלֹּ֫ונוּ				נֵקַל
קַלֹּותֶם				תֵּקַ֫לּוּ
קַלֹּותֶן				תְּקַלֶּ֫ינָה
קַ֫לּוּ		יֵקַ֫לּוּ	juss.	יֵקַ֫לּוּ
		תְּקַלֶּ֫ינָה	juss.	תְּקַלֶּ֫ינָה

THE ALTERNATIVE PREFIX CONJUGATION FOR THE REGULAR AND STATIVE GEMINATE VERB

pref. conj. stative	pref. conj. nonstative
אֶקַל	אֶסֹב
תֵּקַל	תֵּסֹב
תֵּקְלִי	תֵּסֹּבִי
יֵקַל	יֵסֹב
תֵּקַל	תֵּסֹב
נֵקַל	נֵסֹב
תֵּקְלוּ	תֵּסֹּבוּ
תֵּקַלְנָה	תֵּסֹּבְנָה
יֵקְלוּ	יֵסֹּבוּ
תֵּקַלְנָה	תֵּסֹּבְנָה

THE *NIPHAL* FORMS OF THE GEMINATE VERB

inf. cs.	suff. conj.	cons. pret.	volitives		pref. conj.
הִסֵּב	נְסַבּוֹתִי	וָאֶחַל			אֶסֵּב
	נְסַבּוֹתָ		הִסֵּב	impv.	תִּסֵּב
inf. abs.	נְסַבּוֹת		הִסַּבִּי	impv.	תִּסַּבִּי
הִסּוֹב	נָסַב/נָמֵס		יִסֵּב	juss.	יִסֵּב
	נָסֵבָּה		תִּסֵּב	juss.	תִּסֵּב
ptcp.	נְסַבּוֹנוּ				נִסֵּב
נָסָב	נְסַבּוֹתֶם		הִסַּבּוּ	impv.	תִּסַּבּוּ
נְסַבָּה	נְסַבּוֹתֶן		הִסַּבֶּינָה	impv.	תִּסַּבֶּינָה
נְסַבִּים	נָסַבּוּ		יִסַּבּוּ	juss.	יִסַּבּוּ
נְסַבּוֹת			תִּסַּבֶּינָה	juss.	תִּסַּבֶּינָה

THE *HIPHIL* FORMS OF THE GEMINATE VERB

inf. cs.	suff. conj.	cons. pret.	volitives		pref. conj.
הָסֵב	הֲסִבֹּ֫תִי				אָסֵב
	הֲסִבֹּ֫תָ		הָסֵב	impv.	תָּסֵב
inf. abs.	הֲסִבֹּות		הָסֵ֫בִּי	impv.	תָּסֵ֫בִּי
הָסֵב	הֵסֵב/הֵסַב	וַיַּ֫סֶב/וַיָּ֫חֶל	יָסֵב	juss.	יָסֶב/יַסֵב
	הֵסֵ֫בָּה	וַתָּ֫חֶל	תָּסֵב	juss.	תָּסֵב
ptcp.	הֲסִבֹּ֫ונוּ		נָסֵ֫בָּה	cohort.	נָסֵב
מֵסֵב	הֲסִבֹּותֶם		הָסֵ֫בּוּ	impv.	תָּסֵ֫בּוּ
מְסִבָּה	הֲסִבֹּותֶן		תְּסִבֶּ֫ינָה	impv.	תְּסִבֶּ֫ינָה
מְסִבִּים	הֵסֵ֫בּוּ	וַיָּסֵ֫בּוּ	יָסֵ֫בּוּ/יָסֵבּוּ	juss.	יָסֹ֫בּוּ/יָסֵבּוּ
מְסִבֹּות			תְּסִבֶּ֫ינָה	juss.	תְּסִבֶּ֫ינָה

On page 279 the paradigm for the *qal* for the "strong verb" is given; no color is used. The paradigms for the derived stems are given in their respective chapters: *niphal* on page 116, *hiphil* on 128, *piel* on 141, *hitpael* on 149, and *polel* on 207.

For the III-weak roots (pp. 280–81), the similarities of endings among the four paradigms for *qal*, *niphal*, *hiphil*, and *hitpael* stems have been highlighted in blue for the prefix conjugation, the imperative, the suffix conjugation, the infinitive construct, and the participles.

For the type 2 I-weak roots (pp. 282–83), the manner in which the I-weak consonant reappears among the paradigms for *qal*, *niphal*, and *hiphil* stems has been highlighted in blue. For the *qal* stem this is done only for the prefix conjugation, the cohortative and the jussive, and the consecutive preterite; it is done for all the paradigms in the *niphal* and *hiphil* stems.

For the II-weak roots (pp. 284–85), the similarities across the paradigms among the first consonants and the vowels that follow (and the substitute for the missing second root consonant) have been highlighted in blue throughout the paradigms.

For the geminate roots (pp. 286–88), only those forms in which a consonant with *dagesh* represents the geminated second and third consonants have been highlighted in blue. In those forms, the doubled consonant, plus the vowel that follows the doubled consonant, has been highlighted.

◄ FURTHER READING ►

The following works are considered helpful for any student of Biblical Hebrew and essential for those seeking to move beyond the first semester of her or his studies.

All students of the Hebrew Bible should have an authoritative and reliable edition of the Hebrew (and Aramaic) text. The Hebrew Bible most frequently used in academic work is commonly referred to as the *BHS*. This is the *Biblia Hebraica Stuttgartensia* (5th corrected edition; Stuttgart: Deutsche Bibelgesellschaft, 1997). This Hebrew Bible is gradually being updated and replaced by fascicles of the *BHQ*, often referred to as "Quinta." The *Biblia Hebraica Quinta* (Stuttgart: Deutsche Bibelgesellschaft, 2004–), when completed, will no doubt serve as the standard critical edition of the Hebrew Bible. The *BHS*, which is used in this textbook, includes not only the text of the Hebrew Bible but also modern scholarly text-critical information as well as other pertinent information in an apparatus found at the bottom of each page. In addition to this more recent scholarly information, the *BHS* includes selected notes from the ancient Masoretes that are found in the margin of each page and that provide the reader with additional information such as how often a given word or set of words occurs in the Hebrew Bible. The *BHS* also includes an apparatus between the Hebrew text itself and the modern scholarly apparatus at the bottom of the page that points the reader to the locations in an ancient work called the Masorah magna where the notes in the margins can be found.

The unusual and rarer markings found in the scholarly editions of the Hebrew Bible can be found in William R. Scott's *A Simplified Guide to BHS: Critical Apparatus, Masora, Accents, Unusual Letters and Other Markings* (Berkeley, Calif: Bibal Press, 1987), which explains a number of the detailed markings found in the *BHS* quite clearly.

A reliable dictionary or lexicon is needed by all students of Biblical Hebrew. The dictionary most often used in English-speaking countries is commonly referred to by the initials of its authors and translator, BDB: *The Brown-Driver-Briggs Hebrew and English Lexicon: With an Appendix Containing the Biblical Aramaic*. The work is in the public domain and available in various editions (e.g., Peabody, Mass.: Hendrickson, 1996, is a reprinting of the 1906 edition by Houghton, Mifflin & Co.). BDB is arranged, like many dictionaries of Semitic languages, alphabetically according to Semitic root. Each verbal stem of the root is noted, and any nouns, adjectives, adverbs, or other words that can be derived from the root are listed below the information about the verb.

The other scholarly dictionary frequently used in English-speaking countries is commonly referred to as *HALOT*. *The Hebrew and Aramaic Lexicon of the Old Testament* (5 vols.; Leiden: Brill, 1994–2000) is the English translation of the latest version of the *Hebräisches und Aramäisches Lexikon zum Alten Testament* (5 vols.; Leiden: Brill, 1967–1996). It is available from the publisher in a less expensive two-volume "student's edition." Unlike BDB, however, *HALOT* lists words alphabetically and not by root. This makes looking up a word a bit simpler, while losing the advantage of discovering other Hebrew words found in the Hebrew Bible that are related to the given Semitic root.

For any serious student of Biblical Hebrew, two reference grammars, covering the vast details known about the grammar of Hebrew that is found in the Hebrew Bible, are commonly used in Biblical Hebrew classes in the English-speaking world. The older, but reliable, work is commonly referred to by the authors' and translator's names, GKC: *Gesenius' Hebrew Grammar* (ed. E. Kautzsch; trans. A. E. Cowley; 2nd ed.; Oxford: Clarendon, 1910). A second and equally fine reference grammar commonly referred to by the author's name, Joüon, is *A Grammar of Biblical Hebrew* (2nd repr. of 2nd ed.; Rome: Editrice Pontificio Instituto Biblico, 2009). It was originally written in French by Paul Joüon and translated into English, revised, and updated by T. Muraoka.

In addition, Bruce Waltke and M. O'Connor's *An Introduction to Biblical Hebrew Syntax* (Winona Lake, Ind.: Eisenbrauns, 1990) is a compilation of Biblical Hebrew grammatical information, but with an emphasis, as the title suggests, on syntax. This book is a reference grammar of everything from typical grammatical categories to syntax to a history of the biblical text. It is filled with biblical examples for each of its assertions.

Two small books take beginning students through the vocabulary of the Hebrew Bible from words that occur most often to those that are rare (10 occurrences and above). Larry A. Mitchel's *A Student's Vocabulary for Biblical Hebrew and Aramaic* (Grand Rapids: Zondervan, 1984) lists nouns, verbs, and other words strictly according to their number of occurrences in the Bible, while George M. Landes's *Building Your Biblical Hebrew Vocabulary: Learning Words by Frequency and Cognate* (Atlanta: Society of Biblical Literature, 2001) presents words in three different categories. The first and largest category in Landes's book consists of verbal roots that occur frequently, plus the nouns, adjectives, and other parts of speech that are related to them. The second category consists of nouns and other parts of speech that themselves occur frequently but that are related to rare verbal roots. The third category lists nouns and other parts of speech that are not related to an extant verbal root.

◄ INDEX ►

This index points to the section(s) of the lessons (rather than to page numbers) where the topic is discussed. In alphabetized lists, Hebrew words follow English words. The portion of this index devoted to Hebrew words that are discussed in the lessons follows the indexed English portion.